*Social Histories of
the Secondary Curriculum:
Subjects for Study*

Studies in Curriculum History 1

# Social Histories of the Secondary Curriculum: Subjects for Study

Edited by

## Ivor Goodson

The Falmer Press

A member of the Taylor and Francis Group
London and Philadelphia

UK     The Falmer Press, Falmer House, Barcombe, Lewes, East Sussex, BN8 5DL

USA     The Falmer Press, Taylor & Francis Inc., 242 Cherry Street, Philadelphia, PA 19106-1906

---

First published 1985

**Library of Congress Cataloging in Publication Data**

Main entry under title:

Subjects for study.

   (Studies in curriculum history; 1)
   Bibliography: p.
   Includes index.
   1. Education—Great Britain—Curricula—History—
Addresses, essays, lectures.   I. Goodson, Ivor.
II. Series.
LB1564.G7S8   1948   375′.00941   84-18676
ISBN 1-85000-016-6
ISBN 1-85000-015-8 (pbk.)

Typeset in 11/13 Garamond by
Imago Publishing Ltd, Thame, Oxon.

Jacket design by Leonard Williams

*Printed in Great Britain by Taylor & Francis (Printers) Ltd, Basingstoke*

# Contents

Contents

To Professor Foster Watson,
pioneer in the
study of school subjects

The reason why I preferred to use the past is that as a rule people have already made up their minds what they think about the present. About the past they are more susceptible to clarity of vision.

*J.G. Farrell*

# Towards Curriculum History

## Ivor Goodson

This collection of papers originates from a belief in the need to develop further our 'sense of history' about curriculum. Personal involvement in curriculum reform and research over the past two decades has accentuated my conviction that this is a worthwhile enterprise. With very few exceptions sociological studies of the school curriculum have maintained an obsessive contemporaneity at the expense of any serious consideration of historical context. However, in providing an antidote to such omissions, historians of education have often inverted the problem and largely failed to link insights into curriculum past with perspectives on curriculum present. We then have sociological snapshots of contemporary curriculum juxtaposed with periodized histories of past curriculum: two kinds of study developed by different scholars in different places at different times. As a result past and present seldom meet. The result of this disengagement, of this profound absence of a dialogue across the generations, is I believe one aspect of the paralysis which has often afflicted both our curriculum reform and curriculum research endeavours.

Of course this diagnosis is far from new. A number of sociologists have worked in this way (the work of Margaret Archer being a prime example) and others have warned of the dangers of ignoring historical contexts. For instance Blumer has drawn attention to this problem when studying large-scale organizations and argues a need 'to recognize that joint action is temporarily linked to previous joint action'. He warns that 'one shuts a major door to understanding any form or instance of joint action if one ignores this connection'. This 'historical linkage' is important because 'the designations and interpretations through which people form and maintain their organized relations are always in degree of carry-over from their past. To ignore this carry-over sets a genuine risk for the scholar'.[1]

Paradoxically, since Blumer wrote this in 1969 some developments in sociology have tended to move in the opposite direction to the one he advises, thereby involving the 'genuine risk' to which he refers. For example, interactionist studies, with their focus on emergent perspectives and definitions, have stressed situation rather than background and history. In this work the backcloth to action is often presented as a somewhat monolithic 'structural' or 'cultural' legacy which constrains, in rather disconnected manner, the actors' potentialities. But in overreacting to more deterministic models, interactionists are in danger of failing to present any clear connection with historical process. Of course, we can agree that 'any process of interaction is never fully determined by social, structural or cultural forces' and 'social structures and cultures emerge out of and are sustained and changed by social interaction'.[2] But the danger of such stress on personal potential is that historical linkages will remain undeveloped or, at any rate, underdeveloped.

In studying the school curriculum the dangers of such an approach have been clearly evidenced in the past decade. Classroom practice, a crucial and often neglected area, can, by interactionist over-reaction, be presented as the sole context wherein patterns of knowledge transmission are defined. One unfortunate side effect of this focus is that when attempts to reform classroom practice fail, the teacher, who is the immediate and visible agency of that failure, may be presented as exclusively culpable. In seeking to understand curriculum change we need a strategy that is curative of the classroom myopia exhibited in such accounts.

Another major development in sociological studies, the sociology of knowledge, has laid claim to providing one such curative strategy. Knowledge is seen as evolving in response to the promotional and presentational agency of particular subject groups who act to defend and expand their 'interests'. Similarly, knowledge patterns are viewed as reflecting the status hierarchies of societies through the activities of the dominant groups within them. Very often, however, such work has failed to present the evolutionary, historical process at work. Studies have developed horizontally, working out from theories of social structure and social order to evidence of their application. Such an approach inevitably obscures, rather than clarifies, both those historical situations in which 'gaps, discrepancies and ambiguities are created within which individuals can manoeuvre'[3] as well as the varying arenas into which policy is fed and from which it emanates.

The ahistorical characteristics of interactionism and the sociology of knowledge may partly be a reflection of the historical period in which these 'new directions' developed. A review of the documents and statements of the curriculum reform movement inaugurated in the 1960s reveals a widespread belief that there could be a more or less complete break with past traditions. Besides the all pervasive term 'innovation' there was a great deal of reference to 'radical change in education', 'revolutionizing classroom practice' and 're-drawing the map of learning'. At a time when traditions were thought to be on the point of being overthrown it was perhaps unsurprising that so many studies paid scant attention to the evolution and establishment of those traditions. In the event radical change did not occur. We are left in the position of needing after all to examine the emergence and survival of that which is seen as 'traditional'. Significantly the study of the invention and maintenance of 'traditions' has engaged a number of historians in other fields recently. There is every reason to undertake this work in the field of curriculum.

Historians of education have of course provided a most valuable and important antidote to the ahistoricality of much curriculum study — although it should be noted that in the United Kingdom the History of Education Society was founded as recently as 1967 and has only produced its valuable journal since 1972. But, paradoxically, a refined awareness of some of the problems cited above has led to an often over-reactive posture to the sociological abuse of 'raiding' for contemporary or theoretical purposes; Silver, for example, speaks of 'raiding the past'.[4]

Writing of the work of curriculum specialists with respect to historical perspectives, Marsden judges that they 'have often been deficient and can roughly be divided into those which are *ahistorical* and *unhistorical*, insofar as the categories can be isolated from one another'. He defines an ahistorical approach as:

> one which disregards the historical perspective, the writer perceiving it to be irrelevant and/or uninteresting ... Thus work proceeds, almost naively, in a temporal vacuum.[5]

An unhistorical approach is characterized somewhat haughtily:

> as one inconsistent both in gross and in refined terms with the accepted canons of historical scholarship, purveying inaccurate, over-simplified and otherwise distorted impressions of the past. Attention is drawn to the past, not for its own sake but as a means of sharpening a particular contemporary axe.

Alongside this 'misuse' of history Marsden places those curriculum studies 'in which the past is scanned for support of some broad socio-political interpretation or theory'.[6]

Historians have rightly reacted to the misuse of history for 'sharpening contemporary axes' or 'supporting broad socio-political interpretations or theories'. In my view that reaction has gone too far. The result is that history of education has often been rigidly 'periodized'; it has normally pursued a policy of 'splendid isolation' from the messy and unresolved contemporary situation. This is to limit both its aspiration and its importance.

History of education should clearly obviate any concern with 'sharpening contemporary axes'. But such a correct reaction should not be taken as disbarring a concern with contemporary events. The danger of whig interpretations of history must of course be conquered, but this is not to disarow a concern, where possible, to elucidate the precedents, antecedents and constraints surrounding contemporary curriculum and practice. Likewise, the reaction against theoretical enterprises should be conquered. Historical study has a valuable role to play in challenging, informing and sometimes generating theory. This role should not be emasculated through a fear of theoretical misuse by others.

Beyond the ambivalence over contemporary situations and theoretical enterprises much history of education shares a further characteristic which argues for a growing dialogue between historians and curriculum specialists. In many ways history of education has taken an 'external' view of curriculum focusing on political and administrative contexts and on general movements in education and schooling. Partly this is a reflection of the more readily available documents which often relate to central regulations, edicts or commissions on education and curriculum. This is a long way from curriculum as enacted, transacted, realized and received. Rudolph has warned that:

> The best way to misread or misunderstand curriculum is from a catalogue. It is such a lifeless thing. So disembodied, so unconnected, sometimes even intentionally misleading. Because the curriculum is a social artefact, the society itself is a more reliable source of curricular information.[7]

The 'externality' of much history of education argues for a growing dialogue between historians of education and curriculum specialists.

Exhortation, of course, is easier than action. Kenneth Charlton pointed out the problems of generating such a dialogue with characteristic diplomacy some time ago:

> To the curriculum theorist's question: 'Can history contribute to curriculum theory and development?' the historian might

well reply: 'It depends first of all on what kind of theory you have in mind; and it depends, secondly, on what precisely it is you are theorizing about'. For unless the historian is clear as to what is meant by 'curriculum', and what kind of theory is considered appropriate for it, he would be hard pressed to know where to start.[8]

American writers have been less diplomatic. Hazlett has written:

> Where lies the impediment to writing curriculum history? I suggest that the answer rests in the nature of the curriculum field, defined as professional endeavour engaged in by the professoriat. As such, curriculum does not bear the marks of a field of disciplined inquiry in a formal sense. It is, more characteristically, a field of practical, normative activity carried on with urgency in a crisis atmosphere.[9]

Some American writers have moved further to conclude that the answer to the 'externality' of much history of education is not so much dialogue as takeover. By this view the only way to bring historical perspectives to bear on curriculum in a way which recognizes the complexity of curriculum issues is to hand the task over to curriculum specialists. Franklin sees curriculum history 'as a speciality within the curriculum field, distinct from educational history. Its practitioners should be individuals whose primary training is in curriculum, not educational historians ... '.[10] The reasons for the separation are made clear later:

> Because the concerns and foci of the two studies are different. Most important in this respect is that the educational historian's lack of training in curriculum will lead him to either overlook or misinterpret those issues which are of most importance to the curriculum field. Above all this is because the educational historian focuses on those issues in curriculum most relevant to the general issues of education and schooling, rather than the other way round.[11]

In fact the last sentence of this plea for liberating curriculum history from educational historians begins to settle on some of the problems. The issue is not to get rid of 'external' histories, which are important, but to ensure a complementary approach to internal issues which historians have so far proved inadequate in covering. But it is vital not to throw the baby out with the bathwater. The development of 'external' histories is important. How important depends on the aspiration. If, however, an understanding of curriculum and curriculum change is given priority such 'external' histories must be closely related, if not deliberately interlinked, with modes of study which focus on and analyze 'internal' curriculum issues. A number of the papers in this book begin to develop integrated approaches in this way. It is of course only a beginning. Reid's paper, for instance, shows how external and internal factors can be analyzed as they have affected the sixth form curriculum.

The historical studies in this collection have a common intention: in following the evolution of thought and action through historical time, they seek to better understand 'school knowledge'. So far studies of the history of contemporary knowledge, let alone school knowledge, have tended to resemble the pre-parradigmatic stages of disciplines. The studies have been conducted in several places at different times and have often been undertaken by non-specialists who have brought the 'enthusiasm of pioneers' to their work. Macdonald and Walker have recently argued that for school curricula 'by extending our sense of history we can develop a different way of viewing the species'.[12] Mary Waring's work on Nuffield Science originated from a similar perspective:

> If we are to understand events, whether of thought or of action, knowledge of the background is essential. Knowledge of events is merely the raw material of history: to be an intelligible reconstruction of the past, events must be related to other events, and to the assumptions and practices of the milieu. Hence they must be made the subject of inquiry, their origins as products of particular social and historical circumstances, the manner in which individuals and groups have acted must be identified, and explanations for their actions sought.[13]

The justification for historical studies of the evolution of school knowledge can be found at the level of thought and action. First, such work will improve our knowledge of the school curriculum. Historical studies can elucidate the changing human process behind the definition and promotion of school subjects. Employing this strategy shifts the emphasis from questions of the intrinsic and philosophic value of subjects, from their existence as objective realities, to the motives and activities immanent and inherent in their construction and maintenance. Further, historical scrutiny offers insights into the existence of patterns and recurring constraints: why, for instance, certain 'traditions' in the school curriculum survive and others disappear. Whilst historical studies do not, as their major intention, seek to prove particular theories, nonetheless they may use and contribute to theory.

Secondly, at the level of school practice historical studies can aid analysis. Such studies might even help to explain the emergence and maintenance of anti-research traditions among teachers. Partly, teachers' antipathy derives from the point Shipman makes about the curriculum project he was involved with: 'The end product of the project was determined in the field, in contact with the school, not on the drawing board . . . in the end it was what worked that survived.'[14] But the autonomy of the teacher, his capacity for active reinterpretation should not be overestimated, for major constraints do exist. Hence, Shipman's judgment in a sense misses the point: only what is prepared on the drawing board goes into the school and therefore *has a chance* to be interpreted and to survive. Exploring the editing process which takes place on the drawing board of history with respect to the school curriculum is more than static historicism. By understanding this process we can define a range of constraints that are immanent in the teachers' work.

Thirdly, historical case studies should inform and influence policy and practice. A greater knowledge of historical precedents, antecedents and traditions can facilitate more sensitive management and implementation of contemporary curriculum.

### References

1 BLUMER H., 1969, p. 60.
2 HAMMERSLEY, M. and WOODS, P., 1976, p. 3.
3 WALKER, R. and GOODSON, I., 1977, P. 225.
4 SILVER, H., 1977, p. 17.
5 MARSDEN, W.E., 1978, p. 81.
6 *Ibid* p. 82.
7 RUDOLPH, F., 1977, p. 6.
8 CHARLTON, K., 1968, pp. 63–4.
9 HAZLETT, S., 1979, p. 131.
10 FRANKLIN, B., 1977, p. 73.
11 *Ibid* pp. 73–4.
12 MACDONALD, B., and WALKER R., 1976, p. 86.
13 WARING, M., 1975, p. 12.
14 SHIPMAN, M., 1974, p. 2

### Bibliography

BLUMER H. (1969) *Symbolic Interactionism. Perspective and Method*, Englewood Cliffs, Prentice Hall.
CHARLTON K. (1968) 'The contribution of history to the study of curriculum' in KERR, J.F. (Ed.) *Changing the Curriculum*, London, University of

London Press.

FRANKLIN B. (1977) 'Curriculum history: its nature and boundaries,' *Curriculum Inquiry*. 7, 1.

HAMMERSLEY M. and WOODS P. (Eds.) (1976) *The Process of Schooling*, London, Routledge and Kegan Paul,

HAZLETT S. (1979) 'Conceptions of curriculum history,' *Curriculum Inquiry*. 9, 2.

MACDONALD B. and WALKER R. (1976) *Changing the Curriculum*, London Open Books.

MARSDEN W.E. (1978) *Post War Curriculum Development*: *An Historical Appraisal*, History of Education Society Conference Papers. (Mimeo)

RUDOLPH F. (1977) *A History of the American Undergraduate Course of Study since 1636*, San Francisco, Jossey Bass.

SHIPMAN M. *et al* (1974) *Inside a Curriculum Project*, London, Methuen.

SILVER H. (1977) 'Nothing but the past, or nothing but the present?', *Times Higher Education Supplement*, 1 July.

WALKER R. and GOODSON I. (1977) 'Humour in the classroom', in WOODS P. and HAMMERSLEY M. (Eds.) *School Experience*, London, Croom Helm.

WARING M. (1976) *Aspects of the Dynamics of Curriculum Reform in Secondary School Science*, PhD. University of London.

# Subjects for Study: Case Studies in Curriculum History

*Ivor Goodson*

## Themes and Approaches

In the introductory chapter I argued both that curriculum history is currently at a pre-paradigmatic stage and that a major launching point could be a 'growing dialogue between historians and curriculum specialists'. This collection of papers seeks to provide a catalyst both for the definition of new approaches to curriculum history and for the development of dialogue between curriculum scholars.

In seeking to further such a dialogue the collection deliberately presents a variety of different approaches to curriculum history, undertaken by scholars from a range of disciplines and orientations. Several of the contributors have been largely identified with what might be called 'mainstream history of education', many are curriculum specialists, some are sociologists. As a result a number of the case studies — the majority — focus on particular subject histories. (It should be noted, of course, that subject histories and curriculum histories are neither synonymous nor coterminous — a point that is developed below.) Other papers pursue mainly sociological themes using historical data. We have, then, 'primary' curriculum histories largely derived from original sources alongside historical sociology or 'secondary' histories employing historical data to examine or exemplify sociological and curriculum themes. The disadvantage of blurring the definition of 'curriculum history' should be more than compensated for by the potential for cross-reference and dialogue between a range of curriculum scholars. At the present stage this would seem a necessary prerequisite for any attempts formally to define the 'field' of curriculum history. Territorial dialogues should precede territorial definition (the papers however warn that in the real world territorial scrutiny may be the prelude to territorial warfare).

Substantively all the papers point to the complexity of curriculum change and direct attention to a number of previously neglected levels or arenas where analysis should be undertaken. A number of the papers point to the vital role played by subject teaching associations: the Geographical Association (Goodson), the Mathematical Association (Cooper), the National Association for the Teaching of English (Ball), the Christian Education Movement (Bell), British Association for Language Teaching and the Modern Language Association (Radford). Bucher and Strauss in their study of professions have stressed their character as 'loose amalgamations of segments pursuing different objectives in different manners and more or less delicately held together under a common name at particular periods in history'.[1] The analogies between professions and school subjects are then clear but Bucher and Strauss also show how professional associations emerge when conflicts over the gaining of institutional control over recruitment and over external relations with other institutions are most intense. Moreover the development of large (in a sense more united) associations can mark the consolidation of gains or newly acquired status. The change from the Association for Improvement of Geometrical Teaching, founded in 1871, to the Mathematical Association, which was founded in 1897, is one such example. Hence with subject teaching associations the major period of inauguration in England preceded the definition of the Secondary Regulations (1904) and the launching of the School Certificate (1917). The Modern Language Association was founded in 1892, the Geographical Association and the Classical Association in 1893, the Mathematical Association in 1897, the Association of Public School Science Masters in 1901, the English Association in 1907. The subject associations thus emerged as lobbies at precisely the time when the secondary school curriculum was being negotiated and defined by the state. The continuing power of the associations can be clearly evidenced in the curriculum case studies in this volume.

In his paper on English, Ball shows how informal 'networks' as well as formal associations can act in defining and promoting versions of the subject. Building on the work of Griffiths and Mullins he analyzes the stages of evolution and activity in the informal networks that have operated in the curriculum history of English throughout this century. Clearly curriculum history needs to pursue an understanding of the way informal as well as formally constituted groups define and promote versions of the subject.

Beyond the focal role played by subject associations and networks in curriculum history a number of papers show the importance of sustaining external 'constituencies' and traditions in the development of school subjects. Reid argues that 'the idea of external "constituency" can provide a link that is at once stabilizing and flexible between the inventions and initiatives of educators, and the restraint and impulse of outside forces'. Likewise, McCulloch's paper points to the enduring problems of developing an external constituency to support technical schools: 'The leaders of the Association (of Heads of Technical Schools) felt that they and their schools were persistently misunderstood and misrepresented, and that this largely accounted for the failure of the schools to establish themselves.' Waring provides an exemplificatory study of a 'sustaining tradition' in school science. She argues that the most powerful tradition in English science education is individual practical work and shows how this tradition was conceived, developed and promoted in one particular period and place. The tradition has also been developed and defended elsewhere and 'the outcome has been a deeply-entrenched faith in a tradition which has, for many, assumed the status of an absolute and fundamental conservatism (conservationism, if you will) about what school science "is" and should be'.

Following on from the definition and promotion of curriculum there is the vital question of the realization and experience of curriculum in classrooms. A number of papers (for example, Franklin, Waring) deal with the perilous translation from curriculum as statement or rhetoric to curriculum as practice. The elucidation of the relationship between 'rhetoric' and 'reality' remains one of the most profound challenges to future curriculum histories. A number of papers also point to the differentiation of curriculum (and hence of curriculum experience). Cooper's paper shows how, despite major shifts in the contents of mathematics teaching, mathematics curricula continued in the 1950s and 1960s to derive their character from the earlier patterns of tripartite differentiation. Besides this differentiation by 'ability' he also considers the factor of differentiation by gender and, implicitly, by class. June Purvis follows the latter two categories of differentiation in her study of domestic subjects. For the 'less able', working class girls domestic subjects were distinctively designed to train for domestic service and were notably different from those versions offered to middle class, assumedly 'able', girls.

The danger of focusing the case studies in this book mainly on school subjects should be clearly faced. Seeley (1966) has developed the distinction between the 'taking' and the 'making' of problems. If we 'take' subjects as the focus, we are in substantial danger of confirming their 'taken-for-grantedness'. A historical view will confirm that the reinstatement or reaffirmation of school subjects *per se*, and certain subjects in particular, reflects a new regime of social and political control. Whilst it can be argued that research needs to follow these changes we must never forget that the focus reflects actions grounded in a new political climate, the orthodoxy of a dominant subject-based curriculum is the opposite of 'take-for-granted' or 'given' school worlds; it is in fact an index of intervention. The constraints of a focus on school subjects need then to be acknowledged and indeed broadened. It is also true that the focus is on secondary education; clearly in future work studies must be undertaken at all levels of the educational system and must deal with the relationship between these levels.

For this reason a number of papers (for example, McCulloch), deal with aspects of curriculum not solely focused on traditional subjects. Reid is clear on the importance of this broader focus and has argued elsewhere that:

> too much concentration on the idea of the 'subject' may lead researchers to neglect programmes like art or physical education which are essentially activity-based. The use of topic/activity avoids this problem and enables us to ask questions about how topics/activities are marshalled into various curricular patterns and called 'subjects' or shared and exchanged between subjects.

## Case Studies in Curriculum History

As has been noted, the papers in this collection have been chosen mainly to exemplify the range of styles and methods that might be employed in curriculum history. This has been the prime concern rather than coverage of the full range of subject and curriculum categories. Nonetheless, it is hoped that sufficient coverage has been achieved to point up the major features of the historical terrain with regard to the recent stages in the evolution of the secondary curriculum.

Stray's paper provides a case study of Classics in English Education since 1800. This is the first of a section of three papers that might be characterized as historical sociology. The concern is to provide insights into change and stability in Classics Education over almost two centuries, but with an emphasis on techniques, concepts and themes largely drawn from sociology. For Stray the case study might be read 'as a case study in the relations between cultural transmission and social reproduction'. He notes that the account 'rests on a political economy of cultural transmission which has been derived from the salient features of the career of Classics'.

For any student of secondary school curriculum the decline of Classics provides a fascinating case of a high status subject which has rapidly fallen from grace. Stray's work therefore provides a pioneering study of this area and will hopefully stimulate other scholars to research further in this complex area. Historical study could certainly be employed to disentangle painstakingly some of the issues to which he directs our attention.

Ball likewise relies on 'analytical techniques and concepts derived from sociology'. In the model of curriculum change that is presented a useful distinction is drawn between the 'conditions of change', that is 'the changes in the economic and social conditions of schooling which allowed, inhibited or provided for changes in the process and content of 'school knowledge' and the 'relations of change' or 'those activities and strategies which actually initiated the change'. The relations of change are examined using the analyses by Mullins and Griffiths on the emergence of specialisms within subjects. Their accounts analyze the communication 'networks' within a discipline and they provide a theory of intellectual innovation which this case study draws upon. As a result curriculum change is presented as a 'long-term and inter-personal process, based on the establishment of subject paradigms via networks of communication and apprenticeship'.

Cooper's concern is also primarily sociological though elegantly set against a detailed review of stability and change in mathematics curricula over three decades. He concentrates on 'changes in the independent dimension of the degree of differentiation of the mathematics curriculum by "ability", type and, to a much lesser extent, by sex'. His study shows a strong degree of continuity in the form of tripartite differentiation and he notes that the one 'major shift away from it — the introduction of modern "abstract" algebraic and geometrical topics into the CSE syllabus for the "average child" — produced a strong negative reaction from those sharing dominant assumptions on ability'. The manner in which the ebb and flow of differentiation is captured in different historical periods provides a dynamic model of sociological analysis and presentation. We are reminded then that there is a spectrum of relativity in the theme of knowledge and control which is at odds with more static and monolithic theories of reproduction and correspondence.

Mary Waring's paper develops a more recognizably historical approach to case study. As in all her work she is highly cognisant of the elements of uniqueness and idiosyncracy in each historical situation. Hence she warns that her account is not 'making any claim that the London Board led the way in developing an ideal of practical and experimental science'. What we have then is a painstaking recreation of one attempt to establish this tradition in a particular period in one place. It is an example of the way, to use Reid's terms, 'curriculum invention' is established. How that invention was generalized into a fundamental tradition of what school science 'is' and should be is of course a field for further historical study.

June Purvis explores a theme which is also touched upon in Mary Waring's paper which is the schooling of girls and the persistent influence on curriculum of ideas about the role of women in the wider society. Purvis examines this theme through a history of domestic subjects from 1870 to the present day. Besides the pervasiveness of sexual differentiation the chapter also provides an evolutionary perspective on curriculum differentiation according to 'ability' and class. Domestic subjects were considered most appropriate for working class and 'less able' girls. The link to future occupational destinations in domestic service was clearly articulated for this group whilst a different conception of domestic subjects was purveyed to middle class girls.

Whilst Waring and Purvis focus on the realization and experience of curriculum, Bell's study concentrates on the changing 'rhetoric' of agreed syllabuses in Religious Education (RE). He points to the progressive 'abandonment of the Christian hegemony in agreed syllabuses'. Significantly, in the light of the previous comments about the central role of subject teaching associations, he directs attention to their activities. He argues that the emergence during the 1960s 'of an articulate, non-ecclesiastical professionalism among RE teachers was obviously one factor behind the Church's voluntary concession of its traditional hegemony over the RE curriculum'.

Radford's study of modern languages follows the subject's history, with a degree of necessary brevity, from the Norman Conquest through to the present day. Radford shows that modern languages have always been at the heart of curriculum conflict particularly since they provide an academic 'discipline commonly associated with failure'. The history of the subject deals with the central struggle for recognition and resources and shows how this brought 'partisans of modern languages into competition with rival disciplines — Classics, the Sciences, English'. It also caused tensions within the subject between traditionalists and progressives, in particular reconciling the obvious utilitarian advantages of their subject with the intellectual aspirations of a discipline inevitably likened to the classical languages as a medium of humane learning, or more recently pressure from the teachers of so called 'minority' languages to overthrow the despotism of French.

Barry Franklin in his chapter develops an 'internal' study of the Minneapolis Modern Problems course during 1939–1976. As was noted earlier Franklin has been a leading advocate of curriculum history undertaken by curriculum specialists precisely so as to ensure illumination of the complexity of internal curriculum process. The study shows that the translation of curriculum ideas and rhetoric into curriculum practice must follow a tortuous route. Above all he draws our attention to the 'local mediating factors' involved in the day to day operation of the Minneapolis schools. One of the results of these mediating factors he argues has been 'to disrupt what our conventional wisdom has told us is a simple correspondence between efficiency ideas and school practices. If what we have found about the relationship between curriculum theory and practice in Minneapolis is true for other school systems, we will need to revise our understanding of that relationship'.

Whitty also deals with social studies curricula, alongside political education. His concern is not however to provide a curriculum history *per se*. Rather he uses data on three periods of curriculum reform because 'in looking at attempts to challenge the prevailing state of affairs, we can see something of the complexity of the influences that have sustained the mainstream curriculum model and contributed to its reproductive effects'. In the later section he provides a brief discussion of the value of curriculum history in examining sociological theory and argues that 'detailed studies in curricular history can help us to interrogate and refine those theories and this, in turn, can generate a form of theory better able to inform future studies of curricular continuity and change'. But beyond the theoretical enterprise he sees value for those concerned with curriculum action and change: 'Certainly our three case studies make it clear that social and political educators in the past have often based their strategies on an inadequate analysis of the context in which they have chosen to intervene'.

Reid is also concerned with examining theories (particularly in this case those developed by John Meyer) and with judging if curriculum history can illuminate the nature of curriculum change. Reid's case study is grounded in the extensive study of the evolution of the English sixth form which he has recently completed with Jane Filby. He uses these data to illustrate how particular curricula 'inventions' become generalized by the development of sustaining traditions, a supportive rhetoric and crucially, he argues, an external constituency. He shows how schools and constituency collaborate in developing an informing rhetoric and how 'the rhetoric, once established, became the means of shaping and stabilising what schools did. Inventions contributed to a curricular orthodoxy and could be changed only to the extent that the orthodoxy was not interfered with'.

McCulloch looks at what he calls 'the legend of the alternative road', a concept first publicized in the Crowther Report, and examines the relationship between the 'alternative road' rhetoric and the Association of the Heads of Secondary Technical Schools from 1951 to 1964. He illustrates the persistent ambiguities and tensions which sheltered behind the slogan of the alternative road. He then goes on to examine the use made of this unresolved concept by those promoting the new Technical and Vocational Education Initiative (TVEI). He concludes that with respect to the Association of Heads of Technical Schools 'the idea that they were pioneers of an alternative road has encouraged a distorted view of history and maintained the belief that there exists a single "practical" approach in education'. Likewise the original rationale used to promote the TVEI 'shows how "raids" on the past, involving highly selective interpretations of history, may be employed for the purposes of current policy aims'. This chapter therefore warns us that politicians as well as academics can abuse and misuse history to further their own ends. It is part of the task of curriculum history to make such raids on the past more difficult.

In the final chapter Goodson, drawing from his work in *School Subjects and Curriculum Change*, seeks to draw together some conclusions. In particular some tentative guidelines are developed which provide explanatory frameworks for the future study of school subjects.

## Notes

1 BUCHER, R. and STRAUSS, A. (1976) p. 19.

## References

BUCHER, R. and STRAUSS A. (1976) 'Professions in process', in HAMMERSLEY M. and WOODS P. (Eds.) *The Process of Schooling*, London, Routledge and Kegan Paul.

GOODSON, I. (1983) *School Subjects and Curriculum Change*, London, Croom Helm.

REID, W.A. (1984) 'Curricular topics as institutional categories — implications for theory and research in the history and sociology of school subjects', in

GOODSON I. and BALL S. (Eds.) *Defining the Curriculum: Histories and Ethnographies*, Lewes, Falmer Press.

SEELEY, J. (1966) 'The "making" and "taking" of problems', *Social Problems*, 14.

# From Monopoly to Marginality: Classics in English Education Since 1800

*Christopher A. Stray*

The primary concern of this chapter is to provide a case study in the historical sociology of education by considering the changing content and status of Classics in English education since 1800. The role of classical knowledge for most of this period as a symbolic badge of elite membership, and its recent detachment from that role, make its history of more general interest. The account can therefore also be read as a case study in the relations between cultural transmission and social reproduction in England and Wales. The theoretical shape of the account, in fact, rests on a 'political economy of cultural transmission' (of which a tentative outline will be found below), which has been derived from the salient features of the career of classics.

The current decline in demand for Classics in schools began in the late 1950s, when Cambridge and Oxford abandoned their long standing insistence on a pass in O level Latin as a general entrance requirement. This effectively destroyed the major institutional support for the provision of Classics in schools. In 1960, as a direct result, the level of entries to the O level Latin examination began to decline in relation to entries in other subjects; by 1965, the decline had become absolute. In the independent sector, the survival of a Victorian 'gentlemanly' tradition was reflected in the continuing provision of 'full Classics' (Latin, Greek, ancient history). In the state grammar schools of the thirties, forties and fifties, however, the preponderant element in the teaching of classics was the O level Latin course, whose centre of gravity lay not in classical culture, but in the mastery of grammatical and syntactic paradigms. This mastery was demonstrated initially by repetition, subsequently by its deployment in Latin prose composition. 'Literature' played a subordinate part, in the form of 'set books': learnt off by heart by pupils, and in examinations treated largely as corpuses of linguistic material. Ancient history and classical civilization received lip-service as 'essential background', but no more than perfunctory treatment. Within the selective system, the supposed virtues of the 'grammar grind' — precision, rigour, complexity, alienness from everyday experience — rendered it an ideal encapsulation of the tradition of academic humanism which the grammar schools claimed to maintain. It also increased the subsequent unpopularity of Latin at the end of the fifties, when the Cold War, Sputnik, and opposition to both principle and practice of secondary selection combined to bring into disfavour the 'academic' and the 'humanities'.[1]

In the academic sphere itself, Latin grammar was attracting criticism from within the expanding field of structural linguistics, whose practitioners challenged its adequacy as a universal paradigm of linguistic form. It was symbolically appropriate, then, that structural linguistics was drawn on in the mid-sixties in the construction of a radically new O-level Latin course. The Cambridge Latin Course (hereafter referred to as CLC) represents an attempt to distance the subject from its received ideological basis. The declared aim of the course, which is now used by almost half the total entry to O-level Latin, is to promote the fluent reading of Roman literature, rather than the mastery of Latin grammatical forms. The course material, in fact, avoided all mention of formal grammar, employing instead the repetition of sentence patterns embedded in a sociocultural context. The earlier units of the course consist of synthetic Latin narratives set in Pompeii in the first century AD; the traditional textbook is replaced by folders, pamphlets and audio-visual supporting material. CLC was designed to be attractive, to be accessible to pupils over a much wider ability range than the traditional O-level Latin entry, and to take pupils to O level in much less time than had normally been allowed for conventional courses.[2]

When CLC became commercially available in the late 1960s, the initial reaction of most teachers was favourable. By 1973, however, when I began interviewing Classics teachers for the research on which this chapter is based, disillusionment had set in among the great majority, who had been socialized into the values of what one teacher called 'the ordinary, straightforward, traditional Latin'. To be confronted simultaneously, as some were, with a reorganized school, a 'new kind of pupil', and a Latin course which forbade the explicit teaching of grammar or syntax, provoked feelings of frustration and, in some cases, of despair. Here again is the teacher I have just quoted, this time at greater length: this passage is given in full, since it links biographical troubles to the larger issues of institutional and social structural change.

> Classicists have been recruited into the civil service to such a
> large extent ... I think it's that kind of person it produces: a

person who can think clearly, who's methodical, self-controlled
. . . now they don't like to discipline themselves mentally . . . or
physically, it's part of today . . . this dreadful thing we're in . . .
the teenage vandalism and all that . . . it's all linked up with it.
Everything I say is going to be a criticism of everything the
comprehensive system has produced. I'm a part of it, but a part
that can't do anything about it. The English I'm doing now, I
feel quite frankly I can't teach it . . . well the CSE English
group, they keep on making the same grammatical mistakes. I
can't get them right somehow . . . and it's entirely due to the fact
that we don't teach grammar as such any more . . . But what can
you do, you can't go against . . . friends and colleagues. We did
a lot more English grammar when I was at school, so the terms
of reference were heard *across*, it wasn't just done in Latin and
nowhere else . . . with the Cambridge course you've no terms of
reference, you're lost.[3]

This lament points beyond biography, in that it invokes the sense
of a shared generational identity through which 'that kind of person'
was created by 'terms of reference' which were 'heard across' the
specialist boundaries of the grammar school curriculum. But not far
enough beyond. In the first place, it rests on an ahistorical primitivism,
already apparent in the earlier reference to 'the ordinary, straightforward, traditional Latin'. The lament looks back to the historically
specific domination of Classics teaching in the state grammar schools of
the thirties, forties and fifties by the 'grammar grind' of Latin. Such
primitivism, of course, allows of only two states — Paradise and After;
the Fall, in this case, coming with the abandonment of the Oxbridge
Latin requirement at the end of the fifties. What this myth *conceals* is
that the mid-century domination of Latin was initiated, in the 1920s, by
the collapse of an earlier conception of Classics. This was the Victorian
gentlemanly idea of Classics as an organic cultural unity, which suffered
a severe blow from the postwar condemnation of gentlemanly amateurism and its inadequacies. The crucial events took place in and around
1920; just as the current phase in the career of Classics was initiated by
the abandonment of compulsory Latin, so its predecessor was initiated
by the abandonment of an Oxbridge requirement for compulsory
Greek.

As I have suggested above, this earlier conception of Classics
persisted through to the 1950s in the independent sector, alongside the
Latin-centred tradition of the state grammar schools. This points to the
second limitation of the 'lament' quoted above: its experiential categories are class-specific. As I shall argue in more detail below, the

emphasis on 'clear thinking and self-control' reflects the ideological location of the 'grammar grind': it was a central component in the socialization of the professional middle-class groups of the 1930s whose self-legitimation rested on the new-found respectability of Reason (as opposed to Culture) in the 1930s. The theoretical shape of the account which follows is implicit in the criticisms I have levelled at the primitivistic 'lament' quoted above. The differential distribution of different kinds of Classics to separate social groups, and the recurrent shifts, and current decline, in its provision: all these run counter to the tendency to see 'cultural transmission' as the straightforward repetition of a homogeneous societal consensus. Rather, they suggest a picture dominated by the changing definition, evaluation and distribution of curricular knowledge. Because of this, I preface the historical account below with a sketch of a 'political economy of cultural transmission' which focuses on the production, distribution and consumption of knowledge.[4]

We can begin with the assertion that the continuity of a society over time is achieved by the production of social goods (people) and cultural goods (knowledge). These two kinds of goods are different, but are alike ranked in terms of the society's currently dominant values. As new social members are produced, therefore, we can expect them to be 'matched' with specific areas of knowledge in the cultural repertoire; and this process constitutes a system of legitimate allocation. The ideal-typical extremes of such a system are *command* allocation (all members are initiated into the entire repertoire) and *market* allocation (each member selects freely from it). Between these utopian extremes lie a whole range of empirically possible alternatives, presenting a given society with a problem of choice: *who may learn what?* We can therefore expect any society to possess rules of legitimate allocation, which will take the form of *compulsion* or *prohibition* toward the 'command' extreme, and of *availability* toward the 'market' case.[5]

These necessarily abstract statements can be made more specific by applying them to the particular case of modern industrialized societies. Here a division of social labour obtains, within which the state's monopoly over the legitimate transmission of culture is delegated to a specialized occupational group (teachers). The formal education system is thus the legitimate *locus* of this transmission, the curriculum its legitimate *form*. When the division of labour extends from the production of material goods to the sphere of cultural production — knowledge and ideas as well as things — this 'legitimate form' becomes that of the marketplace: a collection of specialized commodities made available to consumers. At the secondary level in particular, teachers have thus belonged to a *double* division of labour. They possess delegated authority to teach both pupils and knowledge, each expertise being certified through accredited courses of study (typically, degree course and teacher training). These structural features of teachers' occupational experience appear strange, once stated, because we take them for granted as permanent features of their world. Yet this is in fact a recent phenomenon which has emerged from a lengthy ideological struggle — the long debate on the relation between culture and the division of labour. From the point of view of those who saw the latter as disintegrative of the unity of human moral experience, the unity and coherence of educational knowledge was an important target. The categories of this debate, and their realization in successive forms of school Classics, provide a central theme in the account which follows.

## Classics and the Division of Labour, 1800–1930

### *The emergence of a curricular market, 1800–1900*

In 1800 the Oxford curriculum was dominated by Classics, as was the Cambridge curriculum by Mathematics. In both cases, what was taught was the conventional knowledge appropriate to successive generations of a noble elite. In Gillispie's succinct summary,

> One could argue that much of the prestige — or at any rate the snob value — of classical studies as a general instrument of education in the modern English-speaking world derives from the fact that in the early nineteenth century Oxford tutors, who were determined to maintain their monopoly of university teaching, did not know anything else to teach. They believed in their wares and valued their positions, and were forced in self-defence to elaborate a persuasive justification of the manner in which the English upper class was being educated. Publications of Cambridge dons claimed for the study of mathematics the same pedagogical benefits which in Oxford were attributed to Classics — a circumstance which supports the impression that the manner rather than the matter of the education was what ultimately gave rise to the theory developed to defend it.[6]

The attack on Oxford in the 1800s was led by the *Edinburgh Review*. Invoking the Enlightenment ideals of progress and rationalism, it denounced Oxford as a reactionary nest of elitist Classics and religious restriction, its scholarship out of date and its provision for professional training hopelessly inadequate. The leading defenders of Oxford rejected these premises in favour of those of Burke's reaction to the Enlightenment. The university, they claimed, was an evolving organism, to be judged as an integral part of contemporary English society, in which (for example) rank counted for more than intellect. Oxford, in their view, did not owe a duty to England as a 'national foundation': its Englishness rested precisely in its being independent rather than 'national'. The awful example of France was instanced to demonstrate the perils of reason and revolution — irrational evolution was the English way, and Oxford should hold to it. Rationalist premises were implicitly accepted, however, in the debate on the merits of Oxford classical scholarship. Both sides, in fact, spent most of their time wrangling over the minutiae of syntax and grammar, thus diverting attention from the related but separate issue, whether and what Classics should be taught at Oxford.[7]

By the 1830s, the intransigence of the defenders of 'Oxford and old England' had given way to accommodation and reform. During the first generation after industrial take-off (circa 1830–60), the challenge to classical education generated by the expansion of bourgeois power was deflected by the emergence of an assimilated noble-bourgeois elite. At the heart of this assimilation lay the classical education provided in the reformed public schools, led by Arnold at Rugby (1828–42). Arnold's self-appointed task was one of transformation, rather than of the reproduction of an existing elite. In place of the elegant versifying of the eighteenth-century gentleman, he developed a programme of reading and composition in Latin and Greek designed to provide moral lessons and a sense of history. Within their isolated rural enclaves, the public schools transformed (in Arnold's words) 'savage boys' into 'Christian gentlemen'. At the same time, they transformed *financial* into *cultural* capital — the manners which gave access to polite society. This was crucial for the expanding professional classes, who were concerned to veil the dependence on fees which formed the material basis of their 'gentlemanly independence'. Arnold's parallel acceptance of the division of social labour as offering, within limits, an important stimulus for necessary social innovation, marked a significant shift from the eighteenth-century opposition of 'virtue' and 'commerce' to which the Oxford tutors of the 1800s had clung.[8]

Paradoxically, it was the tutors' intransigence which paved the way for the increasing influence of the division of labour on the Oxford curriculum. Taking for granted the monopoly of Classics, they had hardly referred to its content as something in need of evaluation. Their liberal successors of the 1830s seized on this lacuna and transformed it into the *positive* notion of 'free academic reason'.

> The reformer had ... to walk a tightrope between 'liberal education' and 'practical, professional education' ... it was at this point that the ideal of an academic profession became crucial. Clearly, the main goal of these reformers was to reorganize the studies of the university to provide more direct training for the professions. At the same time, they had to avoid 'low, utilitarian' notions. The solution was to argue that physiology ... [etc.,] were all ... sources of abstract 'mental culture', and that the teachers of these subjects must be *students of truth* not practitioners for gain'.[9]

In this way, specialized knowledge was rendered legitimate, buttressed by the academic ideology of the shared quest for truth. As a result, the Oxford curriculum became a market economy of culture. The range of curricular commodities increased as new specialisms became respectable; a process facilitated by the contemporary acceptance of faculty psychology, since the promoters of new subjects were able to identify, define — or invent — a faculty which their knowledge was especially fitted to train. At the same time, the absence of any clear or agreed idea of what *counted* as a faculty militated against any genuine debate on the nature and status of the new subjects.[10]

By the 1860s, the consolidated noble-bourgeois elite was firmly established. The new public schools, acting in concert for the first time, succeeded in removing state interventionist clauses from the Endowed Schools Bill before it became law in 1869. The collective autonomy thus asserted was soon formally established by the founding of the Head Masters' Conference, and reflected in their adoption of a common Latin primer.[11] In his *Essays on Educational Reformers*, published in 1868, R.H. Quick declared that 'One of the great wants of middle-class education at present is an ideal to work towards. Our old public schools have such an ideal'. The ideal was still largely that of the classically-educated gentleman, and it retained its attraction, which was maintained not only by the HMC schools, but also by large numbers of the schools released by the 1869 Endowed Schools Act from the restrictive terms of their original endowments. At the same time, the outlines of a curricular market of specialized commodities were appearing *within* Classics, as the new ('provincial' or 'civic') universities were founded, usually with separate departments of Greek and Latin. The connections between this variety of definitions of Classics and the essentially stratified nature of the curricular marketplace can be seen in the report of the Schools Inquiry Commission of 1868. The commissioners suggest that 'Education ... can at present be classified as that which is to stop at about 14, that which is to stop at about 16, and that which is to continue till 18 or 19 ... It is obvious that these distinctions correspond roughly, but by no means exactly, to the gradations of society'.

They then discuss parental demand for the several grades; and (what is to the point here) the discussion is conducted in terms of perceived demand for Classics ('first grade', that is till 18 or 19), and for Latin ('second grade', that is till 16). As far as the second grade was concerned, parents were classified as those who wanted Latin but not Greek, and those (for example, 'the mercantile classes') who 'seem disposed barely to tolerate Latin, if they will even do that'.[12]

### Command intervention: the Board of Education, 1900–1930

By 1900, the formal transmission of culture at the secondary level and above had come to resemble a market economy; albeit a market in which access to 'publicly available' commodities was in fact stratified. Yet the turn of the century also witnessed the emergence of an explicitly 'command' element, in the form of intervention and regulation by central government. A major stimulus to this came from the failure of economic laissez-faire to deliver the goods on a global scale. Free trade, which had ensured the earlier predominance of British exports, now promoted the interests of France, Germany and the USA, all of whom had built more positively on their industrial take-off with technological development and technical education. Such well-publicized indicators as the relative failure of British products at the 1867 Paris Exhibition, compared with their sweeping success at the Great Exhibition of 1851, encouraged interest groups pressing for the expansion of scientific and technical education (for which grants were provided by the Science and Art Department, set up in 1853 with the profits from the 1851 Exhibition). This department functioned entirely separately from the Education Department, which had been set up as a committee of the Privy Council in 1839 to administer educational grants, and which was largely staffed by gentlemanly products of Oxbridge and the public schools. As one of them later observed, 'They were scholars, poets, philosophers and musicians etc., and they were ready to discuss — and discuss well — any subjects under the sun except education'.[13] By the 1890s, however, it became clear that some kind of unified central organization was necessary. France and Germany were both currently carrying out such organization; the problem, as it was generally seen in England, was how to become more organized and efficient without becoming 'unEnglish' and, more particularly, 'Prussianized'.

The concern to provide both for national survival, and for means to it which ran with the English grain, is evident in the report of the Royal Commission on Secondary Education (1895).

> Education ... needs organization, but it would be destroyed by uniformity ... we mean by 'system' neither uniformity nor the control of a Central Department of government. Freedom, variety, elasticity are, and have been, the merits ... in English education ... The 'system' which we desire to see introduced may rather be described as coherence, an organic relation between different authorities and different kinds of schools.[14]

The Bryce Commission's report led to the 1899 Act which set up the Board of Education, a regulatory rather than initiating body which combined the responsibilities of the old Education Department and the Science and Art Department. The interventionist potential inherent in the Board's regulatory powers were, however, forcefully realized by its first Permanent Secretary, Robert Morant. In Morant's view, without 'control by "knowledge" in the sphere of public education of all grades ... a democratic state must inevitably be beaten in the international struggle for existence, conquered from without by the concentrated directing brain power of competing nations, and shattered from within by the centrifugal forces of her own people's unrestrained individualism'.[15]

Control was exercised over the curricula of the new county secondary schools through the Board's power to provide or withhold grants. Morant exercised this control to promote the organic unity of culture as a counter to 'centrifugal forces' such as individualism and the division of labour. The regulations for schools in receipt of grant, first set out in 1904, contained a preface in which Morant insisted that any course of instruction 'must be general; that is, must be such as gives a reasonable degree of exercise and development to the whole of the faculties'. Only when the habit of such exercise had been formed should specialization begin. In advanced work, where specialization was inevitable, some kind of coherence could be maintained by requiring *balanced* provision of subjects. Its Second Secretary said of the Board in 1916 that 'its special duty appears to be ... to try to hold the balance even as possible between various groups of study'.[16] The self-image of the Board as an impartial referee, however, did not preclude interventionist measures to restore a balance perceived to have been disturbed: as, for example, between scientific and classical/literary education. In the 1890s, large numbers of schools had taken up the relatively generous grants offered by the (then autonomous) Science and Art Department for science courses. Morant later commented that 'their influence . . . in the curricula of secondary schools was decidedly mischievous . . . this resulted in a lopsided development. But in 1903 we swept all that away, and started a proper arrangement whereby our Grants were paid in respect of the curriculum as a whole . . .'.[17]

This 'proper arrangement' was started, in part, because of the situation revealed by J.W. Headlam, one of the Board's inspectors, who carried out an investigation of schools in 1902. He warned that

> In the majority of the schools . . . the nature of the literary education . . . requires the most serious attention . . . In many of the schools . . . no attempt is now made to give a classical education . . . it is becoming increasingly difficult for a professional man who cannot afford to send his son to an expensive boarding school to procure in the grammar school of his district an education which will prepare him for a professional career.[18]

The 1904 Regulations laid down that if two languages other than English were taught, one must be Latin, unless its exclusion could be justified to the Board. This clause remained in the amended Regulations of 1907, and was defended in a Board circular on the curriculum (1913), on the grounds of 'Latin's great educational value . . . and its consequent inclusion in the syllabuses of the examinations which admit to many professions and to practically all university degrees in arts'. In general, however, the Board's 1913 circular evidences a retreat from the certainties of 1904. In place of the 'discipline of faculty', we have a definition of the aims of secondary education which reveals the influence of childcentrism: 'to provide for each pupil a good general education. The curriculum must therefore be sufficiently comprehensive in range to avoid undue narrowness of outlook and sufficiently varied in character to arouse latent interests and dormant capacities.' Similarly with the discussion of curricular content: '. . . the progress of knowledge during the last century has involved the introduction of new subjects . . . with the progress of knowledge there is a constant shifting of the relative values assigned to different branches of learning.'[19]

The Board attempted to deal with these problems of change and specialization by promoting both balanced provision of subject groups and the 'organic unity' of their content. In the 1913 circular, it had proposed a new course, to be called 'Modern Humanistic Studies', which was to consist, like Classics, of two languages and some history.

In 1917, it offered grants for the teaching of three such 'Advanced Courses': (A) Science and Mathematics, (B) Classics, and (C) Modern (Humanistic) Studies. The subsequent variation in the approved content of the groups is of some interest. The Board's declared preference for 'organic unity' rather than 'an arbitrary collection of disparate subjects'[20] did not prevent it from including Latin in group C, since it was 'for long the common language of Europe'. Most of the course proposals received from schools, however, specified *classical* Latin, and eventually the Board felt obliged to remove Latin from the Group. Meanwhile, a large number of schools (mostly girls' schools) were complaining that they could not staff Group B in its entirety, and asked for a new Group containing Latin, English and History. This was eventually offered, as Group D, in 1921; it was apparently acceptable as an 'organic unity' because it contained history and two languages. If so, the organic notion was surely being stretched to breaking point.

The Advanced Courses were supported by grant from 1917 until 1935. If the take-up of grant for Groups A, B and C is compared over this period, it can be seen that the 'organic unity' of Classics fared none too well, even with the Board's support.[21]

Table 1    Take-up of grant for advanced courses 1917–35[21]

|         | A: Science/Maths | B: Classics | C: Modern Studies |
|---------|------------------|-------------|-------------------|
| 1917–18 | 82               | 20          | 25                |
| 1918–19 | 155              | 27          | 78                |
| 1919–20 | 189              | 29          | 118               |
| 1920–21 | 216              | 35          | 152               |
| 1921–22 | 230              | 37          | 180               |
| 1935    | 246              | 37          | 171               |

The relative failure of the Board's support for Classics was due, in part, to the staffing problems already mentioned. More important, however, was the abandonment of compulsory Greek requirements at Oxford and a greater share of the school timetable. The classicists had two very dissimilar associations to rely on: the Classical Association (1903) and curricular interest-groups began pressing their claims to increased status and a greater share of the school timetable. The classicists had two very dissimilar associations to rely on: the Classical Association (1903) and the Association for the Reform of Latin Teaching (1911). The former was much the larger and more conservative, and devoted its efforts to a defence of the existing content and position of Classics. It has operated largely through its local branches, which link teachers and their pupils to the nearest university department, providing programmes of lectures and reading competitions. The school/university overlap is also evident in its journal, *Greece and Rome*, which publishes semi-popular articles and book reviews, and is aimed at sixth formers, teachers and undergraduates. The ARLT was, and is, much smaller, and has no branches. It was the brainchild of W.H.D. Rouse, headmaster of the Perse School, who created it as a vehicle for the promotion of direct method teaching in Latin and Greek. At the outset, it suffered severe setbacks which prevented large-scale success. Rouse failed to convince the (largely traditionalist) Head Masters' Conference to endorse his proposals for direct method teaching. Then just as the Association's annual summer schools were about to attract international support, in 1914, the Great War put an end to any hope of immediate links, especially with Germany, whose dominant position in classical scholarship made such links particularly welcome. The War also decimated Rouse's 'bright young men', the potential leaders of the next generation. But the final blow came from the Prime Minister's Committee on Classics, whose report *The Classics in Education* appeared in 1921. The committee read Rouse's books, and some of its members watched him and his colleagues teaching; but though they found his approach stimulating, they concluded that it could not be recommended for general use by teachers and pupils of average endowments.[22]

The Classics Committee was one of four such committees set up at the end of the War, their reports appearing between 1919 and 1921 (the others dealt with natural science, English and modern languages). Amid the mutual jostling for curricular time which formed a central part of this postwar revaluation, the Board of Education continued to see its role as 'holding the balance even'. In 1921 an internal staff committee was appointed to consider the consequences for curricular planning of adopting the recommendations of the reports. Fisher, the Board's President, declared in his remit that the committee's task was a simple one, since the four committees were basically in agreement (PRO Ed. 24/1192). The staff advisory committee on Classics, however, commented at about the same time on the 'acute conflict' between the views of the Classics committee and those of the other three (PRO Ed. 12/221. S888, 17.10.21). Not surprisingly, however, the published circular stressed the 'general agreement displayed as to the main purpose of secondary education and ... the frank recognition of the claims of other subjects'.[23]

The most significant part of the circular is its tabulation of the 'legitimate claims' of the four Committees with the probable 'minimum claims' of other subjects. The result of this exercise was a total of 'claimed' time which equalled or exceeded what was available in a typical school timetable (*ibid*, p. 2. Many girls' schools at this time worked markedly shorter hours than this 'typical' picture implies). The 'squeeze of subjects' was not a recent problem, but 'is becoming increasingly acute' (*ibid*, p. 3.). The Board's solution was to allow more freedom and variation in school curricula, confident that 'the force of tradition and public opinion will tend to preclude for the present more than a limited divergence from the normal curriculum'. This shift of position away from 'command interventionism' was completed in 1926, when the Board ceased laying down curricular prescriptions for secondary schools.[24]

## The Division of Cultural Labour: Academic Latin 1930–1960

In the thirties, the curriculum of the state grammar schools moved steadily away from the 'Edwardian' pattern of organic unity and balance, which the Board had tried to promote, to a 'Georgian' pattern of separate subjects.[25] The unity of these 'collections' of subjects was deemed to derive from the interests of the individual children who chose them. Thus, paradoxical though it may seem, this child-centred approach fostered specialization. As the Spens Report commented: 'We have ... urged that the educative effect inheres not in a subject but in the spirit of study, and are therefore prepared to agree ... to a reduction in the number of subjects studied at any one time'.[26] The culmination of this trend came in 1950 with the introduction of the GCE *subject* examination, following the Norwood Committee's recommendation: 'that is to say, an examination in which pupils would take whatever subjects they wished without restriction as to minimum number of subjects or "groups" of subjects'.[27] Morant would surely have denounced this trend as strengthening the 'centrifugal forces of [the] people's unrestrained individualism' by allowing pupils to amass a 'collection of disparate subjects'. How are we to account for the new-found legitimacy of 'subjects'?

To understand these changes, we have to place them in the context of the broader cultural and social structural changes of which they formed a part. Most fundamental was the impact of world war and economic recession in shattering the relative stability of Edwardian England. As Whitmarsh puts it, '... in the 1920s there were faint hopes of a return to the world that had been lost, the world of 1914. But after

1931 there was a general understanding that this was no longer possible. The thirties offered to its intellectuals a planning mission . . .'[28] Since the past was irrecoverable, the future must be planned and created: thus 'reason alone' became respectable. In addition, it could now be contrasted favourably with powerful contemporary irrationalisms. The widely-popularized work of the elitist social psychologists, such as Trotter and MacDougall, was a force in this direction. By the 1930s, moreover, the power of reason could easily be seen not as a solvent of stable values, but as a beacon light for democracy in a world of irrational extremism, whether fascist or communist. As a result, professional groups, once denounced as potential threats to social solidarity, were now commonly seen as the bulwarks of a free, democratic (and incidentally capitalist) way of life. It was this ideological complex which was reflected in the curriculum of the state grammar schools, which, nurtured and protected from 'undesirable competition' from the elementary schools, became the major source of recruitment to the professions and a central avenue of mobility into the relative security of a middle class career.[29]

The grammar school curriculum in many ways constituted a market economy, in which pupils selected from among alternative and equivalent commodities — equivalent because each could train the pupil's reason, irrespective of content. Thus 'unrestrained individualism' was contained by the market's ideological basis, which centred on *academicity*: the separation between 'subjects' and everyday knowledge. What has to be understood, however, is how this ideology of academicity functioned within a stratified education system in a period when, as Spens declared, 'the emphasis in educational theory has shifted from the subject to the child'.[30] The crucial factor was the absorption of the developmental psychology of interests, which in the USA had formed part of a 'democratic' psychology of individual differences, into the English conservative tradition of *group* differences. In the latter tradition, the 'natural, immanent' development of the individual resulted in membership of a category which formed part of a *de facto* hierarchy. Hence the 'organic system' lauded as typically English by the Bryce Commission functioned to legitimate the stratification of educational provision. The doctrine is found in classical form in the Norwood Report, which dismisses the claims of professional psychology to categorize children in favour of 'English practice': 'The evolution of education has in fact thrown up certain groups, each of which can and must be treated in a way appropriate to itself . . . For example, English education has in practice recognised the pupil who is interested in learning for its own sake . . .'[31]

One of Norwood's contemporaries commented with some irritation that 'he regards himself as entrusted with the task of charting the scope of grammar schools in the wide field of secondary education'.[32] Norwood's success can be gauged by the similarity of his proposals to the White Paper on educational reconstruction of 1943, and to the Education Act of the following year. In the debate on the White Paper, R.A. Butler, then President of the Board of Education, said that 'a certain philosophy runs through the whole scheme ... We shall retain in our system a diversity of choice, while attempting at the same time to fuse the parts and weld them into an organic whole' (debate in House of Commons, 29 July 1943). The ideological categories are those of Norwood, of Bryce, — and of Copleston, ≏ the assertion of the 'English tradition': freedom and diversity, organic unity rather than centralized uniformity. The wartime resurgence of patriotic emotion regenerated this ideological tradition. It also diverted and defused opposition from the Labour Party, which was in any case still torn, as it had been in the 1920s, between outright rejection of selective education and qualified support for grammar schools as avenues of social mobility.[33]

Yet despite the apparently successful compromises of the 1944 Act and the consequent prolongation of selective education into the 1950s, it was in that decade that the pressures built up which brought about the end of the grammar school and its tradition of academic humanism. With that tradition went 'compulsory Latin', generally seen as a symbol of social elitism and obsolete humanism. The disappearance of the Oxbridge Latin requirement led not just to reduced recruitment to Classics, but to a legitimation crisis. Since the 1920s, I have argued, Latin had occupied an exemplary status in the school curriculum as a paradigm case of academic rigour, buttressed by a contemporary ideology of clear thinking and self-control as the necessary qualities for citizens of a liberal democracy, charting its future in an uncertain and irrational world. Within this tradition, successive groups and generations of pupils were socialized into legitimate embodiments of stable values; history was constantly confirmed by biography. Since the 1960s, this has no longer been the case. The construction of new courses (notably the Cambridge Latin Course), as well as the adoption of an active — at times aggressive — approach to the denigrators of Classics since the early 1960s is largely due to the founders of the Joint Association of Classical Teachers, an umbrella organization set up in 1963. JACT has published a journal which has set high standards in both content and production (*Didaskalos*, recently succeeded by *Hesperiam*), and has organized a series of influential conferences, one of which led to the foundation of the Council of University Classical

Departments (CUCD). Loosely affiliated to JACT are a number of local associations of classical teachers (ACTs) which negotiate with LEAs over the position of Classics.

In the final section of this chapter, the analysis similarly moves to the local level. The reasons are twofold. First, not only is the legitimacy of Classics heavily contested, but the decisive struggles often take place in negotiation between teachers and others in schools and LEA areas. Second, a micro-level analysis of local and organizational politics requires the extension of the 'political economy of cultural transmission' to the institutional level; and I think it a salutary requirement that I should develop it, and the reader appraise it. What follows, therefore, is an attempt to analyze the ways in which the status of curricular knowledge is negotiated in relation to the legitimate allocation of knowledge to pupils. The material used here is drawn from interviews with teachers in the Welsh town I shall call Llangarr in 1973, 1978 and 1983.[34]

## Comprehensive Classics: Negotiating Content & Status, 1960–83

Llangarr has a long history of Labour domination in local politics. In the 1950s, the LEA built two multilateral schools, which then began to siphon off some of the 11+ passes formerly shared by the local grammar schools. Together with the removal of 'compulsory Latin', this gradually eroded recruitment to O-level Latin in the early 1960s. The memory of one teacher that 'When I came here in 1962, Latin was established ... everybody was against the impression that Latin could ever change' recalls the last moments of an era. Another teacher's recollection goes to the heart of what change felt like:

> '... fifteen, twelve years ago [*ie.* 1958–60] English began to move away from grammar to free expression and creative writing ... and then ... about a decade ago [*ie.* 1963] pupils questioned the point of doing a subject in which it seemed you had no chance of success unless you had mastered all that grammar. One sensed that the translation into Latin became more and more inaccurate ... the rules of grammar more and more unfathomable. English was followed by French, with the audiovisual course ... then German ... so Latin was left on its own'.

In the mid-sixties, then, the writing was already on the wall in Llangarr. The 'terms' were no longer 'heard across', and O-level Latin classes were shrinking. In some schools, Latin became optional, set against (most commonly) Biology and nonlinguistic Classical Studies; and where this happened, the numbers opting for Latin steadily declined. The LEA responded swiftly to Circular 10/65, proposing to operate a fully reorganized system from 1970; and as part of its preparation for this, set up subject committees on which teachers were represented, to make recommendations for the curricula of the new comprehensive schools. At the same time, the local Classics teachers were visited by members of the project team then engaged in the construction of the Cambridge Latin Course (CLC). The course material was publicly approved by the area HMI and the Classics lecturer at the local university's department of education. It also gained the approval of the LEA adviser in charge of the subject committees mentioned above. The LEA had good reason to support the introduction of the Cambridge course. Constraints of finance and of existing school accommodation meant that the 1970 reorganization would create a patchwork system: all-through (11–18), 11–13 and 13–18 schools were scheduled, with some 13–18 schools fed by three or four 11–13 schools. Curricular standardization was therefore at a premium, and CLC offered a convenient solution. In the event, the LEA agreed that CLC and its associated nonlinguistic (Classical Studies) course should be provided in 11–18 and 13–18 schools; and that Classical Studies *should*, and CLC *might*, be taught in 11–13 schools. It was this 'charter' which marked the end of the initial phase of negotiation, a phase which closed, for the Classics teachers, amid more optimism than could have been guessed at in the mid-sixties.

Despite the 1970 'charter', however, the Llangarr Classics teachers soon found reason to be apprehensive for the future. What the LEA had guaranteed was the *fact*, not the *nature*, of the provision of Classics. Exactly what is taught to whom, and how, in an individual school is to a considerable extent a matter for negotiation; and it is the negotiation of Classics, as it developed through the 1970s, which will be examined next. Before we plunge into ethnographic detail, however, something needs to be said about the analytic perspective within which the account is organized. This requires that we extend the notion of a 'political economy' of cultural transmission, outlined earlier in the chapter, to incorporate the negotiation of knowledge/pupil allocation at the institutional level.

We can begin by noting that Classics teachers bring to this negotiation the resources, and limitations, of professionals whose delegated authority within the division of social labour provides them with rights and duties. (The exact definitions of these rights and duties, we can add, are themselves negotiable.) The implications of this can be drawn out by considering the work of Johnson and Burns. In *Professions and Power*,[35] Johnson discusses the ways in which professionals and their clients negotiate the definition of the content of professional services. Johnson argues that the division of labour both unites and divides us, creating specialized producers but unspecialized consumers, and setting up relations of both dependence and distance among social members. The consequent tensions, he suggests, are resolved in favour either of specialists (collegiate control by professionals); of clients (systems of patronage); or of a third party — historically the most important example being that of the state. *State mediation* takes place when professional/client negotiation is carried out under the aegis of the state, which lays down the rules of negotiation. The situation of specialist teachers belongs in this last category, but is of particular interest because of the teachers' double division of labour. The legitimacy of their claims to knowledge of *pedagogy* and of *subject content* derives, with varying degrees of immediacy, from the state via training and certification.

If we consider the situation of specialist teachers at the institutional level, it becomes clear that their duality of identity-bases and of reference-groups makes for a potentially complex process of negotiation. I propose to approach this by drawing on Burns's analysis of the 'plurality of social systems'.[36] Like Johnson, he begins from the juxtaposition of solidarity and division, co-operation and competition, which characterizes social groups. What we join in valuing, divides us because we compete for it. More specifically,

> All social *milieux* in which such competition occurs have codes
> of rules, explicit and implicit, which distinguish illegitimate
> behaviour from legitimate . . . The existence of such codes . . .
> bespeaks the presence of a specific class of acts and relationships,
> with its own normative rules . . . *ie.* of a social system . . .[37]

Burns goes on to point out that within a single organization, it may be 'normal' to legitimate action in terms of one's *rights* in one system, but one's *duties* in another.

> It is only backstage, so to speak, that the imputations of
> empire-building . . . occur. In universities . . . in faculty meet-
> ings . . . the only legitimate reference is to the needs of students
> and to the advancement of . . . learning. Allegations . . . of
> careerism . . . are entirely improper in faculty meetings, yet may
> be entirely . . . legitimate in other settings. Indeed, in certain

gatherings it might be imprudent to the point of social suicide to impute higher motives than self-interest . . . to reformers.[38]

Classics teachers can be considered to inhabit three analytically separate social systems, which I shall call the *knowledge, occupation* and *organization* systems. They belong to the first of these because of their claim to classical knowledge; in this system, they (like other specialist teachers) distribute to pupils knowledge they have not themselves produced. They belong to the occupation system as transmitters of culture, claiming a practical mastery of pedagogy. Finally, they belong to an organization system in which they are subordinated to an administrative hierarchy invoking norms of efficiency. Our major concern here, the legitimate allocation of knowledge to pupils, constitutes an issue in all three systems. In the organization system, such allocation entails the creation of pupil-groups which are 'proper' in terms of ability, size, and location in time and space. In the other two systems, it sets up tensions between teachers' roles as distributors of cultural commodities on a curricular market (knowledge) and as agents of cultural transmission (occupation). This tension arises because, given the existence of *specialist* teachers, the allocation of pupils to knowledge entails their allocation to teachers. The question which lies at the heart of the analysis at the *institutional* level, therefore, is not only 'Who learns what?' but also 'Who teaches whom?'

### Llangarr School, 1970–83

In order to make the analysis easier to follow, and thus to criticize, I have chosen to show how these questions are raised, and answered, in a single school — here called Llangarr School. This school has been selected for several reasons. First, it is the only school in which I have interviewed staff other than Classics teachers (over thirty in all). Second, it is the only school to which I have returned (in 1978 and 1983) after the initial interviews in 1973–4. Third and most important, Llangarr School was atypical in several ways which made it of particular interest (hence my repeated and extended interviewing). It was created in 1970 by the merger of two single-sex grammar schools and a secondary modern school, whose staffs mixed uneasily for some years in the new comprehensive. In particular, because of the difficulty of redeploying staff, the LEA had been forced to reappoint heads of subject departments, so that each department in the new school had joint heads. As a result, the school was officially regarded as 'overpointed'; in other words, very few additional graded posts were available within it. By 1973, this had already generated friction among members of staff. By 1978, the prospect of falling rolls had intensified this friction, especially among junior staff who saw no prospect of promotion. In addition, the school had by now developed a pastoral/administrative hierarchy, for whose members 'points', somehow, were always available; hence, of course, antagonism on the part of classroom teachers. In this situation, the Classics department was in an especially sensitive position. It had inherited three staff from the two grammar schools, and was thus the largest Classics department in any state school in South Wales. Furthermore, all three classicists held graded posts: two as heads of department, the third as a Greek specialist. It therefore became, as will be seen, a target for resentment in some quarters.

Having given some sense of the context of interaction in the school, let me turn to the 'micropolitics' of curricular allocation. The central mechanism of allocation consists of the organized presentation of optional subjects to thirteen-year old pupils. Subjects chosen at this point are usually pursued to the point of examination at sixteen. For teachers of the subjects made available in this curricular marketplace, much hangs on the outcome of choice. The nature of the pupil-groups which result from it, and of the courses of study underwritten (both immediately and, by implication, at the sixteen-plus level), affects both the status of subjects and their teachers and the quality of the latter's daily working lives.

What are the factors which affect the status of a subject in this (market) sector of the curricular economy? Status is enhanced by inclusion in a high status 'pool' (group) of subjects; but this may bring with it severe competition. On the other hand, status is enhanced by allocation to high status pupils — the prizes for which teachers compete — and this can be achieved by inclusion in a 'stratified' pool. In other words, a pool is assembled containing high, medium and low status subjects, and is offered to a similarly-stratified group of pupils. In addition, some subjects are placed in more than one pool, thus (as teachers put it) 'getting another bite at the cherry'. In Llangarr School, the market was open only to the upper bands (A and B), which made up the top eight from a total of thirteen streams.

Constraints on choice were not limited to the organization of pools. Once the selections made by pupils were tabulated to produce teaching groups, a variety of 'adjustments' took place. Most commonly, courses (and teachers) which were over- or under-subscribed had their recruitment adjusted, usually by reference to pupils' other choices; their perceivedly relevant previous performance; and their declared career interests. The negotiation of allocation, in fact, can best be understood as an annual cycle of interaction, involving teachers, pupils, parents and others, through which the overall 'matrix' of pupil-knowledge allocation is constructed. From the 'adjustments' of spring and the tabulations of summer emerges, in autumn, a new timetable, whose logistic awkwardnesses and perceived biases will generate criticism and further revision.

With this background in mind, we can now consider the changing position of Classics in the school since 1970. Throughout the seventies, pupils were taken at thirteen from three 11–13 feeder schools. Latin and Classical Studies were taught at all these schools, but in very different conditions: one school served the affluent western part of the town, a second the working-class east, and in the third, which was centrally located, Latin was timetabled for one afternoon every ten days — as an option against games. In the first year after reorganization, their ex-pupils arrived at Llangarr having reached different stages in the CLC syllabus. An agreement was later reached to standardize the target for Latin teaching in the feeder schools; but by that time another problem had appeared. Pupils presented with option forms to fill in at the end of their 11–13 career had discovered that Latin was a 'form subject' (ie, compulsory) for the top two classes in the A band at Llangarr, and were choosing Latin to make sure that they were allocated to these classes. Such requests could be denied; but the scale on which they were made brought the elitist position of Latin to general notice. The Llangarr head therefore decided that Latin would have to become optional.

> In the head of departments' meeting ... the head confronted us with a sheet of paper which showed the options ... we were horrified to see that Latin had been put against for instance History. Whereas at present in the third form it was a class subject for the top two classes ... it was proposed to make Latin optional ... it was eventually fixed at Latin versus RI completely, no other subject ... on the ground that we were creating specialist classes ... so they put it right through the A band ... RI was devised ... as the only subject which might not have a deleterious effect on the number of pupils taking Latin.[39]

The slippage from a high status 'command sector' position into the 'market sector' of the pool system was a traumatic experience for the Classics teachers. This serious and, as they must have assumed, irreversible demotion was in consequence handled by the head with some care. The teacher quoted above told me later that 'This time last year we were having the carrot dangled ... that the option should be Latin/ Scripture ... so that we'd have larger numbers than in the previous year'. Underlying this command/market slippage was the confrontation of the grammar-school tradition of knowledge- and pupil-stratification with the emerging ideological field of the comprehensive. This is thrown into sharp relief by a comment from the school timetabler about History, which became optional at the same time as Latin did.

> CAS  How does the curriculum come to be the way it is? How is it that some subjects are classed as compulsory, others as suitable for options?
>
> TT  The main thing is tradition. English and French are compulsory, always have been. German has as good a case, but tradition supports French. History has always been compulsory, but this year it was decided to put it in a pool, and the results were interesting. Last year 180 had to do it; this year 104 chose it, compared to Geography 131, Chemistry 136, Biology 135. On these figures, it seems that these other subjects had a more valid claim to be compulsory subjects. But tradition has held History to be a valuable subject; that tradition is dying slowly.

Grammar school 'tradition' and the comprehensive ideology of availability can be regarded as opposed equivalents: they provide for 'automatic' allocation of knowledge to pupils. Between them lies the middle ground of negotiation where allocation can be argued for, where a case can be made and tested. Tradition itself can, of course, be appealed to in negotiation; but seems usually to be invoked (i) by those with a power of fiat to dress up an autocratic decision, (ii) by the powerless, or those unwilling to struggle, to dress up a lost cause. (One local Classics teacher, for example, told me that when his head had reduced his Latin timetable from five periods a week to four, he had protested, in vain, that he had *always* had five.) How then, does 'tradition' relate to the process of negotiation? The following, relatively sophisticated analysis was offered by one of the Llangarr School classics teachers.

> CAS  Who does decide what gets taught?
>
> SC  I'm not sure. In a sense we're still running on tradition. There has always been Latin and Greek, so in a sense it's an automatic process. So who's causing the difficulties? There are four areas, I think. There's the LEA ...

economic viability. So that's a pressure, but I'm not sure
how it operates. Then there's the head; I'm never quite
sure about him ... he's not at all decisive, and I
sometimes suspect he uses his indecision as a way of
saying no to people. Then there's the timetabler; I know
nothing about this. My two colleagues ... have suggested that ... in doing the timetable ... this is why
Greek mysteriously didn't appear in the options this
year. The fourth one ... I'm told in head of departments'
meetings there's pressure from other subjects. They
normally say 'the scientists' ...

The scientists are familiar competitors, inherited from the grammar
school. The Classics teachers, however, now have among their colleagues 'several people who don't see why a subject they think is on the
decline should have two graded posts; points are taken away from their
own departments such as ... practical subjects. They see themselves as
more relevant to the comprehensive set-up than Classics'.

The Llangarr head was concerned to avoid this kind of staff
conflict, and so encouraged the expansion of (nonlinguistic) Classical
Studies teaching as a way of filling up the classicists' embarrassingly
empty timetables. From *their* point of view, the allocation of Classical
Studies to the B band had the advantage that it deflected resentment
against the elitist tradition of Classics teaching. Just as French was made
'comprehensive' by teaching it right through the B band (where
necessary as 'French Studies', or as one teacher put it, 'French without
the language'), so the provision of Classical Studies helped to make
Classics respectable. The head, however, aroused widespread resentment because of the definitional subtleties he used to support the new
course. Some comments were:

Classical Studies is protected by being in a language group; the
head said it was really a language wasn't it? It isn't of course, but
the head said it was.

Well the head says, it is a language of a sort isn't it? Which beats
me ... Latin for the A band, if not you're palmed off with
Classics, and it *is* palmed off ... it's given to boys who can't
cope with French or Welsh ... it's being provided ... as a third
option for the less able streams.

In setting it against French and Welsh, in fact, the head had created a
stratified pool, one which ensured recruitment to Classical Studies, but

also guaranteed that this recruitment would come from the 'lower depths'.

If the 'less able' were 'palmed off' with Classics, then, the Classics teachers similarly felt they had been palmed off with lower B band pupils — to them at least, a 'new kind of child'. 'We get the poorer children, the difficult children. Now in a sense you may say this is justice, since we've had the cream in the past ... but by virtue of the choice, the pupils we're getting, they're the rejects of ... they're rejects as far as we're concerned.' And again: 'I do more than a third of my timetable Classical Studies I suppose ... It's not what I came into teaching to do ... Thursday is the day, my timetable is 4B, double 5B, 3B ... it's tough going.' On the other hand, the classicist who was allocated the bottom stream of the B band to teach found them ignorant and dull, but quiet and willing to learn; and this discovery that the 'new kind of child' might be a pleasure to teach raises the question of the *variety* of the 'prizes' for which teachers are in competition.

I have already mentioned the case of the 11–13 pupils who tried to secure places in the top streams by choosing Latin. Within the senior school, similarly, it is common for pupils to attempt to complete option forms in such a way that they can be sure of securing (or avoiding) particular teachers. (Pressure from parents to have teachers identified, alongside the courses they teach, has been resisted, so far successfully, by the head.) For teachers, the prizes at stake in negotiating allocation consist of, or stem from, access to valued pupils. Most of the teachers I interviewed hoped to have pupils who were able, docile or both. They felt that status accrued to a subject insofar as it attracted large numbers; old, able and male pupils. On the other hand, not all teachers actively sought such pupils. There was, in fact, a clear division between those who wanted a tolerable timetable and pupils and to be left alone, and the seekers after a 'subject empire', with large A-level sets, several staff, university scholarships and so on. Several teachers in this latter category had a reputation for canvassing able pupils with excessive vigour. More subtle means than browbeating were available: since relevant past achievements are taken into account in 'adjusting' the groups generated by options, some teachers simply marked up pupils they wanted to retain at a later stage. A related tactic could be used when the pupil had no experience of the subject offered for choice: 'The ones who choose Greek ... mostly they're good at Latin, and they know (well, I *tell* them!) that Greek works the same way.' The same teacher gave several examples of irrelevant or mistaken reasons for choosing Latin which he had heard advanced by colleagues, parents and pupils, and added that he tended not to correct them: 'If that's immoral, I'm certainly immoral!'

This 'immorality' is defined in relation to the 'codes of rules ... which distinguish illegitimate behaviour from legitimate' (Burns, quoted above, p. 36). In this case, the rules mediate the tension between the rights of distributors and the duties of transmitters; between knowledge and occupational systems and identity-bases. The norm most commonly invoked by the Llangarr staff was that of *fairness*. This generally inchoate notion was commonly given precision by tying it to concrete parameters. For example, some teachers defined a 'fair time-table' in terms of a balance between 'good' and 'bad', 'easy' and 'difficult' pupils. On the other hand, in the larger departments a teacher was often given better timetables (in these terms) with increasing seniority, so that one year's timetable was assessed as part of a temporal series. Again, we have already seen one of the classicists reconciling himself to teaching 'difficult' children by invoking 'justice' over time ('We've had the cream in the past ...').

'Fairness' can also be given substance by tying it to a *primary* value — for example, 'the ideals of comprehensive education'.[40] The Llangarr staff, however, displayed little agreement at this level. 'The comprehensive ideal' was variously invoked *against* Classics (as irrelevant to comprehensives), and *for* Classics (on the ground that comprehensives were supposed to offer curricular variety). Just as important as this incoherence at the level of ideas was the lack of solidarity and of collegiate debate. The merger of three different staffs and the tensions caused by 'overpointing' and the scarcity of promotions, in particular, discouraged open discussion; instead, points were made via the sarcastic joke, the mutter in the corridor, separate individual trips into the 'administrative suite'. This was the visible site, as it were, of the organization system; the focal environment of the pastoral/administrative hierarchy of the school, which requires some discussion at this point.

In the traditional grammar school, with its relatively small size and stable — if not static — patterns of curricular allocation, decision-making on a wide range of issues typically lay with the head and a 'cabinet' of senior staff. All this changed with expansion and reorganization:

One thing I find rather chastening in the new comprehensive set-up is that the head of department status has declined ... there's no point in saying things because the decision has already been taken. In the old set-up it was the head, deputy head and heads of departments ... now it's head, deputy heads, academic registrar, heads of upper, middle, lower school ... all these administrative posts.

To this list, which dates from 1974, can now be added: year tutors, senior master, heads of Arts and Science faculties, and soon, according to rumour, a Director of Studies. Several teachers complained to me about what they saw as the effective demotion of 'the classroom teacher' — 'too many generals who never visit the line of battle'; 'more chiefs than Indians'. The classicists had a further cause for concern, in the hostility to their subject displayed by the incumbents of some of these administrative posts.

> Some of the secondary modern teachers were transferred to the girls' grammar school, because we had more pupils, and the type of pupils coming in of course, the existing staff had had no experience of this kind of child ... as the comprehensive developed, so it seemed that some of them were eminently suitable to deal with the troublesome type of child who existed in the old secondary modern school. They became year tutors, then graduated to, for example, head of middle school.

By 1974, the Llangarr classicists had thus suffered successive dislodgements towards an uncertain and marginal position. Underlying this process was a shift in the relations, and relative power, of the knowledge, occupation and organization systems. In the grammar school, the first of these was both powerful and ideologically consonant with the other systems. In the new world of the comprehensive, however, the pastoral-administrative complex has become dominant. 'Subject' and 'specialist' teaching, in the administrative pronouncements reported by teachers, connoted the selfish elitism of grammar-school staff, who were now urged to teach 'down the streams'. This shift is dramatically emphasized, of course, by the movement of ex-secondary modern staff into the organization system. The classicists have thus lost out on two fronts: power in the school, and autonomy in the classroom. In 1974, the 'Classics empire' was expanding — but into regions (the B band) which were alien and largely depressing to teach in. In their A band teaching, meanwhile, they were restricted by the CLC's prohibition of formal grammar and syntax, the cornerstone of the Latin they had learnt. Thus their creative praxis as masters of pedagogy was stunted, and they were relegated to the role of distributor of others' products, even within the occupational sphere of transmission.

By the time of my second visit, in 1978, the situation had further deteriorated. The steep gradient of the final year in the CLC course had led to very small numbers of passes at O level, and so recruitment to Latin lower down the school had contracted by half. One of the classicists had only one Latin class, and believed that even this might disappear if insufficient numbers passed a forthcoming mock examination. Recruitment to Greek had dropped below the head's 'viability' levels, so the subject was no longer taught. The prospect of having no language teaching at all seemed close.

In 1983, in contrast, the prospects for Classics at Llangarr looked much brighter. One of the three classicists had just taken early retirement, thus deflating some of the resentment against the department. The school was in the process of becoming an all-through comprehensive, and Latin and Classical Studies were being taught to the new second-form groups. As a result, the amount of Classics taught had increased, and part-time help from other departments was being employed, for the first time since the early seventies. On the other hand, the O-level Latin numbers had again been halved, leaving only one class. One of the classicists commented that 'about half are good academic children ... the others certainly have an interest in the subject ... which is all I can ask for really ... these days ... We use cooperatively-produced leaflets to add vocabulary and grammar ... but CLC is well done, it attracts and holds the attention of linguistically weak pupils, we've got several of them through O-level.'

Perhaps the most interesting feature of the current situation is the evidence of a new sphere of negotiation: the cooperative revision of CLC by local teachers. Their production of leaflets re-introducing formal grammar and syntax has increased the solidarity of local classicists, and has shown, contrary to what appeared the case in 1978, that CLC is itself negotiable.[41] And as the above quotation suggests, the course material has gained the approval of teachers for its practical virtues in attracting and holding the 'linguistically weak'. Finally, the addition of 11–13 pupils to the school has extended the time available for teaching to O-level, as well as providing potential recruits to Latin.

Elsewhere in the LEA area, the prospects for Classics are much poorer. About half the schools which had Classics of some sort in 1974 now have none at all. Classics is now the responsibility of the LEA chief adviser, an English specialist, who is open in his belief that Classics should be abolished. The LEA is also trying to restrict language provision at 11–13 to English plus two other languages, of which one will be Welsh. All these factors, together with a continuing fall in school rolls, make anything more than a continued minority recruitment to Latin, at least, highly unlikely.

The situation of Classics at the national level is uncertain and difficult to establish, especially as centrally-collated examination statistics are now inadequate or non-existent. The numbers passing O-level Latin have probably dropped below 20,000. Greek numbers have 'bottomed out', having shed all but a hard core of (mostly independent) schools. On the other hand, there has been a rapid, though small-scale, growth in the provision of non-examined 'scratch' courses and summer schools, first in Greek and now in Latin. A new Greek course has appeared, building on the lessons of CLC, which is aimed at the sixteen-plus level and has sold very well both in the UK and the USA. One of the issues dividing Classics teachers' associations at the moment is that of 'sixteen-plus Latin'. Should the fight to keep Latin going in the middle school be given up as hopeless? If so, a sixteen-plus course like the new Greek course is needed. Or will Latin at that level only survive with recruitment from the middle school? The issue is an open one at the moment. In the long term, one of the major questions is whether enough linguistically competent classicists can be produced to teach Classics — including nonlinguistic Classics. The success of Classical Studies degree courses has been almost embarrassing in some universities, where student numbers in Classics departments are very high, but the proportion learning a language is very low.

### Conclusion

In this chapter, I have considered the changing content and status of Classics in England and Wales since 1800 as a case-study in the historical sociology of education. I have argued that for most of this period, its content and status have been linked by a succession of corporate self-images held by dominant social groups: noble elegance, gentlemanly moral integrity, and bourgeois orderliness and self-control. Since about 1960, however, this kind of linkage has been broken, and the content and status of Classics has been essentially negotiable.

The connecting thread of the narrative has lain in the relationship of Classics to the division of social labour. In the first half of the nineteenth century, classical knowledge formed a primary resource in an organicist cultural reaction against the division of labour. Later, as a division of *cultural* labour emerged, Latin in particular became an exemplar of respectable, academic specialization. As Edward Thring, headmaster of Uppingham, asserted in 1894: 'Though it is quite immaterial to the theory of teaching what subject has to be taught, it is not immaterial what subject is taken as the most perfect illustration of the theory ... language, and Greek, and Latin, are the most perfect training-ground in the world for training mind.'[42]

With the growth of state secondary schooling and the civic universities, a curricular market of separate academic commodities emerged, among which Latin and Mathematics functioned as exemplars of the market's ideological basis: the developmental emergence of free human reason. Alongside this 'disparate collection of unrelated subjects' (to quote the Board of Education's phrase) stood the continuing gentlemanly tradition of 'organic unity', maintained in the independent schools and at Oxbridge. In the interwar years, when 'reason alone' became respectable as the bulwark of democracy against the irrational extremisms of fascism and bolshevism, Latin became central to the academic certification which led to bourgeois careers; the mundane alienness and precise rigours of the 'grammar grind' symbolized both the ideology and its class location. Despite its prolongation into the years of postwar educational expansion through the efforts of Norwood, however, both the grammar school and the 'grammar grind' received mortal blows in the late fifties.

It is at this point that a disjunction appears between the ideological and institutional contexts of Classics teachers and their biographies and self-images. Latin was not to 'go on for ever'; the 'terms' would soon cease to be 'heard across' the curriculum. The new Classics syllabuses of the sixties reintegrated language into society and culture, and Latin and Greek became embedded, rather than discrete, structures of meaning.[43] The everyday alienness of Latin grammar gave way to the alien everyday of ancient Pompeii, the transmission of esoteric form to the distribution of exotic content. From its distant days of monopoly, Classics has become first an *exemplary* commodity, expressing the values of the market's ideological basis; and now a *marginal* commodity on the periphery of an ideologically reorganized market.

I have argued in this chapter that the career of Classics in English education suggests the need for an analysis of cultural transmission which goes beyond the idea of homogeneous repetition. It also suggests, however, what the salient features of such an analysis might be; and these I have sketched in the outline of a 'political economy' of cultural transmissions. When this is employed at the institutional level, the teacher's occupational role of cultural transmission and specialist's role of knowledge distribution are visible as a combination subserving both continuity and change. In this way, we may be able to understand the mechanism which brings it about that a society *changes*, yet remains the *same society*. The tragedy of the Classics teachers' situation is that they have been doubly dislodged from a transmission role: first by the slippage of Classics from its exemplary position, secondly through the overshadowing of the classroom teacher's transmission role by the pastoral/administrative hierarchy of the comprehensive school. In the days of 'ordinary, straightforward Latin', history and biography were mutually and continually reinforcing, and 'tradition' served to explain their continuity. A generation later, there is a serious possibility that this tradition may become a memory.[44]

## Notes

1 Figures for Latin, Greek and Ancient History are as follows. (All figures are for passes, summer examinations.) O-level Latin peaked in 1964 at 33996, A-level in 1965 at 6012. O-level Greek peaked in 1962 at 2152, A-level in 1964 at 1252. The pattern for Ancient History, for various reasons, is less clearcut. O-level rose from 251 in 1960 to 717 in 1973, then declined. A-level rose from 974 in 1960 to 1145 in 1971, but has fluctuated around 1000 for some time. For full statistics 1960–1974, see STRAY (1977), p. 181.
2 For the linguistics underlying CLC, see WILKINS (1969), (1970).
3 The research is reported in STRAY (1977).
4 1977 was a good year for the political economy of cultural transmission: see COLLINS (1977), COWEN (1977), GARNHAM (1977) and O'KEEFFE (1977). As usual, Wright Mills was there before: MILLS (1963).
5 The notion of a 'command economy' used here derives from Franz Neumann's classic study of National Socialism: NEUMANN (1944).
6 GILLISPIE (1950), p. 37.
7 The key figure at Oxford was Edward Copleston, whose several 'Replies to the calumnies of the *Edinburgh Review* . . .' are quoted in STRAY (1977), pp. 55–64.
8 On 'virtue and commerce' see POCOCK (1972); on the public schools and the new elite, ARMSTRONG (1973) and WIENER (1981). The Victorian retreat into the home (and school) as moral fortress is described by GIROUARD (1979).
9 ENGEL (1975), p. 323. See too ROTHBLATT (1968) and (1973).
10 See, for example, KAZAMIAS (1960), LAYTON (1973).
11 See ROCHE (1969).
12 Quoted from the extracts in MACLURE (1965), pp. 92–93.
13 JOHNSON R. (1972), p. 128.
14 MACLURE (1965), p. 147.
15 Quoted from Morant's report on Swiss education (1898) by SEARLE (1971), p. 210.
16 W.N. BRUCE, in a memo in file Ed. 24/1174, Public Record Office.
17 Memo of 13 March 1911, file Ed. 24/387, PRO.
18 HEADLAM (1903). Morant later wrote that 'if I remember rightly, we *got* the Headlam report in order to support the changes we were anyhow going to make'. See EAGLESHAM (1962), p. 155.
19 BOARD OF EDUCATION (1913).
20 BOARD OF EDUCATION (1914).
21 Source: Board reports for individual years. The report for 1923–24 contains a brief 'history of the Advanced Course' at pp. 25ff.
22 Report of the Committee appointed by the Prime Minister to inquire into the position of Classics in the educational system of the United Kingdom, London: HMSO, 1921, pp. 144–7.

23 BOARD OF EDUCATION. The curricula of secondary schools in England, London: HMSO, 1922, p. 1.

24 For parallel moves in the primary sphere, see WHITE (1976); and for the shift from command to market provision, the suggestive discussion in VALLANCE (1973).

25 These terms are taken from the fascinating insider's view given by PETCH (1947), p. 14.

26 BOARD OF EDUCATION (1938), p. 188.

27 BOARD OF EDUCATION (1943), p. 47.

28 WHITMARSH (1972), p. 1.

29 The classic analysis, and eulogy, of the professions is CARR-SAUNDERS and WILSON (1933). For the elitist social psychologists, see SOFFER (1969).

30 BOARD OF EDUCATION (1938), p. 143.

31 BOARD OF EDUCATION (1943), p. 2.

32 The quotation is from a Board of Education internal memo dated 23 December 1941, filed in Ed. 12/478 at the PRO. (This file, which is devoted to the Norwood Committee, deserves fuller investigation than it seems to have received.)

33 On this subject, see the discussion in CCCS (1981) Ch. 3.

34 STRAY (1977). The degree to which the situation this describes was representative, and of what, is a complicated question for which there is no room here. Note, however, the 'Welsh factor': that is, the way in which educational provision in Wales is recognisably part of national arrangements, yet a consistently 'skewed' part. See, for example, the comments in the Ministry of Education's report for 1950 on the 'markedly high percentage of Welsh children of secondary school age by comparison with those in England who receive grammar school education ... a distinctive feature of Welsh education which has developed in a sense in defiance of the declared educational opinions of the Board and Ministry' (MINISTRY OF EDUCATION (1951), p. 119.). Compare Sutherland's description of Wales as 'a special case where justice and national pride appeared to demand simultaneously a provision for secondary education more generous than that in England and a rejection of intelligence testing.' (SUTHERLAND (1978), p. 8.)

35 JOHNSON (1972).

36 BURNS (1966).

37 *Ibid* pp. 165–6.

38 *Ibid* p. 167.

39 All unattributed quotations are from interviews with the Classics teachers at Llangarr School.

40 On 'fairness' as a secondary value, see MACINTYRE (1967).

41 A second edition of CLC, revised on the lines of the teachers' informal supplements, has just appeared (1983).

42 THRING (1894), p. 120.

43 This integration of content, carried out within a persisting division of cultural labour (Latin, Greek, Ancient History), had some interesting consequences. For example, 'new-style' Latin and Greek syllabuses, with enlarged provision for 'background', overlapped heavily with 'new-style' Ancient History, which included discussion of literature and architecture.

44 See ROTHBLATT (1976), p. 205.

## References/Bibliography

BOARD of EDUCATION (1913) *Curricula of Secondary Schools* (Circular 826), London, HMSO.

BOARD of EDUCATION (1914) *Memorandum on Curricula,* (Circular 849), London, HMSO.

BOARD of EDUCATION (1938) *Secondary Education, with Special Reference to Grammar Schools and Technical High Schools* (Spens Report), London, HMSO.

BOARD of EDUCATION (1943) *Curriculum and Examinations in Secondary Schools* (Norwood Report), London, HMSO.

BURNS, T. (1966) 'On the plurality of social systems', in LAWRENCE J.R. (Ed) *Operational Research and the Social Sciences,* London, Tavistock.

CARR-SAUNDERS, A. and WILSON, P. (1933) *The Professions,* Oxford University Press.

CCCS (1981) *Unpopular Education,* London, Hutchinson.

COLLINS, R. (1977) 'Some comparative principles of educational stratification', *Harvard Educational Review,* 47, pp. 1–27.

COWEN, R. (1977) 'The legitimacy of educational knowledge . . .', *Annals of the New York Academy of Sciences,* 285, pp. 282–96.

EAGLESHAM, E. (1962) 'Implementing the Education Act of 1902', in *British Journal of Educational Studies,* 10, pp. 153–74.

ENGEL, A. (1975) 'Emerging concepts of the academic profession at Oxford, 1800–1854', in STONE, L. (Ed.) *The University in Society,* Princeton University Press, 1, pp. 305–52.

GARNHAM, N. (1977) 'Towards a political economy of culture', in *New Universities Quarterly,* 31, pp. 341–57.

GILLISPIE, C.C. (1950) 'English ideas of the university in the 19th century', in CLAPP, M. (Ed) *The Modern University,* Ithaca, Cornell University Press, pp. 27–55.

GIROUARD, M. (1979) *The Victorian Country House,* 2nd ed., New Haven, Yale University Press.

HEADLAM, J.W. (1903) 'Report on the teaching of literary subjects in some secondary schools for boys', in BOARD OF EDUCATION *Report,* London, HMSO.

JOHNSON, T. (1972) *Professions and Power,* London, Macmillan.

KAZAMIAS, A. (1960) 'What knowledge is of most worth? . . .', in *Educational Review,* 30, pp. 309–30.

LAYTON, D. (1973) *Science for the People,* London, Allen and Unwin.

MACINTYRE, A.C. (1967) *Secularisation and Moral Change,* Oxford University Press.

MACLURE, J.S. (1965) *Educational Documents, England and Wales 1816–1963,* London, Chapman and Hall.

MILLS, C.W. (1963) 'The cultural apparatus', in HOROWITZ, I.L. (Ed.) *Power, Politics and People: the Collected Essays of C. Wright Mills,* New York, Oxford University Press, pp. 405–22.

MINISTRY of EDUCATION (1951) *Education 1900–1950,* London, HMSO.

NEUMANN, F. (1944) *Behemoth: the Structure and Practice of National Socialism, 1933–1944,* New York, Oxford University Press.

O'KEEFFE, D. (1977) 'Towards a socio-economy of the curriculum', *Curriculum Studies*, 9, pp. 101–09.

PETCH, J.A. (1947) 'Some aspects of the growth of secondary school examinations', in *Proceedings of the Manchester Statistical Society*, pp. 1–46.

POCOCK, J.G.A. (1972) 'Virtue and commerce in the 19th century', in *Journal of Interdisciplinary History*, 3, pp. 119–34.

ROCHE, J.W. (1969) 'The great Latin primer question', *British Journal of Educational Studies*, 17, pp. 251–5.

ROTHBLATT, S. (1968) *The Revolution of the Dons*, London, Faber.

ROTHBLATT, S. (1973) 'The 18th century idea of a liberal education and its aftermath', paper given at the Atlantic Conference, Edinburgh.

ROTHBLATT, S. (1976) *Tradition and Change in English Liberal Education*, London, Faber.

SEARLE, G.R. (1971) *The Quest for National Efficiency*, Oxford, Blackwell.

SOFFER, R.N. (1969) 'New elitism: social psychology in prewar England', in *Journal of British Studies*, 8, pp. 111–40.

STRAY, C.A. (1977) *Classics in Crisis: the Changing Forms and Current Decline of Classics* ..., MSc (Econ) thesis, University of Wales.

SUTHERLAND, G. (1978) *Mental Testing and Education in England and Wales, 1880–1940*, SSRC Report HR 4204, SSRC.

THRING, E. (1894) *The Theory and Practice of Teaching*, Cambridge, Cambridge University Press.

VALLANCE, E. (1973) 'Hiding the hidden curriculum: an interpretation of the language of justification in 19th century educational reform', in *Curriculum Theory Network*, 4, 1, pp. 5–21.

WHITE, J. (1976) 'The end of the compulsory curriculum', in *The Curriculum* (Doris Lee Lectures for 1976), London, Institute of Education.

WHITMARSH, G.W. (1972) *Society and the School Curriculum: the Association for Education in Citizenship, 1934–57*, SSRC Report HR 1096, SSRC.

WILKINS, J. (1969) 'Teaching the classical languages-I', in *Didaskalos*, 3.1, pp. 168–97.

WILKINS, J. (1970) 'Teaching the classical languages-II', in *Didaskalos*, 3.2, pp. 365–409.

# English for the English Since 1906[1]

## Stephen J. Ball

The view of school subjects implicit in much of the recent work in the sociology and philosophy of the curriculum is of unitary and monolithic epistemic communities. Analysis has tended to be concentrated upon relations between subjects rather than the disputes and differentiations occurring within them. Perhaps one of the major reasons for this emphasis on communality is the ahistorical nature of the research methods and theoretical perspectives normally employed. Generally, sociologists interested in the curriculum have tended to pay little attention to the socio-historical determinants of school knowledge. In this paper I shall be exploring the 'curriculum history'[2] of one school subject — English — but I will be employing analytical techniques and concepts derived from sociology. The view of subject disciplines advanced is of internally differentiated epistemological communities prone to disputation over the content of subject knowledge and appropriate methodology. I shall not attempt a detailed descriptive history of English teaching, for a very thorough account already exists.[3] Rather, I will hope to identify the origins of those major subject *paradigms* which can be found to exist and compete in the teaching of English at the present time and to examine those factors which have contributed and continue to contribute to the development of English as a school subject.

### Prehistory

It is probably fair to say that before the turn of the century English did not exist as a separately identifiable school subject at either elementary or secondary level. There were certainly very few teachers who could be called or would have called themselves teachers of English. It was not until 1904 that the Board of Education included in its *Regulations* a directive requiring all state secondary schools to offer courses in English literature and language. Prior to that English was studied by most children from age eight upwards in the form of orthography, etymology and syntax. English teaching consisted of subjecting children to systematic instruction in the principles of English grammar. In other words, Enlgish took its subject matter and its pedagogy directly from those of the teaching of Classics. Indeed many of the teachers were themselves trained in the Classics.

Most of the work done in 'English' during this period, or in what were in fact normally separate composition and grammar lessons, was based on imitation for composition work and parsing for grammar work. And in this composition remained 'a poor relation ... merely a testing device, the proof of the grammar pudding'.[4] As for Literature, in 1872, 71,507 children (3.6 per cent of all those in elementary schools) were examined in 'specific subjects', and grammar was the second most popular of these specific subjects with 18,426 being examined, English literature was the fourth most popular with 11,085. By 1882 the number of examinees in English literature was up to 140,772. However, the Board of Education, *Report* 1910, does point out that 'these figures might, however, easily give rise to quite erroneous impressions unless the scope and meaning of the term "English literature" as explained in the list of "specific subjects", be clearly defined'.[5] The syllabus for the examination of English literature as a 'specific subject' in 1876 was as follows:

> 1st year ... One hundred lines of poetry, got by heart, with knowledge of meanings and allusions. Writing a letter on a simple subject.

> 2nd year ... Two hundred lines of poetry, not before brought up, repeated; with the knowledge of meaning and allusions. Writing a paraphrase of easy prose.

> 3rd year ... Three hundred lines of poetry, not before brought up; repeated; with knowledge of meanings and allusions. Writing a letter or statement, the head of the topics to be given by the Inspector.

For the period 1882–90 the Report notes 'the continuance of the emphasis in English which had prevailed in the previous period'.[6] But for the period 1902–10 it goes on 'Grammar instead of being taught as an isolated subject was taught in relation to composition.'[7] Indeed in the first ten years of this century there was a marked degree of opposition to the teaching of grammar as a separate and predominant aspect of English.

Three matters of issue emerge from this brief examination of the teaching of English during the earliest period of state education. One is the occurrence of territorial disputes involved in the claims made for English to be a specific, separate and coherent subject entity included in the curriculum of all elementary and secondary schools. Another is the emergence of competition and conflict within the boundaries of English between rival claimants to the definition of the corpus of knowledge and associated pedagogy which should constitute the subject. The third is a process of curriculum change marked by a considerable complexity of influences and slowness of pace. It is with those main themes that I shall be concerned in the remainder of this paper.

### First Struggles 1906–1917

During this period a campaign was begun to disassociate English from the overbearing domination and competition of Classics teaching, to establish English once and for all as a separate subject in its own right, with its own content and at secondary level its own specialist teachers. But this was not a campaign that was easily or quickly won. While English was established fairly quickly, if not over confidently, as a separately timetabled subject, the role of the teaching of grammar continues to be one basis of disputation within the subject until the present time, as we shall see later.

An important part of the strategy of establishing English as a separate subject with its own content was the inauguration, in 1906, of The English Association. The Association was set up with the explicit aims of promoting English as a subject in its own right with its own place in the curriculum and to counter the stultifying and conservative influences of the Classical tradition. In the original articles of the Association, article (c) states that the association is 'to promote the due recognition of English as an essential element of national education'.

It is clear that the Association came into being very much as a source of support for the establishment of an autonomous epistemic community for English teachers and a response to the pressures from the opposition of the Classicists: 'As Classics, Modern Languages and other subjects had supporting associations, one was needed to uphold the claims in education and otherwise of the mother tongue' (F.S. Boas Undated Paper).[8] Ruddock notes that: 'participants at this first Annual

Meeting of the Association thought fit to urge that the general overall purpose of the new Association was to secure "a prominent if not a foremost place" for English in the curriculum of every school and college in the Empire'.[9] In 1907 the Association had 300 members, by 1927 over 7000 members. And over a period of thirty years from its inception, members of the Association were to have considerable influence upon the thinking about the teaching of English in schools.

By 1906 the lines of battle were drawn for a conflict which in effect continues to the present day. We must recognize that during the 1910s and 1920s, at least, this battle was to be fought on two fronts: on the one hand it is a territorial dispute between English as a subject and Classics; on the other hand, there are the origins of an internecine dispute within English about the definition of the subject. This latter is a dispute between a view of the subject as 'grammar' and a view of the subject which gives a central position to the role of 'literature' and pupil expression. The former view has embedded firmly within it a conception of English teaching as being concerned with the 'correct' use of English, based on the belief, reiterated in the 1909 *General Report on the Teaching of English in London Elementary Schools*, that 'the use of English . . . is a fine art, and must be taught as a fine art'.

The early phase of the development of 'English' in competition with the teaching of the Classics parallels closely Bucher and Strauss's account of the problems ensuing from the emergence of new specialisms or segments in the medical profession:

> The emergence of new segments takes on a new significance when viewed from the perspective of social movements within a profession. Pockets of resistance and embattled minorities may turn out to be the heirs of former generations, digging in along new battle lines. They may spearhead new movements which sweep back into power. What looks like backwash or just plain deviancy, may be the beginnings of a new segment which will acquire an institutional place and considerable prestige and power.[10]

The segmental conflict in English is clearly evident in pamphlets published by the English Association right through into the 1930s, so too is what Bucher and Strauss refer to as 'the sense of mission'.[11]

Interestingly and significantly, the intellectual battle to establish English as a discipline in schools was closely related to and allied with the very similar battle to establish English as a contemporary discipline in the universities. English was accepted as part of a Bachelor of Arts degree at London University in 1859 and was subsequently adopted by several other provincial universities, but in every case it remained an essentially linguistic rather than a literary area of study and held an uneasy and subordinate intellectual position, somewhere between History and Grammar. Oxford and Cambridge were less ready to recognize English as a subject worthy of their attention and such courses as were introduced were based on philology and the study of old English.

Thus, in common with some other subjects which emerged in the school curriculum during this period, the advocates of English had no established academic 'plausibility structure', and no extant epistemic community available in the universities, to further their cause.[12] Support came solely from those teachers, inspectors and interested others who identified with the 'sense of mission' of English teaching in schools. Thus many of the prime movers in the establishment of an alternative conception of English to that embodied in the classical tradition were either practising teachers, like George Sampson, originally headmaster of an elementary school — later local authority inspector and author of *English for the English* —, or writers, like Henry Newbolt and Arthur Quiller-Couch. The familiar model of influence passing downward from the universities to the school is inappropriate here. It was the 'classical' conception of English teaching that had its origins and its plausibility structure in the universities.

Nonetheless, the impact of the 'new English' was marked enough in the 1902–10 period for the 1910–11 Board of Education Report to note significant changes in the elementary school curriculum:

> Where a few years ago there would have been two lessons in dictation and one in composition, the proportion is now reversed . . . the subjects too on which they write are different. The formal essay on an abstract or general subject is more rarely set. Instead, the children write mainly from their own experiences. Formal grammar, instead of being treated as a more or less isolated subject, is soundly taught in connection with composition.[13]

And indeed the Board of Education itself provided support for those teachers anxious to divest themselves of the excesses of the Classical Grammarian method. The 1905 *Suggestions for the Consideration of Teachers and Others Concerned in the Work of the Public Elementary Schools*, urged teachers to give greater emphasis to expression and less to analysis:

> The analysis of the parts into which a well-constructed sentence may be divided should be made in every case by the children and

should not be pursued further than their thought feels need of it. Mere verbal distinctions and the laborious divisions of phrases or clauses into their constituent parts are valueless and tend to obscure rather than reveal thought ... There should be no grammar teaching apart from the other English lessons, it should arise naturally out of the reading and composition lessons.[14]

Here then is a distinct shift from a subject-centred to a child-centred approach to English language. Emphasis is given for the first time to naturally occurring language. This was accompanied by suggestions that greater concern should be given to children's talk in lessons, other than in the form of recitations. Similar kinds of exhortations were aimed by the Board at the teachers of English in secondary schools. The Circular 753, *The Teaching of English in Secondary Schools*, published in 1910, which had had representatives of the English Association involved in its drafting at the Board of Education, argued that:

Grammar should not bulk largely in the regular school teaching of English, and it should not be isolated from composition and literature and made into an abstract exercise. Whole lesson periods should not be systematically given up to formal grammar, and it should never be assigned as a separate subject to a teacher who takes neither literature nor composition.[15]

The Circular provides some indication of the extent of the progress made in establishing English as a separate and specialist curriculum subject. Indeed the place and role of English is categorically reaffirmed: 'In issuing a circular in the teaching of English in secondary schools the Board do not think it is necessary to dwell upon the importance of the subject. The claim of English to a definite place in the curriculum of every secondary school is admitted'.[16]

It is important to note that neither the establishment of English as a separate subject nor the changes in English teaching during this period, as noted previously, would have been possible, despite the work of the English Association, without the demise of the Revised Codes. The 1902 Education Act, setting up the LEAs and giving considerable autonomy to individual headmasters, considerably weakened the hitherto pervasive influence of the public schools on the state system and presented teachers with an historical situation in which their room for manoeuvre was considerably increased at both school and classroom level.[17]

At the elementary level autonomy was stressed for individual teachers both in the much broader purposes attached to the elementary school in the 1904 *Code of Regulations*[18] and in their greater freedom and responsibility in the fields of curriculum and method outlined in the 1905 *Handbook of Suggestions*. In addition, the emancipation of the elementary school was furthered by the new and more benign role given to the 'dreaded' school inspectors. But at secondary level the constraints of inspection were quickly being replaced by the constraints of public examination. And in 1917 the Board of Education set up the Secondary School Examinations Council to coordinate the standard of University Board examinations. In 1918 the Board issued a regulation that no external examinations should be taken in grant-earning secondary schools below the standard of the School Certificate.

In the case of English the incorporation of the subject in the Modern Studies group of Advanced courses had a profound status-confirming effect. English had arrived as a subject. Omission from the list of advanced courses or allocation as a subordinate subject, which occurred when the list was published initially, could have been disastrous in the campaign to establish English firmly in the secondary curriculum. F.S. Boas made this clear in his introductory address to the 1919 Conference of the English Association.

In the Regulations for the scholastic year that is now ending there was contained the first provision for 'Advanced Courses' for boys and girls between 16 and 18. This important 'step forward' in education was hailed with unanimous approval, but for those especially concerned with the teaching of English there was one blot on the scheme. In the 'Modern Studies' Group opportunity was given for the teaching of History and of the languages and literatures of Western Europe, but English was allotted only a subordinate place. Many of us felt that much of the work of recent years for the development and consolidation of the higher study of English was gravely imperilled, representations were made to the Board from various quarters, and it is very satisfactory to find that they have been fully and frankly met. The Board have decided, while restricting the Group subjects to two modern languages with History, to allow English to be taken as one of the two modern languages. The field is therefore open to teachers of English, and it behoves them to equip themselves as fully as possible for their increased responsibilities.[19]

## The Twenties, Thirties and Forties

It would be a mistake to portray the growth and penetration of the 'new English', as I have dubbed it, as a contested but inevitable process or indeed as a very rapid process. While the revised conceptions of English as a literary and expressive discipline continued to make steady headway in the elementary schools from 1904 onwards, change in the secondary schools was significantly slower and in certain respects more conflictual. What needs to be considered is why the grammarian paradigm in English teaching continued to be so resilient against the challenge of alternative 'assertive' paradigms right up until the 1950s, and why it continues to be represented in the teaching of English even today. In examining these concerns we must face an immediate analytical problem, that is, whether these competing paradigms of English teaching are to be considered simply in terms of their rhetorical development in the writings of respective advocates, and/or in 'official' pronouncements of the reports, recommendations and suggestions issued by the Board of Education, or in terms of the realities of classroom teaching. Obviously, all three are important, and they cannot be treated as mutually exclusive fields of activity, but it would be naive to take them to be synonymous. However, there is a further difficulty, in that any attempt to portray the classroom teaching of English during this period must rely upon the indirect accounts of commentators, rather than first hand accounts of researchers or practitioners. What emerges from these former sources is a fairly standard picture, at least at secondary level, of the continuing pre-eminence of a grammarian classicist approach to the teaching of English. The dominant image of the period, at least at secondary level, is of the pervasive and conservative influence of the public school curriculum.

> In the majority of secondary school syllabuses up to and including the 1950s the language element predominated. Drill in the mechanisms of writing: spelling, punctuation, paragraphing and so on, practice in identifying and explaining the various parts of speech — this has been the stuff of English since the turn of the century.[20]

> As recently as 1960 English as a school subject was in a state of suspended animation that had hardly changed over forty years.[21]

> For over fifty years this Latin-based norm of 'correct' English was firmly entrenched in Schools. It was enshrined in the School

Certificate and in the ordinary language syllabus and once established there it was difficult to dislodge.[22]

One of the reasons for the persistence of the grammarian tradition during the 1920s, 1930s and 1940s, a 'pale substitute for Classics', as Shayer puts it, is undoubtedly the continued importance of the Classics at university level and in the public schools. But there are a number of social and situational factors that also had their part to play. English literature, in particular, had become accepted much more readily as a subject for girls. The preponderance of single sex schools in the secondary sector thus tended to isolate boys' schools from many of the developments in English teaching. Also, importantly, despite the founding of the English Association and the steady stream of reports, suggestions and recommendations from the Board of Education and elsewhere, English continued to be regarded as a subject that all teachers were capable of teaching. This fact was noted in the 1910 Circular 753 issued by the Board of Education: 'The teaching of English in a school is not only being treated as a water tight unit, but is being taught by any member of staff who can be induced to "take a few periods" to fill in time'.[23] While the widespread practice of using non-specialists for English teaching continued, both the credibility and the progress of English was inhibited. Meanwhile the universities continued to produce 'English' graduates imbued with philology and language studies. Additionally, the structural stability of the schools themselves did not encourage a rapid dissemination of new educational ideas. The structure of teacher employment during the inter-war years provided for stable staffs and little geographical mobility. And the teaching profession did not escape the effects of the world depression of the 1930s, and this brought its own stultifying influence to bear upon the teaching of English.

However, the state of affairs in the secondary schools during this period is not indicative of a total lack of development in the state of thinking about English as a discipline and the teaching of English in schools and universities. Rather the opposite is the case, for an examination of the work of the English Association and the members of what came to be called the Cambridge School of English reveals the emergence and establishment of two separate but related paradigms of English teaching that were to come to have a major impact upon classroom practice during the 1950s and 1960s. Abbs[24] distinguishes these as the 'Cambridge School of English' and the 'Progressive Movement' — the latter advocating and promoting the importance of self-expression and individuality and the role of play in learning English. The key figures in the progressive movement in its early stages were: Percy Nunn, Greening Lamborn, Edmund Holmes, W.S. Tomkinson and Caldwell Cook. Later came Marjorie Hourd and Herbert Read. In discussing Read and Hourd, Abbs notes that they: 'emphasize the power of creativity in education, to recognize the place of feeling and of imagination, to perceive the value of psychic wholeness'.[25] This approach to English teaching had its impact most directly upon the elementary schools and later more broadly contributed to the underlying philosophy of practice of the progressive primary schools of the 1960s. Interestingly, the material on which Hourd's *The Education of the Poetic Spirit* is based emanates from work done in one of the high schools of the Girls Public Day School Trust, and the findings presented refer only to girls. Hourd's work was an attempt to bridge the child-centred/subject-centred views of English teaching, to reconcile literature and psychology and she argued, taking a lead from Dewey, for the necessity of the teacher to 'psychologize' the subject. 'This was the teacher's job to discover how his subject could become part of child experience'.[26]

The extent of the impact of this Progressive Movement upon English teaching is extremely difficult to gauge. It is clear that the nineteenth century bias towards grammar and composition continued to hold sway in many elementary schools throughout the 1920s, 1930s and 1940s. So that Shayer, describing this period, reports that 'While "activity" was gaining respectable psychological ground, the time lag that invariably operates between theory and accepted classroom practice continued'.[27]

If the Progressive Movement is best represented in the progressive primary school, then the Cambridge School probably had its apotheosis in the post World War II grammar school sixth form. The Cambridge School vision was preeminently represented by F.R. Leavis in the University, and by George Sampson — somewhat earlier ≃ at the school level. Sampson places himself firmly in the elite cultural tradition of Coleridge and Arnold. He saw English as having a humanizing influence and, as a basis of opposition to the destruction of the British cultural tradition, he wrote of English 'that it is the one school subject in which we have to fight, not for a clear gain of knowledge, but for a precarious margin of advantage over powerful forces of evil'.[28]

Sampson's crusading work was carried on, in particular, by Thompson through a journal for teachers — *Use of English* — and in direct proselytizing in schools. But it was Leavis who articulated most clearly and vehemently the 'Arnoldian Literary-Critical Tradition' and I.A. Richards, a Cambridge contemporary, who, by working out alternative forms of literary criticism, provided a methodological alternative to Latinate parsing. Richards received considerable praise in the Ministry of Education's Pamphlet No. 26. *Language: Some Suggestions for Teachers of English and Others in Primary and Secondary Schools and Further Education.*[29] Discussing Leavis' personal contribution, Abbs writes: 'In new and worsening cultural circumstances he gave a powerful currency to the notion that the teacher, critic and artist had no choice but to oppose the destructive and seemingly inexorable drift of industrial civilization.'[30] And of the contribution of 'the Cambridge School' generally, he says:

> 'In the context of English teaching this school provided a critical method of reading, a method for the analysis of mass culture, and an informed awareness as to the place of literature in society.'[31]

Nonetheless, it would be misleading to attribute the shift towards literature in the teaching of English, gradual as it was, solely to the influence of the Cambridge School and Leavis' acolytes. The move away from grammar and the classical tradition is clearly marked in the work of the English Association in the first twenty years of the century. The role of literature was strongly affirmed by George Sampson, and by the findings of the 1921 Newbolt Committee, of which Sampson and Quiller-Couch and three other English Association men were members. And F.S. Boas, vice-president of the English Association, addressed the 1918 conference of the Association in the following terms: 'We realize that for pupils of different ages, and for schools of different types, elementary, secondary and continuation, there must be diverse schemes of English work. But what else the scheme, it must be well balanced and include something more than the beggarly elements. Literature should be the predominant partner.'

At the point of the outbreak of World War II the three paradigms of English teaching so far introduced were clearly articulated, both in theory and practice, and contending with one another for predominance — with, in practical terms, 'the progressive movement' making headway against grammar in the elementary schools and 'the Cambridge School' making inroads in the secondary schools.

It is possible to begin to conceptualize the reasons for the emergence of these competing paradigms in two ways: first, in terms of the inexorable adjustment of the school curriculum to the needs or forces of the social structure; or, second, as the outcome of the strategies, pressures and influences of particular groups or individuals with investments in the teaching of English. In practice I intend to go some way towards conflating these approaches by discussing both the *conditions of change* — the changes in the economic and social conditions of schooling which allowed, inhibited or provided for changes in the process and content of school knowledge — and the *relations of change* — those activities and strategies which actually initiated change. The latter, the relations of change, have been explored and analyzed, in such a way as to be extremely relevant to the issues at hand, in the case of American sociology and several specialisms in the natural sciences, by Mullins[32] and Griffiths and Mullins.[33] Mullins deals with the emergence of *subject specialisms* (a concept which can be equated clearly with that of *subject paradigm* used here) in terms of a model of stages of group development. This account rests upon the analysis of the communication structure within a discipline, and a theory of intellectual innovation and concomitant group formation. The communication structures described by the model are based on 'trusted assessors of work'.

The essential question is, who does the practitioner turn to for critical assessment of his work? In teaching this can be considered in terms of three kinds of social relationship: communication (serious discussion about teaching practices); apprenticeship (at school or in university education or teacher-training); and colleagueship. According to Mullins' account there are four stages in the emergence of any specialism 'each stage being marked by empirically demonstrable social and intellectual characteristics'.[34] They are: normal; network; cluster; and speciality. In the *normal stage:* 'The general scientific communication structure is quite loose ... There is a low degree of organization both within the literature and within social relationships ... Little coordinated effort is made to solve any particular problem.'[35] In the case of English teaching this stage can perhaps be equated with the period up to 1906, where the content of English teaching in schools was constrained and defined both by the overbearing classical tradition and by the prescriptions of the 1862 Revised Code. The move into the next stage, the *network stage*, may be marked by the founding of the English Association in 1906:

> A major discovery, a new idea or an especially cogent criticism of the present state of affairs may begin to attract attention to one or several persons. Directly or indirectly, these persons come to focus on *each other* consistently ... A consensus gradually begins to develop among this group as its members focus on crucial intellectual issues.[36]

The English Association provided a focal point for the advocates of both the literary critical and to an extent the expressive paradigms in

English teaching and from it emerged several influential figures who were able to articulate a cogent critique of the existing dominant paradigm. George Sampson was one such critic of the old and representative of the new, Arthur Quiller-Couch was another. Both took part, as we have seen, in the influential 1921 Newbolt Committee. Sampson was author of the influential *English for the English* and Quiller-Couch became the first professor of English at Cambridge in 1912 and was author of *On the Art of Reading*.[37] This latter point is significant for another aspect of the *network* stage as Mullins describes it, 'the appearance of a few students and the creation of student-teacher links'.[38]

The transition to the next stage is, according to Mullins, 'a major change'. In the *cluster stage:*

> communication becomes even more ingrown. Clusters of students and colleagues form around the key figures in a group in one or a few institutions … It constitutes a first institutionalization and is based on colleague and teacher-student relations rather than the less stable, informal relations of the network stage … Intellectually, such a group concentrates on the specific set of problems defined by the program statement.[39]

The *cluster stage* can undoubtedly be identified with the founding of the 'Cambridge School' and the intellectual leadership of Leavis. And the book *Culture and Environment* by Leavis and Thompson[40] can perhaps be taken to be the major programmatic statement of the school. Mathieson notes: 'Bringing rigour and purpose to English studies at Downing, Leavis inspired many graduates to enter teaching, to introduce his critical methods into schools, colleges and university education departments. They envisaged the exercise of critical dissemination as a form of continuous warfare against hostile forces in the environment.'[41] Leavis taught and inspired two generations of students, many of whom were themselves to make considerable impact upon the teaching of English in schools, colleges and universities. His students included: David Holbrook, Richard Hoggart, Fred Inglis, William Walsh, G.H. Bantock, Ian Robinson, Raymond Williams, Boris Ford, Frank Whitehead, Douglas Barnes, Edwin Mason and Denys Thompson. And via this process it can be argued that the Cambridge Literary-Critical School of English established itself as a speciality in English studies. According to Mullins the movement to the *speciality stage* '… begins as the students became successful themselves, and both they and others were towed away from their original location.'[42] A process of routinization also occurs as '(1) the students begin to develop divergent

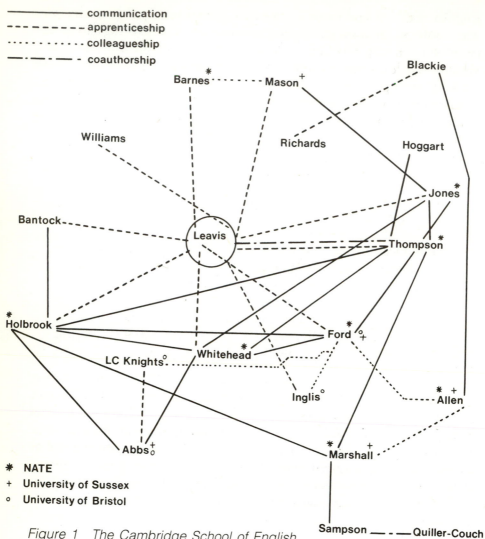

——————— communication
– – – – – – – apprenticeship
· · · · · · · · · · · · colleagueship
—· — ·— · coauthorship

*Figure 1   The Cambridge School of English*

✱ NATE
+ University of Sussex
o University of Bristol

interests and (2) text books, critical material, and secondary works are written in order to maintain the priority of the group's theoretical reformation'. Finally, yet another indicator of the speciality stage was accomplished by the establishment of the journals *Scrutiny* (1932–1953) and *English in Schools* (1939–49), which then became *Use of English* (1949).

Thus some penetration of the work of Leavis and his students into the schools is apparent in both direct and indirect ways, to quote Mathieson again: 'the Cambridge English School has, since the 1930's, produced not only professors and senior lecturers in university English and Education Departments throughout the country, but authors of many influential journals, and many secondary school teachers passionately committed to Leavis' critical approach to English.'[43] However, again it would be unfair and inaccurate to identify movements in the teaching of English in the 1940s and 1950s solely with the impact of the Cambridge School. Another institutional centre of opposition to the classical grammatical paradigm of English teaching was emerging during this period, based in the London Day Training College (now the University of London Institute of Education). James Britton, a student of the college writes:

> I began my teaching career in 1930 in a storm of controversy about the teaching of English grammar. It was not at that time a question of *whether* to teach it, but *how*. The mast my colours were nailed to was that of 'the reform of grammar teaching'. And certainly the enemy was a real one — the best-selling English textbooks were mines of unproductive busywork.[44]

Britton was a student of Percival Gurrey and says of him 'If the study of Grammar does not occupy today the place he saw for it in the English curriculum it is in large part because other concerns he indicated to us have overtaken it'.[45] Gurrey and Britton were founding members, in 1947, of the London Association for the Teaching of English. (Other early contributors, also from the London Institute, or the University of London colleges, included: R. Firth, John Trim, Randolph Quirk and Michael Halliday.) While the 'Cambridge School' addressed itself primarily to the Grammar school, the 'London School' was much more closely associated with the spread of comprehensive education. As early as 1957, there was a comprehensive school discussion group within LATE, meeting under the chairmanship of Guy Rogers, headmaster of Walworth School.

In 1963, LATE was swallowed up in the founding of the National Association for the Teaching of English (the English Association was virtually dormant by this time), which was the initiative of, and in its inception was dominated by, Leavis men. Boris Ford was the first chairman (then Director of the Institute of Education at Sheffield), Denys Thompson was a prime mover and member of the panel (editor of *Use of English*), and Frank Whitehead was chairman in 1967. However, in contrast to the Cambridge School, the London Institute approach to English teaching had continued to develop the emphasis on the role of language, rather than literature, as is suggested in Britton's account of his early teaching experiences (quoted above); an emphasis, as Britton sees it, that involves 'distinguishing sharply be-

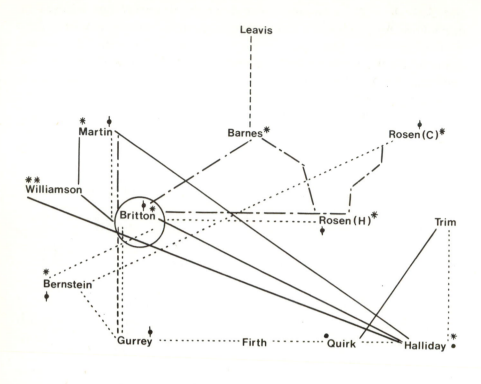

*Figure 2   The London Connection*

tween *using* the mother tongue and *studying* it'.[46] This formed the basis
for the emergence of what I shall refer to as the 'English as language'
paradigm of English teaching, which was to come to fruition in the
1960s through the work of Barnes, Rosen, Martin and Britton himself,
all LATE and London Institute or University people (see *Figure 2*). The
development and articulation of this paradigm provided for, as we shall
see, a fundamental split in the ranks of NATE and a considerable
reorientation of the teaching of English in secondary schools. In
swallowing up LATE in its organization NATE had incorporated
within itself a militant dissenting incubus. And many of the LATE

members already listed above emerged as leading figures in NATE in the late 1960s and 1970s, and were directly involved in moving NATE away from the pervasive influence of the Cambridge School and towards greater concern with the naturally occurring, written and oral language of school children. Indeed the 'Britton-Martin model of language' was established by the 1970s as the NATE orthodoxy.

Despite the above, it would be naive to see this *paradigm shift* simply in terms of an intellectual *coup d'état*. Once again it is necessary to raise questions about the extent to which movement at the rhetorical level was reflected in changes in the actual day to day classroom practices of English teachers; but perhaps more importantly the *relations of change* outlined here must be set against the *conditions of change* affecting education nationally and internationally. Obviously, the impact and influence of an Association such as NATE is impossible to calculate accurately. Membership figures provide only a crude guide (by April 1964 NATE had 1000 members and 40 branches, by 1968 4000 members and 49 branches). But a former Joint Secretary of the Schools Council made the following assessment:

> . . . the most successful associations in England have so far been the Association for Science Education, the National Association for the Teaching of English and a small group of associations which centre their interests on school mathematics. In each of these a marked awareness has been visible from the mid-60's and earlier about the challenge of curriculum reform.[47]

As we shall see, NATE was involved in a number of curriculum development projects in the 1960s and 1970s which addressed themselves very closely to the needs and practices of classroom teaching.

The mid-1960s were marked universally by a change in the climate of opinion about education. In Britain, there was a marked re-thinking of the role, content, structure and process of educational provision. Also in Britain there was a massive concatenation of contextual variables, *conditions of change*, stimulating and reflecting educational change. These included the spread of comprehensive education, the restructuring of the teaching profession, the introduction of the CSE examination, and latterly the Raising of the School Leaving Age. In English the response to these changing conditions is marked by the swift ascendancy of the 'English as language' paradigm. From the mid-sixties onwards the work of the London School (and to a lesser extent the linguistics programme of Halliday and Doughty at Birmingham) brought about a redefinition of 'English as language'. A major turning point in the debate between the Cambridge lobby and the advocates of 'English as language' was the outcome of the 1966 Dartmouth Seminar, a joint English-American conference of English teaching specialists. At the conference, what were called the 'skills' (grammarian) and 'cultural heritage' (literary) models of English teaching were rejected in favour of 'language and personal growth'.[48] 'Language and personal growth' stressed the need for English teaching to begin with the pupils' performance and to be related directly to their experience. Social and personal relevance were being stressed as the main bases on which personal growth would be achieved.[49] From this point on the establishment and dissemination of the 'English as language' paradigm with its institutional base at the London Institute of Education (more specifically Britton's Writing Research Unit), is marked by a series of prestigious projects,[50] funded by the Schools Council, and the publication of a number of research studies and programmatic statements.[51]

Foremost among the published texts is Britton's *Language and Learning*[52] which became a key reference point for the whole range of work which took up the 'English as language' position during the 1970s. Drawing in particular on the work of American psychologist George Kelly, Britton argues that language provides the child with a representational system through which predictions about the world may be constituted and tested out. In other words language is the basis of experience and experience serves to differentiate for persons their unique 'world representation'. The implications drawn for teachers were that 'talking-and-doing must be given major stress throughout the primary school' and that 'language must continue to grow roots from first hand experience.[53]

But it is important to recognize that within the 'English as language' movement there are a series of important sub-divisions and differences of emphasis, which have often been blurred or misread by critics. In simple terms these differences can be teased out by considering the degree of emphasis placed on the *social*, at one extreme, as against the *linguistic*, at the other extreme. Although in both cases primary concern is with the child as learner and performer. The *social* is most strikingly represented in Dixon's early work, particularly the collection of materials *Reflections* (published with other teachers from Walworth Comprehensive).[55] Here English is drawn in the direction of social studies and 'the explicit and continuous discussion of social and moral issues ... a pedagogic version of social realism'.[56] This 'social realist' position, taken up in the work of Commission 7 at NATE conferences, implies a radical stance towards both subject knowledge, rooting English in the 'cultural present of the average and the "less able child"'[57] and subject pedagogy, in an attempt to break with the 'transmission process that binds knowledge, teacher and pupil into a more traditional and more hierarchical set of relationships'.[58] On both counts it may be set directly against the assumptions of the Cambridge School. The *linguistic* position is presented by Halliday and Doughty and the *Language in Use* programme, first published in 1971.[59] This is a course book for teachers aimed at involving pupils in a reflexive analysis of how language works in a wide variety of different situations. The starting point is the pupils' own experiences of language and the scheme draws on the pupils' cumulative experiences of using language to live (see Doughty, Pearce and Thornton, *Exploring Language*;[60] Doughty and Doughty, *Using Language in Use*;[61] and Keen, *Teaching English: a Linguistic Approach*.[62]) Britton's concerns with language and learning occupy the middle ground between the social and linguistic, stressing both the different functional uses of language (transactional, expressive and poetic) and the central relevance of the child's own social experience of life.

While the 'English as language' paradigm may have established itself as the new orthodoxy, at least as far as NATE is concerned (the debates and conflict in the association cannot be taken to indicate a national shift), the advocates of the Cambridge School were certainly not content to allow themselves to be completely overwhelmed. They still controlled the *Use of English* after all, and Whitehead in an article printed in that journal in 1976 launched an attack on the book *Growth through English*, which had been republished in the previous year. In particular Whitehead claims that the overbroad definition of literature used in the book 'has done a disservice to teachers by assimilating pupils' stories and poems (the literature of the classroom) into the mature products of real authors'.[63]

Abbs is also strident in his criticisms of both the linguistic emphasis of the new orthodoxy, which he sees as representing 'an unfortunate adaptation to the dominant technocratic thrust of our civilization'[64] and the social realist component which he argues is posited as 'theoretically "neutral" although in fact often started ideologically to the left'.[65] Similar criticisms were voiced by Mathieson[66] and Hoggart[67], the latter highlighting what he saw as 'the danger of too contemporary a slant in English studies'.

In effect Hoggart's argument is for stronger boundary-maintenance in English in the face of a shift towards what Bernstein refers to as the *integrated code*, 'the *subordination* of previously insulated subjects *or* courses to some *relational* idea, which blurs the boundaries between the subjects'.[68] Thus Smith reports that 'in the early 1960s English was becoming so diffuse that it looked in danger of disappearing altogether.'[69] Links forged at this time between some English teachers and those teaching the social sciences were based on common political concerns about the role and structure of educational provision and on the attractions of social science methods. And, as Bucher and Strauss[70] suggest, a methodological orientation towards other disciplines can exacerbate already existing divisions within a subject group. Even sixty years after the founding of the English Association, teachers of English remained highly insecure about the status of their subject. Indeed, in part at least, the insecurities felt by the founders of NATE are based upon very similar problems to those experienced by the initiators of the English Association. We have already noted the challenge stemming from the relationships established with other curriculum subjects. A second factor of concern to both groups was the large number of non-specialists engaged in the teaching of English. We can compare the *1910 Board of Education Circular No. 753. The Teaching of English in Secondary Schools* with comments made in the 1970s. The former stated categorically: 'Teachers of English, quite as much as the teachers of any other subject, require definite qualifications for their work. They must have studied it before they can be competent to teach it,' whereas in 1973, George Allen is writing: 'Much English, often most, was and still is taught by teachers whose own specialist studies lay elsewhere; all too often they know very little about English generally.'[71] The ensuing problems are not solely felt at a national level. The work of non-specialists can also have its effect upon intra- and inter-departmental politics at the school level (see for example the case studies of Oak Farm and Furzedown schools in Ball and Lacey[72]). Recently, the Bullock Report, *A Language for Life*, reported that at the time of its survey one third of those teaching English in secondary schools had 'no discernible qualification'[73] and 38 per cent were teaching the subject for less than half their time.

A contemporary picture of English in schools emerges which is not starkly dissimilar in many respects from the situation that existed when English was first established as a separate curriculum subject. There is: (1) disputation within the subject involving a very real struggle for intellectual sovereignty with competing paradigms seeking to control the definition of analytic problems and methods, and the pedagogic form for the realization of the subject; (2) threats to the continuing independence of English as a school subject from the inroads of adjacent curriculum areas; (3) a large component of non-specialists teaching the subject. However, the contemporary situation differs in the degree of complexity involved in the competition with the subject community.

As noted previously, the opposition between paradigms involves both issues of content and issues of method (pedagogy). Implicit in the former is the polarization of *élite* and *mass* concepts of culture, and in the latter is a concomitant separation of child-centred and subject-centred orientations. The dimensions and structure of the current state of allegiance and conflict in English teaching are represented schematically in Figure 3.

In all cases it is possible to equate the separately identified positions on the matrix more or less with the work and advocacy of particular contributors to the field of English studies. Furthermore by isolating

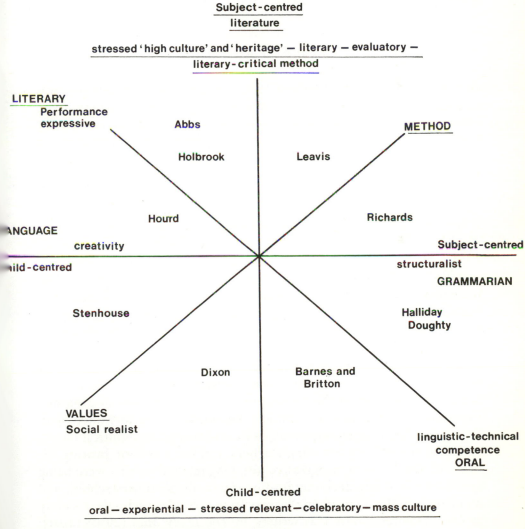

Figure 3 Paradigms of English Teaching

particular axes on the matrix it is possible to plot the current state of controversy or the changes over time either in the rhetoric of educationalists and commentators and/or in the practices of school teachers. For example if we take the language axis, stretching from an emphasis on *grammar* at one end to an emphasis on the role of pupil *creativity* at the other, then it is possible to identify changes over time, discussed previously, with a shift in emphasis from the former to the latter. But what is more, the move from the latinate form of 'taught' grammar, to 'natural' grammar, 'self-expression', and 'social relevance' also embodied a shift in the dominant conception of the pupil as learner, the learning process and the aims of education.

## Standards, Bullock and the Aftermath

In the period between 1965 and 1975 English as a school subject was changed and redefined, at least within the arenas discussed here, to an extent unmatched in all the previous sixty years of its existence. The conditions of change identified previously provided a background to a whole range of innovatory programmes in education in a brief 'moment' of 'progressive consensus'. Few subjects were not affected in one way or another by the need that was felt to exist to experiment with new forms of knowledge and teaching practices. The spread of the comprehensive school demanded that teachers re-think the curriculum and their working relationships with pupils; or so it seemed at the time. However, while the 'noise' of educational reform was not necessarily matched by widespread changes in actual practice, in the public imagination, orchestrated by the mass media, a picture was created of massive and increasingly 'dangerous' changes in the educational experiences of pupils in schools. In the early 1970s these public concerns, fuelled by the hysterical response of right wing commentators, in the *Black Papers* and elsewhere, had reached the state of a national moral panic. Even the normally sedate *Times* newspaper spoke of the need to tame 'the wild men of the classroom'. Comprehensive education and innovations in teaching and subject knowledge were identified with falling standards, increasing violence in schools and the political indoctrination of pupils by left wing teachers. English was soon bearing the brunt of attacks upon 'progressive' teaching methods which were being specifically linked to declining reading standards in primary schools and an increase in illiteracy among leavers from secondary schools. As early as 1968 Dolores Moore was writing in *The Daily Mail* (28 October): 'Read the numbers, published now and then, of illiterate school leavers each year. Notice at an open day, just how few seven-year-olds, and even eleven-year-olds, can actually write and spell correctly. Look at the standard of reading books. It is generally low. Sometimes very low. Yet more money is spent each year on educating our children.' In 1972, an NFER report was published suggesting a measurable decline in reading standards in the late 1960s among certain groups of children.

In response to this 'climate of public concern' Mrs Thatcher, then Secretary of State for Education, was moved to set up an inquiry under Sir Alan Bullock, 'to consider in relation to schools, all aspects of teaching the Use of English, including reading, writing and speech.' The report *A Language For Life*, published in 1975, attempts to review the state of English teaching from the earliest development of pre-school language skills through to the teaching of English literature to 16–19 year-olds studying for A-levels. But as the title indicates the emphasis of the report is on the development of language skills. 'The time has come', the report concludes, 'to raise language as a high priority in the complex life of the secondary school.' However, in response to the critics of 'progressivism' the committee's detailed research provides no evidence that formal work in English was decaying 'in a climate of unchecked creativity.' The report is critical of 'the notion of English in the secondary school as almost exclusively a source of material for personal response to social issues'[74] which was regarded as often lacking in direction and tending to produce cliches in pupils' work. This approach was seen by the committee to be diminishing the pupils' experience of English work. Alongside this, literature is strongly defended against the inroads of 'thematic' work. (Perhaps it is John Dixon's 'social realist' view of English that is most clearly under attack here.) The undue emphasis on 'creativity' in the primary classroom was also seen as worrying when other types of work were 'neglected'.

Strong encouragement was given for the need for teacher intervention in pupils' work.[75] (Here then the traditional teacher role is reinforced over and against attempts to develop less hierarchical forms of classroom relationship.) In many respects the report attempts to steer a middle course and to establish a 'coherent' basis for English teaching which draws together some of the diverse and competing versions of school English that had been in contest during the period 1960 to 1975. Thus alongside the criticisms of 'unchecked creativity', the teaching of 'grammar' as an isolated topic is roundly condemned; 'Competence in language comes above all through its purposeful use, not through the working of exercises divorced from context.'[76]

And while 'social realism' and 'grammar' are given little support in the report both 'English as language' and 'English as literature' receive positive reinforcement. And the paradigm of literature teaching which is clearly underwritten in the report is that sponsored and developed through the work of F.R. Leavis and the Cambridge School of English, the tradition of literature teaching 'which aims at personal and moral growth' and stresses 'the "civilizing" power of literature.'[77] The ideas in the report about 'English as language' clearly draw on the work of Britton and 'the London School', which is specifically mentioned in the report. Considerable attention is given to oracy, the report argues that 'a priority objective for all schools is a commitment to the speech needs of their pupils and a serious study of the role of oral language in learning.' Also support is given to the role of linguistics in English teaching and teachers are encouraged to acquire 'an explicit understanding of the operation of language'. Two central themes — language and learning, and reading — lie at the heart of the report. A continuing programme, aimed at the development of pupils' language from pre-school to school leaving is the main recommendation, with the 'reading curriculum' seen as an integral part of the total 'language curriculum'. Two keywords widely taken up from the report into educational discourse reflect these primary concerns. First, the notion of 'basic skills', which in the report refer not simply to the starting point of language development but to a concern with language competence throughout the pupils' school career. Second, is the concept of 'language across the curriculum',[78] the need that is for schools to have a language policy which addresses the problem of language development across all the subjects of the curriculum. Both of these keywords sparked off a considerable barrage of 'noise' in schools, local education authorities and the media. Following the publication of the report, hundreds of schools — both primary and secondary — established working parties to examine and devise a policy for 'language across the curriculum'. Equally, in many schools teachers were given posts of responsibility for 'language across the curriculum' and numerous in-service education courses were soon being offered under this title. However, to reiterate one of the familiar themes in this paper, the widespread translation of this 'noise' and activity into changes in the classroom practices of teachers remains questionable.

More generally the symbolic and political functions of the Bullock report are probably in the long run of greater significance than its specific findings. In one sense it demonstrated the power of 'public opinion' and the mass media to stimulate government action to intervene in teachers' classroom decision-making. This intervention was achieved not directly by legislation but by a publicly conducted procedure of boundary definition. The Bullock report effectively attempted to impose limits upon the range of activities that could legitimately pass as English teaching. Certain traditional practices were reinforced and some elements of innovation had received commendation, but the 'excesses' were clearly identified and censured. Probably most significantly the basic concern of English teaching with pupil *skills* is established in the report. It is this more than anything else which has probably made an impact on teachers' thinking and planning for work in English lessons.

However, the Bullock report clearly did not satisfy all its audiences. *The Daily Mail*, that model of objective reporting on educational issues, received the report in the following ironic terms: 'WHITEWASH spells whitewash. Sir Alan Bullock's report on the teaching of English shrouds the reality in trendy pieties' (19 February 1975). Clearly, from *The Mail*'s point of view the report had failed to come to grips with the 'realities' of the situation, the 'realities' to which *The Mail* itself had privileged access. And a great deal of the press attention centred not on the main findings of the report itself — which included a refutation of the suggestion that reading scores were declining — but on the minority report of the one dissenting member, a *Black Paper* contributor who argued for a return to traditional forms of teaching English in the primary school.

The Bullock report was in fact only to be the precursor of a much broader and more fundamental struggle to shift the control of educational matters away from schools and teachers towards 'the community' and 'the political centre' — the 'Great Debate'. The main public concerns associated with the setting up of Bullock — 'standards' and 'accountability' — were to be played out in even grander form across the whole educational scene. The DES, the Inspectorate and the Secretaries of State for Education were beginning from the mid-1970s to reassert their 'rights' to 'walk in the secret garden of the curriculum'.[79] As far as English was concerned the major threat in this process lay in the 'stealthy'[80] behind the scenes development of the Assessment of Performance Unit. Launched in 1975, as part of an initiative concerned with the 'educationally disadvantaged', by 1978 the APU was moving towards the establishment and monitoring of national standards in pupil performance across a range of subjects. And writing in 1980, Lawton[81] saw the development of the APU as both dangerous and anachronistic and the establishment of testing on a national basis as likely to have massive 'backwash effects' in the classroom: ... 'having moved away from the Scylla of *laissez-faire* the DES show no signs of possessing an adequate theoretical base for curriculum change and is in danger of getting too close to the Charybdis of behaviouristic, mechanistic approaches to curriculum and evaluation.'[82]

As it turns out the APU's development has not so far produced the sorts of national standard setting that were envisaged at this time and the work of the Unit has been confined mainly to small-scale studies and a concentration on mathematics and science. But the importance of the publicity and anxiety surrounding the development of the APU and the 'Great Debate' lay not so much perhaps in their concrete effects as in the change in climate that they brought about and the considerable undermining of teachers' morale which resulted. The initiative for change in the curriculum was, to a great extent, wrested from teachers and professional organizations and taken on by central agencies (APU, HMI, MSC etc.).

In this situation it could certainly be argued that conditions were ripe for a reassertion of more traditional and elitist forms of English teaching. The work done by the *Black Papers* and the media had clearly begun to undermine many of the curriculum changes achieved in the late 1960s and early 1970s. And the advocates of the Cambridge School were certainly not slow to exploit the possibilities of the situation. For example, Fred Inglis, writing in *Use of English* (the Cambridge School Journal) in 1977, reviewing the work of the journal, saw the time as right to restate the central importance for English of the work of F.R. Leavis. The paper is clearly written in adversorial terms:

> It seems timely to restate the centrality of his [F.R. Leavis's] place in any study of the use of English. There are plenty of English teachers these days to prate on about Leavis's alleged elitism (though how you have an intelligentsia without elites is a question not be asked). Reactionary, elitist, authoritarian, absolutist, these are the tinny valuations of the mindless — the vulgar or carbuncular egalitarian whose only permitted discriminations are against economic privation and the restriction of social access. The point about Leavis's importance for this magazine is that *Scrutiny* — and Leavis, for us and *The Use of English*, was *Scrutiny* — gave a believable account of the movement of civilisation together with a programme of resistance.[83]

For Inglis the mighty tradition of English literature is set against the 'subversive values' of those who would assert the 'hatefulness and banality' of 'popular culture', '*Skinhead, Crossroads*, the foulmouthed exchanges of ROSLA sixteen-year-olds on the Kop'.[84] Inglis also recognizes elements of value in the attempts of those (Britton, Barnes and Rosen) who have drawn the attention of teachers to the 'peculiarly contextual nature of linguistic experience' and is not against a 'radical pluralism' in English teaching, but what he sees as central to the teacher's task is to go beyond the 'grossnesses, absences and distortions' of the language of children and to 'purify and enrich' it, 'to teach', 'to revalue and mediate official culture'.[85] Behind the powerful rhetoric of Inglis' arguments lies a plea for synthesis (on his terms). He sees teachers of English as having been 'abandoned by a bankrupt Schools Council, a bloodless and wizened NATE, and a cynical union'[86] and needing to find a new unity in their work. Calls for a resolution, a compromise between opposed positions and entrenched ideologies in fact provide a major theme in post-Bullock publications for English teachers.[87] Commentators saw themselves as addressing a teacher audience which has been confused, bemused and misled by the debates and contradictory proposals aimed at it during the previous period.

One writer at least takes a much more uncompromising position. Holbrook, writing in 1979, rejects entirely as 'false and impractical . . . the implication that linguistics offers us a means to foster and control language development.'[88] He cannot accept the 'functional' view of language presented in Bullock, as a means of 'processing experience' and representing the world to ourselves: 'So convincing is the seeming commonsense in Bullock that we fail to notice how its whole view of language is arid and inadequate'.[89] The answer to Bullock, for Holbrook, is once again to be found in Leavis: 'Leavis's concern is with values we recreate in ourselves, as we read literature, and take on our language, which is the way in which the 'Human World' is constructed.'[90] Holbrook accepts neither 'basic skills' nor 'popular culture' as matters for the teacher of English.

In some respects it may be that Holbrook is as much out of step in the post-Bullock period as those enthusiasts who continued to argue for English to be based upon the 'inevitable creativeness of ordinary everyday life'.[91] But it is important always to recognize that behind the Cambridge School position there lies not only an explicit literary elitism but also an implicit social elitism. Arthur Pollard, *Black Paper* writer, in an article entitled *Conservatives, Culture and Education*, published by the Social Affairs Unit in 1982, quotes that other doyen of the Cambridge School, T.S. Eliot: 'There is no doubt that in our headlong rush to educate everybody we are lowering our standards and more and more abandoning the study of those subjects by which the essentials of our culture . . . are transmitted.'[92] In the current context education and training are becoming increasingly separated in government education policies, there is no longer a 'headlong rush to educate everybody'. And while Holbrook and Inglis and Abbs would be the first to want to reject such a reading of their work, it is within these limits of tolerance that different views of English teaching must currently be understood and explored.

## Making Sense of Curriculum Change

The changes in the politico-economic climate of the late 1970s have brought about *conditions of change* which have allowed a reassertion of the utilitarian functions and 'high culture' traditions of English teaching in schools. As regards the former, 'The school needs to be seen, by both pupils and parents, as a facility (for which they have paid) provided for their use'.[93] 'Correctness' and the improvement of standards of language used by children are once again major issues on the classroom agenda for teachers of English.

In many ways in attempting to explain this reassertion the *conditions of change* can be identified and specified more straightforwardly than the *relations of change*. In the post-Bullock era it is the public dimensions of educational policy that have come to be of prime importance, the *relations of change* must once again, as in the very earliest period of the development of English, take into account the role played by the state in influencing and affecting the definition of the subject. But at any point in time, there is a whole set of influences at work in shaping and changing a particular school subject. While it is possible to accept at an abstract level that school knowledge 'is a selection from the available knowledge within the culture' and that, 'those in positions of power will attempt to define what is to be considered as knowledge',[94] it is much more difficult to identify those in 'positions of power', the extent to which their attempt is successful, and the extent to which alternative definitions compete for ascendancy within any subject. Nor is it very clear whether the process of definition concerns simply states of knowledge or must also be taken to include ways of knowing and matters of pedagogy. It should be clear from the discussion so far that there was a considerable autonomy for schools in the selection and organization of subject knowledge, at least since the demise of the Revised Codes and until the 'Great Debate', which rendered the practices of teachers relatively immune to the *recommendations* and *suggestions*, etc. of government and the educational civil service. Certainly those models of explanation for classroom change which may be culled from the literature on English teaching suggest that curriculum innovation is very much a matter of *gradualism*. As Shayer[95] puts it, what we find here is a considerable time lag between the acceptance of theory and the impact of that theory upon actual classroom practice. If we concentrate on the secondary school once again, then one of the explanations for changes in the teaching of English, often relied upon by commentators, relates the time-lag noted by Shayer to change via the impact and dissemination of personal experience. For example Smith[96] sees this kind of change as taking place through several generations of teachers and pupils in the 1920s, 1930s and 1940s.

And this kind of passage of influence has been noted specifically by some of those teachers who came to effect changes in the teaching of English in the 1950s and 1960s, James Britton[97] for instance is clear about the influence on his work of Percival Gurrey. The impact of experience as pupils has tended to be underemphasized in studies of teachers and their methods. Mardle and Walker[98] present one of the few arguments for the necessity of recognizing the pupil experience as a major contribution for the socialization of teachers. And Lortie[99] presents a closely related account of the influences affecting American teachers at work. A similar set of assumptions of dissemination and change taking place via personal experience and influence is central to Griffiths and Mullins'[100] account of the emergence of subject specialities discussed previously. They also stress the considerable time lag involved in such a process.

What emerges from this analysis of curriculum change is a model of curriculum innovation which is perhaps at the same time both humanistic and reactionary. Curriculum change is seen to be a long-term and inter-personal process, based upon the establishment of subject paradigms via networks of communication and apprenticeship (with many of the teachers who are not directly exposed to experience of these paradigms being influenced marginally, or not at all, by them). It would appear that the most profound influences upon the English teacher, in terms of his or her conception of English as a school subject and its concomitant pedagogy, is equally as likely to be the teacher's own experience as pupil as their university or college training. The impact then, at school level, of the process of curriculum change presented, is through the sedimentation of generations and groups of teachers trained at particular institutions, with particular allegiances, in competition with one another; with occasionally one or other position losing ground as 'only a few elderly hold-outs remain'.[101] But then again the emergence of new paradigms is not itself a matter of chance. Large scale social and educational changes, which also affect teachers directly, may tend to inhibit or promote this process. Its promotion in particular is often the result of changes in educational policy, like the introduction of comprehensive education, which present the classroom teacher with new problems. So that as Kuhn notes, in the case of science, 'probably the most prevalent claim advanced by the proponents of a new paradigm is that they can solve the problems that have led the old one to a crisis.'[102]

If the account presented here is a realistic way of representing some aspects of curriculum change in schools, or the absence of change, then it must inevitably throw new light upon the dominant traditions of the curriculum development movement. If taken as a general model of curriculum development it fundamentally challenges the basic rational-technical premises of the Research, Design and Dissemination approach to curriculum development, and it may go some way towards explaining the failure of those projects based upon this model to alter the ways in which most teachers conceive of their subject and go about teaching it. It may also offer some support for the current move away from project-based curriculum innovation towards school-based curriculum development and in-service education. It might also suggest that the increased control of the espoused curriculum by state agencies will not be any more successful in redirecting the enacted curriculum in the classroom than other centre-periphery attempts at curriculum change. However, it is clear that the 'hysteria'[103] surrounding the 'Great Debate' and the recent spate of cuts in spending on education have profoundly altered the climate of educational thinking within which change is possible. Established networks have been disrupted and devalued, other dormant or hidden networks of social relationships have been resuscitated, and new coalitions are at work on the educational scene.

## Notes

1 This is a revised and expanded version of a paper titled 'Competition and conflict in the teaching of English: a socio-historical analysis' which appeared in *Journal of Curriculum Studies*, Vol. 14, No. 1. pp. 1–28. I am grateful to Ivor Goodson for his useful comments as to ways of developing the previous version. A more detailed analysis of the period 1906–35 can be found in Ball (1983).
2 See Goodson (1984) for an account of 'curriculum histories'.
3 Shayer (1970).
4 Shayer, *ibid*, p. 22.
5 G.B. Board of Education (1910), p. 4.
6 *Ibid.*, p. 14.
7 *Ibid.*, pp. 24–25.
8 Quoted in Rudduck (1979).
9 Rudduck (unpublished).

10 Bucher and Strauss (1976), pp. 24–25.

11 *Ibid.*, p. 20.

12 See Goodson (1983).

13 G.B. Board of Education (1911), p. 6.

14 G.B. Board of Education (1905), p. 38.

15 G.B. Board of Education (1910), p. 11.

16 *Ibid.*, p. 2.

17 The 1902 Education Act made clear the limitations on the superintendence 'of matters relating to education in England and Wales' given to the Board of Education when it was set up by the 1899 Board of Education Act.

18 G.B. Board of Education (1904).

19 English Association, The (1919), p. 6.

20 Saunders (1976), p. 19.

21 Allen (1973), p. 30.

22 Smith, (1973), p. 3.

23 *Ibid.*, p. 33. .

24 Abbs (1980).

25 *Ibid.*, p. 9.

26 Hourd (1949), p. 12.

27 Shayer, *op. cit.*, p. 42.

28 Sampson (1921), p. 14.

29 G.B. Min. of Education (1945), p. 145.

30 Abbs, *op. cit.*, p. 4.

31 *Ibid.*, p. 5.

32 Mullins (1973).

33 Griffiths and Mullins (1972).

34 Mullins *op. cit.*, p. 18.

35 *Ibid.*, pp. 20–21.

36 *Ibid.*, p. 21.

37 Quiller-Couch (1920).

38 Mullins *op. cit.*, p. 22.

39 *Ibid.*, p. 23.

40 Leavis and Thompson (1933).

41 Mathieson (1974), p. 122.

42 Mullins *op. cit.*, p. 25.

43 Mathieson *op. cit.*, p. 138.

44 Britton (1973), p. 18.

45 *Ibid.*, p. 18.

46 *Ibid.*, p. 14.

47 Owen (1973), p. 122.

48 Dixon (1975), p. 4.

49 *Ibid.*, p. 13.

50 Some of the major projects were: —

    The Written Language of 11–18 Year-Olds 1966–71 James Britton and Nancy Martin.  £33.517.

    Writing Across the Secondary Curriculum 1971–74 Nancy Martin.  £31,000.

    Language Development in the Primary School 1969–71 Connie Rosen (Goldsmiths College).  £50,000.

> English in the Middle Years of Schooling 1970–72. Bernard Newsome (Goldsmiths College). £18,000.
> Oracy 1967–72. Andrew Wilkinson (Birmingham). £15,750.
> English 16–19 1975–79 John Dixon (Bretton Hall). £77,000.
> Linguistics and English Teaching 1964–71 M.A.K. Halliday and Peter Doughty (Birmingham). £156,000.

51 For example, Stratta, Dixon and Wilkinson (1973), *Patterns of Language: Explorations in the Teaching of English;* Burgess *et al* (1973), *Understanding Children's Writing;* Britton *et al* (1975), *The Development of Writing Abilities;* Mallet and Newsome (1977), *Talking, Writing and Learning 8–13.*

52 Britton (1970).

53 *Ibid.,* p. 137.

55 Dixon and Stratta.

56 Abbs, *op. cit.,* p. 24.

57 Hodgson, *op. cit.,* p. 442.

58 *Ibid.,* p. 442.

59 Doughty, Pearce and Thornton (1971).

60 Doughty, Pearce and Thornton (1972).

61 Doughty and Doughty (1974).

62 Keen (1978).

63 Whitehead (1976), p. 13.

64 Abbs, *op. cit.,* p. 23.

65 *Ibid.,* p. 10.

66 *Op. cit.,* p. 223.

67 Hoggart (1964), p. 167.

68 Bernstein (1971), p. 53.

69 Smith, *op. cit.,* p. 7.

70 G.B. Board of Education (1910), p. 7.

71 Allen (1973), p. 30.

72 *Op. cit.*

73 G.B. D.E.S. (1975).

74 G.B. D.E.S. (1975), p. 7.

75 *Ibid.,* p. 8.

76 *Ibid.,* p. 528.

77 *Ibid.,* p. 125.

78 This was taken from the title and subject of the 1971 NATE annual conference.

79 Referred to in a speech by Sheila Browne, Senior Chief HMI to a conference of local education authorities in July 1977.

80 Lawton (1980), p. 50.

81 *Op. cit.*

82 Lawton, *op. cit.,* p. 48.

83 Inglis (1977), p. 40.

84 *Ibid.,* p. 45.

85 *Ibid.,* p. 47.

86 *Ibid.,* p. 47.

87 Allen (1980), Abbs (1982), Sharp (1980).

88 Holbrook (1979), p. 52.

89  *Ibid.*, p. 58.
90  *Ibid.*, p. 64.
91  Inglis, *op. cit.*
92  Pollard (1982).
93  Cashdan (1979), p. 18.
94  Young, *op. cit.*, p. 32.
95  Shayer, *op. cit.*
96  Smith, *op. cit.*, p. 7.
97  Britton (1973), p. 13.
98  Mardle and Walker (1980), p. 10.
99  Lortie (1973), p. 487.
100  Griffiths and Mullins, *op. cit.*, p. 963.
101  Kuhn (1962), p. 159.
102  Kuhn, *op. cit.*, p.153.
103  Simon (1977), p. 204.

## References/Bibliography

ABBS, P. (1980) 'The reconstitution of English as art', *Tract*, 81, pp. 4–31.

ABBS, P. (1982) *English within the Arts*, London, Hodder and Stoughton.

ALLEN, D. (1980) *English Teaching Since 1965: How much Growth?*, London, Heinemann.

ALLEN, G. (1973) 'English: past, present and future', in BAGNELL, N. (Ed.) *New Movements in the Study and Teaching of English*, London, Temple Smith.

APPLE, M.W. (1979) *Ideology and Curriculum*, London, Routledge and Kegan Paul.

ARNOLD, M. (1908) *Reports on Elementary Schools 1852–82*, London, HMSO.

BALL, S.J. (1983) 'A subject of privilege: English and the school curriculum 1906–1935' in HAMMERSLEY, M. and HARGREAVES, A. (Eds.) *Curriculum Practice*, Lewes, Falmer Press.

BALL, S.J. and LACEY, C. (1980) 'Subject disciplines as the opportunity for group action: a measured critique of subject subcultures' in WOODS, P.E. *Teacher Strategies*, London, Croom Helm.

BARNES, D. (1976) *From Curriculum to Communication*, Harmondsworth, Penguin.

BARNETT, P.A. (1902) 'English literature and English schools', *Journal of Education*.

BERGER, P. (1969) *A Rumour of Angels*, Harmondsworth, Penguin.

BERNSTEIN, B. (1971) 'On the classification and framing of educational knowledge' in YOUNG, M.F.D. (Ed.) *Knowledge and Control*, London, Collier-Macmillan.

BERNSTEIN, B. (1974) 'Sociology and the sociology of education: a brief account' in REX, J. (Ed.) *Approaches to Sociology*, London, Routledge and Kegan Paul.

BLACKIE, J.M. (1969) *English Teaching for Non-Specialists*, London, Faber.

BOARD OF EDUCATION (1904) *Code of Regulations*.

BOARD OF EDUCATION (1905) *Suggestions for the Consideration of Teachers and Others Concerned in the Work of the Public Elementary Schools.*

BOARD OF EDUCATION (1909) *General Report on the Teaching of English in London Elementary Schools.*

BOARD OF EDUCATION (1910) *Report.*

BOARD OF EDUCATION (1911) *Report.*

BRITTON, J. (1970) *Language and Learning,* Harmondsworth, Penguin.

BRITTON, J. (1973) 'How we got here' in BAGNALL, N. (Ed.) *New Movements in the Study and Teaching of English,* London, Temple Smith.

BRITTON, J. et al (1975) *The Development of Writing Abilities (11–18),* Schools Council Research Studies, London, Macmillan.

BUCHER, R. and STRAUSS, A.L. (1961) 'Profession in process', *American Journal of Sociology,* 66, pp. 325–34, January.

BURGESS, C. et al (1973) *Understanding Children Writing,* Harmondsworth, Penguin.

CASHDAN, A. (1979) *Language, Reading and Learning,* Oxford, Basil Blackwell.

CENTRE FOR CONTEMPORARY CULTURAL STUDIES (1981) *Unpopular Education: Schooling and Social Democracy in England since 1944,* London, Hutchinson.

CURRIE, W.B. (1973) *New Directions in Teaching English Language,* London, Longman.

DIXON, J. (1975) *Growth Through English,* Oxford, Oxford University Press for the National Association for the Teaching of English.

DOUGHTY, P., PEARCE, J. and THORNTON, G. (1971) *Language in Use,* London, Edward Arnold.

DOUGHTY, P., PEARCE, J. and THORNTON, G. (1972) *Exploring Language,* London, Edward Arnold.

DOUGHTY, A. and DOUGHTY, P. (1974) *Using Language in Use,* London, Edward Arnold.

DYHOUSE, C. (1976) 'Social-Darwinistic ideas and the development of women's education in England 1880–1920', *History of Education,* 5, 1, pp. 41–58.

EAGLETON, T. (1976) *Criticism and Ideology,* New York, New Left Books.

EDMONDS, E.L. (1962) *The School Inspector,* London, Routledge and Kegan Paul.

ENGLISH ASSOCIATION, THE (1919) *The Teaching of English in Schools,* a series of papers edited by E.J. MORLEY.

GALLIE, W.B. (1955–6) 'Essentially contested concepts', *Proceedings of the Aristotelian Society,* 56.

GOODSON, I.F. (1983) *School Subjects and Curriculum Change,* London, Croom Helm.

GOODSON, I.F. (1984) 'Subjects for study' in GOODSON, I.F. and BALL, S.J. (Eds.) *Defining the Curriculum,* Lewes, Falmer Press.

G.B. DES (1975) *A Language for Life,* London, HMSO.

G.B. DES/APU (1977) 'APU — Questions and Answers', London, HMSO.

G.B. DES/APU (1978) 'APU: An Introduction', London, HMSO.

GRIFFITHS, B.C. and MULLINS, N.C. (1972) 'Coherent social groups in scientific change', *Science,* 1 September, pp. 959–64.

HODGSON, J.D. (1975) Change in English Teaching: Institutionalisation, Transmission and Ideology, unpublished PhD, Institute of Education, University of London.

HOGGART, R. (1964) 'Schools of English and contemporary society 11', *Use of English*, 17, 3.

HOLBROOK, D. (1979) *English for Meaning*, Slough, NFER.

HOURD, M. (1949) *The Education of the Poetic Spirit*, London, Heinemann.

INGLIS, F. (1977) 'The use of English and the use of English', *Use of English*, 29, 1.

KEEN, J. (1978) *Teaching English: a linguistic approach*, London, Methuen.

KUHN, T.S. (1962) *The Structure of Scientific Revolutions*, Chicago, Chicago University Press.

LAWTON, D. (1980) *The Politics of the School Curriculum*, London, Routledge and Kegan Paul.

LEAVIS, F.R. and THOMPSON, D. (1933) *Culture and Environment*, London, Chatto and Windus.

LORTIE, D.C. (1973) 'Observations on teaching as work', in TRAVERS, R.M.W. (Ed.) *Second Handbook on Research and Teaching*, New York, Rand McNally.

MARDLE, G. and WALKER, M. (1980) 'Strategies and structure: some critical notes on teacher socialization' in WOODS, P.E. (ed.) *Teacher Strategies*, London, Croom Helm.

MATHIESON, M. (1975) *The Preachers of Culture*, London, George Allen and Unwin.

MINISTRY OF EDUCATION (1954) *Pamphlet No. 26 Language! Some Suggestions for Teachers of English and others in Primary and Secondary Schools and Further Education*, London, HMSO.

MULLINS, N.C. (1973) *Theories and Theory Groups in Contemporary American Sociology*, New York, Harper Row.

MUSGROVE, F. (1965) 'The contribution of sociology to the study of the curriculum' in KERR, J.F. (Ed.) *Changing the Curriculum*, London, University of London Press.

MUSHET, J. (1912) *Exercises in English*, Edinburgh.

OWEN, J. (1973) *The Management of Curriculum Development*, Cambridge, Cambridge University Press.

PETCH, J.A. (1953) *Fifty Years of Examining the JMB 1903–53*, London, Harrap.

PETTY, M.F. and HOGBEN, D. (1980) 'Explorations of semantic space with beginning teachers: a study of socialization into teaching', *British Journal of Teacher Education*, 6, 1, pp. 51–61.

QUILLER-COUCH, A. (1920) *On the Art of Reading: Lectures delivered in the University of Cambridge, 1916–17*, Cambridge, Cambridge University Press.

RUDDOCK, J. (1979a) 'A study of traditions in the development of short in-service curriculum courses for teachers', unpub. PhD thesis, University of East Anglia.

RUDDOCK, J. (1979b) 'Notes on the English Association and National Association for the Teaching of English', unpub. CARE, University of East

Anglia.

SAMPSON, G. (1921) *English for the English*, Cambridge, Cambridge University Press.

SAUNDERS, M. (1976) *Developments in English Teaching*, London, Open Books.

SCHIFF, H. (1977) *Contemporary Approaches to English Studies*, London, Heinemann for the English Association.

SHARP, D. (1980) *English at School: The Wood and the Trees*, Oxford, Pergamon.

SHAYER, D. (1970) *The Teaching of English in Schools*, London, Routledge and Kegan Paul.

SIMON, B. (1977) 'Marx and the crisis in education', *Marxism Today*, Vol.

SMETHERAM, D. (1978) 'Identifying strategies', paper given at SSRC-funded Conference 'Teacher and Pupil Strategies', held at St Hilda's College, Oxford, Sept. 15–17.

SMITH, A.E. (1954) *English in the Modern School*, London, Methuen.

SMITH, L.E.W. (1973) *Towards a New English Curriculum*, London, Dent.

SMITH, L.M. and KEITH, P.M. (1971) *Anatomy of Educational Innovation: An Organizational Analysis of an Elementary School*, Chichester, Wiley.

STRATTA, L., DIXON, J. and WILKINSON, A. (1973) *Patterns of Language: Explorations in the Teaching of English*, London, Heinemann.

THOMPSON, D. (1970) 'Introduction' in SAMPSON, G. *English for the English*, Cambridge, Cambridge University Press.

WHITEHEAD, F. (1976) 'Stunting the growth', *Use of English*, 28, 1.

YOUNG, M.F.D. (1971) 'An approach to the study of curriculum as socially organized knowledge' in YOUNG, M.F.D. (Ed.) *Knowledge and Control*, London, Collier Macmillan.

# Secondary School Mathematics Since 1950: Reconstructing Differentiation

*Barry Cooper*

It is widely accepted that there has been a substantial change in the mathematics taught in secondary schools in England since the 1950s. Certainly, the content of textbooks used in courses leading to external examinations has been considerably modified by the work of such groups as the School Mathematics Project (SMP).[1] The activities of this coalition of selective and independent school teachers and university mathematicians, supported by large industrial concerns, ensured the entry into the O-level syllabuses of a variety of 'modern' mathematical topics.[2] Such projects also argued strongly for a new pedagogical approach in mathematics teaching, stressing the 'structure' of the subject and a more discovery-based approach in the classroom.[3] It appears, however, that, in practice, less change has occurred on this latter dimension of the curriculum than on that of content.[4] My focus in this paper, however, is on neither content nor pedagogy *per se*, but on changes in the independent dimension of the degree of differentiation of the mathematics curriculum by 'ability' type and, to a much lesser extent, by sex. It is clearly possible for the syllabus, for example, to change in various ways while the degree of differentiation remains constant. In particular, I ask whether there has been any major move, since the 1950s, towards a more common curriculum in mathematics. A key concern is to describe, for this period of comprehensivization, subject members' perspectives of mathematical 'ability', its distribution and the related issue of the 'appropriateness' of particular definitions of school mathematics for pupils of differing 'abilities'.

I therefore begin by describing the mathematics curriculum of the post-war tripartite system, concentrating on its differentiated nature and the assumptions which served to legitimate this. I then look at some of the curriculum reform projects of the 1960s, examining the extent to which their originators and eventual users accepted or challenged certain dominant assumptions of the tripartite era. I show that their challenge, though significant, was a partial one. I then consider the reaction in the 1970s to the changes in differentiation that were perceived by many to have occurred during the period of reform, showing that real and perceived shifts in the degree of differentiation can produce violent reactions. Lastly, I consider the implications of the patterns of stability and change examined in the paper.

## The Tripartite Mathematics Curriculum

The secondary school mathematics curricula of the 1950s were based in the distinct educational subcultures termed, by Lawton, the public school and elementary traditions, whose origins lie in the Victorian period.[5] The Taunton Commission, in 1868, had argued, in discussing the curriculum of the secondary schools, for 'mathematics' to be included for the upper middle and professional classes, for 'arithmetic' and 'the rudiments of mathematics beyond arithmetic' for pupils from the 'mercantile classes', and for 'very good arithmetic' for the sons of 'smaller tenant farmers, the small tradesmen, [and] the superior artisans'.[6] For the working classes, the Revised Code of 1862 had specified elementary arithmetic.[7]

The selective school mathematics of the 1950s derived from this 'mathematics' of the independent schools of the 1860s referred to by Taunton. For pupils aged up to sixteen this had come to include, alongside the Euclidean geometry favoured in the independent schools for its classical associations, trigonometry, pre-1800 algebra and, sometimes, calculus.[8] This development of the Victorian curriculum had been largely controlled by the Mathematical Association, a body of selective school and university mathematicians founded in the late nineteenth century, originally to promote change in geometry teaching.[9] The domination of policy-making in this Association by the public school/university axis can be seen from the information presented in *Table 1*.[10]

This selective curriculum was internally differentiated, both by 'ability' and sex. In the Inspectorate's *Teaching Mathematics in Secondary Schools* (1958), it is not only argued that, where possible, mathematics should be taught in sets but also that these sets were, and should be, receiving appropriately different courses.[11] A less 'academic', more 'practical', course is recommended for the less 'able' in the grammar school.[12] Various remarks suggest that, in reality, grammar school pupils thus categorized mainly received arithmetic.[13]

Alongside this differentiation by 'ability' there also occurred that

Table 1  Membership of the Teaching Committee, and sub-committees, of the Mathematical Association for various reports

| Report | University | Training College | HMI | Member's Location | | | | | |
| --- | --- | --- | --- | --- | --- | --- | --- | --- | --- |
| | | | | Independent School | Direct Grant School | Grammar School | Technical College | Elementary and Central Schools | Uncoded |
| Arithmetic (1932) | — | — | 2 | 9 | — | 2 | — | 2 | 2 |
| Algebra (1934/57) | — | — | 2 | 8 | — | 2 | — | 2 | 2 |
| Geometry (1938) | — | — | 1 | 7 | 1 | 2 | — | 1 | 1 |
| Trigonometry (1950) | 2 | — | — | 8 | 1 | 1 | 2 | — | 2 |
| Calculus (1951) | 2 | — | — | 4 | — | 2 | — | — | 1 |
| Higher Geometry (1953) | 4 | — | — | 5 | — | — | — | — | — |
| Sixth Form Algebra (1957) | 2 | — | — | 3 | 2 | 1 | — | — | — |
| Analysis I (1957) | 3 | — | — | 2 | — | 2 | — | — | — |

Source: Cooper (1982), chapter 3.

by sex. The Crowther report, for example, using entries for English language O-level as a basis for comparison, noted that 87 per cent of boys, but only 53 per cent of girls took O-level mathematics in the period 1956–1958.[14] Even this , of course, represented a major change from the situation in late Victorian England.[15]

Having briefly described the selective school curriculum, I shall now turn to the 'mathematics' taught to pupils in the secondary moderns. If the selective curriculum can be seen as deriving from Taunton's suggestions for the 'first grade' of secondary education, that is as largely 'academic' in nature, that received by most pupils in the postwar secondary moderns might be seen as deriving from the arithmetic of the Revised Code and as 'practical' in nature. This simple picture was, of course, becoming complicated, in the late 1950s, as pupils in the modern schools were increasingly entered for GCE examinations and some came to share grammar school mathematics.[16]

Many of the general subjects teachers who taught mathematics in the modern schools had first worked in the elementary sector,[17] and the more immediate sources of the postwar modern school curriculum can be found in the theory and practice of the inter-war elementary schools and their senior departments. Because of this crucial link, I shall briefly describe the mathematical work recommended for senior departments of elementary schools before 1944. *The Handbook of Suggestions for Teachers* (1937) states:

> The course will fix and extend the knowledge and skill in arithmetical operations gained in the junior school, and teach the children to apply their new powers to the affairs of daily life and school; it will also have to prepare them to deal with situations requiring numerical knowledge that lie ahead of them. Their experience of accounts, gained in school affairs such as meals, concerts, savings banks and societies, school journeys, excursions, gardening or poultry-keeping will introduce ideas that are current in the larger world of finance, and will be used to lead up to such questions as buying by instalments, investments, pensions and insurance. The use of graphical methods will provide them with a new means of representing and interpreting arithmetical data. Their work in practical subjects, mechanical drawing, surveying and design will serve as a basis for the study of geometry.[18]

The 'practical', 'non-academic' orientation is clear, as is the emphasis on applied arithmetic. This recommended course will be seen below to have shared much in common with that of the postwar modern schools.

Indeed, one early book on the secondary modern school, by the Chief Education Officer for Southampton, had no section on mathematics, only one on arithmetic. Nor did mathematics appear in either the list of contents or index.[19] Chapman's useful survey of 1600 secondary modern schools, carried out in the late 1950s, illustrates the continued importance of this tradition in these schools.[20]

Chapman summarizes his data on the content of secondary modern mathematics thus: 'It would seem that a rough division acceptable to schools, is that half the time should be spent on arithmetic and the other half on geometry and algebra, with a greater proportion on geometry than on algebra.'[21] This summary, however, does not convey the extent of curricular differentiation that existed within these schools. His case studies make it clear that this summary refers to no real 'average' pupil: the curriculum was clearly differentiated by 'ability' and sex. For example, in one boys' school:

> Here the content of mathematics appears under three headings: the mathematics *necessary* for everyday life, as, for example, in money, simple length, time, etc.; mathematics *useful* in everyday life, as, for example, in interest rates, proportions, averages and statistics; and mathematics as a *mode of thought*, as in problems in arithmetic, algebra and riders in geometry. This school provides all except the near-ineducable with the first of these mathematical aims, and as many boys as possible with the second. Only, however, with a few of the boys is it possible to attempt the third aim. The claim of any topic for inclusion in this mathematical scheme of work depends ... on whether it is within the powers of comprehension of a boy.[22]

Of another (mixed) school, where 'the A class children are expected to reach a standard of mathematics not much lower than that obtained by the lower forms at a grammar school', he quotes from his questionnaire responses thus:

> On the other hand, in the D stream, we shall be struggling with pupils to whom the manipulation of figures is almost a closed book. It is reasonable to assume that the demands of mathematical ability will be very small on these latter children. The ability to reckon up their wages and to obtain correct change for purchases made will be the limit of mathematical demands upon them. It is, therefore, of paramount importance that the teacher has in mind the subsequent demands that are likely to be made upon the child.[23]

Such differentiation of aims by 'ability' appears throughout his report. The A stream were often likely to receive a mathematics course broadly of a grammar school type, while the lower streams received courses in the elementary tradition of applied arithmetic. It is in this latter area that evidence of differentiation by sex is most clear. Under the significant heading 'Adapting Mathematics for Girls', Chapman describes the following typical topics from a girls' school: 'Household arithmetic of furnishing, the covering of areas of floors and walls, curtain calculations, heating and lighting and calculations relating to apparatus and equipment for third year children, and for the fourth year household accounts and the planning of a household budget.'[24] In boys' schools a different emphasis appears. For example: 'So far as domestic affairs are concerned, the scheme points out that there are always plenty of jobs in a house awaiting the householder who has had a school training in handicrafts, requiring such skills as space measurements and planning to ensure an economical use of materials.'[25] Other differences are also detailed in his report.

Further evidence on the nature of the differentiation of secondary modern mathematics, in particular on its relation to 'ability' and sex, can be found in the survey carried out for the Newsom report. This shows that girls were more likely than boys to be confined to arithmetic.[26]

The differentiation by 'ability' was legitimized by a perspective on pupils' capacities similar to that set out in the Norwood report of 1943. There, it was argued that three broad types of intellectual capacity existed, and that, in response, there should exist three appropriately different educational programmes ranging in emphasis from the academics to the concrete.[27]

Earlier, in 1934, *Senior School Mathematics*, from the Board of Education, had expressed similar views on the curriculum and 'ability' in relation to the elementary schools:

> The variation of pupils in natural capacity needs no elaboration . . . . The plan of dividing the senior school into two, three or even four streams . . . with appropriate differences in curriculum, timetable and methods of teaching, has become common practice, and mathematics is rightly considered as one of the chief subjects in which differences of treatment must be made . . . . [Each] senior school must normally provide at least two alternative courses in mathematics.[28]

This position was paralleled in 'mainstream' books published in the 1950s. In *The Teaching of Modern School Mathematics*, by James, for example, a training college lecturer and secretary of the Mathematical

Association's subcommittee on secondary modern mathematics, we find: 'Not many modern schools have a mathematics staff large enough to allow the pupils to be placed in sets for mathematics. A few schools divide their pupils into streams using mathematical ability only .... The advantage in mathematics is obvious ... [No] other subject is so difficult to teach to a class with a wide range of ability.'[29] Of the 'modern school child', he wrote: 'For most modern school pupils the mathematics course must be based on practical situations with the mathematical ideas growing out of these. Indeed, for many of our pupils we shall never get away from this; the less able the pupil, the more tied to practical considerations the mathematics course must be.'[30] And, while geometry should be taken with all streams:

> The difference will be in the treatment given and the range covered. Whereas some of the work of the A stream can be deductive and can deal with generalisations, that of a C stream will be entirely practical, measurement and observation taking the place of intellectual activity.[31]

Similar views were expressed by Olive Morgan, deputy head of a Middlesex Comprehensive, in her *The Teaching of Mathematics in the Secondary Modern School*, who also argued for setting.[32] I shall quote at length to illustrate her somewhat ambiguous perspective:

> The majority of people who teach in the secondary modern schools were taught in the grammar schools and were, by definition, above the average in intelligence. The secondary modern school is the school for the average and below average child, the slow learner, the 'non-academic' type, the child with handicaps of all kinds....
>
> For the so-called 'bright' child, ability to leap from concrete experiences to generalisations and abstract ideas is the hallmark of intelligence. It is an intellectual process which demands great mental effort, and the difference between the bright, nimble-minded, intelligent child and the 'dull', or 'slow', or 'non-academically minded' child is the difference in his ability to make this effort.
>
> In the secondary modern school there will be some children who have the innate ability to think easily in abstract terms, but the majority will have to be trained to do so.... There will be some children who will never be able to perform any but the

simplest exercises in abstract thought, because they are either unwilling or unable to make the necessary mental effort. . . .[33]

The Mathematical Association's report on secondary modern mathematics shared these assumptions: 'Only the older abler pupils in modern schools are mature enough mathematically to pursue very far the study of mathematics as an abstract system . . .'[34] The Inspectorate's report of 1958, referred to earlier, provided official support for such a perspective.[35]

It must be stressed of all these documents that, while they were reformist in the sense of wanting more non-selective pupils to receive more than mere arithmetic, they simultaneously provided a set of legitimatory principles explaining why such pupils could not actually be expected to progress very far beyond arithmetic. Such comments as James' 'the solution of right-angled triangles using sine, cosine and tangent is as far as most modern school pupils will go in trigonometry' and Morgan's 'it will only be the minimum number of children who will be able to tackle algebra with understanding' abound.[36] In this respect they echoed earlier perspectives within elementary education. *Senior School Mathematics* had argued, for example: 'For most senior school pupils, any systematic geometry based on definitions, axioms and postulates, is unsuitable either as a means of disciplining their minds or of giving them a knowledge of space. In any case, they will gain far more mentally and practically, from a study of the useful and interesting applications of geometry.'[37]

Although I have no space to discuss the legitimation of differentiation by sex here, it is noticeable that these writers of the late 1950s expressed much more concern for a common curriculum for boys and girls of comparable 'ability' than had their predecessors in the 1930s. Several still argued, however, for some differentiation in line with the then perceived roles of the sexes.[38]

Various critiques of the content and pedagogic approaches comprising the 1950s curriculum were mounted in the late 1950s and early 1960s. It is to the reforms which followed these and their effects on the degree of differentiation by 'ability' that I turn next.

## The 1960s: Reform

In the early 1960s, in a context in which a variety of interested parties within schools, universities, industry and politics believed selective school mathematics to be in need of change, a number of groups, such as

SMP and MME, worked to create new syllabuses, textbooks and examinations. I have analyzed the origins of these events in some depth elsewhere[39] and, here, merely intend to examine the extent to which the activities of these groups, and the eventual implementation of their proposals in schools accepted and/or challenged the differentiated nature of the secondary mathematics curriculum of the 1950s. I shall concentrate on SMP since, with hindsight, it can be seen to have been a particularly 'successful' project. Since this success may, however, be thought to be partially explicable in terms of SMP's relative lack of challenge to dominant differentiating assumptions, it is important also to consider other projects, such as MME, whose names are now less well known.

SMP's immediate origins lay in three major conferences held between 1957 and 1961 between teachers, university lecturers and representatives of large-scale industry and commerce.[40] These had been convened because of an increasing concern in academic and industrial circles over the relevance of selective school mathematics to pupils' future 'needs' within the universities and industry. At them, various sub-groups within the school and university mathematics communities competed with each other, and with extra-subject interests, to gain legitimacy for their favoured definition of school mathematics.[41] It can be seen by examining the occupational locations of the participants (*Table 2*) that any proposals from these meetings would be likely to be primarily concerned with O and A-level mathematics rather than the whole range of school mathematics, and would reflect the interests of educational actors involved with the selective sector and the universities.[42]

This was indeed the case. The Southampton conference, for example, organized by Thwaites — a co-founder of SMP — produced proposals for reform of O and A mathematics and university mathematics.[43] SMP, a group of mainly independent school teachers, began soon afterwards to produce textbooks for new O and A-level courses.[44] Only later, when it became clear that there was, within the context of comprehensive reorganization, a larger market for their product did the group decide to produce a new version of their textbooks aimed at CSE pupils. In taking this decision, they remained largely within the dominant psychometric assumptions described earlier. Thwaites gave this account of the change of policy:

> Our initial objective was to rewrite just the O and A-levels. But 1–5 were being used for sub-O-level ability pupils. This was a bad thing — perhaps positively harmful — since they were not

*Table 2*   Participants at the Oxford, Liverpool and Southampton
conferences on Mathematics Education

| Location | Oxford (1957) | Liverpool (1959) | Southampton (1961) |
|---|---|---|---|
| Universities | 16 | 18 | 34 |
| Other Higher and Further Education | 4 | 40 | 2 |
| Private and Nationalized Industry, and Government Science | 24 | 49 | 18 |
| Independent Schools | 30 | 11 | 27 |
| Direct Grant Schools | 7 | 28 | 10 |
| Other Selective Schools | 20 | 62 | 30 |
| Non-selective Schools (including Comprehensives) | — | 3 | 6 |
| HMI/Ministries/ Educational Administration | 2 | 5 | 1 |
| Unclassified | — | 2 | 2 |

*Source:* Cooper (1982).

> written for such less able pupils. We had to decide whether to
> put this right, and decided to try to cope with the demand for
> SMP from lower down.[45]

Howson, also associated with the project in its early days, agreed:
'People were already using books 1–5 lower down. They needed
stopping, the books weren't right for this ability range. We were
following consumer demand.'[46]

Given this acceptance of the need for differentiated materials, a new
type of writer was required. A new team, including people with
experience of teaching across the 'ability' range, was quickly
assembled.[47] It was their CSE series, based on the earlier texts, which
was to become SMP's most successful main school course within the
comprehensive sector. In 1976, for example, when I surveyed the
mathematics courses available within the secondary schools of two
Southern LEAs, twenty-eight out of thirty-seven comprehensives responding were using primarily SMP textbooks and, of these, a majority
were employing the CSE series (which was eventually added to end-on
to provide a course to O-level).[48] This CSE series, although developed
from within a perspective which accepted the need for marked differentiation by 'ability' represented, in so far as it was used with pupils

who had previously not been entered for O-level, a reduction of the former gap in content between the 'top 20 per cent' and 'average' pupils.

The assumptions about differentiation held by members of MME, the major rival to SMP in the early 1960s, were similar but not identical to those of SMP. MME had originated within the Association for Teaching Aids in Mathematics (ATAM), a recent rival to the Mathematical Association, whose membership was located more widely throughout the tripartite system than that of the older Association, and whose major concern had been, throughout most of the 1950s, with promoting pedagogic reform.[49] In the late 1950s, however, increasing criticism came from within the ATAM of the content of secondary mathematics, both from secondary modern teachers who, for a variety of motives, wished their schools to be more concerned with mathematics (as opposed to arithmetic) and from college lecturers and selective school teachers who believed that 'modern mathematics' was of relevance to the majority of secondary school pupils.[50] Hope, a college of education lecturer who was jointly to found MME, argued, for example: ' . . . so much of modern mathematics offers simple direct techniques which make a solution almost inevitable. This has its point for the majority of the population.'[51] He did not, however, move far outside of dominant assumptions. In his various contributions to the Association's journal, he seems to have accepted streaming, for example, as the natural way of teaching mathematics. Although, however, the initial proposals of MME were, like those of SMP, for a new O-level,[52] the project did include many secondary modern staff and pupils in its work. The consequences of this focus of the initial moves towards reform on the O-level course for participation are illustrated in *Table 3*, from which it can be seen that MME, as indicated above, was more involved in working out the implications of reform across the 'ability' range, with a major interest in introducing 'modern maths' to non-selective pupils earlier in its life than SMP.[53]

Other projects originating at this time, such as Mathematics in

Table 3   *SMP and MME Schools (1963/64)*

| | Independent | Direct grant | Grammar | Technical | Comprehensive | Secondary Modern |
|---|---|---|---|---|---|---|
| SMP | 10 | 3 | 24 | 2 | 1 | 1 |
| MME | — | — | 4 | 4 | 1 | 14 |

*Sources:* Thwaites (1972); Midlands Mathematical Experiment (1967).

Education and Industry (MEI), initially confined themselves to selective school mathematics.[54] In the terms developed by Young in *Knowledge and Control*, projects such as SMP were examples of 'those in which existing academic curricula are modified but there is no change in the existing social evaluation of knowledge.'[55] As he argued in a subsequent article, such reforms take their direction from university 'subject experts'.[56] This can be shown to have been the case with the reforms of the early 1960s discussed so far.[57]

Before moving to discuss a second type of project identified by Young, it is important to consider briefly why materials like those of SMP, designed mainly within the independent sector for O-level pupils, came to be so widely adopted within the secondary system as a whole and, secondly, why those of SMP in particular were taken up rather than, for example, those of MME, developed in the state system. First, as I have already noted, during the late 1950s and early 1960s more and more secondary modern pupils were entered for GCE examinations, a development in which some parents and teachers shared interests. This increasing emulation of selective schooling within the non-selective sector tended to ensure that the reform of selective school mathematics initiated by groups like SMP would eventually affect pupils outside of selective schools themselves — at least those taking O-levels and CSEs modelled on O-levels.[58] This development might be seen as part of the general tendency, noted by Bell and others, for the curriculum of elite groups to be imitated by lower status actors.[59] Differentiated curricula in stratified societies, where the desire for and possibility of upward mobility exist, might be seen, that is, as inherently likely to result in attempts at imitation from below. Such attempts, of course, serve, sometimes explicitly and sometimes implicitly, to concede the desirability of elite definitions.

On the second question, leaving aside the difficult issue of perceived quality, I have argued elsewhere that SMP overcame its rivals through having access to greater resources of finance, status, time and connections with which to publicize and legitimize its materials in the early phase of reform.[60]

Young also suggested in *Knowledge and Control* that, in the absence of major social change, a second type of curricular reform was likely to occur within the secondary sector. Here, the innovation would 'disregard the social evaluations implicit in British academic curricula' but would be restricted in its availability to 'less able' pupils.[61] The clearest example of such an approach within mathematics during the 1960s was the Mathematics for the Majority Project (1967–72) and its Continuation Project (1971–75), both sponsored by the Schools Council. These developed from the Council's Working Paper Fourteen, *Mathematics for the Majority*, concerned with 'pupils of average and below average ability in mathematics'.[62] Kaner, the director of the Continuation Project (MMCP), argued that these children should receive a version of mathematics radically different from that received by 'able' pupils. For these children: 'It would be wrong to believe that the objectives of mathematics teaching need to be defined in terms of mathematics or, necessarily, in mathematical language. For all but a very few people, maths is a means to an end.'[63] Elsewhere, he outlined the aims of his project thus: 'We want to convey to pupils the ways in which mathematical thinking is relevant to their other studies and convince them that mathematics is a tool worth using outside the school ... We intend the materials to be an agent for change towards a realistic form of education for non-academic children.'[64] This would involve the creation of a 'new subject', which he later terms 'Mathematics Studies', to be offered as an 'alternative choice' to existing courses in mathematics.[65] The approach taken was to derive mathematical topics from environmental themes, such as 'Buildings' and 'Communications'.[66]

The approach of MMCP clearly does not challenge curricular differentiation by 'ability' but tends rather to reinforce it, justifying this in terms of the 'needs' of the 'less able' for a certain curricular approach. However 'appropriate' MMCP's approach might be for 'less able' pupils, and however much some might want to defend its educational value, it was always likely, in so far as it tended to deny certain pupils access to high status versions of mathematics, to be received with mixed feelings by them.[67] In my survey, previously referred to, twelve of the fifty-two comprehensives and secondary moderns responding were using these materials in some way with 'less able' pupils. The Schools Council Impact and Take-Up Project found at least one teacher using them in 26 per cent of schools surveyed.[68]

The other major type of innovation in secondary mathematics — individualized schemes of work such as SMP's 7–13 scheme and the Kent Mathematics Project (KMP) — perhaps represent more of a shift away from the practice of categorizing pupils into a few types and providing 'appropriate' curricula, though not necessarily away from psychometric assumptions about 'ability' itself. SMP's advertizing for its scheme stresses its capacity to 'cater for a wide range of ability', for example.[69] Banks, of KMP does, however, talk of 'mathematical ability' being 'developed', a significant shift in perspective from that dominant in the 1950s.[70] One discussion of the Secondary Mathematics Individualized Learning Experiment (SMILE), the individualized scheme produced within ILEA which owes much to KMP, does, however, reproduce dominant psychometric assumptions: 'The children seem to be happy with their own "tailor-made" matrix and prefer it to work set from a formal textbook when a few bright ones are bored and the less able are completely lost.'[71]

What these schemes presumably will allow is a more flexible form of differentiation by 'ability' within a range of organizational settings, including 'mixed-ability' classrooms, where they may also alleviate control problems.[72] Although there is, arguably, a qualitative difference between differentiation on a group and individual basis, the recent HMI survey of mathematics teaching suggests that, at most, these schemes are employed in about 10 per cent of secondary schools. This difference may not therefore prove important for the argument developed in this paper. It is, perhaps, more important here to turn to another, more general, question. Given the multitude of projects in the 1960s and the variously motivated commitment of many in the comprehensives to a more common curriculum, has there been any major change in the nature and/or degree of curricular differentiation in mathematics during the period of reorganization?

It can be noted first of all that, organizationally, 'mixed-ability' teaching is not widespread in mathematics. In my survey (1976) of two LEAs I found that, in the comprehensives, only eleven of the thirty-seven responding used this method in their first year. The figures reduced to eight in the second year and two in the third year, by when twenty-eight were employing setting. The more recent HMI national survey found figures for the first three years of 46 per cent, 19 per cent and 7 per cent respectively for the full-range comprehensives in its sample.[73] Most children, therefore, for most of their time, are not in 'mixed-ability' classes for mathematics. I have already noted that only a small minority experienced individually-paced schemes of work. By the third year, 81 per cent of children in the national survey schools were receiving 'traditional class teaching' in mathematics.[74] An organizational basis for curricular differentiation by 'ability' type therefore clearly still existed, in most schools, after comprehensivization.

The HMI survey also throws some light on the degree and nature of the curricular differentiation the majority of children in comprehensives are now experiencing, at least in their fourth and fifth years. *Table 4* shows a clear, though imperfect, relationship between 'ability' and type of course received.[75] Non-examination pupils in particular were highly unlikely to experience 'modern' mathematics. A significant number of CSE pupils, however, were. In fact, taking together those categories in Table 4 which include elements of 'modern maths', we can

*Table 4    Type of course and examination target of pupils in years four and five in full-range comprehensive schools*

| Course type | Percentage of Schools: Course Objective | | |
| | GCE O-level | CSE | Non-Exam |
| --- | --- | --- | --- |
| Modern only | 32 | 22 | 7 |
| Compromise only | 27 | 36 | 31 |
| Traditional only | 32 | 27 | 53 |
| Modern + Compromise | 2 | 4 | 2 |
| Modern + Traditional | 3 | 6 | 1 |
| Compromise + Traditional | 4 | 6 | 5 |
| Total | 100 | 101 | 99 |

*Source:* DES (1980) p. 23.

see that O-level and CSE pupils are similarly distributed, though 'modern only' courses are, nevertheless, received by 45 per cent more O-level than CSE pupils. It is here, in the introduction of 'average' pupils to newer versions of mathematics originally intended for 'able' pupils, that there has probably been the most significant change in the degree and form of differentiation of the mathematics curriculum during comprehensivization.

Some idea of what this significantly modified differentiation around the base of 'modern' mathematics looks like in detail within the schools can be obtained from two case studies I carried out in 1977 relating to a boys' and girls' comprehensive respectively.[76] Both were employing SMP materials, having recently introduced them. The head of department in the boys' school had produced a scheme of work differentiated for three bands. When interviewed, he described it thus:

Well, for the top 30 per cent, the same philosophy as the old grammar schools. Appreciation of the subject for its own sake, elegance. We don't do totally modern but we can do as much as we want to with the top groups. They're the sort of kid receptive to the philosophy behind the modern maths . . . . The middle 40 per cent, the CSE candidates, the good to moderate: maths is a subject like any other for them . . . . They must be able to do the basics and know something of the rest. I develop a few things in depth, that's all they can take. We're preparing them for apprenticeships. I carefully select topics from modern maths. I wouldn't do matrix algebra with them. Nor topology, not for the average school leaver and technical apprentice . . . . Mostly we do pragmatic maths .... The bottom 30 per cent: My concern here is to give them success, stuff they can get right ... They have a limited span of concentration .... Number work, money, metric units, some appreciation of what you can do with fractions and decimals .... Any modern topics are strictly for entertainment value only. Optimism and confidence-boosting are critical and accepting that their level of performance will be limited, even in arithmetic.

Other mathematics teachers in the school shared his assumptions about 'ability', if not about 'modern maths'. One fifty-seven year-old ex-secondary modern teacher argued, for example:

It all depends on ability levels. With the average pupil and downwards, maths is all about getting a job .... I avoid the modern sort of rubbish. I prefer traditional maths as it has been in syllabuses up till now. CSE is far too wide. Most of the modern topics should go. There aren't a lot of applications for reflections, or whatever they call them now ... Modern maths is an attempt to teach maths to kids who shouldn't be doing maths anyway. It's too time-consuming ... Arithmetic is enough for those with IQs of less than a hundred and the more formal the better.

Another, emergency-trained after the war, shared this view:

I'm not favourably impressed by the SMP books. They're too wordy. There's too much reading and not enough exercises ... It's all unrelated to real life. We should talk about things like car cylinders. SMP is only suitable for brighter children. Women tend to go for it ... as it's soft.

A third, whose comments may have been coloured by his having lost his department on reorganization, was no less clear. Again an emergency-trained, ex-secondary modern teacher, he argued:

Half a person's life is spent calculating. It's an everyday activity. This is surely the main reason for maths for most children — not those in the grammar stream though. But even of those only a few will go on to do maths. Most will just need calculating. Most kids now can't use maths after school, especially with the modern syllabuses. Modern maths is not very relevant, except perhaps for the top grammar school pupils ... The kids usually ask me what's the point of it ... For them there is no point.

The head of department in the girls' school shared these assumptions:

> I believe a lot of what is done is really a waste of time, trying to
> teach the less able a lot of what we teach them. They should
> know basic arithmetic to cope with everyday life, plus some
> maths — measuring, drawing — for physical co-ordination . . .
> We use *World of Maths* for the less able, not SMP. I believe all
> children should have some real maths, not just arithmetic. But
> with the less able, in the last two years, I should say you can
> forget algebra, trigonometry and geometry and just do arithme-
> tic topics that will help them when they leave school.

If these schools are at all typical of comprehensives, and the HMI
survey suggests they might be, then, although there may have been a
significant change of degree, the mathematics curriculum of the comprehensives remains one differentiated in a tripartite manner. The 'able' are
more likely than other pupils to receive the redefined selective school
mathematics of the 1960s, the mathematics described as 'real mathematics' by a *Times'* editorial of the day.[77] The 'average', CSE pupils, are
more likely to receive a mixed diet of the previous and newer definitions
of O-level mathematics, suitably 'watered-down'. This probably represents a considerable change from the arithmetic-based courses they
would have received in many secondary moderns. The 'less able,'
however, probably still tend to receive mainly applied arithmetic of the
type recommended in the 1937 *Handbook* or, in a minority of schools,
specially designed courses based around materials of the type produced
by MMCP. Only in the minority of schools, where individualized
schemes are in use, are pupils likely to be receiving a less categorically
differentiated curriculum than this. The dominant legitimating assumptions within the schools seem, therefore, to have undergone no major
change.[78]

The HMI survey, however, did not reveal a perfect correlation
between 'ability' and curriculum type. It is possible that it was even less
perfect some years before. A change in the degree of differentiation
certainly seems to have occurred during the period of comprehensive
reform. As a result, more 'average' or CSE pupils had come to study an
academic version of mathematics, derived from contemporary university definitions via such projects as SMP, rather than a version comprising
applied arithmetic and varying amounts of geometry and trigonometry
seen, at least for boys, as relevant to their future lives in work. This
change in the degree of differentiation and in content, insofar as it was
seen to result in these pupils studying 'inappropriate' versions of

mathematics, was to produce a considerable negative reaction in the 1970s.

## Reaction

We have already seen that some older, ex-secondary modern teachers within the comprehensives I studied were highly critical of what they saw as attempts to introduce inappropriate mathematical topics into courses for 'average' and 'less able' pupils. Their critique, based on a clear view of their pupils' occupational futures, drew on the subcultural assumptions of the postwar secondary moderns and, ultimately, it can be argued, on those of the elementary tradition. Similar criticisms of the diffusion 'downwards' of 'modern maths' were to come from sources outside the schools as well. While some sections of industry had supported SMP's initial reform of the O and A-level syllabuses, in the hope that these changes would lead to an alleviation of the problems of the school/university transition and to an increase in numbers of mathematics and science graduates, many industrial and commercial concerns were to be less happy with the actual and perceived diffusion of 'modern mathematics' into courses studied by future routine clerical and manual employees.

In February 1974, for example, a number of such criticisms were reported in *The Times Educational Supplement*.[79] These came from the Engineering Industry Training Board, the Shipbuilding ITB, the Air Transport ITB, Huddersfield Technical College, and the Director of Education at the CBI. All concentrated their attacks on the 'inadequate' preparation of apprentices. Longbottom of the Shipbuilding ITB argued: 'We have a constant complaint from our craft training managers that we need the old maths for drawing plans, and for development work.'[80] Such a response to the diffusion 'downwards' of 'modern maths' might have been predicted from the remarks of Langdale, of ICI, at the 1959 Liverpool Conference, where he had carefully delineated the mathematics needed by various categories of craft apprentices within his company — only 10 per cent of whom came from the grammar schools.[81] Some of these topics were then covered in some secondary modern courses for 'average' pupils; all of them were then covered in 'traditional' O-level courses.

Over the next few years, such criticism of the teaching of mathematics, especially 'modern mathematics', was to be given increasing publicity by the mass media in a climate of opinion where state education, especially in comprehensives, was under a general political attack.[82]

Perhaps the strongest criticism of the now supposedly much less differentiated mathematics curriculum, however, came from within the educational system, from Margaret Hayman of Putney High School (GPDST) while carrying out her duties as president of the Mathematical Association. In 1975, in her presidential address, 'To Each According to his Needs', she claimed that, before the war, education and work had been well-related for most children:

> For the majority of children mathematics was interpreted rather narrowly as arithmetic, but in this field they were competent, confident and could tackle the numerical work involved in their subsequent jobs. Many pupils went from school to apprenticeships of some kind, where the work they had done at school was seen to be relevant and an adequate base from which to develop technical skills . . . .[83]

But after the war, Labour Party philosophy had encouraged the move towards the comprehensive school, and:

> Unfortunately, the doctrine of an equal opportunity for suitable education became confused with an equal opportunity for the same education, and I think that it is here that we find the major cause of many of the educational problems of today . . . Because a highly academic abstract education had been seen to be economically profitable for a few, it was assumed that it was a desirable thing for everybody. And so the old grammar school course was taken over — learned more slowly, watered down, pepped-up with practical illustrations, subjected to new classroom techniques — but no one had the courage to ask if this was basically what the majority of children were capable of enjoying or would find satisfying either in their future work or for its own sake.[84]

She related this to SMP:

> In the early 1960s there was a feeling that a new approach to mathematics would be helpful and the School Mathematics Project . . . was started. This developed from a very academic base, among pupils where the previous system had been most, rather than least, successful. The writers produced some very interesting textbooks suitable for the top 10 per cent of the ability range . . . . This, of course, did nothing towards solving the real problem. To quote again from the bulletin of the CBI: 'Many arguments have been put forward to explain this lowering

of standards, and the one that is most often heard is that mathematics teaching in schools, particularly in modern mathematics courses ..., does not include enough arithmetic to give young people the necessary grounding in basic computerized skills upon which industry heavily relies.' I think this is fair criticism in so far as many modern syllabuses stress ideas rather than techniques. SMP ... are pursuing the myth that if you speak a foreign language sufficiently slowly you will be understood; that the difficulties within the subject are due to the speed at which it is taught, rather than the nature of the mathematical concepts involved.[85]

She partially legitimated her arguments by referring to Brown's research on children's ability to 'abstract', arguing that this showed that many children were 'incapable of understanding ... mathematical principles ... once these are divorced from practical situations from which they arose'.[86] Furthermore, if pupils were forced to study the 'academic' mathematics favoured by reformers then 'anti-social behaviour', resulting from 'mathematical frustration', would follow.[87] 'Mixed-ability' teaching was also attacked: 'in a class of thirty there may only be one really mathematical child'.[88] In conclusion, she recommended a well-differentiated mathematics curriculum for the comprehensives:

> The satisfaction of achievement and the intrinsic beauty of mathematical relationships is sufficient justification for the course for more able pupils. For the rest of secondary school pupils we need a new and different approach, but not the same for all. The next 20 per cent of the ability range have some capacity for abstraction, and a course similar to some of the present CSE courses with an emphasis on the practical rather than the abstract mathematics would be suitable. Again, much more practice of basic arithmetic and some simple algebra would add to the pupils' confidence and their capacity to cope with work after school ... For the rest ... I think we must differentiate between the first three years, when the subject can be taught in the context of the classroom, and the other two years when ... there must be a much closer integration between the school and the outside world ... To summarize, I think that much of the disorder in schools is because children are being asked to do work in all subjects, but particularly in mathematics, which is beyond their inherent capabilities, and this will continue until we recognize that different children need basically

different courses .... We must stop trying to teach abstract mathematics to all pupils, and concentrate on mathematics for some pupils and competence in arithmetic as a first priority for the majority.[89]

This strong restatement of tripartite assumptions received considerable publicity through *The Times Educational Supplement*.[90] Such criticism from within the educational system, coupled with that from employers, coalesced during the middle 1970s to produce a climate of 'crisis' in relation to mathematics education similar, ironically, to that of the early 1960s which had produced the wave of reforms now under attack. In February 1975, in a letter to *The Times*, Professors Halberstam and Armitage argued that a Bullock report was needed for mathematics.[91] In September 1977, in the climate created by Callaghan's Ruskin speech, a House of Commons Committee, after a year investigating the standards of school leavers, took up the idea, arguing that the DES should set up a national inquiry into mathematics education.[92] This was set up in March 1978 and the membership announced in September. The Committee, chaired by Cockcroft, Vice-Chancellor of the New University of Ulster, included representatives of schools, further and higher education, and industry.[93] SMP was represented by Hersee, then executive director of the project.

The main thrust of the report of the Committee, published in early 1982, was that a more differentiated mathematics curriculum should be established in secondary schools.[94] This proposal rested on a view of 'ability' seen as different rates of learning:

> Whether or not it is true ... that each person has a mathematical ceiling ... it is certainly true that children, and adults, learn mathematics at greatly differing speeds ... This means that there are very great differences in attainment between children of the same age. A small number reach a standard which enables them to study mathematics at degree level, but many others have time to advance only a very short distance along the mathematical road during their years at school. Because of the hierarchical nature of mathematics these pupils do not reach a position from which they are able to tackle the more abstract branches of the subject with understanding or hope of success, though some can and do continue their advance after they have left school.[95]

They were also reacting to what they felt had been a too rapid diffusion of 'modern mathematics'.

A further, and very rapid development, was the extension of modern mathematics courses to pupils whose attainment was lower and the introduction of modern syllabuses in CSE mathematics examinations. Not all teachers possessed a sufficient mathematical background to enable them to appreciate the intentions underlying the new courses they were teaching. In consequence the material ... was often not presented as part of a unified structure but as a collection of disconnected topics whose relevance to the mathematics course as a whole did not become apparent to pupils.[96]

The report argues that modern abstract algebraic concepts in particular 'have proved difficult for many pupils to understand', and their 'purpose and use have not been evident to them'.[97] It argues that this undesirable situation, in which many children experience only failure in mathematics, has resulted from an 'understandable pressure that O-level and CSE syllabuses in mathematics should be "compatible", that is that they should contain substantially the same mathematical topics' in order to allow course changes for as long as possible during a pupil's career.[98] It is claimed:

We believe it is clear ... that the changes in the examination system and in the organization of secondary schools which have taken place in recent years have influenced the teaching of mathematics in ways which have been neither intended nor sufficiently realized. At the present time up to 80 per cent of pupils ... are following courses leading to examinations whose syllabuses are comparable in extent and conceptual difficulty with those which twenty years ago were followed by only about 25 per cent of pupils. We have therefore moved from a situation in which ... there was in our view too great a difference between ... syllabuses ... to one in which ... there is far too little difference in the mathematics syllabuses ... followed by pupils of different levels of attainment. Because ... it is the content of the O-level syllabuses which exerts the greatest influence, it is the pupils whose attainment is average or below who have been most greatly disadvantaged.[99]

They summarize their position thus: 'Very many pupils in secondary schools are at present being required to follow mathematics syllabuses whose content is too great and which are not suited to their level of attainment.'[100] Their solution is straightforward:

Syllabuses for pupils of lower attainment have been developed from [O-level syllabuses] by deleting a few topics and reducing the depth of treatment of others; in other words, they have been constructed 'from the top downwards'. We believe that this is a wrong approach and that development should be 'from the bottom upwards' by considering the range of work which is appropriate for lower-attaining pupils and extending this range as the level of attainment of pupils increases.[101]

They begin their task of outlining a 'differentiated curriculum' — 'the provision of different courses to meet the differing needs of pupils', by setting out a 'foundation list' of topics which should form part of the syllabus for all children and 'by far the greater part' for the 'lowest 40 per cent of the range of attainment in mathematics', those for whom CSE is not intended.[102] Except that logarithms are replaced by the use of electronic calculators, the list is remarkably similar to that set out for the senior elementary school in the 1930s.[103] Furthermore, as then, the approach is to be 'practical' and 'relevant', and the mathematics is to be related to work in other subjects. For all the radical sounding overtones of the 'bottom upwards' approach, it serves here, in conjunction with low expectations of what the 'less able' can achieve based on their response to previous differentiated practice, to legitimate a narrow, largely arithmetic-based, curriculum for these pupils.

The report then discusses two more 'reference levels'. The syllabus for those currently taking the CSE and achieving Grade Four 'should not be very much greater than that of the foundation list', but: 'At a higher level, we consider that a syllabus whose extent is comparable to that of existing 'O' level syllabuses represents a suitable examination target for pupils in the top 20 per cent of the range of attainment in mathematics.'[104] A 'need' is also identified for a syllabus between these two latter levels.[105] Their proposals will lead, they argue, to no 'lowering of standards', since: 'We believe that if pupils follow a course whose content is better matched to their level of attainment and rate of learning, they will achieve not only greater confidence in their approach to mathematics but also greater mastery of the mathematics they study. This should contribute to improvements in attainment, attitudes and confidence and so to a raising of standards overall.'[106] When discussing forms of classroom organization the Committee's main concern is again that pupils should receive 'appropriate' courses. The educational disadvantages of streaming and setting are played down.[107]

The Cockcroft report seems, then, to be a return to the tripartite assumptions of the 1950s. Pupils can be classified into types and directed into appropriate courses. One difference, however, is that, instead of this being discussed directly in terms of 'ability', it is legitimized in terms of the different — but related — concepts of 'levels of attainment', 'rate of learning' and the 'needs' of pupils. The latter concept does not, however, always refer to psychological characteristics, but sometimes to pupils' likely occupational futures, a form of legitimation shared with the 1937 *Handbook of Suggestions for Teachers*. One major difference between the *Handbook* and the report, however, lies in the greater attention paid in Cockcroft to the differences in achievement between the sexes. There is a much less apparent concern to differentiate the mathematics curriculum by sex in the later document and a more explicit concern to improve girls' achievements.[108]

Since Cockcroft another strong case for differentiation has been made by the Joint Council for Sixteen Plus National Criteria. They argue that no common paper need be taken by all candidates in any future 'common' sixteen plus examination and for a number of well-differentiated courses similar to those proposed by Cockcroft.[109] It appears, therefore, that in the face of a partial, though significant, move away from the particular form of differentiation of the 1950s in the comprehensives, a major move is currently underway within mathematics education to re-legitimate and re-establish a form of curricular differentiation whose origins lie even further back in English history, in the Victorian period: 'real mathematics' for some, mainly arithmetic for others.

## Conclusion

Shipman, discussing comprehensive reorganization in 1969, was already concerned that the differentiation of curriculum and life chances that had characterized the tripartite system was being reproduced within the comprehensive school.[110] While he believed that the 'diluted academic curriculum' previously experienced by 'average and below average' children in modern schools had been 'a source of frustration for both staff and pupils' he was worried about the possible consequences of its reform:

> The new curriculum, involving topic-centred approaches, interdisciplinary enquiry, projects taking the children outside the school ... will probably increase the motivation of the pupils and give them an insight into the working of the world around

them. They are often lacking in real academic discipline .... But regardless of their worth, they could separate the education of the Newsom child from that of the future elite as effectively as when these groups were educated in different schools or systems. The content of these courses is diverging from that found in O-level and A-level syllabuses and there has been a simultaneous separation in the teaching methods employed. The Newsom report continued a tradition of separate kinds of schooling and these developments, however praiseworthy in themselves, may prove a way of maintaining this divide.[111]

The evidence referred to in the second section of this paper suggests that, at least for the case of mathematics, Shipman over-estimated the extent to which this type of curriculum would be introduced for the 'average and below average'. MMCP, for example, was only used in a minority of schools. Furthermore, taken together, the HMI survey and my case studies both suggest that a tripartite form of differentiation of mathematics has continued to exist in most schools, though in a significantly modified form. The major shift away from it — the introduction of modern 'abstract' algebraic and geometrical topics into the CSE syllabus for the 'average' child — has produced a strong negative reaction from those sharing dominant assumptions on 'ability'.

It is quite likely, therefore, if the Cockcroft recommendations are heeded, that, while the content of mathematics — especially for the 'able' — may remain different from that of the tripartite era, the curriculum will nevertheless be differentiated on similar lines to that of the 1950s or, even, the 1930s. The similarity of Cockcroft's foundation list to the suggestions of the 1937 *Handbook* lends some support to such an interpretation.

Mainstream debate on mathematics education in England has, in fact, since the beginning of state education, assumed that mathematics is intrinsically difficult and that only a minority will ever succeed in its study. (In the USSR, by contrast, over 90 per cent of children are apparently currently expected to study calculus to our O-level standard.[112]) While differentiation by sex, at least for the 'able', has been considerably reduced,[113] differentiation by 'ability' — in the past highly correlated with social class[114] — has apparently been maintained.

While, however, many mathematics teachers do clearly support a substantial degree of quantitative and/or qualitative curricular differentiation by 'ability' type, the differentiated curriculum in mathematics, and in other subjects with market value, is perhaps inherently unstable. Since the higher status academic mathematics leading to O-level is associated with increased life chances parents will tend to insist on something like it for their children. Furthermore, many teachers of 'less able' children, for a mixture of ideological and career-related reasons, will also continue to strive to teach a diluted version of it to non-O-level children.[115] For these reasons, it is likely, as occurred to some extent both in the secondary moderns of the 1950s and the comprehensives of the 1960s, that some reduction in the degree of curricular differentiation through imitation will tend to occur regularly. It is perhaps in the reaction to such developments that we can most readily discern the basically differentiating nature of the English educational system. Whatever one considers to be the relative merits of 'academic' and 'practical' approaches to education, it is difficult to disagree with Shipman's concluding comment in his 1969 piece:

> Social scientists can take much of the credit for illuminating the relation between education and social background. But the unanticipated result of their recommendations may have been to alter only the way in which this relation is maintained rather than to reduce the unfairness which it produces. It may even be that the maintenance of inequality through the curriculum is not only more subtle, but also more effective than depending on more obvious selection procedures.[116]

In the light of such initiatives as Cockcroft, it is this we must continue to explore.

### Acknowledgements

I should like to thank Ivor Goodson, Trevor Pateman, Colin Lacey and Stephen Ball for their helpful comments on an earlier draft of this paper.

### Notes

1 See, for example, the '11 to 16 Syllabus Analysis' in MATHEMATICAL ASSOCIATION, (1968a).
2 See COOPER (1982; 1983; 1985) for an account of these activities.
3 See, for example, THWAITES (1972) and HOPE (1963).
4 See, for example, COOPER (1976) and DES (1980), chapter 6.
5 See LAWTON (1973), p. 79.
6 See MACLURE (1973), pp. 92–95.
7 *Ibid.*, p. 80.
8 See, for example, COOPER (1982), pp. 42–43.

9 *Ibid.*, chapter 3.
10 For details on the compilation of Table 1, see COOPER (1982), chapter 3.
11 See MINISTRY OF EDUCATION (1958), p. 24.
12 *Ibid.*, p. 103.
13 *Ibid.*, p. 104.
14 See CENTRAL ADVISORY COUNCIL FOR EDUCATION (1959), p. 212.
15 See, for example, BARNARD (1969).
16 See TAYLOR (1963) and CENTRAL ADVISORY COUNCIL FOR EDUCATION (1959), p. 76.
17 See, for example, RUBINSTEIN and SIMON (1969) and TAYLOR (1963).
18 BOARD OF EDUCATION (1937), pp. 144–145.
19 See DEMPSTER (1949).
20 See CHAPMAN (1959).
21 *Ibid.*, p. 120.
22 *Ibid.*, pp. 113–114.
23 *Ibid.*, p. 112.
24 *Ibid.*, p. 117.
25 *Ibid.*, p. 112.
26 See CENTRAL ADVISORY COUNCIL FOR EDUCATION (1963), p. 240.
27 See MACLURE (1973), pp. 201–204.
28 See BOARD OF EDUCATION (1934), pp. 15–16.
29 See JAMES (1958), p. 5.
30 *Ibid.*, p. 7.
31 *Ibid.*, p. 82.
32 See MORGAN (1959), pp. 21–22.
33 *Ibid.*, pp. 14–15.
34 See MATHEMATICAL ASSOCIATION (1959), p. 19.
35 See MINISTRY OF EDUCATION (1958).
36 See JAMES (1958), p. 105 and MORGAN (1959), p. 20.
37 See BOARD OF EDUCATION (1934), p. 47.
38 See COOPER (1982), pp. 61–63, for a discussion of this.
39 See COOPER (1982).
40 See, for example, THWAITES (1972), p. viii.
41 See COOPER (1982), chapters 5 and 6.
42 For details of the compilation of *Table 2*, see COOPER (1982).
43 See THWAITES (1961) for details of these.
44 See COOPER (1982), chapter 7.
45 Interview with THWAITES, March, 1977.
46 Interview with HOWSON, March, 1976.
47 See THWAITES (1972), p. 121.
48 Thirty-seven of a possible fifty-five replied to my postal questionnaire.
49 See COOPER (1982), chapter 4, for an account of the activities and perspectives of the ATAM during the 1950s.
50 *Ibid.*, chapter 4.
51 MIDLANDS MATHEMATICAL EXPERIMENT (1964), p. 11.
52 See, for example, his review of the Mathematical Association's report on secondary modern mathematics, HOPE (1959), and HOPE (1963).
53 *Table 3* has been compiled from THWAITES (1972) and MIDLANDS MATHE-MATICAL EXPERIMENT (1967).

54 See MATHEMATICAL ASSOCIATION (1968a) for details.
55 See YOUNG (1971), p. 39.
56 See YOUNG (1972), p. 207.
57 See COOPER (1982), especially chapter 7.
58 On the content of CSEs in mathematics, see MATHEMATICAL ASSOCIATION (1968b).
59 See, for example, BELL (1971).
60 See COOPER (1982), chapter 7.
61 See YOUNG (1971), p. 39.
62 See SCHOOLS COUNCIL (1967), p. 1.
63 SEE KANER (1973), p. 9.
64 See KANER (1972) p. 2.
65 See KANER (1974).
66 See WATSON (1976), chapter 11.
67 See SPRADBERRY (1976).
68 See SCHOOLS COUNCIL (1980), p. 2.
69 See, for example, *THE TIMES EDUCATIONAL SUPPLEMENT* for 23.4.76.
70 See BANKS (1975).
71 See FROST (1975).
72 See, for example, BALL (1981), pp. 212–215. For a different view see BUSWELL (1980).
73 See DES (1980), p. 26.
74 *Ibid.*, p. 27.
75 *Table 4* is from DES (1980), p. 23.
76 For more details, see COOPER (1982), chapter 7.
77 See *THE TIMES*, 20.2.63.
78 See BALL (1981) and KEDDIE (1971) for relevant work.
79 See *THE TIMES EDUCATIONAL SUPPLEMENT*, 1.2.74.
80 *Ibid.*
81 See COOPER (1982), pp. 151–152.
82 See, for example, HOPKINS (1978) chapter 3, and CENTRE FOR CONTEMPORARY CULTURAL STUDIES (1981), chapter 9.
83 See HAYMAN (1975), p. 138.
84 *Ibid.*, p. 138.
85 *Ibid.*, p. 139.
86 *Ibid.*, p. 142.
87 *Ibid.*, p. 143.
88 *Ibid.*, p. 144.
89 *Ibid.*, pp. 147–148 and p. 153.
90 See *THE TIMES EDUCATIONAL SUPPLEMENT*, 4.4.75. and 3.10.75.
91 See *THE TIMES*, 28.2.75.
92 See *THE TIMES EDUCATIONAL SUPPLEMENT*, 23.9.77.
93 See *THE TIMES EDUCATIONAL SUPPLEMENT*. 17.3.78 and 29.9.78.
94 See COCKCROFT (1982), chapter 9.
95 *Ibid.*, pp. 67–68.
96 *Ibid.*, pp. 81–82.
97 *Ibid.*, p. 82.
98 *Ibid.*, pp. 129–130.
99 *Ibid.*, p. 130.

100 *Ibid.*, p. 132.
101 *Ibid.*, p. 133.
102 *Ibid.*, p. 134.
103 See Cockcroft (1982), pp. 134–140, and Board of Education (1937), pp. 534–559.
104 *Ibid.*, p. 144.
105 *Ibid.*, p. 144.
106 *Ibid.*, p. 145.
107 *Ibid.*, pp. 150–152.
108 *Ibid.*, pp. 62–64 and Appendix 2.
109 See The Times Educational Supplement 18.2.83, p. 8.
110 See Shipman (1971).
111 *Ibid.*, pp. 103–104.
112 See Wilson (1983).
113 See, for example, the changing ratio of male/female 'O' level passes in mathematics since the war.
114 See, for example, Douglas (1964), and Halsey *et al* (1980).
115 On the tendency for teachers to 'upgrade' their practice, see Goodson (1983).
116 See Shipman (1971), p. 106.

### References/Bibliography

Ball, S.J. (1981) *Beachside Comprehensive: A Case Study of Secondary Schooling*, Cambridge, Cambridge University Press.

Banks, B. (1975) '. . . and how the KMP progresses', *The Times Educational Supplement*, p. 51, 3 October.

Barnard, H.C. (1969) *A History of English Education from 1760*, London, University of London Press.

Bell, R. (1971) *Thinking About the Curriculum*, London, Open University Press.

Board of Education (1934) *Senior School Mathematics*, London, HMSO.

Board of Education (1937) *Handbook of Suggestions for Teachers*, London, HMSO.

Buswell, C. (1980) 'Pedagogic change and social change', *British Journal of Sociology of Education*, 1, 3, pp. 293–306.

Central Advisory Council for Education (1959) *15 to 18*, The Crowther Report, London, HMSO.

Central Advisory Council for Education (1963) *Half Our Future*, The Newsom Report, London, HMSO.

Centre for Contemporary Cultural Studies (1981) *Unpopular Education*, London, Hutchinson.

Chapman, J.V. (1959) *Your Secondary Modern Schools: An Account of Their Work in the Late 1950s*, London, College of Preceptors.

Cockcroft, W.H. (1982) *Mathematics Counts*, London, HMSO.

Cooper, B. (1976) *Bernstein's Codes: A Classroom Study*, Education Area Occasional Paper No. 6, University of Sussex.

Cooper, B. (1982) *Innovation in English Secondary School Mathematics: A*

*Sociological Account*, D. Phil, University of Sussex.

COOPER, B (1983) 'On explaining change in school subjects', *British Journal of Sociology of Education*, 4, 3, pp. 207–222.

COOPER, B (1985) *Renegotiating Secondary School Mathematics* Lewes, Falmer Press.

DEMPSTER, J.J.B. (1949) *Education in the Secondary Modern School*, London, Methuen.

DEPARTMENT OF EDUCATION AND SCIENCE (1980) *Aspects of Secondary Education in England: Supplementary Information on Mathematics*, London, HMSO.

DOUGLAS, J.W.B. (1967) *The Home and the School*, London, Panther.

FROST D. (1975) 'What is SMILE?', *The Times Educational Supplement*, p. 49, 3 October.

GOODSON, I.F. (1983) *School Subjects and Curriculum Change*, London, Croom Helm.

HALSEY, A.H., HEATH, A.F. and RIDGE, J.M. (1980) *Origins and Destinations: Family, Class and Education in Modern Britain*, Oxford, Clarendon Press.

HAYMAN, M. (1975) 'To each according to his needs', *Mathematical Gazette*, Vol. 59, pp. 137–153.

HOOPER, R. (Ed.) (1971) *The Curriculum: Context, Design and Development*, Edinburgh, Oliver and Boyd.

HOPE, C. (1959) Review of Mathematical Association's *Mathematics in Secondary Modern Schools*, *Mathematics Teaching*, 11.

HOPE, C. (1963) 'A new 'O' level syllabus in mathematics', *Mathematics Teaching*, 22, pp. 36–41.

HOPKINS, A. (1978) *The School Debate*, Harmondsworth, Penguin.

JAMES, E.J. (1958) *The Teaching of Modern School Mathematics*, Oxford University Press.

KANER, P. (1972) 'Editorial', *Newsmaths*, 3.

KANER, P. (1973) 'MMCP: a complex mixture of awareness and ignorance', *Newsmaths*, 6/7, pp. 4–9.

KANER, P. (1974) 'Back to Square One: a long look at MMCP', *The Times Educational Supplement*, p. 70, 4 October.

KEDDIE, N. (1971) 'Classroom knowledge', in YOUNG, M.F.D. (Ed.), pp. 133–160.

LAWTON, D. (1973) *Social Change, Educational Theory and Curriculum Planning*, London, Hodder and Stoughton.

MACLURE, J.S. (1973) *Educational Documents*, London, Methuen.

MATHEMATICAL ASSOCIATION (1959) *Mathematics in Secondary Modern Schools*, London, Bell.

MATHEMATICAL ASSOCIATION (1968a) *Mathematics Projects in British Secondary Schools*, London, Bell.

MATHEMATICAL ASSOCIATION (1968b) *A Report on Mathematics Syllabuses for the Certificate of Secondary Education*, London, Bell.

MIDLANDS MATHEMATICAL EXPERIMENT (1964) *Report 1962–63*, London, Harrap.

MIDLANDS MATHEMATICAL EXPERIMENT (1967) *Report 1963–65*, London, Harrap.

MINISTRY OF EDUCATION (1958) *Teaching Mathematics in Secondary Schools*, London, HMSO.

MORGAN, O.I. (1959) *The Teaching of Mathematics in the Modern School*, London, Harrap.

RUBINSTEIN, D. and SIMON, B. (1969) *The Evolution of the Comprehensive School: 1926–1966*, London, Routledge and Kegan Paul.

SCHOOLS COUNCIL (1967) *Mathematics for the Majority*, Working Paper No. 14, London, HMSO.

SCHOOLS COUNCIL (1980) *Impact and Take-Up Project: A Condensed Interim Report ≃ Secondary Schools*, London, Schools Council.

SHIPMAN, M. (1971) 'Curriculum for inequality' in HOOPER, R. (Ed.), pp. 101–106.

SPRADBERRY, J. (1976) 'Conservative pupils? Pupil resistance to curriculum innovation in mathematics', in YOUNG, M.F.D. and WHITTY, G. (Eds.), pp. 236–243.

TAYLOR, W. (1963) *The Secondary Modern School*, London, Faber.

THWAITES, B. (1961) *On Teaching Mathematics*, Oxford, Pergamon.

THWAITES, B. (1972) *SMP: The First Ten Years*, Cambridge, Cambridge University Press.

WATSON, F.R. (1976) *Developments in Mathematics Teaching*, London, Open Books.

WILSON, B. (1983) 'Russian roulette', *The Times Educational Supplement*, 4. March.

YOUNG, M.F.D. (1971) 'An approach to the study of curricula as socially organized knowledge' in YOUNG, M.F.D. (Ed.), pp. 19–46.

YOUNG, M.F.D. (Ed.) (1971) *Knowledge and Control*, London, Collier-Macmillan.

YOUNG, M.F.D. (1972) 'On the politics of educational knowledge', *Economy and Society*, 1, pp. 194–215.

YOUNG, M.F.D. and WHITTY, G. (Eds.) (1976) *Explorations in the Politics of School Knowledge*, Driffield, Nafferton Books.

# 'To make the mind strong, rather than to make it full'[1]: Elementary School Science Teaching in London 1870–1904

*Mary Waring*

## Arguments for 'Hand' and 'Eye' Training

Elections for the first London School Board were held in November 1870, only two months after the passing of Forster's Education Act which, after years of bitter struggle, committed the government to the establishment of a national system of elementary schools. These were to be provided wherever needed and run by local School Boards, with authority to draw on the rates. Since Board members were to be elected by ratepayers, there would clearly be little incentive for educational 'extravagances'.

Elementary schools were not schools for an entire age group in the population; they were intended mainly for the working class — for the 'labouring poor' and the growing population of industrial and commercial workers. They were not first, or primary, schools: they were to provide all the education that the majority of their clients would receive. Their purpose was essentially utilitarian: part protective in ensuring a basically literate and numerate workforce who knew and accepted its place in society; part response to the economic needs of an industrializing society.

With hundreds of thousands of children dependent upon the quality of the schooling it provided, the responsibilities of the new London School Board were considerable and, throughout its existence, its membership included a number of able and committed men and women, some of them very distinguished indeed, and its size gave it a measure of financial independence and security. Material provision was therefore largely a matter of good book-keeping and it was possible for the Board to contemplate a variety of curricular experiments, as new ideas and needs arose.

The late 1860s had seen a period of intense activity and pamphleteering by scientific pressure groups, urging government action on scientific and technical instruction. The response took the form of a twenty-year long series of commissions, which sat against a background of deepening economic recession and gloom. The concern and uncertainty could, however, be used effectively to press the case for elementary science in the education of future workers. Linked with growing pressures for 'hand and eye' training through practical courses of all kinds,[2] and with faculty psychology, instruction in science could, it was argued, be much more than the provision of important knowledge. If experimental, that is, practical, work were included, valuable skills, faculties and habits would be inculcated. Initially, it seems to have been assumed that it was sufficient for learners merely to watch demonstrations, but later the value of experiments performed by pupils themselves was stressed. For many, manipulative training was the *raison d'être* for practical work. Others argued that it had no place in the school: '[Is] an artisan ... a man made in God's own image, or ... a mere ambidextrous monkey? ... The true education of the labourer is to make him an intelligent being, not a mere dextrous manipulator.'[3] 'Developing the intelligence', it came to be argued, could best be done by linking the training of hand, eye, body *and* mind in appropriate practical activities.[4] Clearly, an intelligent workforce was not only desirable in itself; it was an essential prerequisite for industrial and commercial progress and for social stability.

Linking practical work in science with the training of specific faculties, themselves associated with 'scientific method', was a very important step for science education, for it gave rise to the idea that school science could — and should — be some sort of simulation exercise. Under the descriptor, 'heurism', this belief was first explicitly formulated by Meiklejohn[5] in the seventies, and it was taken up and put into action in London schools by Armstrong and his disciples in the eighties and nineties. For heurists, invoking 'scientific method' in order to train certain important faculties, namely observation, communication and reasoning, meant putting the learner in the position of the discoverer, in carefully-sequenced experimental situations, in which the solution of one problem always led to the next. The model was that of induction, and every step of an inquiry was carefully and accurately recorded, not only as a means of communication, but so that valid conclusions could be drawn from the facts and patterns of facts 'discovered', and new questions raised.[6]

For supporters of science, introducing science teaching into schools of all kinds was important for another person — to open up pathways for the most able. Huxley told the Devonshire Commission:

> In the scientific education of the great masses of people the great object appears to me to be to construct such a scheme as shall enable you to sift, to get hold of, the men who have real scientific ability ... to pick out the men of intellect from the men who are only fit to carry water and hew wood.[7]

Such a need implied not only science teaching, but a scholarship ladder 'from the gutter to the university',[8] for which Huxley and others pressed.

To ensure that local needs were met, School Boards had been given a measure of say on curriculum matters and, with men like Huxley and J.H. Gladstone as leading figures on the London Board from 1870 to 1894, it is hardly surprising to find that, from the outset, science for all was accepted as a *desideratum* to be achieved as soon as possible.[9] Whatever the intentions, however, a wide range of constraints existed and it took many years. At first there were enormous logistical problems of accommodation, teaching force, school attendance and poverty. Classes remained very large, and teachers were ill-equipped to do more than hand on the factual knowledge most had acquired in an examination-ridden system. All problems were particularly severe in girls' schools.[10]

In addition, instruction had to be in line with the Regulations issued by the Department of Education at Whitehall, which defined the range of subjects, compulsory and optional, and, for all but the last few years of the Board's existence, the syllabuses of instruction. Compulsory subjects comprised mainly the three Rs and, for girls, 'Needlework and Cutting Out' and there were many, including HMI, who viewed the provision of anything more in elementary schools as a 'fancy education', 'educational luxuries that should not be provided at the public's expense'.[11]

Optional subjects were divided, after 1875, into 'class' subjects (taken by classes above standard I) and 'specific' subjects, open to individual scholars above standard IV. Specific subjects were intended to meet the needs of older pupils with special abilities and of teachers with special interests and qualifications (usually Science and Art Department certificates). Although the Board took steps to ensure, support and improve object lessons and elementary science (there was considerable overlap) in the lower standards, it is with science as a specific subject that this paper is concerned.

Until 1895, when inspection replaced examination, all subjects were examined annually by HMI, and grants were made to schools on the basis of the results ('payment by results'). Class achievement formed the basis for grants in compulsory and class subjects; individual achievement in specific subjects. Attendance and, after 1892, 'merit' grants made up the government grant to schools. The remaining cost of elementary education had to be met by drawing upon the rates. (Science and Art grants were available for pupils above standard VII, but were not significant in London.)

Inevitably, then, teachers and schools were under considerable pressure to enter pupils for government examinations wherever possible, and to get them through. An HMI complained wearily,

> I wish that I could think that the choice of a specific subject was more often determined by a special fitness for teaching, or any special aptitude for learning it. It is too much regarded as a possible streamlet from the Parliamentary milch-cow, towards which the teacher is guided by an intelligent forecast of its grant-earning capacity. Having established the probable advantage, he sallies out to buy a textbook, with the contents of which he may hope in a year to make a select class familiar, and the boys are set to work upon diagrams of the human skeleton, or illustrations of the phases of the moon, upon a calculation of their *remunerative*, rather than their scientific and educational value.[12]

With pupils viewed as examination fodder, it is not surprising to find pupil-teachers advised: 'In giving a series of elementary science lessons on any subject, it is a good plan to get all the sets of examination questions upon the subject you can find, and to see that your class can answer all that come within the range of your work after you have given the lesson.'[13]

The inadequacy of the preparation of teachers for teaching science as anything other than accumulated and examinable facts was a particular concern of Gladstone and his fellow supporters of science on the London Board. Although special consideration was given to applicants for posts who had science certificates, this guaranteed only the possession of facts. Few had any experience of practical work and, as the emphasis on it grew, the Board experimented with ways of encouraging teachers to make it a central feature of science lessons. The most important experiments were (i) the introduction, in 1885, of a peripatetic system of teaching mechanics (and, later, physics and chemistry), and (ii) the introduction of evening classes for teachers.

### Peripatetic Lecture — Demonstrators

A one-off, small-scale, experiment was tried in 1882. It is interesting in that it reflected growing concern about practical science, soon to become manifest in peripatetic experiments, and because it must represent one of the earliest entrepreneurial initiatives in science education. A Thomas Twining obtained permission to circulate 'lecture boxes' in seven Board schools at fortnightly intervals. Each 'lecture box' contained text, diagrams and apparatus for one of ten lecture-demonstrations on physics, chemistry, natural history or physiology, based on his *Science Made Easy* series, and selected 'with a constant and obvious view to the practical advantages of the working classes, teaching those things, and those things only, which have a correct bearing on daily life . . . [and affording] . . . a groundwork for the duties of the workshop, as well as for the comforts of a well-ordered home'.

Twining sent the Board five letters 'of a very satisfactory character' from participating schools and told them that the Washington Bureau of Education and the New South Wales Government had ordered sets. These had been put together by Messrs Griffin of Garrick Street who, Twining assured them, would give the Board a very fair quotation should they wish to extend the experiment.[14]

It appears, however, that no further action was taken. Other plans were, in any case, germinating in the minds of Gladstone and his supporters. The establishment of the First Royal Commission on Technical Instruction (1881–4) had resulted in the setting up of a Technical Education Sub-committee by the Board, with Gladstone as its first chairman, to make recommendations on ways of facilitating later technical instruction through elementary school work.[15] Although not prepared to consider anything in the way of vocational training in elementary schools, the committee concluded that 'hand and finger' training, a prerequisite for manual work, was certainly within its province. They therefore recommended that drawing be taught in all schools; that freehand drawing from models and elementary science be given more attention in boys' schools (girls, they argued, already had practical training in needlework and cookery classes); and that local experiments be tried with woodwork, mechanical drawing and clay-modelling classes.

As far as science was concerned, their attention focused on the specific subject, mechanics, which they regarded as 'perhaps the most appropriate subject for boys with a mechanical bent'. Yet, they pointed out, only 165 of the 17,000 boys currently taking specific subjects took mechanics, there was little apparatus readily available, and few teachers were qualified to teach it. The sub-committee therefore recommended that the 'peripatetic plan of teaching mechanics', which had already proved very successful in Liverpool and Birmingham, be tried out in one London district.[16]

As soon as the Board's approval had been granted, W.H. Grieve, a 'Special Teacher of Science' in a pupil-teacher school, was appointed as 'Science Demonstrator' in Tower Hamlets and Hackney.[17] He was to visit each of twenty-one schools once a fortnight, taking with him the necessary apparatus and equipment, which he would keep in a room allocated in one of his schools. (From the fact that he claimed expenses for cab fares, it can probably be assumed that Grieve did not push a handcart from school to school as did his counterparts in other towns.) The lecture-demonstration was watched by the class teacher, who then repeated the lesson during the intervening period. On leaving, Grieve gave the teacher a list of questions which boys were to answer in writing before his next visit. The scheme was very popular, and Grieve was told that attendance improved noticeably on science days. He was delighted when many of his 2090 pupils illustrated their written answers with sketches of the apparatus used to demonstrate experiments; still more so when, early on, two standard VI boys brought along models of the Barker's Mill with which he had illustrated his last lecture. These had been made entirely on the boys' own initiative, taking up their free time, and, when tested in front of the class, 'were found to work just as true as the original'. This suggested to Grieve what was to become a major feature of much peripatetic mechanics teaching — the making of models by the boys. It added manipulative training to the benefits of the course and, as Grieve pointed out in his report to the Board, afforded an opportunity for less able boys to shine. It was not long before a manager at Teesdale Street School became so interested that he offered cash prizes for the best models.[18] And, in 1889, the 'Scholars' Section' at the Melbourne Exhibition included Barker's Mills, spouting jars, common pumps, force pumps, valves and windlasses, all made by boys taking peripatetic mechanics and, too, diagrams, notebooks and specimen examination papers.[19]

In his first report, Grieve pointed out that, quite apart from the interest aroused, the obvious relevance of the work might encourage boys to stay on at school beyond standard V. This, in turn, would mean a larger number of entries for annual examinations and so larger government grants to schools. The scheme might even become self-supporting: 'Assuming that 75 per cent of the 2000 pass ... at the rate of 4 shillings per head, a return of £300 is made to the Board, equal to the sum allowed for apparatus, salary and working expenses'.[20]

Two of the Board's Inspectors watched Grieve in action on several occasions in 1886–7. They reported that, although it was too soon to make judgments based on examination success, they were impressed by Grieve's performance and by the evident interest and enjoyment of the boys. One had reservations about the effectiveness of this combination of lecture-demonstration and teacher-operated lesson in training observation, statement and reasoning, because it made few demands on the boys. The second observed that it was a pity that, even in these lessons, government examinations could loom so large: in one lesson on expansion, there were 'so many allusions to Her Majesty's Inspector that he seemed to be a force higher than heat, and a phenomenon more interesting than expansion!'.[21]

The Technical Education Sub-committee was well satisfied with the experiment and, early in 1887, proposed the appointment of three additional Demonstrators for schools in the Board's other three divisions. Some Board members opposed the proposal vigorously. Were these 'special professors' necessary in view of the high salaries paid to the teachers? Was it really true that ordinary teachers could not do the work — it was relieving them of duties that they were paid to perform. Was the Board going beyond its province and providing secondary education? Would it not overcrowd the curriculum quite unnecessarily?

In reply, Gladstone and his supporters argued that increased government grants had been earned by schools in the scheme; that teaching mechanics did not constitute secondary education; that mechanics was the very foundation for the future mechanical and technical training of artisans; that very few teachers were appropriately qualified (only 25 of the 700 who had obtained science certificates in 1875 had passed in mechanics); and that the approach was a temporary measure until training colleges could take on the responsibility for ensuring that all teachers studied science. The Department of Education, moreover, approved of the scheme, which had been successful in all three cities where it had been tried. After much wrangling, approval was granted for a further three years' trial and for the additional appointments.[22]

It is clear that opinion outside the Board was just as divided on the merits of the scheme, though for different reasons. A report to the National Association for the Promotion of Secondary and Technical Education in 1889, for instance, argued that it did good in stimulating pupils' interest in natural phenomena, but could hardly amount to systematic scientific instruction.[23] And HMI Aldis drew attention to the problems inherent in a situation in which teacher and pupils were relative strangers and, in particular, to the difficulty of ensuring that boys were stretched. He also believed that the subject was mathemati-

cally too demanding for all except a few.[24] Aldis had examined all
twenty-one schools in 1887 and, although older boys did well, the
results in standard V had been very disappointing. For example, at
Dempsey Street School — which Grieve regarded as one of his best —
all twenty-three from standards VI and VII had passed, but only
eighteen out of thirty-nine in standard V. The school had withdrawn
from the scheme.

Grieve argued that the examination was to blame. The paper, which
required written answers, offered a very limited choice and, moreover,
tested only 'crude theories'. Yet the Code demanded that the subject be
taught 'mainly by experiment and illustration'. The paper required a
knowledge of scientific terms which was quite beyond the younger
pupils (who were only eleven or twelve) — and he included seven
questions to illustrate this. Two, by no means untypical, questions were:

Q5 *Compressibility* is due to the approach of the *molecules*. It
is a proof of *porosity*. Explain the words underlined.

Q4 A nail driven into a piece of wood is not a case of
penetrability. Explain this.[25]

Grieve's complaint was referred to the Technical Education Sub-
committee, who agreed that the questions were 'not framed in the best
manner for testing the intelligence of the scholars', and Gladstone
agreed to speak to the HMI.[26] The matter was also referred to the Cross
Commission on Elementary Education in one of several attempts to
have HMI appointed who had scientific backgrounds.[27]

There was probably some justification for both points of view, but
the problem remained. Only a year later, for instance, another demonstrator complained that the very different examination results in his
two districts could only be ascribed to the fact that two HMI had
carried out the examinations.[25]

After five years of experiment only twenty-five schools were able
to carry on on their own,[29] and it was clear that more was needed to
help teachers to overcome their anxiety about practical work. Demonstrators had already started to hold occasional evening classes to
demonstrate methods of performing experiments and of manipulating
models.[30] At their request, the Board sanctioned the establishment of
regular courses of eight or ten sessions.[31] In addition, they gave three
months' leave of absence every year to those teachers who had shown
special aptitude, to enable them to attend summer schools at South
Kensington.[32] Doubts were growing, however, about the effectiveness
of lecture-demonstrations for achieving the desired ends with pupils. It

was felt that hand and eye training should be linked with mind training in order to 'train the intelligence'. To achieve this linkage, it was argued, pupils themselves needed to perform experiments. This idea that individual practical work was somehow effective in achieving cognitive, affective and manipulative ends often remained no more than a vague assumption. Even so, it was powerful enough to become a major tradition in English science education.

### Heurism and 'Scientific Method'

A more specific version was, however, developing in parallel. This was *heurism*, and it was already in operation in at least two London independent schools.[33] Gladstone had heard Armstrong lecture on heurism in the early eighties. In 1891, when one of the demonstrators emigrated to Australia, one of Armstrong's former students, Hugh Gordon, was appointed in his place. Gordon told the Board that he was concerned, 'not with inculcating a large assortment of unorganised facts, but to point out and to imbue the children with scientific method'.[34] He lost no time in reorganizing peripatetic mechanics in Tower Hamlets and Hackney (which he took over after a re-shuffle) and in devising a new course of 'Elementary Natural Philosophy'. As soon as he obtained permission to treat the latter as an alternative to mechanics, a phasing-out operation began.[35] Based upon a course for elementary schools devised by Armstrong for the British Association, Elementary Natural Philosophy covered relatively standard content, but did so in the carefully structured progression typical of an heuristic approach. It achieved full recognition when it was incorporated in the Code in 1894 as 'Elementary Physics and Chemistry'.[36]

Though Gordon retained the pattern of fortnightly visits to schools, the whole orientation of the lessons changed. Each started with questions designed to elicit any difficulties or misapprehensions that might have arisen during the previous fortnight, and to clarify the point reached in the inquiry. Gordon then invited suggestions for the next step, though he later admitted that a good deal of guidance was often necessary. Then two to four boys got out the apparatus, fitted it up and did any necessary weighing. After this, they — or other boys — performed the experiment while the class watched. Before Gordon's next visit, the class teacher repeated the lesson, recapitulating the steps of the inquiry; then boys wrote up their own notes, while small groups, in turn, repeated the experiments for themselves.[37]

Clearly, this approach was something of a compromise in heuristic terms, but the size of classes, the everpresent constraints of cost, and the problem of teacher inadequacy made it inevitable. It did not, however, stop Gordon from making what can only have been extravagant claims about pupils' learning, claims based, moreover, upon purely subjective judgments. His positiveness, and his dismissive attitude towards the efforts of his colleagues did not endear him to them, or foster co-operation. He wrote to the Board, claiming that existing mechanics courses consisted of little more than 'conjuring tricks with explanations' and that their 'so-called practical work' failed to teach 'what science really is' and to develop 'good habits and scientific methods'.[38] His successor, Mayhowe Heller (another Armstrong protégé) claimed that, although Gordon's methods were 'more conducive to intelligent teaching', more interesting, and really practical in instilling scientific method, Gordon had encountered 'considerable prejudice and many difficulties'.[39] The records suggest that this may well have been so, but that it was at least as much a product of the ill-feeling created by the public criticisms, not just of Gordon, but of Armstrong and other heurists.[40]

Both Gordon and Heller ran evening classes for teachers that were specifically designed to overcome the difficulties that teachers experienced in changing from their long-standing didactic methods to heurism. Each session started with a brief lecture on the topic for the coming fortnight, followed by discussion of difficulties. Then teachers spent the rest of the evening performing experiments. When they left, they took with them a cyclostyled summary of the lecture and a set of questions for the boys which would form the basis of their practical work. Heller later claimed that a 'goodly percentage' of teachers 'became genuine teachers of scientific method, while the others, even if their opinions were not fully re-moulded, at any rate saw greater possibilities and higher ideals in the teaching of science than previously'. Even he had to admit, eventually, that it took a year's attendance 'to make a teacher understand the new interpretation to be put upon science teaching and it was more often than not three years before he could be considered as having fully grasped the possibilities'. Eight months came to be regarded as a minimum period.[41]

## Science Teaching for Girls

Fitting elementary school girls for their place in adult society implied a preparation for domestic duties and responsibilities in the interests of (i) the physical, moral and mental health of the working class; (ii) the supply of domestic servants for the middle class. Two specific subjects were of clear relevance: animal physiology (the nature and functions of the body and the laws of health) and domestic economy, described by one of the Board's Inspectors as 'that curious jumble of scientific scraps'.[42] To encourage the teaching of domestic economy, the Department of Education made it one of the specific subjects in 1875 and, two years later, required that it be the first choice for all girls taking these options. Partly as a result, partly because of overlap between domestic economy and animal physiology syllabuses (food and the laws of health), partly because of women teachers' lack of qualifications, and partly because there were still many who had reservations about the suitability of animal physiology as a subject for girls,[43] this subject was left almost entirely to boys for several years. In 1888, for instance, 4869 boys and only 468 girls studied it.[44]

In an attempt to foster the subject in girls' schools, the National Health Society started offering annual prizes on the results of a special examination, to be taken by girls and examined by a Board Inspector. But, in 1876, only seven candidates were entered from three schools and, by 1880, the number was just 215, from eleven of the Board's 234 girls' departments.[45]

Domestic economy came under steady fire from Inspectors of both Board and Education Department. At the heart of the problem, they believed, was a failure to teach girls even the most basic scientific principles, a deficiency which reflected their teachers' own inadequate training. In 1883, one of the Board's Inspectors proposed that domestic economy should have all 'essentially practical operations' such as washing and cooking eliminated, since they were taught elsewhere. This would leave what he called the 'science of domestic economy', a 'sound knowledge of the scientific principles underlying the various operations of domestic life and conducing to a state of comfortable and healthy existence'.[46] Views of this kind were put forward in a number of quarters in the eighties and, in 1889, the Technical Education Sub-committee agreed that the time had come to give girls an opportunity to learn science.[47] It is clear that this 'science' was viewed very much as the basis for a better understanding of domestic tasks and that the experiment envisaged was of a much more limited character than peripatetic mechanics for boys, which, by 1896, was in the hands of four demonstrators and four assistants, all full-time.

On being sounded out, 243 head mistresses expressed considerable interest in the proposal.[48] To test its feasibility, the four Science Demonstrators were asked to give a lecture on 'science appertaining to domestic economy' in each of three of their schools. When this, too, was successful,[49] the Sub-committee felt able to go ahead and ask for a part-time 'lecturer on popular science subjects', able to devote about half of his time. To this end, letters went to Oxford and Cambridge, seeking a 'new graduate, intending to live in London', who would like to supplement his earnings.[50] Francis Newbold, BA, FCS, was appointed, and started work in eleven schools early in 1890. A second appointment was made just before he began; this time of a 'Lady Lecturer in Science', a Mrs Corrie Grant, who had obtained first and second class Honours in the Natural Sciences Tripos at Cambridge (Newnham College).[51] From the nature of her appointment it seems likely that she was known to one of the Sub-committee or to Aldis. She was to give two lectures a day, on four days a week, in twenty-four schools in Tower Hamlets and Hackney.

Both she and Newbold covered topics such as air, water, heat, and chemical change, and both did so by lecture-demonstration.[52] Classes were huge: Newbold wrote of sixty to eighty girls; Mrs Grant of fifty to 120. Although the wide range of ability presented difficulties, it seems clear that the response from teachers and pupils was most gratifying. Newbold told the Board:

> The girls attend well, and seem much interested, following the experiments with evident enjoyment ... Some ... understand everything, and jump to answer every question, while others only marvel and are dumb ... It is noticeable that the more brilliant experiments excite a great amount of interest, but convey less meaning; the burning of phosphorus in oxygen, for example, was evidently regarded with magnificent wonder, but some girls only carried away the idea that oxygen is 'a very bright gas', others that 'oxygen burns very brightly in a jar', while others, who had been all eyes, could not remember, at a subsequent lecture, that oxygen is anything but a synonym for air.[53]

Mrs Grant had had similar experiences and, as a result had, after the first month, avoided 'even the use of acid, as I found some children were inclined to regard acid in the light of a conjuring implement'.[54] She was uncertain about the lasting value, except for the brightest girls. Newbold, who believed that the written answers he had got from the girls were a better guide to their understanding, expressed great confidence in their worth. His view was confirmed by the teachers, who told him that attendance improved on 'science' days, especially when these occurred on Mondays or Fridays. The Sub-committee also canvassed head mistresses directly for their opinions and these, too, were very satisfactory.[55]

Newbold continued teaching in the same schools and along the same lines until at least the end of the experimental period (1896 for girls), fitting his teaching in with his work on legal circuit, and devoting about 130 days a year to it. When the managers of Hart Street Mixed School asked to be allowed to have him lecture, not to girls, but to boys, for whom it would be 'more useful', the Sub-committee responded by taking him out of the school altogether.[56] Mrs Grant withdrew from the scheme in the summer, recommending a Miss Webb — a London science graduate with teaching experience in a middle school — as a replacement.[57] The appointment was confirmed and the new Lady Lecturer drew up her scheme of work, which was based on the classification of animals. This was, clearly, not at all in line with the Sub-committee's intentions, and Gladstone was deputed to intervene.[58] The revised programme, entitled 'Domestic Economy' covered six topics: ventilation, washing, cleansing, clothing and nursing. Its content was far closer to standard courses in domestic subjects, though it did include some scientific experiments.[59] Nevertheless, the Board was satisfied, as were the head mistresses — except one, who said that she was 'disappointed, because the lessons were so very practical, and she had hoped for "pure science"'. All wanted more courses.[60]

Miss Webb's three-month contracts were renewed regularly for another year and she taught courses in physical geography, physiology and the laws of health, and a revised version of her original domestic economy.[61] She resigned in 1892, however, as she was unable to find other part-time work to supplement her income. When she mentioned this to the Sub-committee, they asked the Board to agree to a full-time, permanent post.[62] This was, however, turned down on the grounds that 'increasing the interest and developing the intelligence of scholars of the girls' departments can be obtained without the creation of a permanent office'.[63] Instead, the Board proposed the appointment of not more than four part-time lecturers, at six shillings an hour. Miss Webb did not wish to continue.

Twenty-nine candidates applied for the posts when advertised, and thirteen were interviewed. Only two were, however, appointed.[64] The first was a young London science graduate, with a Cambridge teaching certificate (with distinction). A former Board scholarship winner, she had taught in girls' high schools, and her syllabus was very similar to Miss Webb's. The second, Mrs Wigley, was not a graduate. She had trained at Cheltenham Ladies College where she had also been, for some time, 'Mistress of Method', and she had recently been teaching domestic economy to young women and girls in County Wexford. She was the author of 'several works on domestic economy and kindred topics'. Her proposed syllabus was rather different in appearance, and could conceivably contain a fair amount of science, in spite of one or two eccentricities. It was based on four main topics:

1 Women and girls — their position, influence and work.
2 What they work upon — (a) matter — its properties;
                              (b) elements and compounds.
3 What they work for — (a) health, depending upon
                                  (i) good food;
                                  (ii) pure air;
                           (b) comfort, depending upon
                                  (i) cleanliness;
                                  (ii) good temper;
                                  (iii) good taste;
                           (c) prosperity, depending upon
                                  (i) carefulness;
                                  (ii) thrift;
                                  (iii) good management;
                                  (iv) self-denial.
4 What they work with — (a) household implements and tools;
                              (b) labour-saving machines.[65]

Five weeks after she started teaching, Mrs Wigley sent in what is apparently her only surviving report. Just how far she had got with the syllabus is not clear, although her report refers to three lectures. This is sad, because the reader is led to wonder what it was that received sufficient recognition as 'scientific principles' for her to be retained as a Lady Lecturer in Science until 1895, which means several re-appointments. She expanded upon her three lectures with evident enthusiasm and pride, and it would be a pity to paraphrase most of it. She wrote:

In these first lectures, my aim was to excite in the girls a little extra enthusiasm and earnest thought, respecting their influence and position as daughters and sisters now, and as women by-and-by. Also I want to make these lectures *stand out* (her italics) in their life and thought, as something deeper and more important than any other ordinary school subject. Actually that which would gather up and more firmly impress upon their minds all that was good and advantageous in their other lessons. So it was that I tried to fill their first lesson full of interest, and at the same time to make it the keystone to all that came after.

After comparing their position as schoolgirls with that of children in bygone times, I told them of the old Saxon legends respecting women, how that some women were 'Elle' women, or *hollow*, with nothing at all in their heads, nothing worth having in their hearts and no skills or deftness in their hands. Also that some women were only werewolves — just wolves disguised as women, whose object was only to allure and destroy. Both these kinds of women were to be shunned and dreaded; they could never bless or help, or be a pure and holy influence in the home. And then I told them of the gentle and unselfish hearth spirit, whom our fathers worshipped and honoured, as one who did them good and not evil all the days of their lives. All this interested them very much, and gave me the opportunity of fixing three especial points, which we would try to work out in every succeeding lecture:

1 That those who run the home must not have empty heads.
2 That they must not have hollow hearts.
3 That all their sense powers must be trained to do skilled work.

We finished the lecture with the resolution that every time we meet we will try to accomplish our three-fold aim. I rhymed this for them, because I wished to get it into their heads:

Some wise thing the head should know;
Some wise grace the heart should grow;
Some skilled work that sense should try;
We will search for – you and I.

Each subsequent lesson had apparently started with 'some facts in simple science, with simple experiments which could be applied to a woman's work'. Unfortunately, the report tells us nothing about the science done, for Mrs Wigley was far more concerned to put on record the second part of each lesson which, she wrote, 'naturally' took the form of a moral lesson. (That this was acceptable to schools and Board reflects a widespread view at the time that the central purpose of education was moral training.) She had, she said, already dealt with 'the sweet graces of "Unselfishness" and "Perfect Truth"', and these were to be followed by "Modesty", "Obedience" and "Perseverance". She continued:

I should very much enjoy, if any of these schools gets a flag, to take 'Patriotism', in the history of the *Union Jack*. Then, as regards the practice work, we have taken 'How to make a graceful apology' or to say, 'I beg your pardon'. I have heard from the teachers that these words have been very much in the fashion in all earnest since that talk over them. On the occasion of the third lecture, I have set them to hunt for things *upside down*, *inside out*, or *hind part before*, and to put them right.

The '100–200' children in each class had, she claimed, been interested and attentive, growing 'more and more animated', though the order remained 'just about perfect'. Pupils, teachers and she herself had all been greatly pleased with the series so far, and about thirty neighbouring schools had expressed a wish to be included. (It is not clear whether they knew what was in the course.) She was quite willing and able to take on the extra work, and it would not be costly. She travelled by train, tram and bus wherever possible, and took a cab only where public transport was not available. During the recent fine weather she had walked.[66]

Two more Lady Lecturers were added in 1894. They were both domestic economy and hygiene experts,[67] and their courses were little different from those of ordinary teachers, apart from some extra demonstration experiments.

It was not long before the need for special 'Lady Lecturers' was being questioned. Not only were they offering little that was different, but girls were by this time doing individual practical work in both cookery and laundrywork classes. At the same time, considerable interest had been aroused by a 'Domestic Science' course devised by Heller, which aimed at inculcating scientific method within the context of domestic studies — to many an ideal 'science for girls'. Board Inspectors were asked for their opinion, which, in the event, matched those prevailing on the Board.[68] As a result, the Lecturers' appointments were not renewed and all peripatetic 'science' in girls' schools was abandoned in 1896.

In the following year, the Code incorporated Heller's course as 'Domestic Science — the Science of Domestic Economy and Hygiene', making it an alternative to Domestic Economy. In the new course, the Code warned, instruction should be 'entirely experimental, the experiments so far as possible being carried out by the scholars themselves, and arranged with the object of solving a definite problem. Measurement and exact work should be encouraged'. With Gladstone and Armstrong as leading figures on its sub-committees having to do with education, it was to be expected that the British Association would both recognize and publicize 'Domestic Science' as the ideal course for girls.

Heuristic domestic science for girls clearly demanded teacher-training, and Heller undertook this until his departure in 1897. Responsibility then fell to Miss Edna Walter, senior science mistress at the Central Foundation School, London, and another of Armstrong's disciples. She was later able to exercise considerable influence as a woman HMI.[69]

## Turn-of-the-Century Trends

Whether or not individuals subscribed to heurism, a general belief had, by 1900, become firmly established: that learning science is crucially connected with practical work carried out by pupils. This belief has been a distinguishing characteristics of English science education throughout the twentieth century. Two important difficulties associated with it had already become clear in the nineties. First, there was the problem of reconciling a commitment to practical science with the demands of public examinations of all kinds, including scholarship examinations.[70] Second was the problem of helping teachers to implement it. In the case of elementary schools, the latter problem had proved far more intractable than enthusiasts had anticipated. During the nineties, the Board's priorities in relation to experiments in science teaching had shifted steadily away from classrooms to teacher preparation. In 1898, or early 1899, Dr C.W. Kimmins of the Technical Education Board was commissioned by a newly created 'Special Sub-committee on Science Teaching' to report on science teaching in the Board's schools and on the 'experimental classes for teachers'.[71]

It was clear to many that the content of science teaching needed a major overhaul, to bring it into line with current ideas, and to check the proliferation of specialized courses that had taken place during the nineties, and the Board of Education (as the Department became in 1899) was completely re-thinking its position on syllabuses. The freedom that emerged allowed Kimmins to plan coordinated courses for all types of school in the run-up to LCC takeover in 1903.[72]

The second important outcome of Kimmins' reports was that teachers' courses were reorganized. A first stage of forty (later forty-eight) sessions providing instruction in the elements of 'Experimental Science' and familiarizing teachers with the construction of apparatus and methods of demonstration was followed by a course of 'pedagogical' lectures, staffed by seven newly-appointed 'Science Lecturers'. The courses began, but response dwindled rapidly and, by 1903, only one was in operation.[73] The Board's uncertain future and changed priorities combined to relegate concern about science for the majority of working class children to a position of minority interest. And, by 1902, most peripatetic demonstrators and assistants had been absorbed back into the system; two had left the services of the Board.[74]

## Conclusions

It must not be assumed that this account is making any claim that the London Board led the way in developing an ideal of practical or experimental science. The Board's experiments were a response to changing needs, opinions and beliefs in the wider society, and they had their counterparts elsewhere, although it is clear that being at the centre of the communication network had important consequences. By the turn of the century, a tradition of individual practical work as an important element of school science was firmly and widely established. It assumed certain means-end relationships which had already begun to be associated (often very loosely) with some sort of simulation of scientific activity, for which heurists provided the first explicit prescription. Sex-stereotyped 'science' courses had been tried out, and a belief that science courses for girls would be more 'relevant' and therefore more appealing if given a domestic bias was already set to become a hardy perennial, which survived long after research in the 1930s indicated the reverse.[75] Heuristically-conceived 'Domestic Science' was on the threshold of its hey-day as 'science for girls', and it is interesting to note here that, while London's top independent schools for girls were strong supporters of heuristic methods of science teaching (at least in the lower forms: public examinations made it more difficult in top forms), almost without exception they resisted[76] resolutely the strong pressures to substitute domestic science for science that developed during the Edwardian period, and to which many of their sister schools elsewhere succumbed.[77]

The evolution of courses for London science teachers in the nineties reflected a growing recognition that it was not enough to provide teachers with factual knowledge, or to prescribe and demonstrate a particular new approach — that persuasion, involvement and, above all, conviction, were crucial to, though not guarantees of, 'success'. Yet successive generations of twentieth century in-service providers had to learn the same lesson all over again.

Throughout this century, the most powerful tradition in English science education (apart from early specialization) has been that of individual practical work. Science educators have expended considerable time and energy on the relation between laboratory investigation and the building-up of knowledge, between 'process and product', inquiry and conceptual structure. The rhetoric has therefore sustained, at varying levels of specificity, an ideal of school science as simulation, variously interpreted, in which 'substance and syntax' of science are built up together and, in the process, certain values and attitudes are developed. The tradition was given strong theoretical support by much post-war educational philosophy and by some educational psychologists (which also served to persuade other countries of its value). Practical support came from the fact that children often learn best in concrete situations and that 'doing experiments' is often highly motivating and demonstrably enjoyable. The outcome has been a deeply-entrenched faith in a tradition which has, for many, assumed the status of an absolute, and a fundamental conservatism (conservationism, if you will) about what school science 'is' and should be. Attempts to buttress the tradition in the face of a growing awareness of the limitations that exist in real classrooms have tended to draw attention still further away from the curious fact that *science-trained* educators have been content to leave largely untested their most fundamental nineteenth century assumptions about means-end relationships in 'teaching the pursuit of science', treating them as something to be thought *in terms of, not about*. One result has been that, whatever the spin-off benefits (and they must not be underestimated), much curriculum reform has had more to do with re-arranging old prejudices than with innovation at this very fundamental level — yet it is here that hopes for the provision of meaningful school science for all must lie.

## Acknowledgement

I am grateful to the GLC Archives Office, London, for providing access to the material in this paper and for permission to publish.

## Notes

1 SBL 1414, (1888), p. iv.
2 SELLECK, (1968), chapter 4.
3 LYON PLAYFAIR, in a speech at Edinburgh, 1870, quoted in BLANCHET, (1953), p. 46.
4 SBL 1414, (1888), p. vi.
5 See his inaugural address in GORDON, (1980), pp. 1–42.
6 See DEPT of EDUCATION, (1898), pp. 389–419, or BROCK, (1973), 110–120.

7 PP (1872), XXV, Q333

8 SBL 1324, (1871), pp. 5–6.

9 SCHOOL BOARD of LONDON, (1904), p. 103.

10 See, for example, *Ibid*, p. 95; SBL 1324, (1871), Appendix; *School Board Chronicle*, (1873), X, pp. 508–10.

11 *School Board Chronicle*, (1876), XVI, p. 309 and PP (1888), XXXVIII, p. 328.

12 See HMI ALDERSON in PP (1888), XXXVIII, p. 328.

13 COLLAR and CROOK, (1900), p. 297.

14 *School Board Chronicle*, (1882), XXVII, p. 122.

15 *School Board Chronicle*, (1884), XXXII, p. 641 and *School Board Chronicle*, (1885), XXXIII, p. 5.

16 SBL 795, 3.12.1884, pp. vii–viii; also *School Board Chronicle*, (1885), XXXIII, p. 6.

17 *School Board Chronicle*, (1885), XXXIII, p. 386.

18 *School Board Chronicle*, (1887), XXXVIII, p. 225.

19 *School Board Chronicle*, (1889), XLII, p. 293.

20 SBL 790, 16.11.1885.

21 *School Board Chronicle*, (1887), XXXVIII, pp. 199–200.

22 *School Board Chronicle*, (1887), XXXVII, p. 163.

23 ACLAND and LLEWELLYN-SMITH, (1889), p. 85.

24 PP (1888), XXXVIII, pp. 339–40.

25 *School Board Chronicle*, (1887), XXXVIII, pp. 224–5; also SBL 898, 25.4.1887; also, PP (1888), XXXV, pp. 31–5.

26 SBL 898, 25.4.1887.

27 *School Board Chronicle*, (1890), XLIV, p. 330; also PP (1888), XXV.

28 *School Board Chronicle*, (1889), XLII, p. 294 (Todd); also *School Board Chronicle*, XXXIX, p. 259 (Hubble).

29 SBL 898, 25.3.1889.

30 See *School Board Chronicle*, (1890), XLIII, pp. 562–3.

31 *School Board Chronicle*, (1890), XLIV, pp. 330–1.

32 *Ibid*, p. 480.

33 Cowper Street School and St. Dunstan's College. See BROCK, (1973), pp. 16–20; EYRE, (1958), p. 113; *Nature*, (1933), CXXXI, pp. 194–5.

34 SBL 898, 17.11.1890; also *School Board Chronicle*, (1894), LII, pp. 231–2.

35 SBL 898, 9.2.1891 and 13.7.1891; also *School Board Chronicle*, (1892), XLVIII, p. 310.

36 ARMSTRONG, (1898), p. 397 and *School Board Chronicle*, (1894), LII, pp. 231–2.

37 DEPT of EDUCATION, (1898), pp. 429–33.

38 *School Board Chronicle*, (1892), XLVIII, p. 310.

39 *School Board Chronicle*, (1895), LIV, pp. 255–6

40 See, for example, TEB 4, (Llewellyn-Smith), pp. 31, 37; SBL 900, 17.3.1893; *School Board Chronicle*, (1893), XLIX, p. 224.

41 DEPT of EDUCATION, (1898), pp. 428, 432.

42 *School Board Chronicle*, (1879), XXII, p. 645.

43 See, for example, *School Board Chronicle*, (1879), XXI, p. 344.

44 ACLAND and LLEWELLYN-SMITH, (1889), p. 83.

45 See, for example, *School Board Chronicle*, (1876), XVI, pp. 313–14, and

(1880), XXIII, p. 221.
46 *School Board Chronicle*, (1883), XXIX, p. 287.
47 SBL 898, 25.3.1889; also PP (1892), XXVIII, p. 426 (Aldis).
48 SBL 898, 25.3.1889.
49 SBL 564, 23.2.1894.
50 SBL 898, 28.10.1889.
51 *Ibid*, and also 17.1.1890.
52 SBL 898, 28.4.1890.
53 *Ibid*, also *School Board Chronicle*, (1890), XLIV, p. 331.
54 SBL 898, 13.10.1890.
55 SBL 899, 23.2.1891.
56 SBL 900, 4.11.1892.
57 SBL 898, 7.11.1890.
58 SBL 898, 24.11.1890.
59 SBL 898, 8.12.1890.
60 SBL 899, 20.4.1891.
61 SBL 899, 20.10.1891 and 9.11.1891; also SBL 900, 19.2.1892.
62 SBL 900, 6.5.1892 and 3.6.1892.
63 SBL 900, 24.6.1892.
64 SBL 900, 4.11.1892; also 21.10.1892.
65 SBL 900, 4.11.1892.
66 SBL 900, 29.4.1893.
67 SBL 565, 11.5.1894.
68 SBL 824, 23.3.1896; 19.6.1896; 19.10.1896; 14.12.1896.
69 *School Board Chronicle*, (1897), LVIII, p. 251; also BRITISH ASSOCIATION, (1898), pp. 289–92.
70 TEB 80/39, pp. 200–1; for more detail, see PRO ED 14/20.
71 SBL 836, 17.3.1899; also SCHOOL BOARD OF LONDON, (1904), p. 294.
72 SBL 1434 (1903).
73 SBL 836, 17.3.1899.
74 SBL 795, 23.12.1902.
75 See COMBER, (1938), especially pp. 23, 42, 165–6.
76 See, for example, *School World*, (1912), pp. 452–65.
77 See DYHOUSE, (1981), especially pp. 139–75.

## References/Bibliography

Abbreviations:  PP   = Parliamentary Papers
                PRO = Public Records Office
                SBL  = School Board for London, (GLC Archives, Clerken-well)
                TEB  = Technical Education Board, LCC, (GLC Archives.)


*PRIMARY SOURCES*


SBL 1324, (1871), First Report and Minutes of Evidence of Scheme of Education Committee

SBL 795, (1884), Report of the Special Committee on Technical Education
SBL 1414, (1888), Report of the Special Committee on the Subjects and Modes of Instruction in the Board's Schools.
SBL 790, Miscellaneous Papers on Curriculum
SBL 898, Technical Education Committee ⎤
SBL 899, Technical Education Committee ⎬ Minutes, covering the period 1886–93 only
SBL 900, Technical Education Committee ⎦
SBL 564, School Management Committee Minutes, Vol 75 (of 154)
SBL 565, School Management Committee Minutes, Volume 76
SBL 569, School Management Committee Minutes, Volume 80
SBL 824, (1896), Business Papers on Special Subjects of Instruction
SBL 836, (1899), School Management Committees: Special Reports
SBL 1434, (1903), Science Syllabuses in Physics and Chemistry

## SECONDARY SOURCES

ACLAND A.H.D. and LLEWELLYN-SMITH, H. (1889), *Report to the National Association for the Promotion of Technical and Secondary Education*, London, NAPTSE.

ARMSTRONG, H.E. (1898), 'The Heuristic method of teaching, or the art of making children discover things for themselves', in Department of Education, (1898), *Special Reports on Education, Volume 11*, London, HMSO pp. 389–413.

BLANCHET, J. (1953), *Science, Craft and the State — a Study of English Technical Education and its Advocates, 1867–1906*, University of Oxford, unpulished D Phil thesis

BRITISH ASSOCIATION FOR THE ADVANCEMENT OF SCIENCE, (1898), *Annual Report, 1897*, London, John Murray.

BROCK, W.H. (Ed.), (1973), *H.E. Armstrong and the Teaching of Science, 1880–1930*, London, CUP.

COLLAR, G. and CROOK, C. (1900), *School Management and Methods of Instruction, with Special Reference to Elementary Schools*, London, Macmillan.

COMBER, L.C. (1938), *The Scientific Interests of Children in Relation to the Teaching of Science*, University of London, unpublished MA (Educ) thesis.

DYHOUSE, C. (1981), *Girls Growing Up in Late Victorian and Edwardian England*, London, Routledge and Kegan Paul.

EYRE, J.V. (1958), *Henry Edward Armstrong, 1848–1937*, London, Butterworth.

GORDON, P. (Ed.), (1980), *The Study of Education*, I, London, Woburn.

GREAT BRITAIN, Department of Education, (1898), *Special Reports on Education*, II, London, HMSO.

—— PP (1888), XXV, Royal Commission on the Elementary Education Act, (CROSS COMMISSION), *Report*.

—— PP. (1872) XXV, Royal Commission on Scientific Instruction and the Advancement of Science, (DEVONSHIRE COMMISSION), *Report*.

LLEWELLYN-SMITH, H. (1892), *Report to the Special Committee on Technical*

*Education*, TEB 4.

MEIKLEJOHN, J.M.D. (1876), 'Inaugural Address: St Andrew's University', in GORDON, P. (1980), *The Study of Education*, Volume I, London, Woburn.

*School Board Chronicle*, (1871–1912), Volumes I–LXXXVIII (after 1903, called the *School Board Gazetté*.)

SCHOOL BOARD FOR LONDON, (1904), *Final Report of the School Board for London, 1870–1904*, London, P.S. King and Son.

*School World*, (1912), 'Science in girls' schools', December, pp. 452–65.

SELLECK, R.J.W. (1968), *The New Education: the English Background, 1870–1914* London, Pitman.

SPALDING, T.A. and CANNEY, T.S.A. (1900), *The Work of the London School Board*, London, P.S. King.

# Domestic Subjects Since 1870

*June Purvis*

> There has probably never been a time when it was the ultimate aim of the majority of educators to produce among girls characteristics other than those suited to an ideal home life (Percival 1939: p. 314)

> Child care, child development, mother care and home making are usually regarded as the province of girls (DES 1975: p. 14)

## Introduction

The last decade has witnessed an increasing number of publications on historical, sociological and educational aspects of the school curriculum. In particular, feminist writers have posed searching questions about the curriculum for female pupils.[1] My aim in this chapter is to offer an overview of one part of the school curriculum that over the last 100 years or so has been inextricably linked with the education of working class girls — domestic subjects.

A number of themes will appear throughout this chapter. First, the schooling of girls throughout the period I am considering has been persistently influenced by ideas about the role of women in the wider society outside the school — in particular, the duties associated with a family life of domesticity, wifehood and motherhood. Secondly, though all girls are associated, in varying degrees, with ideas about domesticity, wifehood and motherhood, domestic subjects in schools are considered more appropriate for working class than middle class girls. Thirdly, domestic subjects in schools are linked not only with working class girls but also with 'less able' girls.

The chapter will be divided into two main parts. The first part will look at domestic subjects in the schooling of girls from 1870 to 1944, while the second part will concentrate on the period from 1944 to the present day. Before we begin this main task, however, we must consider what we mean by 'domestic subjects'.

As Wynn[2] has noted, it is impossible to define exactly the term 'domestic subjects' since it has extended over a wide and diverse subject area. In particular, the broad term 'domestic subjects' has often been used interchangeably with other terms such as 'domestic economy', 'domestic science' and 'home economics'. Throughout this chapter, I will use the term domestic subjects to refer to a range of school curricula that over the last 100 years or so have had titles such as cookery, laundrywork, household management, hygiene, nutrition, housecraft, needlework, housewifery, child care, mothercare, family and child, parentcraft and home studies.

## I 1870–1944

No account of the history of domestic subjects for English schoolgirls over the period 1870–1944 would be complete without reference to the dominant ideas about the role of women in the wider society. In particular, ideas expressed by the middle classes about the ideal family form and about the femininity of women were powerful forces helping to shape curricular content for girls. Let us look at this first, before we focus in greater depth on domestic subjects.

### The nineteenth-century legacy : middle class ideas about the family and femininity

Throughout the nineteenth century, we find a mass of statements made by the middle classes about the 'ideal' family form — that of a wage/salary husband and father and an economically dependent full time wife and mother. Such a family form, which was prevalent among the middle classes, was thought to provide a stable environment for the upbringing of children, a source of support and comfort to the male head of household and a force for stability within the wider society. The femininity of all women was linked with domesticity, and within the husband/wife relationship a wife was expected to be patient, self-sacrificing and subservient, administering to the various needs of the 'head' of the household.[3]

These middle class ideas which linked the femininity of women with the home, the family and domesticity were part of the dominant middle-class ideology. For both middle class and working class girls, growing up and learning to be 'feminine' meant socialization into a future ideal of wifehood and motherhood. However, whereas a middle class girl was expected to become a ladylike household organizer, with domestic servants to undertake all manual work, the middle class expected her working class counterpart to become a thrifty, practical housewife who undertook all the manual household chores.

Such class-specific expectations about domesticity for girls were not fully met. While the middle classes believed that girls in their own social stratum might be socialized *by the home* into the domestic ideal of the ladylike household organizer, it was considered that working class girls lacked such a 'civilizing' influence and were not taught how to become thrifty, practical housewives. Thus we find numerous statements, made by the middle classes, about the 'inadequacies' and 'deficiencies' of the working class family — how homes were poorly managed and children uncared for, ill-treated and neglected.[4] In particular, the 'deficiencies' of the working class wife and mother were highlighted. And working class girls, like their mothers, were considered by the middle classes to be ignorant of domestic skills.

One of the means that the middle classes advocated for the 'improvement' of the working class family was education. Education, it was hoped, would help to civilize and reform working people, and prevent certain social problems such as poverty, crime and alcoholism — social problems that threatened the stability of society. In particular, the teaching of domestic subjects to working class girls was seen as an important means of remedying an inadequate home environment. From the point of view of the middle classes, such subjects offered two main advantages. First, they would train working class girls in those skills that would help them to become competent wives and mothers in the future. Secondly, such subjects would also offer a training for employment in domestic service in middle class households. As we shall see, the idea of using domestic subjects in schools as a training for wifehood and motherhood *and* for the vocation of domestic service, was continually reiterated by the middle classes throughout the latter decades of the nineteenth century and well into the twentieth. Indeed, the association of domestic subjects in schools with the working class and with 'women's work', whether it was unpaid work in the family or paid work in domestic service, guaranteed this knowledge area a very low status.

Though domestic subjects were relatively unimportant in the schooling of middle class girls over the period 1870–1944, such subjects were not entirely absent. However, when such subjects were taught they were, as we shall see, usually sharply differentiated from those domestic subjects taught to working class girls. Now let us examine the history of domestic subjects in the schooling of working class and middle class girls in the period 1870–1944 in greater detail.

## Domestic subjects and the schooling of working class girls

Throughout the period 1870–1944, the education of English school-children was clearly demarcated along social class lines. In particular, elementary schooling was the lot of the majority of the working class while secondary education, the most prestigious form of schooling, was primarily an experience for the middle classes. Within these broad social class divisions, the education of girls was usually inferior in comparison with that of their brothers. Before 1870, working class girls might receive the basic rudiments of schooling in a variety of institutions such as Sunday schools, dame schools, charity schools and the day schools of the British and Foreign School Society (largely supported by religious dissenters) and of the much larger National Society for Promoting the Education of the Poor in the Principles of the Established Church (the Church of England). The day schools of the two religious bodies were largely maintained and organized by the middle classes and were key providers of schooling for working class children for much of the century.

Before 1870, the key domestic subject taught to working class girls in charity schools, dame schools and British and National schools was sewing or needlework.[5] The importance attached to this subject was underlined by the government's Revised Code of 1862 which made the teaching of needlework compulsory to all female pupils in schools receiving a government grant. Such a ruling applied particularly to the day schools of the British and National Societies.

The branch of needlework emphasized in these schools, both before and after 1862, was *plain* rather than fancy needlework. And the garments to be made were to be useful, day-to-day clothes. In rural areas, the local gentry often supplied material for sewing or clothes for mending. In urban areas, where this did not happen, elementary schoolgirls were often encouraged to bring garments from their own homes that needed mending. Such a scheme was not always success-ful. Clara Grant,[6] teaching in elementary schools in London in the 1890s recollects that many mothers refused to help in this way: one mother complained that she would not like to send her 'husband's stockings' for mending nor her 'old shifts'. Despite such drawbacks, needlework was seen by the middle classes as a key domestic subject that should be taught to working class girls — it would help them, so it was believed, to become thrifty future housewives who could sew and mend for their families, as well as capable domestic servants. As Dyhouse[7] has noted, by the end of the nineteenth century, needlework had assumed a symbolic importance in the schooling of working class girls since proficiency with a needle implied both femininity and thrift.

By 1890, needlework was not the only compulsory domestic subject taught to working class girls. State provision of education, after the 1870 Education Act, brought a number of changes to the elementary sector. As Lawson and Silver[8] have noted, the 1870 Act did not abolish the voluntary day schools of the religious societies but supplemented them, and it also made possible the introduction of compulsory education, up to the age of 10, in 1880, and free elementary education, in 1891. The 1870 Education Act specified that in districts which lacked efficient and suitable provision for elementary education, a school board was to be established to rectify the deficiency. The new board schools, like the voluntary schools, were intended for working class children (though some lower-middle class children did attend) and were not seen as a stepping stone to secondary education. It is in the post 1870, state maintained, elementary 'public' schools that domestic subjects began to expand in the curriculum offered to working class girls.

In 1878, domestic economy was made a compulsory specific subject for girls in elementary schools, and in 1882, grants were made for the teaching of cookery. Though cookery was studied primarily by girls it was not exclusive to them since by 1912 several authorities, chiefly in seaport towns, had successfully established cookery classes for boys.[9] But these additional subjects were overwhelmingly associated with the elementary schoolgirl and involved, once again, an emphasis upon the learning of practical domestic skills. Domestic economy, for example, could cover topics such as the use, care and repair of clothing; the weekly wash day; the choosing and cooking of food; the cleaning of cooking utensils; the warming, lighting and cleaning of a house; simple cures for slight ailments, and the management of a sick room.[10] Cooking skills were restricted to what was called 'artisan cookery'[11] — plain cooking considered suitable for the lifestyle of the working class, and might cover 'moderately economical' recipes[12] for making such dishes as mutton broth, potato pies, irish stew and bread pudding. Instructions such as the following were frequently inserted in handbooks for the cookery teacher in elementary schools:

The girls in the elementary schools should be taught dishes they can make and cook in their own homes, with the appliances and small open grates found in the houses of the working classes.

The seven primary methods of cooking — 'boiling, roasting, baking, stewing, frying, steaming, and grilling', ≃ should be taught not once, but repeatedly, until the pupils know each method thoroughly. Soup-making, the cooking of vegetables, cheap puddings and cakes, bread-making, children's foods, etc., these are the dishes that will meet the needs of the working classes. No elaborate dishes should be attempted.[13]

Many middle class commentators welcomed the addition of domestic economy and cookery to the curriculum for the elementary schoolgirl and argued for *more* time to be given to domestic subjects generally. Lady Caroline Leigh, for example, advocated in 1887 that 'that unelastic and tyrannous thing, the timetable' should be banished and that domestic economy should be taught every afternoon:

Many a child who now makes but an indifferent scholar might prove a good, happy, sensible wife and mother if early taught the beauty of cleanliness, methodical habits, and how to sew and cook thoroughly. The heart of the nation responds when 'Home sweet home' is sung. Let it be ours to see that the association of the words never bring to any man the recollection of foul smells and heart-sickening disorder.[14]

This statement and numerous others made by the middle classes make it quite clear that learning domestic subjects in schools was associated with sex, social class and ability; that is, it was for working class girls who were, by definition, identified as being academically less able. The statement also emphasizes another common point, that learning practical domestic skills was seen as serving the interests of men, especially husbands. Other influential persons stressed much more forcibly the value of domestic subjects as a training not only for wifehood but also for domestic service. Miss Headdon, for example, a member of the Council of Ladies of the National Association for the Promotion of Housewifery, took this view when she advocated the introduction of housework into the elementary school curriculum:

There is a great demand for *skilled* domestic labour, and no adequate supply to meet it, partly owing, we are assured, to the fact that this natural *womanly taste is neglected* and *its cultivation left out of the girl's education* ...... to the untrained, ignorant girl the idea of domestic work is repugnant, while to the girl who has been *taught to work*, who has *some knowledge and method to guide her*, it is a pleasant exercise.

> That girls are not taught housework *while young* and capable of being taught is the main cause of the incapacity of our domestic servants and working men's wives.[15]

The offical view of the Board of Education was that elementary schools should educate working class girls in domestic skills or 'household duties which devolve more or less on all women',[16] but not offer vocational training for domestic service. Nevertheless, the kinds of domestic subjects being introduced into the elementary school curriculum could serve both purposes. In 1890, grants were made for the teaching of laundry work, and in 1900, a special grant was made for household management, which included such subjects as cookery, laundry work and housewifery. Some authorities too, such as the London School Board, made attempts to offer 'science' with a domestic bias in the belief that this was more relevant for girls than the science taught to boys (see Waring, pp 121–43 in this volume).

The new textbooks that were published to aid the teaching of domestic subjects at this time make it quite clear that such subjects were intended to teach the learning of practical skills *and* to provide some kind of character training.[17] E. Rice, for example, hoped her textbook on domestic economy would be useful to teachers for imparting information, developing the general intelligence of pupils and 'inculcating habits of order, industry, and usefulness'. Margaret Rankin in a textbook on the art and practice of laundry work suggested to the teachers:

> There is nothing more likely to aid in the development of character in children than the thorough inculcation of this science of cleanliness, and the teacher who is earnest and enthusiastic in the work will appreciate the importance of the relation between cleanliness and perfect health. While guiding the pupils into methodical ways of working, she will embrace the opportunity of instilling hygienic principles of cleanliness, and also influence the character of the pupils by the formation of habits such as punctuality, cleanliness, tidiness, carefulness, and order...[18]

The pressure to extend the teaching of domestic subjects in elementary schools continued into the twentieth century. During the first decade of the new century, for example, some schools offered short courses in child care and infant management. Sometimes these courses were taught to final year girls by a nurse or a visiting lecturer, while at other schools the girls attended a 'home-making' centre. In 1910, the Board of Education recommended that infant care should not be taught as an isolated subject but as part of an integrated course in hygiene and household management.[19]

Writers such as Davin (1978), Turnbull (1980), David (1980) and Dyhouse (1981) link these developments in the extension of domestic subjects in the curriculum for elementary schoolgirls to fears about the future of the British race and the decline of the British Empire. The call-up for the Boer War (1899–1902) had revealed that large numbers of potential male recruits were physically unfit for service. In addition, a falling birth rate coupled with a high infant mortality rate aroused fears about the quantity of potential recruits for the defence of the Empire as well as fears about the quality of maternal care. The much debated Report of the Inter-Departmental Committee on Physical Deterioration (1904) contained a mass of statements from middle class people about the poor standard of living amongst working class families in congested urban areas. In particular, the witnesses emphasized the inadequacies of the working class mother — both as a wife and parent. Generally, children were seen as 'a national asset', 'the citizens of tomorrow'.[20] And working class girls were to be prepared for such a future by teaching them appropriate domestic skills.

Not all such attempts were successful, though. Grace Foakes attended a housewifery course where she was taught to sweep, dust, polish, make beds and bath a life-size doll. The pupils did not, however, always conform to the teacher's expectations:

> We had great fun on this course, for it was held in a house set aside for the purpose, and with only one teacher in charge, we were quick to take advantage when she went to inspect some other part of the house. We jumped on the bed, threw pillows, drowned the doll and swept dirt under the mats.[21]

And Dorothy Scannell[22] who attended a housewifery course in the 1920s remembers how she made a disastrous mistake when preparing a meal for the teachers — she was over generous with the margarine and added a whole packet, instead of one or two knobs, to the mashed potatoes: as a result, she did not receive her good housewife certificate.

Before 1944, some working class girls might receive a form of 'secondary' education, usually called 'post-elementary' education, in a range of institutions within the elementary sector. The curriculum of these schools was carefully controlled by various regulations issued by the Board of Education. The emphasis within such schools was upon vocational training for boys and girls, and once again, domestic subjects were offered as an integral part of the curriculum for girls. Higher grade schools, for example, were to develop the education given in the ordinary elementary school and offer 'special instruction bearing on the future occupations of the scholars, whether boys or girls'.[23] However, drawing and manual work for boys, and domestic subjects for girls, had to be included as part of the general or special instruction. The strands of special instruction that were of a vocational nature were roughly classified as humanistic, scientific and manual 'and in the case of girls, domestic'.[24] Pupils were not admitted to the schools unless they were 12 years old and had spent at least two years in an ordinary elementary school. The total number of schools recognized as higher grade was small — in 1916–17, for example, there were only thirty-one in England and Wales.[25] And girls attending the higher grade schools were overwhelmingly outnumbered by the boys. Banks[26] suggests that of the female pupils leaving higher grade schools during the twelve months ending 1st June 1897, 29.3 per cent had unknown destinations, 20.5 per cent became pupil teachers, 12.5 per cent passed on to another secondary school and 12.5 per cent went into business or commercial life. Female pupil teachers going back into the ordinary elementary schools that they had once attended might, of course, teach to female pupils those domestic skills that they had learnt. As I have argued elsewhere[27] female teachers thus became a resource for teaching working class girls those domestic subjects that helped to maintain sexual divisions between girls and boys in the classroom and in the wider society.

Two alternative forms of post-elementary education were the central school and the junior technical school which both offered further specialized training in domestic subjects for elementary school-girls. The general education at the central school included the inevitable needlework and domestic subjects for girls, and after two years a commercial or industrial bias, or both, was introduced. And it was in girls' central schools with an industrial bias that greater emphasis was given to needlework and domestic subjects, as well as art and science, in the last two years. In particular, dressmaking and millinery might be taught in order to prepare girls for employment in these trades.

In some urban areas, the central schools offered additional domestic courses for girls as well as those contained in any industrial course. These additional domestic courses might include housecraft, book-keeping based on household accounts, needlework, sick nursing, and elementary hygiene. Such courses were intended 'for girls who wish either to pursue domestic occupations in the home, or ultimately to become managers or housekeepers in hotels, private houses and institutions of various kinds'.[28] During the 1920s and 30s, fewer and fewer working class girls were prepared to enter domestic service. Nevertheless, these domestic courses in central schools still attempted to prepare working class girls for 'typical' women's work within the private sphere of the home.

By the 1930s, the central schools had lost much of their popularity to another form of post-elementary education — the junior technical school.[29] These schools recruited pupils from the elementary sector at the age of 13 or 14 and the Board of Education intended that such schools should be vocational schools, offering a training in manual skills for the future artisan or rank and file worker in industry. By 1936, 134 such schools had been established, and by 1939 the number had risen to 220.[30] As Sillitoe[31] has noted, the junior technical schools provided yet another opportunity for developing the teaching of domestic subjects on more advanced lines than had been possible in the ordinary elementary school. Nowhere was this made more explicit than in those junior technical schools called 'junior housewifery schools'.

The junior housewifery schools (sometimes also called home training schools) recruited their female pupils at thirteen or fourteen years old. Half of the time was devoted to general education and the rest to a variety of domestic topics that centred on the home. One Board of Education Report stated that the junior housewifery schools were concerned with matters involving the 'intelligent management of a household', and that the courses offered covered a 'wide' range of subjects:

> Personal health and hygiene, including First Aid, cooking, sewing, cleaning, laundry work, ventilation, sanitation, heating, lighting, water supply, the furnishing and decoration of rooms, and the use of various appliances, together require a wide range of knowledge in which simple mathematics, elementary general science and art are obviously essential. Furthermore, a background of history and literature and a considerable vocabulary are essential to enable the pupil to make full use of the many books, magazines and pamphlets published specially in the interests of the home.[32]

The same source also claims that the junior housewifery schools provided an 'excellent training' for 'home duties or domestic service' though many parents apparently believed that the emphasis was solely upon the latter. The schools might also be a springboard for further training for girls intending to become welfare workers or women supervisors in hotels, boarding houses, large stores and the catering trades, or nurses.[33]

The number of schoolgirls experiencing such a domestic training would, however, have been small since by 1939 only nine of the 220 junior technical schools were junior housewifery schools.[34] Neverthe-less, the existence of such schools does underline the fact that when advanced vocational training was offered to girls within the elementary sector it could involve an emphasis upon those things considered appropriate for working class females — namely domesticity and practical domestic skills. Within the junior housewifery schools, elementary schoolgirls were prepared for unpaid work within the home and paid work in low status jobs that were typical of women's employment, such as domestic service, catering supervisors, nursing.

Though I have mainly considered so far clearly defined domestic subjects in the curriculum offered to the elementary schoolgirl, domes-tically related courses and domestic themes could be taught under other names. The teaching of courses on citizenship in the 1930s, for example, could stress domesticity for girls via links with the family, neighbours and the wider community. One textbook on training for citizenship in elementary schools, for example, looks at the part that can be played by various school subjects such as history, geography, economics and science. However, the content of the chapter on training for citizenship through domestic subjects relates implicitly to girls since the term 'citizen' is synonymous with 'housewife', and the housewife's responsi-bilities within and outside the home are emphasized:

> In a beginners' course in domestic subjects education for citizenship is best started by inculcating through actual practice the idea that the individual is a member of group... The idea of the family as a unit in a civic community is developed, and with it the responsibility of the housewife to her neighbours and to her town. The first lessons in housewifery and laundry work, therefore, should be accompanied by training in habits calcu-lated to inculcate this sense of responsibility. The subject of cleanliness in the home should lead on to that of orderliness in the streets and public parks. In all such topics as the disposal of refuse, the extermination of household pests, the treatment of infectious diseases, the avoidance of smoking chimneys, of spreading weeds, the choice of clean shops — the duty of the housewife to her neighbours, and her responsibility for a high standard of public welfare can be continually stressed.[35]

By 1939, both social class and gender divisions were firmly entrenched within the overall pattern of educational provision. The vast majority of working class children were schooled within the elementary sector and domestic subjects were taught primarily to girls — though a small number of boys did have cookery classes. Some working class children won scholarships and free places to the academically oriented grammar and other types of secondary education, but such opportunities were few. In particular, the number of scholarships and free places for which girls could compete was substantially less than the number available to boys. Though the attendance of working class girls in secondary schools was scarce,[36] some middle class girls (especially those whose parents were impoverished) did enter schools in the elementary sector. But the vast majority of middle class girls, like their brothers, were educated outside the elementary sector. Apart from when they were very young, the forms of education for middle class girls were usually separate, inferior and distinct from those of their brothers. And in the single sex education of the middle class girl, little emphasis was given to domestic subjects apart from needlework. Now let us look at the relative unimportance of such subjects for the middle class girl.

### Domestic subjects and the schooling of middle class girls

For most of the nineteenth century, middle class girls were usually educated at home by a governess or a parent or sometimes by both. The home education might be supplemented by attendance at a small, family-like, private school. Like their working class sisters, middle class girls were linked with domesticity and a future life of wifehood and motherhood — but as potential wives and mothers who could afford to employ domestic servants for the routine, manual tasks necessary to maintain a household. Thus the education of middle class girls stressed the acquisition of ornamental knowledge that would make them attractive to potential suitors. A little knowledge of French, German, history and geography, together with ladylike accomplishments in deportment, drawing, painting, needlework (especially decorative sewing), and piano playing were probably common.[37] By the 1870 then, the education of middle class girls lacked that emphasis upon manual domestic skills that was stressed in the schooling of working class girls. It was assumed that a middle class girl would learn those managerial skills necessary for running a household by watching and copying what was done at home.[38]

The major challenge to home education and/or attendance at a small private school came from a range of fee-paying secondary schools for middle class girls that were established from the 1850s. Particularly important were the North London Collegiate, established by Miss Frances Mary Buss and her mother in 1850; the Cheltenham Ladies College, founded in 1854, and of which Miss Dorothea Beale became Principal in 1858, and various day schools, sometimes known as 'high' schools, established by the Girls Public Day School company, founded in 1872. Such schools sought to improve the standard of education for middle class girls and, in particular, to prepare them for those public examinations that their brothers took. As Digby[39] has noted, though these new schools used the domestic vocation of the middle class girl as a conservative rationale for improving her schooling, the subjects offered aimed to provide a moral and intellectual education rather than a practical training for the duties of a household. Thus in the new schools domestic subjects were usually, though not always, avoided.[40]

When domestic subjects were taught in the new schools, the rationale for their inclusion was often quite distinct from that voiced by middle class commentators for teaching working class girls such subjects. Plain needlework, for example, could give a middle class girl a skill that had philanthropic value — the making of clothes for the needy. Thus Miss Buss[41] in her evidence before the Schools Inquiry Commission of 1867–8, claimed that every girl at the North London Collegiate learnt 'plain needlework' and that every year a large quantity of 'plain clothing' was given away amongst the poor of the neighbourhood. This did not mean, however, that such a practical domestic skill as plain sewing was given a high status or regarded as important within the curriculum. A sewing class or 'Dorcas' Society could meet as infrequently as once a month and be regarded as a duty which made little contribution to the overall total marks of a schoolgirl. Thus Molly Hughes, a pupil at the North London Collegiate in the 1880s, recollects that Miss Buss encouraged:

> both plain sewing and Christianity by ordaining a Dorcas meeting once a month. To most of us it was a treat, providing a change from the usual routine ... Since the work was more of a good deed than a lesson, we were allowed to talk a little within reason while we sewed ...
>
> For two hours we sewed horribly coarse cotton, of a dull biscuit colour and queer smell, with little blackish threads poking out of it here and there. It was to become in time chemises for the poor. We were not taught how to cut them out, for our mistakes would have been wasteful. Our duty was to join long stretches of stuff together ... The reward for our noble work consisted in being read aloud to by the form mistress. As she was not required to improve us, she chose some jolly book that she herself liked, and we were encouraged to discuss any little point that arose in it, even while we sewed ... Even here marks pursued us. Since they were not to be taken off

for talking in this blessed instance, ten or less were allotted for the amount of sewing we had achieved ... But.... the Dorcas marks never 'counted'.[42]

Sometimes, too, cookery classes might be introduced, but their content was clearly distinguishable from that taught to working class girls since the emphasis was upon learning theoretical facts rather than the practice of cooking. Thus Molly Hughes remembers that her domestic economy lessons at the N.L.C. involved talking about 'hydrogenous foodstuffs and carbohydrates' and were:

entirely theoretical, as there was neither kitchen nor laundry at our disposal, and I darkly suspected that our teachers had never entered such places. Now I could make a rice pudding blindfold, so mother and I were greatly tickled at my having to write down and learn a recipe for it.[43]

Overall, however, it would appear that by the end of the nineteenth century, the only domestic subject that the majority of the fee-paying schools for middle class girls offered was needlework. Practical domestic skills had little relevance for middle class girls, even as a training for employment. As the Association of Headmistresses said in 1907, domestic work, 'as at present organized', offers no career to the middle class girl, even those who left school at 16 years old.[44] Most of these school leavers hoped to become clerks or teachers.

The fears expressed, around the turn of the century, about the future of the British race and the decline of the British Empire, aided, as we have seen, the expansion of domestic subjects for working class girls educated within the state elementary sector. And the debates about education for wifehood and motherhood did not completely bypass the fee-paying, secondary sector for middle class girls. The Association of Headmistresses frequently debated the issue and a variety of opinion was expressed. Some headmistresses asserted that domestic subjects had no place in the curriculum of their schools, and that their main task was to offer girls an academic and intellectual education that was as near as possible that studied by their brothers. Miss Gardiner, Headmistress of Blackburn High School, for example, warned that 'the intellectual birthright must not be sold for skill in making puddings'.[45] But others within the Association, such as Sara Burstall, Headmistress of Manchester High School, and Margaret Gilliland, Headmistress of Haberdashers' Aske's, favoured the inclusion of domestic subjects.

At Manchester High School, for example, during the 1900–01 session, Miss Burstall introduced a housewifery course for girls who were 'going home and had no intention of following a profession'; the course included instruction in cookery, laundry, hygiene, household management, needlework and household arithmetic as well as lessons in French, English and History.[46] The high schools at Clapham, Blackheath and Streatham also introduced courses with a domestic bias for those who intended to stay at home. Clapham High School, for example, offered a 'brides-to-be' course, and 'Housewives Certificates' were given to those who successfully completed it.[47]

It is important, however, not to overemphasize the extent of provision of domestic courses in the fee-paying girls' schools. Some, but not all, of the girls' schools introduced such subjects. Those girls' schools in receipt of government grants had, eventually, to include practical instruction in domestic subjects such as cookery, needlework, laundrywork, housekeeping and household hygiene. But even if a girls' school was obliged to conform, in order to survive, this does not mean that domestic subjects were rated highly. A Board of Education Report in 1923[48] stated that one of the most important aims of girls' secondary schools, that of 'fitting girls for the duties of motherhood and for working in the home' had been 'unduly obscured' by the academic trend in the curriculum, a trend that was largely due to the necessity of preparing pupils for external examinations. There is some evidence to suggest too that when domestic courses were introduced in the new girls' schools, they were aimed at the 'less able' middle class schoolgirl who could not aspire to academic achievement. Miss Gilliland,[49] for example, was horrified when a female colleague in another girls' school told her that some of her pupils who were 'backward' in academic work learnt cookery.

Over the period 1870–1944, then, middle class girls might study some domestic subjects, especially needlework, in the course of acquiring an education. This applies to home based education, the schooling offered in a small, private, familial institution, and the schooling offered in one of the 'new' high schools.[50] However, even when this was so, domestic subjects were largely devalued, especially in the more academic forms of schooling such as the girls' high schools. The economic and social advantages of middle class girls in relation to working class girls, especially in regard to level of income, life style, accent, dress, manners and employment expectations meant, of course, that the acquisition of domestic skills could never have the same meaning for them as they might for their working class sisters. By the outbreak of the Second World War, domestic subjects in schools were firmly linked with working class girls in elementary schools, and such girls were usually classified as the 'less able'.

### 'Secondary education for all'

In the 1920s and 1930s the two systems of elmentary state education (largely attended by working class children) and secondary fee-paying education (largely attended by middle class children) continued side by side. Pressure grew for an end to such a class-ridden and divided education system. As one critic said in 1927:

> A elementary school education has always meant, and still means, a cheap education. An elementary school text-book means a cheap book, which is carefully adapted in language and content to a wholly derogatory estimate of the needs and powers of the children of a certain sector of society, who are supposed not to require or to be capable of the same kind of education as the children of parents who have more money.[51]

The educational slogan of the 1930s, 'secondary education for all' became a possibility with the passing of the 1944 Education Act which introduced three progressive stages of primary, secondary and further education. However, the main thrust for reform was the inequalities in educational opportunities between the social classes, not between boys and girls. The way that girls could be disadvantaged in education, in comparison with boys, was not an important debating issue in educational circles. In particular, the inequalities and disadvantages that working class schoolgirls might experience in comparison with their brothers were never seriously questioned.

## II 1944 to the 1980s

Amongst other things, the 1944 Education Act specified that secondary education was to offer a variety of instruction and training as may be desirable in view of the different ages, abilities and aptitudes of the pupils. In practice, the provision of a state system of non fee-paying secondary education based on different abilities and aptitudes meant a tripartite system of schooling that reflected the language of the Norwood Committee Report of 1943. The latter had asserted that English education had in practice recognized 'the pupil who is interested in learning for its own sake ... the pupil whose interests and abilities lie markedly in the field of applied science or applied art' and the pupil who deals 'more easily with concrete things than with ideas'.[52] The three kinds of secondary school that largely corresponded to these three types of mind were the grammar school, the technical high and the secondary modern. Pupils were selected for the grammar or technical school in terms of performance in attainment and intelligence tests in English and arithmetic. Though there were wide regional variations in the proportion of children attending any one type of school, one estimate in 1956 suggested that 20–25 per cent of the age group of 11 year olds were selected for the grammar school, and less than 10 per cent for the technical school, while the remaining two-thirds attended the secondary modern.[53] Research in the 1950s and 1960s suggested too that selection at 11+ favoured the middle class child and that the 'unselected' majority in the secondary moderns were mainly of working class backgrounds.

At the time the tripartite system was being established and consolidated, many changes were taking place in the wider society and in the economic and social position of women. For example, the post war period saw the rise of the welfare state with a host of 'free' social services that covered not only secondary education but also health and family welfare. Unmarried and married women had entered what were previously 'men's jobs' during the war, and after the war the number of married women combining the two roles of paid worker and housewife/ mother rose. Some occupations that had previously been the preserve of men admitted women (the Diplomatic Service did so in 1946, though women could still be sacked on marriage). Other occupations intro- duced the principle of equal pay for men and women, for example equal pay for schoolteachers was accepted in 1953. More reliable and efficient forms of contraception led to a reduction in family size and gave more women the right to choose whether they became mothers or not. While such changes implied that the old link between women, domesticity, wifehood and motherhood might be loosening, other forces served to reinforce and strengthen the link. Riley,[54] for example, warns us that we cannot assume that the employment of married and unmarried women in the Second World War led to any great changes in suppositions about 'women's place'; social policy developments at the end of the war, she claims, still saw the family as *the* social unit, and women were seen socially and economically as mothers within and with reference to the family. The emphasis upon motherhood and child care for women continued into the 1950s and 1960s and was fuelled by the influential writings of such people as John Bowlby. Bowlby[55] stressed that 'mother-love in infancy and childhood is as important for mental health as are vitamins and proteins for physical health'. For a mother to engage in full time paid employment outside the home was seen as damaging to a child, shameful and unnecessary — especially in the welfare society that had emerged after the upheavals of war. One writer in the *Picture*

*Post* in 1956 posed a question that many people were probably asking: 'Is it *really* necessary in this Welfare State for a woman to go out to work, or do they do it for the ice cream and the TV?'[56] To sum up, during the 1950s and 1960s a woman's primary role was seen as that of wife and mother. Any other commitments, such as paid employment, were to be fitted into family life so that the needs of a husband and children were not neglected.[57]

These ideas about domesticity, wifehood and motherhood for women were reflected in the various education reports of the 1940s, 1950s and 1960s. Wolpe, for example, suggests that the Norwood Report (1943), the Crowther Report (1959) and the Newsom Report (1963) all make assumptions about the different future roles of boys and girls, and the preparation that secondary schools offer for this. Very broadly, she suggests that these reports conceptualize secondary schooling for boys in terms of a future life in paid employment, as breadwinners with an economically dependent wife and children. For girls, on the other hand, though some consideration is given to future occupational roles, the overriding concern is with their future married state, as wives and mothers.[58] The emphasis upon domesticity for girls within such 'official' government statements was applied particularly to girls in the secondary modern. And it was especially through the teaching of domestic subjects that such ideas were to be given concrete expression.

### Domestic subjects and the secondary modern schoolgirl

Though many of the official statements about the aims of a secondary modern schooling were simply 'vague generalities',[59] it was assumed that such schools would offer a general education with a 'practical', though not vocational bias[60] that was distinctly different from the 'academic' bias of the grammar school. It was usually assumed too that the 'unselected' secondary modern schoolgirl was 'less able', of 'working class origin' and more capable of dealing with 'practical' subjects such as needlework and domestic science than her grammar school counterpart. Of course not *all* secondary modern schoolgirls were of working class origin — indeed Ford[61] suggests that increasing numbers of middle class children entered the secondary modern from 1957 when the first wave of the postwar baby 'bulge' arrived. Neither can it be assumed that *all* secondary moderns developed a practical bias in the curriculum. Reynolds and Sullivan[62], for example, point out that during the 1960s many changes occurred in the secondary moderns, including the entry of increasing numbers of pupils for the external examination system that had previously been tied to the grammar school — the GCE. However, overall it would appear that the content of, and pedagogic approach to, curricula within the grammar school and the secondary modern remained distinctly different, and that the status differentials between the two forms of schooling were maintained.

As Dalloway[63] has observed, every secondary modern schoolgirl had to study domestic science: it could occupy a half or even a whole day of the timetable for each week. Some secondary moderns had well equipped rooms for the study of domestic subjects. Angela Singer, for example, offers the following description of the co-educational secondary modern she attended in the early 1960s: 'Whole blocks were dedicated to domestic science filled with luxuries never contemplated at home like spin dryers... There was a sewing-room with electric machines and we would spend entire afternoons in gleaming kitchens making apple crumble'.[64]

The facilities offered at this secondary modern school would have been approved by the Newsom Report. The terms of the Newsom Committee were to consider the education between the ages of 13 and 16 of pupils of average or less than average ability who are or will be following full-time courses either at schools or in establishments of further education. The Report notes that girls of average and below average ability will enter jobs in offices, in shops, in catering, and in the clothing and other manufacturing trades[65] — all jobs typically entered by the female secondary modern school leaver. However, the Report also states:

> For all girls, too, there is a group of interests relating to what many, perhaps most of them, would regard as their most important vocational concern, marriage. It is true that at the age of fourteen and fifteen, this may appear chiefly as preoccupation with personal appearance and boy friends, but many girls are ready to respond to work relating to the wider aspects of homemaking and family life and the care and upbringing of children.[66]

The emphasis that is given to the vocational concern of 'marriage' is particularly evident in the sections in the Report on practical subjects such as housecraft and needlework. And it is noted that for the 'less able girls' — the lower streams of the secondary moderns, the conditions for housecraft should be as realistic as possible, for example, running a house or a flat for an extended period of time such as a week.[67]

To what extent the teaching of domestic subjects in the secondary modern ever approximated the conditions of the 'real' housewife is debatable since the issue of girls' education in the tripartite system has been inadequately researched. One analysis of information collected from over 3400 secondary moderns does suggest that at least some schools made an attempt to relate domestic science teaching to 'real life situations'.[68] Thus Chapman suggests that a number of schools asked the girls to undertake individual assignments on topics such as 'illness', 'visitors', 'handling other children', 'social life' and 'men in the house'. The content of the questions that the girls were asked to explore, when pursuing any one topic, reveals only too well the continuity between the schooling of working class girls in domestic subjects earlier in the century with what was taking place in some secondary moderns in the late 1950s. Thus an assignment on 'handling other children', given to the schoolgirl at a school in western England, asked her to imagine that:

> your own sister and brother want to go to the Zoo on Saturday and mother says you can take them. Find out the best way to go on the bus. Wash your sister's dress and socks and your brother's shirt. Cut sandwiches to take, and, as it is not too long a journey, make some trifles or jellies or blancmanges, set in cartons or moulds suitable to carry. Pack suitably. Do not forget to take spoons.[69]

The topic on 'men in the house' included the following instructions for girls in a secondary modern school in the north-east of England:

> You have to make a meal for your two brothers who are coming in from school. Darn some socks for them, make some scones for tea, or prepare a meal suitable for a man to carry out to work. Wash and iron two aprons, set a tea tray and make some tea. Make some small buns to have with tea.[70]

As we can see in these two examples, secondary modern schoolgirls in the late 1950s were being taught in domestic subjects to care for, and look after, other people, such as brothers and sisters, and to engage in domestic skills such as washing, cooking and darning. In other words, the domestic science curriculum would appear to be attempting to socialize its female pupils into a maternal role that involved serving others. In particular, the fact that 'men in the house' could constitute a separate topic within a domestic science course reveals how girls might be taught to give priority to the needs of males within the family household.

Needlework was the other main domestic subject that was taught in secondary moderns — and the amount of time spent on this subject could vary from one and half hours to five hours per week.[71] Just as skill with a sewing needle was regarded as a symbol of femininity and thrift for working class girls in elementary schools at the turn of the century, so the legacy of the past lingered into the secondary moderns of the 1950s:

> there is no uncertainty about the value of needlework ... most girls have in mind the idea of ultimately having a house to run and a family to bring up ... A girl who is a competent needlewoman is one who can not only make new clothes but who can also repair, renovate and make children's clothes from adults', make her curtains, and keep household linen in good order. In this way she plays her part in raising the standard of living and setting an example to her children for her home is attractive and well and economically run.[72]

The lofty ideals that were frequently reiterated to support the inclusion of domestic subjects in the secondary modern may not always have been realized. We do find, throughout the literature, isolated complaints about the lack of relevance of domestic subjects for the way the 'real' life outside school, whether in paid employment or in the home, was conducted. Singer,[73] for example, remembers that she could not see how learning about bias binding in needlework or baking powder in cookery would help her earn a living. And Ford[74] suggests that generally secondary moderns may not have prepared girls for the sorts of paid jobs they would enter. Sometimes too, domestic science teachers complained that what was taught in the classroom was different from what occurred in the home:

> All too often during hygiene lessons children wash their hands — only to sit down and continue writing in their books ... So often pupils are made to clean an already gleaming bath. Frequently lessons on the care of teeth are spoilt by the fact that girls clean their teeth, not in the cloakroom or bathroom, but in the domestic science kitchen. Most children start housecraft at the age of twelve nowadays, and time is wasted on cutting bread and making sandwiches. They probably used sliced bread at home, and most of them have done a good deal of baking for their mothers already, so that making sandwiches and a cup of cocoa holds little interest for them.[75]

Whether realistic or not, domestic subjects were an integral part of the experience of schooling for the secondary modern girl. In particular, they embodied the 'practical' approach that favoured the less able girl who could deal 'more easily with concrete things than with ideas'.

## Domestic subjects and the grammar school girl

Within the 'academic' ethos of the grammar school, practical subjects, such as domestic subjects, had a low status. Indeed, a study undertaken into the teaching of domestic science in secondary schools commented that it was 'unfortunate' that a subject which was of importance to all girls was so often excluded from career-based courses in girls' grammar schools.[76] There is some evidence to suggest too that domestic subjects in the grammar school were identified with the less able grammar school girl.

As early as 1948, Sir John Newsom commented on what he considered the common practice in many girls' grammar schools — that while the intellectually able pupils would study a second foreign language, the 'less able' were allowed to take domestic science.[77] Since Sir John believed that all grammar school girls, irrespective of level of ability, should study domestic subjects, he reminded the readers of his book of Samuel Johnson's dictum that 'a man is better pleased when he has a good dinner upon his table than when his wife talks Greek'! However, his recommendation that domestic subjects should be thoroughly taught to the more able as well as less able grammar school girl was not heeded. The Crowther Report (1959), for example, which provided a mass of information on the education of boys and girls between the ages of 15 and 18 noted that with the 'intellectually abler girls', there was little scope in school hours for giving them any education specifically related 'to their special interest as women'.[78] Schools should, on the other hand, make more adjustments for the less able girls who were likely to marry at an earlier age than in the past:

> The prospect of courtship and marriage should rightly influence the education of the [less able] adolescent girl. Though the general objectives of secondary education remain unchanged, her direct interest in dress, personal appearance and in problems of human relations should be given a central place in her education'.[79]

To what extent grammar schools introduced courses on such themes as how to dress, good grooming and so on for less able girls is debatable. But subjects such as domestic science and needlework were part of the grammar school curriculum. And for Irene Payne[80], who attended a single sex girls' grammar in the 1960s, such subjects were, she claims, for those girls not considered to be very clever.

The 1960s saw the growth and expansion of a comprehensive system of secondary schooling that was largely intended, at least in the rhetoric, to eradicate social class inequalities rather than inequalities between boys and girls. The themes of social democratic reformism in education in the 1960s — the themes of expansion, expectation and equality — never questioned the inequalities between the sexes but remained firmly 'masculine'.[81] The 1970s witnessed a near universal system of comprehensive schooling within the state maintained secondary sector but it was a system that retained, rather than challenged, the primacy of the 'academic' subjects associated with the old grammar schools. Thus a clear hierarchy of school subjects emerged within the comprehensive schools. Academic subjects were considered, as in the past, suitable for able students whilst other subjects were not: in addition, they not only enjoyed a disproportionate share of resource allocation but also extended their dominance since 'academic' rules were applied to the mainstream comprehensive school curriculum.[82] Within such a hierarchy of school knowledge, practical curricula such as domestic subjects are accorded a low status. And domestic subjects in comprehensive schools in the 1970s and today are still mainly studied by girls, and probably especially by less able girls.

Certain developments in the 1970s, however, indicated that the strong link between domestic subjects and female pupils might at least be attacked, if not broken. Section 22 of the Sex Discrimination Act of 1975, for example, specified that access to benefits, facilities and services provided by an educational establishment must be provided equally for girls and boys. Whether all subjects are offered to girls and boys on an equal basis, even within the large, coeducational comprehensive schools that organize a wider range of curricular choices than in the separate schools in the old tripartite system, is doubtful. As Deem[83] has pointed out, the expansion of curriculum content that accompanied the growth of the comprehensive system meant, in many schools, an expansion of sex-stereotyped subjects such as typing, shorthand or child-care for girls, and quite different subjects for boys. Let us explore this issue of domestic subjects such as child-care within the comprehensive school in a little more detail.

*Domestic subjects within the comprehensive school*

The DES report on curricular differences between boys and girls in primary, middle and secondary schools, and in further education, found that in secondary schools, various curricular options often segregated the sexes and reinforced the link between girls and domestic subjects. Home economics, for example, is still seen predominantly as a girl's subject, though a number of boys would be prepared to join a cookery class if given the opportunity to do so.[84] The Report highlights the fact that certain restrictions are placed on the supposedly free choice of options open to pupils so that certain 'pre-emptive patterns' emerge.[85] And such a pattern was found too in a study of a coeducational comprehensive school undertaken some five years later, during 1980–81. Thus Grafton *et al* found that not only did the grouping of certain options make it less likely that boys and girls would make 'untypical' choices (for example, it was impossible to study both the motor mechanics and the family and child options during a particular year), but also that more subtle influences via teacher advice might push pupils in the expected direction for their sex:

> Certain subjects, for example, woodwork, metalwork, cookery, technical drawing and family and child, were described as open to both sexes. However, tutors' guidelines requested 'prior discussion' in the case of boys who wanted to take the family and child option. Girls who wanted to take woodwork or metalwork had to 'show a sincere desire' to do so. Needlework was described in terms of its being taken by girls only.[86]

The structuring of optional choices and the pressures that may be exercised by teachers are not, of course, the only influences that may push girls and boys towards stereotyped choices of options in a comprehensive school. Pressures exercised by other pupils, and by parents about expectations for the future may be just or even more important than the factors we have already mentioned. In addition, the messages contained in textbooks may influence 'choice' in rather subtle ways. A textbook that might be used in GCE O and A-level in the 1960s and 1970s, for example, links the home and the quality of family life with the housewife and not the husband and father: 'It is not only the home itself, but its smooth running and the cultivation of good family relationships, which are of vital importance, and as these chiefly devolve upon the housewife, her role is significant and the well-being of her family is very largely in her hands'.[87] Indeed, Turnbull[88] suggests that the representation of gender roles in home economics texts in use in the 1970s show sharply differentiated tasks for women and men: women clean, cook and undertake the more routine and messy aspects of child-rearing, while men do the more occasional tasks like car washing, gardening, repairing and playing with children. This pattern persists, she continues, whether or not women have paid employment since such work is always considered peripheral to home-making.

It is probably the case that domestic subjects in the comprehensive school, and especially those that come under the broad umbrella of parentcraft, are considered particularly suitable for, and studied by, the less able girls (often assumed to be working class). Around the early 1970s, the notion of a 'cycle of deprivation' gained some currency within political circles. In 1972, Sir Keith Joseph, the then Secretary of State for Social Services, raised the issue of whether a cycle of deprivation underlay some of society's more persistent social problems, and whether a policy of preparation for parenthood might help to break it. Sir Keith initiated a number of discussions on the issue with various interested persons, and in 1974 the DHSS issued two booklets — *Preparation for Parenthood* and *Dimensions of Parenthood*.[89] Such ideas helped, though were not solely responsible for, the expansion of parenthood-related courses in comprehensive schools in the 1970s.[90] In particular, the DES report on curricular differences between boys and girls found that the fourth and fifth year options that were usually part of the programme for the 'less able pupils' involved the girls in subjects that were related to the home and to parenthood:

> The range of courses offered to boys includes agriculture, accounts, building, catering, electronics, engineering design, fashion design or surveying. Accounts, catering, electronics and fashion design are offered to girls. Integrated courses labelled, for instance, citizenship, humanities, design for living, environmental studies, urban studies or social education are taken by more girls than boys. Child care, child development, mother care and home making are usually regarded as the province of girls.[91]

Less able pupils are more likely to be entered for the lower status CSE examination than the GCE (though not all less able children take the CSE). If we take CSE and GCE A-level results as crude indicators of less able and able pupils we do find some evidence to support the claim that domestic subjects are not only more popular with female than male pupils but also less likely to be studied at A-level. In the summer of 1979, for example, only 11 boys but 3440 girls passed domestic subjects at A-level while 11,500 boys and 145,720 girls gained passes in these subjects at grade 5 or better in the CSE.[92] Though it is still mainly girls who enter for domestic subjects at A-level and especially at CSE level, some changes in the sex distribution of domestic subjects has occurred over the ten year period 1969–1979. The number of boys and girls gaining grade 5 or better in domestic subjects in the CSE in 1969, for example, was 803 and 47,377 respectively. If we compare these figures with the CSE 1979 figures just quoted, we see that over the period

1969–1979, the percentage increases for pupils achieving grade 5 or better in the CSE in domestic subjects was 114.8 for boys and 38.6 for girls.[93] Despite these changes, however, the bulk of the evidence does suggest that domestic subjects today, as in the past, are overwhelmingly identified with girls, and especially less able girls.

### Conclusion

Throughout this chapter then, we have seen that the history of domestic subjects in English schools over the last 100 years or so has been tied to the schooling of girls, not boys, and, in particular, the schooling of working class and less able girls. We have also seen that the importance of domestic subjects for the female sex is directly related to ideas about the role of women in society, and, in particular, the duties associated with a family life of domesticity, wifehood and motherhood.

Probably more than any other part of the school curriculum, domestic subjects have embodied stereotyped notions about women and femininity that have served not only to depress the educational ambitions of millions of schoolgirls but also to define such subjects as essentially 'feminine' subjects rather than 'neutral' or 'masculine' knowledge areas. Now it seems to me that what is needed in the 1980s is a programme of action in schools that will rid domestic subjects (now often called home economics) of their stereotyped notions about women and men, will develop non-sexist teaching materials and teaching methods and broaden the content of the subjects beyond the 'efficient and capable housewife-well cared for and happy husband and children-happy home-healthy society' syndrome. As the EOC has argued:

> Education in home economics provides young people with those 'life skills' which enable them to leave school equipped with the personal confidence and independence to participate fully in, and exert control over, their environment. Changes in society — more women in paid employment outside the home; more unemployment; more single person households and one parent families — all indicate that many of the assumptions which are made concerning the traditional division of labour between men and women in the household are no longer realistic. Boys and girls, therefore, should have equal access to home economics education within the school curriculum.[94]

Perhaps a start might be made by making a non-sexist domestic subjects/home economics curriculum compulsory for all pupils. Both girls and boys have much to learn from such an experience.

## Notes

1 See, for example, ARNOT (1981), BYRNE (1978), DEEM (1978), DEEM (Ed.) (1980), DELAMONT (1980), KELLY (Ed.) (1981), MACDONALD (1981), SPENDER and SARAH (Eds.) (1980), SPENDER (1982), WOLPE (1974) and WOLPE (1977).
2 WYNN, B. (1974), p. 8.
3 It is impossible within the confines of this chapter to give detailed references to these points. But see DYHOUSE (1981), PURVIS (1981a) and PURVIS (1981b).
4 See, for example, the discussion offered by ANDERSON (1971) pp. 68–69 in regard to the working class family in nineteenth century Lancashire.
5 For an account of the schooling of working class girls in England from 1800–1870 see PURVIS (1981c), and for accounts of domestic subjects see GORDON and LAWTON (1978) pp. 106–115, SILLITOE (1933) and YOXALL (1913, 1965 repr.).
6 GRANT, C. (1931) p. 47.
7 DYHOUSE, C, (1981) p. 89.
8 LAWSON, J. and SILVER, M. (1973) p. 314.
9 SILLITOE, H. (1933) p. 106.
10 *Domestic Economy*, 1880, *Domestic Economy Readers* 1896.
11 SILLITOE, H. (1933) p. 113.
12 BLACK (n.d.) p. 9.
13 DAVIES, H. (1892) p. 5.
14 LEIGH, C.A. (1887) p. 122.
15 HEADDON, Miss (1887) p. 130–31.
16 Quoted in WYNN, B. (1974) pp. 12–13.
17 See DAVIN A. (1979), RICE, E. (n.d.)
18 RANKIN, M. (1900) p. 9.
19 DYHOUSE, C. (1981) p. 99.
20 Quoted in DAVIN, A. (1978) p. 10.
21 FOAKES, G. (1976) p. 47.
22 SCANNELL,, D. (1974) pp. 137–8.
23 BOARD OF EDUCATION (1927) p. 29.
24 *Ibid* p. 30.
25 GRAVES, J. (1943) p. 75.
26 BANKS, O. (1955) p. 191.
27 PURVIS, J. (1981a) p. 336.
28 BOARD OF EDUCATION (1927) p. 113.
29 BANKS, O. (1955) pp. 103–104.
30 BOARD OF EDUCATION (1939) p. 285.
31 SILLITOE, H. (1933) p. 109.
32 BOARD OF EDUCATION (1939) p. 286.

33  *Ibid* p. 286.
34  *Ibid* p. 285.
35  ASSOCIATION FOR EDUCATION IN CITIZENSHIP (1939) p. 114.
36  MARKS, P. (1976) p. 193.
37  See BRYANT, M. (1979) and PURVIS, J. (1982).
38  BURSTYN, J. (1980) p. 38.
39  DIGBY, A. (1982) p. 3.
40  YOXALL, A. (1965) p. 47.
41  BUSS, F. (1867–8) p. 254.
42  HUGHES, M. (1946, 1979 repr.) pp. 44–45.
43  *Ibid* p. 46.
44  BANKS, O. (1955) p. 194.
45  Quoted in DIGBY, A. (1982) p. 6.
46  BURSTALL, S. (1933) p. 149.
47  DYHOUSE, C. (1981) p. 164.
48  BOARD OF EDUCATION (1923) p. 58.
49  GILLILAND, M. (1911) p. 154.
50  It is difficult to estimate the proportions of middle class girls attending these various forms of education up to 1944. Both DYHOUSE (1981) and DIGBY (1982) point out that up to 1914, the 'new' high schools were attended by a minority of the total number of middle class girls. However, as the cost of a home education rose, it is highly probable that there was a substantial increase in the number of middle class girls entering fee paying secondary schools from 1914–1944.
51  Quoted in TAWNEY, R. (1913, 1964 Edition) p. 142.
52  Quoted in LAWSON and SILVER (1973) p. 422.
53  FLOUD, J. and HALSEY, A.H. (1956) p. 56.
54  RILEY, D. (1981) p. 101.
55  BOWLBY, J. (1955) p. 182.
56  Quoted in RILEY, D. (1981) p. 78.
57  BIRMINGHAM FEMINIST HISTORY GROUP, (1979) p. 50.
58  WOLPE, A. (1974) p. 157.
59  TAYLOR, W. (1967) p. 18.
60  BANKS (1955) pp. 214–215, RUBINSTEIN, D. and SIMON, B. (1969) p. 42.
61  FORD, J. (1969) p. 6.
62  REYNOLDS, D. and SULLIVAN, M. (1981) p. 24.
63  DALLOWAY, M. (1965) p. 86.
64  SINGER, A. (1982) p. 11.
65  CACE (1963) p. 37.
66  *Ibid* p. 37.
67  *Ibid* p. 135.
68  CHAPMAN, J. (1959) p. 130.
69  *Ibid* p. 131.
70  *Ibid* p. 152.
71  CHAPMAN, J. (1959) p. 143.
72  *Ibid* p. 135.
73  SINGER, A. (1974) p. 11.
74  FORD, J. (1969) p. 55.
75  ANONYMOUS (1963) p. 88.

76 ASSOCIATION OF TEACHERS IN DOMESTIC SCIENCE (1969) p. 35.
77 NEWSOM, J. (1948) p. 82.
78 CACE (1959) p. 33.
79 *Ibid* p. 34.
80 PAYNE, I. (1980) p. 18.
81 CCCS (1981) p. 122
82 See GOODSON (1984 forthcoming) or BALL (1981) p. 18.
83 DEEM, R. (1981) p. 137.
84 DES (1975) p. 12.
85 *Ibid* p. 7.
86 GRAFTON, T. *et al* (1981) p. 12.
87 DAVIDSON, P. (1978) p. 168.
88 TURNBULL, A. (1980) p. 73.
89 WHITEFIELD, R. (1980) p. 71.
90 GRAFTON, T. *et al* (1981) or DAVID (1983).
91 DES (1975) p. 14.
92 HMSO (1981) pp. 56–58.
93 *Ibid* p. 58.
94 EOC (1983) pp. 4–5.

### References/Bibliography

ANDERSON, M. (1971) *Family Structure in Nineteenth Century Lancashire*, London, Cambridge University Press.
ANONYMOUS (a domestic science teacher) (1963) 'From schoolgirl to house-wife' *Housecraft*, pp. 87–88 March.
ARNOT, M. (1981) 'Culture and political economy: dual perspectives in the sociology of women's education' *Educational Analysis* 3, 1 pp. 97–116.
ASSOCIATION FOR EDUCATION IN CITIZENSHIP (1939) *Education for Citizenship in Elementary Schools*, London, Oxford University Press.
ASSOCIATION OF TEACHERS OF DOMESTIC SCIENCE (1969) *A Survey of the Teaching of Domestic Science*, St. Albans, Campfield Press.
BALL, S.J. (1981) *Beachside Comprehensive*, Cambridge, Cambridge University Press.
BALL, S.J. (1984) *Comprehensive Schooling. A Reader*, Lewes, Famler Press.
BANKS, O. (1955) *Parity and Prestige in English Secondary Education*, London, Routledge and Kegan Paul.
BIRMINGHAM FEMINIST HISTORY GROUP (1979) 'Feminism as femininity in the nineteenth-fifties?' *Feminist Review*, 3.
BLACK, MRS (n.d.) *Household Cookery and Laundry Work*, London, William Collins.
BOARD OF EDUCATION (1923) *Report of the Consultative Committee on Differentiation of the Curriculum for Boys and Girls Respectively in Secondary Schools*, London, HMSO.
BOARD OF EDUCATION (1927) *The Education of the Adolescent, Report of the Consultative Committee*, London, HMSO.
BOARD OF EDUCATION (1939) *Report of the Consultative Committee on*

*Secondary Education with Special Reference to Grammar Schools and Technical High Schools*, London, HMSO.

BOWLBY, J. (1955) *Child Care and the Growth of Love*, Harmondsworth, Penguin Books, first published 1953.

BRYANT, M. (1979) *The Unexpected Revolution*: *A Study in the History of the Education of Women and Girls in the Nineteenth Century*, London, The University of London Institute of Education.

BYRNE, E. (1978) *Women and Education*, London, Tavistock.

BURSTYN, J.N. (1980) *Victorian Education and the Ideal of Womanhood*, London, Tavistock.

BUSS, FRANCES MARY, (1867–8) Evidence to the Schools Inquiry Commission *Schools Inquiry*, vol. V, part II, Parliamentary Papers vol. XXVIII, part IV. London.

CENTRAL ADVISORY COUNCIL FOR EDUCATION (CACE) (1959) *15 to 18*, London, HMSO (The Crowther Report).

CENTRAL ADVISORY COUNCIL FOR EDUCATION (CACE) (1963) *Half Our Future*, London, HMSO (The Newsom Report).

CENTRE FOR CONTEMPORARY CULTURAL STUDIES (CCCS) (1981) *Unpopular Education*, London, Hutchinson.

CHAPMAN, J.V. (1959) *Your Secondary Modern Schools*, London, The College of Preceptors.

DALLOWAY, M. (1965) 'Housecraft in schools today' *Housecraft*, March, pp. 86–7.

DAVID, M.E. (1980) *The State, the Family and Education*, London, Routledge and Kegan Paul.

DAVID, M.E. (1983) 'Sex, education and social policy: a new moral economy?' in WALKER, S. and BARTON, L. (Eds.) *Gender, Class and Education*, Lewes, Falmer Press.

DAVIDSON, P. (1978) *Home Management*, London, Batsford, first published 1973.

DAVIES, H. (1892) *A Handbook of Plain Cookery*, London, McCorquodale and Co.

DAVIN, A. (1978) 'Imperialism and motherhood' *History Workshop* 5, pp. 9–65 Spring.

DAVIN, A. (1979) '"Mind that you do as you are told": reading books for Board School girls' *Feminist Review* 3, pp. 89–98.

DEEM, R. (1978) *Women and Schooling*, London, Routledge and Kegan Paul.

DEEM, R. (Ed.) (1980) *Schooling for Women's Work*, London, Routledge and Kegan Paul.

DEEM, R. (1981) 'State policy and ideology in the education of women, 1944–1980' *British Journal of Sociology of Education* 2 (2) pp. 131–143.

DELAMONT, S. (1980) *Sex Roles and the School*, London, Methuen

DEPARTMENT OF EDUCATION AND SCIENCE (DES) (1975) *Curricular Differences for Boys and Girls*, London, HMSO.

DIGBY, A. (1982) 'New schools for the middle class girl' in SEARBY, P. (Ed.) *Educating the Victorian Middle Class*, Leicester, The History of Education Society.

*Domestic Economy Adapted to the Çode of 1880*, (1880), London and Edinburgh, W. & R. Chambers (no author given though initials I.S.B. to preface).

*Domestic Economy Readers Standards VI and VII* (1896), London, Longman (no author given).

DYHOUSE, C. (1981) *Girls Growing Up in Late Victorian and Edwardian England*, London, Routledge and Kegan Paul.

EQUAL OPPORTUNITIES COMMISSION (EOC) (1983) *Equal Opportunities in Home Economics*, Manchester, EOC.

FLOUD, J. and HALSEY, A.H. (1956) 'English secondary schools and the supply of labour' reprinted in HALSEY, A.H., FLOUD, J. and ANDERSON, C.A. (Eds.) (1961) *Education, Economy, and Society*, New York, The Free Press. The page number refers to the 1961 publication.

FOAKES, G. (1976) *My Part of the River*, London, Futura.

FORD, J. (1969) *Social Class and the Comprehensive School*, London, Routledge and Kegan Paul.

GILLILAND, M. (1911) 'Home arts' in BURSTALL, S.A. and DOUGLAS, M.A. (Eds.), *Public Schools for Girls: A Series of Papers on their History, Aims and Schemes of Study*, London, Association of Headmistresses.

GOODSON, I. (1984 forthcoming) 'Defining a subject for the comprehensive school: a case study' in BALL, S. (Ed.)

GORDON, P. and LAWTON, D. (1978) *Curriculum Change in the Nineteenth and Twentieth Centuries*, London, Hodder and Stoughton.

GRAFTON, T., MILLER, H., SMITH, L., VEGODA, M., and WHITEFIELD, R. (1981) 'Gender and curriculum choice: a case study' paper presented to the Sociology of Curriculum Practice Conference, St Hilda's College, Oxford, 21–23 September.

GRANT, C.E. (1931) *Farthing Bundles*, London, C. Grant.

GRAVES, J. (1943) *Policy and Progress in Secondary Education 1902–1942*, London, Nelson and Sons.

HEADDON, MISS (1887) 'Industrial training for girls' in BRABAZON, LORD, (Ed.) *Some National and Board School Reforms*, London, Longmans.

HMSO (1981) *Statistics of Education 1979 Vol. 2 School Leavers CSE and GCE: England*, London

HUGHES, M.V. (1979) *A London Girl of the 1880s*, Oxford, Oxford University Press, first published in 1946.

KELLY, A. (Ed.) (1981) *The Missing Half: Girls and Science Education*, Manchester, Manchester University Press.

LEIGH, C.A. (1887) 'For lack of knowledge' in BRABAZON, LORD (Ed.) *Some National and Board School Reforms*, London, Longmans.

LAWSON, J. and SILVER, H. (1973) *A Social History of Education in England*, London, Methuen.

MACDONALD, M. (1981) *Class, Gender and Education*, Units 10/11 of OU Course E353, Milton Keynes, The Open University Press.

NEWSOM, J. (1948) *The Education of Girls*, London, Faber and Faber.

PAYNE, I. (1980) 'A working class girl in a grammar school' in SPENDER, D. and SARAH, E. (Eds.) *Learning to Lose*, London, The Women's Press.

PERCIVAL, A.C. (1939) *The English Miss To-Day and Yesterday*, London, Harrap and Co.

PURVIS, J. (1981a) 'Women and teaching in the nineteenth century' in DALE, R., ESLAND, G., FERGUSSON, R., and MACDONALD, M. (Eds.) *Education and the State Vol. 2. Politics, Patriarchy and Practice*, Lewes, Falmer Press in association with the Open University Press.

PURVIS, J. (1981b) 'Towards a history of women's education in nineteenth century Britain: a sociological analysis', *Westminster Studies in Education*, 4 pp. 45–79.

PURVIS, J. (1981c) 'The double burden of class and gender in the schooling of working class girls in nineteenth century England, 1800–1870' in BARTON, L., and WALKER, S. (Eds.) *Schools, Teachers and Teaching*, Lewes, Falmer Press.

PURVIS, J. (1982) 'Review article: the education of girls and women in the nineteenth century,' *Research in Education* 28, November.

RANKIN, M.C. (c. 1900) *The Art and Practice of Laundry Work*, London, Blackie and Son.

REYNOLDS, D. and SULLIVAN M. (1981) 'The comprehensive experience' in BARTON, L. and WALKER, S. (Eds.) *Schools, Teachers and Teaching*, Lewes, Falmer Press.

RICE E. (n.d.) *Domestic Economy*, London, Blackie and Son.

RILEY, D. (1981) 'The Free Mothers: pronatalism and working mothers in industry at the end of the last war in Britain' *History Workshop* 11 pp. 59–118, Spring.

RUBINSTEIN, D. and SIMON B. (1969) *The Evolution of the Comprehensive School 1926–1966*, London, Routledge and Kegan Paul.

SCANNELL, D. (1974) *Mother Knew Best*, London, Macmillan.

SILLITOE, H. (1933) *A History of the Teaching of Domestic Subjects*, London, Methuen.

SINGER, A. (1982) 'The boys in our class smelled of plimsolls' *The Guardian*, 20 May.

SPENDER D. (1982) *Invisible Women: The Schooling Scandal*, London, Writers and Readers Co-operative Society Ltd.

SPENDER D. and SARAH E. (Eds.) (1980) *Learning to Lose*, London, The Women's Press.

TAWNEY, R.H. (1964) *Equality* (with a new introduction by RICHARD M. TITMUSS) London, Unwin Books, first published in 1931.

TAYLOR, W. (1963) *The Secondary Modern School*, London, Faber.

TURNBULL, A. (1980) 'Home economics — training for womanhood?' in LOVE, C., SMITH, D. and TURNBULL, A. (Eds.) *Women in the Making*, South Bank Sociology Occasional Paper 2, London, Social Sciences Department, Polytechnic of the South Bank.

WHITEFIELD, R. (1980) *Education for Family Life*, London, Hodder and Stoughton

WOLPE, A.M. (1974) 'The official ideology of education for girls' in FLUDE, M. and AHIER, J. (Eds.) *Educability, Schools and Ideology*, London, Croom Helm.

WOLPE, A.M. (1977) *Some Processes in Sexist Education*, London, Women's Research and Resources Centre.

WYNN, B. (1974) *Aspects of the Teaching of Domestic Subjects*, dissertation submitted as part of the requirement for MA in the Sociology of Education, London, Institute of Education.

YOXALL, A. (1965) *A History of the Teaching of Domestic Economy*, Bath, Cedric Chivers Ltd., first published 1913.

# Agreed Syllabuses of Religious Education Since 1944

*Adrian Bell*

Religious education (RE) became a compulsory part of each pupil's curriculum with the 1944 Education Act which charged local authorities with the responsibility of devising an 'agreed syllabus' (or with adopting the syllabus of another authority). Under the terms of the Act, the syllabus was to be constructed through a specially convened conference, comprising representatives of: Church of England[1]; other denominations determined by the LEA; the LEA; and teacher associations. All four committees had to agree the proposed syllabus. This, and the repetition of the 1870 Cowper-Temple clause which excluded any 'religious catechism or religious formulary which is distinctive of any particular denomination' were the underpinning notions of agreement in the agreed syllabus machinery produced by the 1944 Act.

The numerous syllabuses which have been produced since 1944 constitute an historical record of views on RE teaching of considerable clarity and temporal precision.[2] The data on changes in agreed syllabuses that will be used here are obtained from a survey of syllabuses published between 1944 and 1982. Three quite distinct styles of syllabus have been produced over this time, and these correspond, with very little overlap, to three sharply defined periods: 1944 to 1965; 1966 to 1974; 1975 to 1982. The transitions are marked by the West Riding syllabus of 1966, and the Birmingham syllabus of 1975.

## The Pattern of Agreed Syllabuses

### 1944 to 1965

The various syllabuses produced from 1944 through to the mid-1960s reveal a remarkable uniformity. The stated aims were overtly confessionalist — to inspire Christian belief and adherence to the Christian Church. The introduction to the widely adopted Surrey syllabus was characteristic:

> The aim of the syllabus is to secure that children attending the schools of the county ... may gain knowledge of the common Christian faith held by their fathers for nearly 2000 years; may seek for themselves in Christianity principles which give a purpose to life and a guide to all its problems; and may find inspiration, power and courage to work for their own welfare, and for that of their fellow-creatures, and for the growth of God's kingdom.[3]

The content of these syllabuses was very largely based upon bible readings, and the dominant strands were: the life and teaching of Jesus; the history of Israel; the history of the Christian church. In many there was also a section on exemplary Christian lives, such as saints or social reformers, again with unselfconsciously confessionalist aspirations. For infants, topics such as food or animals were widely suggested, and always to be taught within a Christian interpretation: 'God's Gifts' or 'God's wonderful world'.[4]

There was a similar uniformity across the syllabuses in the way the content was organized. Invariably it was precisely specified for year groups, sometimes by individual terms. In contrast there was little discussion in these syllabuses of pedagogy, other than phrases like 'the teacher has to put the flesh on the bones'. Pedagogy appeared to be unproblematic, and this was the point of departure into the next phase of agreed syllabuses.

### 1966 to 1974

In the late 1960s a rush of new syllabuses appeared which all bore significant similarities to each other and represented clear departures from the earlier phase. They remained confessionalist in aim. Thus the West Riding syllabus argued that the material had to meet and satisfy the 'religious needs' of pupils and that these 'are only satisfied by the growing discovery that at the heart of the universe there is a God who cares, a spirit who seeks to enter into personal relationships with us.'[5] It was in the manner by which the confessionalist aims might be realized that the break with the previous period was most clearly marked. 'Relevance' became the touchstone — relevance to the lives of the pupils in their contemporary social circumstances. This was to be made manifest through a thematic content: 'We advocate a thematic approach for we feel that this is the way in which the teaching of Christianity may be made most relevant to the lives and experiences of pupils.'[6]

Themes which could be said to connect directly with pupils' everyday experiences became the organizing principle of much of the content in each of these syllabuses. The contrast with the previous biblical approach was illustrated most lucidly in the Wiltshire document which contained two parallel syllabuses: a thematic 'modern' Syllabus A, and a 'more conventional' Syllabus B for teachers 'who feel that the Bible must be the starting point from which all their teaching must proceed.'[7]

In all cases these syllabuses organized the material in three broad developmental stages, rather than in an exact year by year form. Throughout, the insistence on 'relevance', the content of the themes, the importance attached to using pupils' experience as the initial direction indicated a clearly progressive set of pedagogical assumptions. The ILEA syllabus was especially explicit:

> Suitable centres of interest, projects or themes are made the basis of an exploration which integrates work in many different subject areas. Working in this way requires children to be treated as individuals contributing to a group understanding, and the mutual respect which develops between teacher and child.[8]

There was a Plowdenesque optimism in many of the descriptions of appropriate pedagogy. Usually these syllabuses continued to cite biblical references corresponding to proposed themes, but they were to be used, if at all, only when they aptly illuminated the theme under discussion. On this point they were unanimous; the theme was paramount.

### 1975 to 1982

Beginning in Birmingham, a new generation of syllabuses emerged which eschewed the thematic approach and its implicit treatment of religion. They repudiated also any hint of confessionalist aims: 'There can be no question of making it an aim of religious education in schools to convert pupils to any particular religion or ideology.'[9] This was typical of the way in which syllabuses from the mid-1970s onwards distanced themselves from the previous position. The inclusion of RE in the curriculum was now justified on what were repeatedly referred to as 'educational grounds'. Its purpose was stated most economically in the Avon syllabus: 'The principal aim should be to enable pupils to understand the nature of religion and what it would mean to take a religion seriously.'[10] The subject matter was drawn not just from Christianity, but from a range of major religions (and secular philosophies). Furthermore, the nature of religion was presented as multi-dimensional; each of the new syllabuses suggested material not only on doctrine, but on the history, sociology, liturgy, ethics, myths and artistic expression of these religious traditions. Religion thus became an explicit object of study, and in the Birmingham formulation, understanding required the subject to be taught 'objectively'. Later syllabuses tended to speak of 'open-mindedness' or 'sympathetic appreciation'.

A second aim found in each of these syllabuses was that this treatment of the subject would assist pupils in whatever interpretative quest they might be engaged in by, for example, 'raising questions of belief and values in the pupils' minds and encouraging them to seek answers for themselves.'[11] As if to emphasize this, the new syllabuses were organized in the form of a series of rational objectives, specified for each age band. The Birmingham syllabus set one other important trend: the actual syllabus of RE was a mere four pages long within a brief formal pamphlet. This was accompanied by a massive, loose-leaf handbook of content ideas. Subsequent syllabuses followed what amounted to a policy of separating the 'legal requirement of a syllabus from the professional requirement of a teachers' handbook.'[12]

## Accounting for Change

A number of empirically grounded socio-histories of particular school subjects have recently appeared which have taken as their starting point Musgrove's proposal that the research should 'examine subjects both within the school and the nation at large as social systems sustained by networks, material endowments and ideologies.'[13] The single most striking theme to emerge from these accounts has been the evidence of the differentiated nature both of subject communities and of institutions external to the school which have influenced their curricula.[14] Cooper, for example, conceptualizes a subject as 'a set of segments, or social movements, with distinctive missions, or perspectives, and material interests.'[15] In accounting for curricular change, therefore, it is the relationships between these segments within and outside the educational system which constitute the explanatory variables. These relationships themselves are seen as capable of changing, according to variations in different segments' access to resources, and developments in the conditions for action within schools.

Religious education does, however, look singularly appropriate for a structuralist account; it is the one compulsory subject in a school system whose history is deeply infused with ecclesiastical involvement, in a society with an established church which has retained its associations with an aristocratic-gentry culture that has, arguably, been the dominating influence on the curriculum of English schools.[16] This penetration of the Durkheimian association of religion and culture into state education, aptly expressed by the term 'agreed syllabus' even has its moments of appropriate ritual, as with the inauguration of a new RE syllabus:

> ... When the latest Cambridgeshire Syllabus (1949) was published it was solemnly dedicated by the Bishop of Ely at a service in Great St Mary's Church in Cambridge, in which Anglican and Free Church ministers and teachers took part, and a copy of the book was formally presented by the chairman of the local county council to the Bishop who laid it on the altar.[17]

The RE curriculum itself is widely felt to have a moral influence upon young people, and to impart a sense of cultural and national identity. Above all, there is the clear evidence from every survey made since 1944 of overwhelming adult approval for compulsory religious education in state schools.

In spite of these appearances, religious education has not been what Goodson describes as 'a monolithic entity'. The RE clauses of the 1944 Act imposed at a time of intense national unity an obligation upon a subject community which existed in only the most fragmented form. The history of the subject since 1944 is the record of the actions of a plurality of social groups within the educational system and outside it, informed at various times by similar and at other times by competing interpretations of that legal obligation, in a cultural context which has itself become increasingly differentiated. No other subject has proved quite so capable as RE has done of exciting passionate conflicts of values.

### The Agreed Syllabus Formula

At the outbreak of the war half the schools in England were Church schools, and almost a quarter of the nation's children were receiving their education in them. The prospects for any kind of substantial educational reform depended on some kind of settlement to the dual system, and that entailed reaching agreement with the established Anglican Church which owned 85 per cent of the non-provided schools. The lengthy negotiations which Butler conducted produced compromises by the Board of Education and by the church authorities, and in some measure the unique status of RE created by the 1944 Act was one outcome. Years later, Butler was to argue: 'I do not believe we could have got what was described as the settlement of 1944, if we had not included these clauses on religious education as part of the religious settlement which was itself part of the dual system settlement . . .'[18] It was an outcome that incurred virtually no opposition from the general public, and very little from politicians. Behind this very considerable consensus was the wartime crisis.

War greatly enhances national unity, and creates and recreates powerful affective symbols of that unity. Daily, the War which touched every person in the country was depicted as the struggle to preserve national values threatened by a ruthless pagan enemy. The importance of Christianity as the foundation for those values, and therefore the significance of its vitality in national life, was repeatedly asserted. Butler again:

> I shall listen with respect to those who have doubts about religious instruction being compulsory, but I am convinced of the principle which animated us in the flush of wartime — because, my Lords, this was put through while we were living in Church House, with the bombs actually raining at the time, and the sentiments and emotions of the day must not be forgotten . . .[19]

The capacity of organized religion to galvanize those sentiments and emotions of the day was demonstrated by the enormous congregations at nationwide Services of Intercession at the time of the fall of France. It was within Church House, however, that the major disputes over the proposals for a non-denominational religious education in all state schools took place.

When *The Times*, whose editor pledged his personal support to Butler's efforts, argued: 'The future of religious education involves the future of our national life and character and they will not be safeguarded unless unity of aspiration leads, and leads without further long delay, to united action',[20] its irritation was directed at the prevarication among church leaders. This was closely tied to concerns about the future role of church schools. As Cruickshank depicts it: 'Some were less anxious to preserve church schools than to ensure sound Christian teaching for all children in all schools.'[21] For this segment of church opinion, the settlement proposals were attractive. Set against this group was a conservative, high church lobby which insisted on retaining the traditional position of the church school, with its association with the parish church, so that children could be more effectively 'trained for membership of a worshipping community'. The Nonconformists had long been campaigning for the abolition of the dual system completely, while a vociferous Anglo-Catholic group, not especially wedded to Church schools, wanted to secure opportunities for denominational teaching in county schools.

By 1944 Archbishop Temple was able to deliver to Butler the compromise he sought.[22] A major factor here seems to have been the data that Butler supplied which revealed the dilapidated condition of many of the church schools; 90 per cent had been built before 1900, and of 753 schools on the Board of Education's blacklist, 541 were Church of England voluntary schools.[23] The Church could not afford the building programme. But what in the end made an agreement possible was the fact that in every segment of ecclesiastical opinion one assumption could be shared — that the proper aim of religious education was to nurture Christian commitment in the pupil. It was accepted by the Board of Education also, whose White Paper on Educational Reconstruction had asserted that the purpose of ensuring RE a 'more defined place in the life and work of schools' was to give expression to 'the widespread desire to revive the spiritual and personal values in our society and in our national tradition.'[24]

In the Act, religious education was seen as comprising two elements: a daily act of 'collective worship' and classroom 'religious instruction'. The clear understanding was that classroom instruction was to elaborate, in accordance with an agreed syllabus, the Christian beliefs contained in the daily act of worship.

### The First Generation of Syllabuses: 1944 to 1965

In placing upon state schools a major responsibility for the nurture of Christian commitment, the 1944 Act legitimated a singularly influential role for the clergy in shaping the RE curriculum. It was a role that the clergy felt no anxiety in exercising, and one that it had some experience of. The pre-war RE handbooks that a number of local authorities had drawn up had been written substantially by churchmen.[25] The biblical and historical content of the first generation of agreed syllabuses closely followed those earlier teachers' guides which were in turn derived from theology degree courses. The syllabuses were drawn up, the Durham Commission was to conclude, 'more to satisfy scholars and churchmen'.[26] But then they had been drawn up largely *by* scholars and churchmen.

The clerical influence could also be found in the embryonic professional association, the Institute of Christian Education. It had been established in 1935 through the work of the Student Christian Movement (a body strongly connected with universities and public schools) to provide a forum whereby academics and clerics could assist school teachers of RE. It had a public spirited mission and a concern to develop a sense of professionalism among teachers. Professionalism was equated with being competent and up to date with biblical and theological scholarship. Dr Temple was the first president of ICE, and a theological college principal the first editor of its journal *Religion in Education*. Many leading theologians contributed to the journal as part of the effort to equip teachers with contemporary theological knowledge; few teachers did so.

In state schools before and after the war there were very few specialist teachers of RE. The full extent of the shortage was indicated by a report of the ICE in 1954; in the Birmingham LEA, for example, less than 3 per cent of primary schools, 20 per cent of secondary modern and 51 per cent of grammar schools contained any teacher with the barest qualification in the subject.[27] Very rarely was there any department of RE, the norm in secondary as in primary schools being for form teachers to teach the subject.

The consequences for the construction of agreed syllabuses was twofold. First, teacher representation on the conferences was selected by the unions (NUT and AMA), individual members being identified on the basis of church involvement or known conviction. Secondly, it inhibited the formation of a community of RE specialists able to articulate a definition of the subject drawn from classroom experience. Added to this, there were no RE advisers. As late as 1960 not a single LEA had appointed an adviser with specific responsibility for the subject. As later events have demonstrated, the appointment of an able specialist adviser is a significant factor in the development of RE curricula. The absence of this potential influence throughout the first period of syllabus design, together with the fact that specialist teachers were few and isolated, meant that the syllabuses were patterned very much by the vision of the clergy.

'A don's syllabus' was how many teachers in the 1950s described their LEA's agreed syllabus to a Sheffield University Institute survey, which concluded: 'To teach most agreed syllabuses adequately would demand not only the services of an accomplished theologian but also six or more teaching periods a week.'[28] All of that was to change in the 1960s.


### The Goldman Era: 1966 to 1974

The dominant theme in the many cultural changes of the 1960s was an extravagant celebration of individualism. It articulated in colourful and dramatic forms a perception of fulfilment through freely chosen experience uninhibited by societal constraints. Only a small minority were fully enmeshed in its antinomian expression but it symbolized and introduced a far wider section of the population to shifts in expectations and forms of social interaction. It was, as Bernice Martin suggests, 'an index to a whole new cultural style': 'The sixties were the transformation point. They exemplified for society at large, in striking ways, processes which would expand the frames within which expressive possibilities were currently contained.'[29] The frames were weakened across many areas of public and private life. Education at all levels was affected by this cultural shift; so too were the churches, for which it was, claims Vidler, 'a decade of fermentation.'[30]

In the Protestant world there was a series of attempts by liberal theologians to formulate a notion of Christianity that would enable commitment to find a meaningful lodgement in a largely secularized environment.[31] Their central axiom was that the scientific rationality of contemporary man led him to find traditional religious affirmations implausible in his everyday existence. Their efforts were characterized by a shift from assertions of objective truth to subjective forms of understanding religion, a demythologized gospel and a dilution of the boundary between sacred and secular. Within the churches, revised forms of liturgy showed the same deritualizing motif. Behind all this went an earnest concern to translate Christian traditions into a system of belief that would be more relevant to men and women leading their contemporary secular lives. This 'New Theology' was dramatically popularized by the Bishop of Woolwich in *Honest to God*.[32]

This was a paperback best-seller, running through several editions in its first year, and was summarized in *The Observer*. It provoked violent controversy within the church, and this was played out before the widest possible audience. The publication, and responses to it, provided headline news in the popular press and were the themes of numerous television programmes. It was, says Vidler, 'the most famous — or notorious — episode that contributed to the new fermentation.'

'While some of the devout were shocked by *Honest to God*, multitudes of readers welcomed it both as a frank and patently honest acknowledgement of the need for a new deal in theology and as an attempt to express the gist of the Christian faith in a fresh frame of reference.'[33] Fuelling the controversy was the fact that the publication coincided with what became popularly known as the 'new morality' — serious attempts by a number of theologians to reformulate the notion of sin. Much of the invective that was directed by hurt, conservative segments of the Church focused on these descriptions of ethical complexity, and many made causal connections between the propagation of situation ethics and the current Profumo scandal.[34]

But *Honest to God* was addressing the problem with which teachers of RE, especially in secondary schools, were becoming familiar — the indifference of their flock to the traditional subject matter as it was traditionally presented. The Schools Council Enquiry revealed secondary modern pupils ranking RE as almost the least useful and least interesting subject in the entire curriculum.[35] Whereas in the churches the congregation could vote with its feet, in schools RE was compulsory. The fact that it was seen by pupils with a strongly instrumental view of education as having no vocational significance, and little expressive value, made teachers peculiarly vulnerable to their dissatisfaction. Usually the RE teacher lacked the resource for controlling recalcitrant pupils provided by a public examination. The 'New Theology' legitimated the search that many RE teachers were making for a redefinition of the subject that might more effectively engage the attention of their pupils.

The pedagogical issue was addressed directly in a series of publications by educational researchers during the first half of the 1960s. Loukes[36] revealed a picture of teenage pupils disenchanted by 'totally boring Scripture lessons' who could recall little of the knowledge transmitted over ten years of RE. He was the first to advocate a 'problem-centred' definition of the subject, with discussions of moral and religious questions drawn directly from pupils' experience. Acland[37] accounted for pupils' rejection of traditional RE in terms of the impact of the secular culture of contemporary industrial society; his proposals were similar to those of Loukes. Goldman[38] argued that the biblical orientation of agreed syllabuses was intrinsically inappropriate. He applied Piagetian theory and research method to a study of pupils' understanding of biblical stories, and claimed to show that the material was inevitably too abstract for children still in the stage of concrete operations. He too proposed a thematic style of RE. The work of these three was to prove influential in the design of new syllabuses. In the case of Goldman it is difficult to overstate the impact made by his research and the curricular implications drawn from it.

An 'Open Letter to LEA RE Advisory Committees',[39] organized by Goldman in 1965, and signed by six other university and college lecturers in education (including Loukes and Acland) drew attention to 'current inadequacies in the teaching of RE', and made a number of recommendations. Foremost among these were: 'the reform of agreed syllabuses along the lines suggested by recent research, that is, on the broader dimensions of children's needs and capabilities, rather than the narrower dimensions of biblical knowledge'; reinterpretation of the aims of RE as 'personal search rather than the imparting of a body of fact'; and 'support for teachers in any dispute with parents or churches who have not yet fully imbibed current theological ideas'.

The research to which they referred was their own. Five of the seven signatories published important and widely reviewed books on RE between 1961 and 1966, and their work did point towards the ineffectiveness of prevailing agreed syllabuses. It had the power of being the first empirical investigation of significance into the efficacy of RE teaching, and the findings chimed with many teachers' classroom experience. The theoretical bases of their research — the sociological underpinning of Loukes and the Piagetian psychology of Goldman, for example — were thoroughly in tune with the intellectual developments of the 1960s, especially in teacher education. Above all, their recommendations reflected the optimistic progressive thrust of educational ideas during that decade, and more widely, the cultural emphasis on individualism, and the authenticity of subjective experience rather than the authority of received tradition. Theologically, they embraced the liberal response to the *Honest to God* debate. It was absorbed rapidly into the colleges and departments of education.

The authors of that open letter were confessed Christians; they were also able to identify themselves as 'professional educators'. They were in fact providing the intellectual leadership for a segment of RE teachers and lecturers that was redefining its sense of professional identity. An important factor behind this was the departmentalization of secondary modern schools. Lowndes[40] points out that by 1965 in only a handful of such schools was it still policy for RE to be taught by all form teachers to their own form. Although this process created the opportunity for specialized teaching (a requisite for professional identity), the continuing shortage of qualified RE teachers meant that the RE department was unlike that in any other subject area. Typically it was a head of department and a collection of other specialists occupying a proportion of their timetable with RE. The DES Secondary Survey indicated only about one third of all RE lessons were taken by teachers with an RE qualification.[41]

For the RE specialist this posed particular difficulties of control over the RE that was actually taught, especially since many of them were young, recently graduated from colleges of education and were required to direct the teaching of experienced staff often holding senior positions in the school. Connection with a subject association lent some authority to teachers in this position. A further source of status ambiguity stemmed from the ambiguous nature of the subject as it was currently defined. It lacked the academic standing of other subjects; few pupils took public examinations; manifestly anybody could teach it since anybody was liable to be asked to teach it by a headteacher in the final stages of constructing the timeable; and it was overlaid with non-academic expressive functions. In the staffroom the RE specialist could find himself the target of the kinds of jokes that outside would have been directed at parsons. These characteristics of the work situation, together with limited opportunities for career mobility (since rarely were departmental heads offered large posts of responsibility) contributed to a growing sense of shared professional identity among a significant number of secondary specialists. It was shown in their anxiety about whether the Schools Council would accept RE as one of its subject panels, and their relief when it did. Through the 1960s the term 'professionalism' was used increasingly, and used to signal a claim to independence from ecclesiastical control.

A major impetus to this movement came with the amalgamation of the ICE and the SCM in schools to form the Christian Education Movement (CEM) in 1965, and the creation two years later of its Professional Teachers Committee. The CEM expanded into a national organization with salaried regional staff who provided an advisory service to individual teachers, schools and LEAs. The link forged with many LEAs was especially important; not only did they make substantial grants to CEM, many came to regard it as an alternative to providing their own advisory staff. CEM produced a volume of printed material and had a mailing list of several thousand individuals and schools. By 1970 it had a network of some seventy local branches (typically meeting twice per term). The drive had come from the secondary specialists, but in 1971 a primary department was set up and several thousand more schools were affiliated.

The CEM also assumed responsibility for the bi-monthly journal *Learning for Living*.[42] Loukes was its first editor; Goldman wrote regularly as did many other 'professional educators' teaching in schools and in university departments and colleges of education. The journal constantly articulated the view that teaching RE in contemporary Britain was deeply problematic. The theme of 'pluralism', and the implications this held for how RE was to be taught, recurred in issue after issue, and although there was no strict editorial policy, it generally reflected the liberal 'New Theology'.

Yet within the profession, as outside among Church members, there were sharp disagreements and some visible attempts to preserve the traditional character of the subject. An alternative 'Open Letter' was published a year after Goldman's.[43] It stressed the value of biblical content, without which, it claimed, 'children could not be expected to discuss religion sensibly at all'; it dismissed any classroom significance for 'New Theology' arguing that 'many teachers (supported by a growing body of scholarly opinion) see no reason to abandon traditional Christian beliefs after they have scrutinized recent theological thought'.

The traditional definitions of RE were also sustained in a number of other professional associations. The National Association of Teachers of RE and the Association of Christian Teachers (ACT) maintained the confessional stance, but by far the most active among those seeking to re-affirm the original understanding of the 1944 Act was the Association of Religious Education (ARE). This organization was created in the late 1960s by a group of earnest evangelical Christian teachers, angered by the low status of RE, the seemingly widespread indifference to its importance, and impatient with CEM which they regarded as being too theoretical, insufficiently concerned with classroom practice and too liberal in its theological position. Through its journal, *Area*, a campaign was conducted against what was described as the 'Cinderella status' of the subject, and for several years ARE articulated the frustrations felt by many upholders of the traditional mission of religious education. Its major impact was probably on the CEM. The development of the Professional Committee within CEM was, to some degree, a response to the activities of ARE.

All these associations that asserted a more traditional view of RE remained far smaller bodies than CEM. Their message was distinctly out of tune with the secular cultural developments of the decade, and they formed few alliances with any strategic groups within the education system. The CEM, on the other hand, developed close links with the LEAs, the bodies formally responsible for agreed syllabuses, and traditionally it had enjoyed the highest ecclesiastical connections. It was increasingly through CEM that a new notion of 'professional RE' was channelled.

In 1961 the first LEA adviser with specific responsibility for RE was appointed, in the West Riding. The work of revising the syllabus was begun, and Goldman was co-opted to advise the conference. It was a critical event in this phase of RE syllabuses. It enabled the redefinition of the subject to be translated rapidly into a new pattern of agreed syllabuses, and they echoed, when they appeared in the second half of the 1960s, the same concerns that had led to attempts earlier in the decade to redefine theology. They too began with an acknowledgment of the secular context of children's lives; they strove for 'relevance' and the formation of individualized, subjective understandings of Christian belief as a way of interpreting everyday life.

### Multi-Faith RE: 1975 and after

In 1970 a commission to inquire into religious education, established by the Church of England Board of Education and chaired by Dr Ramsey, Bishop of Durham, published its report. This was the first authoritative renunciation of confessionalist aspirations for the subject in state schools. The report argued that the cultural, theological and educational changes since 1944 constituted a 'minor revolution' for RE. It elaborated a justification for the inclusion of RE within the curriculum, but one that was based upon what the report called 'educational criteria' rather than on any position of unique privilege.[44]

A corollary to relinquishing confessionalist aims was transferring more control of curriculum design to educationalists. The Durham Report advocated this, describing the legal machinery of the agreed syllabus as a 'relic of the ecclesiastical era in religious education', and to some extent it was already taking place. It was shown by the influence of professional opinion in the syllabuses of the late 1960s, and the development in some LEAs of handbooks of classroom materials by teachers which effectively by-passed the agreed syllabus.[45] It was to be extended: the 1971 syllabus in Cornwall was, with the agreement of the churches, designed entirely by teachers; the conference in Cheshire determined as its first principle that teachers should be in the majority on all its working parties.

The emergence during the previous decade of an articulate, non-ecclesiastical professionalism among RE teachers was obviously one factor behind the Church's voluntary concession of its traditional hegemony over the RE curriculum. But that itself was symptomatic of the process of social differentiation which had gradually removed established religion from its position of pre-eminence in political and cultural life to a more narrowly confined sphere. The presidency that the Anglican Church enjoyed in 1944 was, by 1970, significantly diminished. Its social influence was widely felt to have declined along with the status and the number of its clergy.

In the year after the Durham Report set the stage for a new round of agreed syllabuses, the Schools Council Working Paper, *Religious Education in the Secondary School*[46] was published. It was here that the 'phenomenological' treatment of the subject — a non-confessionalist but empathetic endeavour to understand religion as a multi-dimensional phenomenon of human life wherever it is lived — was presented before a wide professional audience. Its principal author, Smart, was head of the Department of Religious Studies at Lancaster University, and was to give a consistency to the new syllabuses as Goldman had done a decade earlier.[47]

What the Schools Council report offered was an academically coherent programme to a religious education that was no longer being required to induct pupils into Christian faith. If RE was to justify itself on educational grounds, Smart provided a rationale and a content. It was a content that appealed to many teachers of the subject on a number of counts. In the first place it held out the promise of academic status in the staffroom in a way that no previous confessionalist definition of the subject had done because it sought to make religion an explicit object of study through a public methodology, and RE as intellectually demanding as any other subject in the curriculum. This would not be a religious education that any teacher could teach. Secondly, it suggested another possible solution to the secondary teacher's problem of capturing the interest of pupils. Despite the hopes of those who had constructed the 1960s syllabuses that the thematic style would transform RE into a classroom experience that pupils would perceive as having some relevance to themselves, this had not proved to be the case. A survey commissioned by the Anglican Board of Education reported in 1977 that: 'If one could choose just one summary word for our interviewees' responses (to RE in schools) it would be *boring* in capitals and six underlining strokes.'[48] It went on to point out that although many reported finding the discussions interesting, they had found it difficult to accept as 'really RE' or as 'particularly useful'. They seemed to want clear subject boundaries, and this the Schools Council approach could provide.

Finally, the 'phenomenological' definition of RE that Smart and his colleagues were proposing contained an answer to the question of how the subject could be taught in a pluralist society. This, more than any other issue, had come to dominate professional discussion. Whether

Britain could be thought of as a pluralist society is a matter on which sociologists are divided. Martin,[49] for instance, argues that while there is a multiplicity of faiths adhered to, the uniform indifference to religious questions shown by the majority of the population makes for anything but pluralism. What is significant here, however, is that, as the pages of *Learning for Living* demonstrated, many teachers defined the social context of their teaching as pluralist and that very indifference of which Martin speaks was seen as part of its pluralism. Although this view, and the intellectual and moral concern that it entailed, was not restricted to those inner city teachers who faced the children of immigrant parents, it is not surprising that the first translation of the new definition of RE into an agreed syllabus was in Birmingham.

The previous syllabus in that authority (constructed in 1950 and revised in 1962) had displayed the hallmarks of that era: 'We speak of religious education, but we mean Christian education (and) the aim of Christian education in its full and proper sense is quite simply to confront our children with Jesus Christ.'[50] When the new syllabus was first published in 1974 it saw these aims as inappropriate because 'there has been a revolution in the understanding of its (RE's) nature and purpose' and also because the city 'now contains sizeable groups of people each loyal to their own particular religious or non-religious commitment, and, in addition, many with no deep commitment of any kind.'[51] From the outset, the multi-faith syallabus was seen as having the function of assisting community relations. The conference contained representatives of non-Christian religions; it also co-opted a prominent member of the British Humanist Association.[52]

The syllabus outlined that each pupil (at secondary level) would study, 'objectively and for its own sake' two major world religions and a 'non-religious stance for living', either Communism or humanism. When, as agreed by the conference, it was passed to the city council it provoked a violent dispute, following party political divisions, and the syllabus was withdrawn. There followed months of debate in council, often passionate correspondence in the local newspapers, and questions in Parliament. Finally, on legal advice from the DES, the conference was re-convened. References to Communism were removed from the sylla-bus outline (but not from the handbook) and the revised edition was published.[53]

Communism was the focus of the Birmingham controversy, but it disguised two broader issues: the extent to which RE should encompass faiths other than Christianity; and whether or not the RE teacher should endeavour to nurture commitment to Christian belief. On these two issues there were groups outside the educational system which felt very deeply, and in the aftermath of the row in Birmingham they campaigned urgently.

The Order of Christian Unity was the most active of the pressure groups that sought to preserve a Christian evangelical interpretation of the 1944 Act. It organized conferences, wrote pamphlets and petitioned Parliament under slogans such as 'Curriculum Christianity'.[54] The targets were identified as 'comparative religion' and 'the dilution of Christian content in RE' and its charter spoke of the 'urgent need to promote and defend Christian education.' Its concerns also embraced broadcasting ethics, and changes in divorce and abortion laws. It was, in short, a moral crusade against the cultural thrust of the 1960s, and it was supported by other leading figures of that movement, such as Lord Longford and Rhodes Boyson. Another was Mrs Whitehouse, whose 'Save RE in State Schools' petition attracted over half a million signatures in 1976.

Partly through these connections, the character of RE in state schools was the subject of three parliamentary debates during 1976 and 1977. Here, and especially in the two which took place within an unusually packed House of Lords, were repeated assertions of an inextricable association between a traditional form of RE and the moral development of young people, the quality of national life, and (in the view of some) the very survival of Britain. The sentiments and turn of phrase echoed the debates of 1944, and as in 1944, there was a strong conservative lobby within Church House. The Durham Report's recommendation of a non-confessionalist 'educational approach' to RE had been followed by similar expressions of opinion from the Free Church Federal Council[55] and the British Council of Churches.[56] When the General Synod discussed these three documents in 1976, it rejected a motion calling for a recognition that 'county schools cannot be expected to take responsibility for Christian nurture among their pupils'. Instead it demanded recognition of the 'partnership which exists between LEAs and the Church in joint responsibility' for that function.

Yet none of this campaigning made any significant impact upon the conferences which devised the new syllabuses in the late 1970s. Under-lining all the extra-educational activity was the assumption that teaching RE should be equated with Christian moral socialization.[57] The precise notions of morality differed between the various segments of opposition to the new definition of RE — the puritan tones of Mrs. Whitehouse could be distinguished from the orthodox Anglicanism in the Lords debates — but the fundamental equation was the same, and it was one that influential segments of professional RE teachers had come to reject.

The Durham Report had argued for a distinction to be clearly drawn between RE and moral education. Before that, in the 1960s, there were many signs of interest in moral education, separately defined (and in some schools, separately located on the timetable). The Schools Council had clearly endorsed this view by simultaneously funding curriculum projects in both areas. The ambiguous status of the confessionalist interpretation of RE and the indifference of pupils to that mission had persuaded many teachers to define the subject as a distinct activity governed by the same intellectual canons as any other in the curriculum. Among those who faced significant numbers of immigrant pupils, representing a plurality of faiths other than Christianity, a non-confessionalist, multi-faith form of RE seemed an imperative. The extent to which this view had spread among RE teachers can be gauged by the fact that it was becoming endorsed in the latter half of the 1970s by professional associations such as ARE and ACT which had earlier espoused a more evangelical position.[58]

The phrase that was used in a number of new syllabuses to typify that definition of RE, that 'the principal aim should be to enable pupils to understand the nature of religion and what it would mean to take a religion seriously' was a quote from an influential book published in 1975, *Teaching Religion in Schools*.[59] Its author, Jean Holm, head of an RE department in a college of education, a member of the Schools Council RE Committee and on the Council of CEM, was often asked to address agreed syllabus conferences. It was this kind of professional voice, rather than appeals from outside education calling for a return to the original understanding of the 1944 Act, that commanded the conferences. This was not simply because the Church groups had conceded control to the teacher group; many of the clergy were also sympathetic to the multi-faith idea in RE. They too had encountered pluralism, which, as Berger points out, makes claims to monopoly on the truth difficult to maintain: 'Inasmuch as religion essentially rests upon superempirical certitudes, the pluralistic situation is a secularizing one and, ipso facto, plunges religion into a crisis of credibility.'[60] They had witnessed in the 1970s the growth of the black Churches in Africa and the sudden process by which (not only in Britain) the plight of the Third World's inhabitants had become a central theme of theological and church activity. These experiences had made many clergy impatient with that segment of opinion most frequently found among the lay members of the established Church which appeared to equate Christianity with, in Martin's words, 'the common civic sense of the British people'.

This was the conception of Christianity that had butressed the popular consensus in 1944, and which probably continues to support the widespread approval that exists for compulsory RE in schools. Thus Martin argues:

> A broad assent exists to what is perversely believed to be 'Christian' morality: do-as-you-would-be-done-by is the most frequently quoted summary of morals. It is as a basis for morality or 'civilization' that Christianity is so widely applauded, and especially as a means for inculcating distinctions between right and wrong amongst children.[61]

The redefinition of RE (academic, non-confessionalist, multi-faith) that was successfully advanced by the most influential segments of professional opinion, supported by significant groups of churchmen and by the Schools Council, represented a minority view within the population as a whole. Groups who campaigned, from outside the educational system, against this definition often drew attention to this fact in their speeches and literature, but were unable to mobilize popular support behind their traditional cause. While there was much tacit support for the legal status of RE which was seen as having a gentle socializing influence and as representing some cultural continuity, the actual lesson content was never a salient issue. For that considerable majority to whom religion was equivalent to basic decency, and strident assertions of commitment were somewhat suspect, it probably never had been.[62]

## Conclusion

In the years immediately after 1944, agreed syllabuses were shaped by the dominant influence of churchmen and university theologians; forty years later they were being constructed by conferences that primarily reflected the influence of a professional community of RE teachers, lecturers and researchers in teacher education, and advisers. The syllabuses themselves had changed radically; RE in fact had been redefined.

During the early years the Church had been intimately associated with the state; it was a significant symbol of national unity and the message that it propagated widely interpreted as comprising the moral concepts central to British life and cultural history. Compulsory RE in state schools was acknowledged as providing an essential initiation into that moral order over which the Church representatives were the legitimate guardians. Since then, much of that overarching influence has been lost, and recognized as having been lost.[63] The RE curriculum is one of many areas of social life over which the Church has curtailed its claim to that of being one specialist opinion among a plurality of legitimate views. The processes by which this has occurred have not been without conflict.

Within the churches there have been divergent reactions to the experience of secularization, especially to the loss of moral authority that seemed to many to characterize the 1960s, and later to the presence of substantial numbers of non-Christian immigrants. Broadly these have represented the two options of defense and accommodation[64]: some segments have continued to assert the traditional objectivities while others have attempted to re-cast them so as to render them subjectively more meaningful in a secular and increasingly pluralized society. Among RE teachers, there were identical sets of responses to the same problems as they were encountered in classrooms. The teachers were differentiated into segments which paralleled those among the clergy and among the lay members of the churches. The alliances and disputes between these segments, which represented the varied reactions to the declining influence of organized Christian religion, cut across those institutional boundaries.

It was the accommodating vision that was to find itself manifested in the new RE syllabuses. The pressure towards accommodation leant more heavily upon those within the educational system than on those outside, since the teachers were obliged to face an often uninterested, but captive population of pupils who held a strongly instrumental view of education. Usually these teachers did not have access to the instrumental control of the public examination. This encouraged redefinitions of RE that were naturally closer to the shifts in secular cultural emphasis that took place throughout this period: the optimism and search for individual relevance in the 1960s; the concern for racial harmony in a pluralist society in the 1970s. The segments within the churches and the profession of RE teachers which articulated this view formed important alliances with the Inspectorate and the LEAs (which were responsible for agreed syllabus design) and the Schools Council. Its message was effectively communicated through an expanding professional association, the CEM, which was itself, institutionally and financially, connected to the LEA structure.

If the disputes within the educational system were pursued with less passion than those within the established Church, it is because they coincided with the expansion of a distinctly professional voice that was independent of ecclesiastical control. For the Church, the disagreements that had always been present were exacerbated by the sense of contraction and waning influence. RE continues to be capable of touching deeply felt values among a number of people, but control of the syllabuses rests largely with the professional RE teachers and opposition to new definitions of the subject have come chiefly from lay members of the churches.[65] Compulsory RE was born in a moment of acute national crisis that pulled Church and state into close union, but that relationship has not remained static. Hull is quite correct in pointing out that 'the abandonment of the Christian hegemony in the agreed syllabuses represents a small but significant shift in the relations between Church and state.'[66]

## Notes

1 Except in Wales and Monmouth.
2 By contrast we have remarkably little data on the extent to which agreed syllabuses have shaped classroom practice. A survey of agreed syllabuses officially in use, conducted in 1981 by the CEM, suggests that there is probably considerable variation between one local authority and another in this relationship. If this is the case, an important variable would seem to be the differential capacity of RE advisers to mobilize local resources for in-service programmes.
3 SURREY (1945), p. 5.
4 CARLISLE, CUMBERLAND and WESTMORLAND (1951), p. 189.
5 WEST RIDING (1966), p. 3.
6 INNER LONDON EDUCATION AUTHORITY (1968), p. 6.
7 WILTSHIRE (1967), p. 36.
8 INNER LONDON EDUCATION AUTHORITY (1968) p. 42.
9 BIRMINGHAM (1975), p. 5.
10 AVON (1976), p. 4.
11 NORTHAMPTONSHIRE (1980), p. 9.
12 See PRIESTLEY (1981), p. 7 for a discussion of this point.
13 MUSGROVE (1968) p. 101.
14 See especially BALL (1982), GOODSON (1981, 1982)
15 COOPER (1983), p. 220.
16 MUSGROVE (1979), pp. 61–65.
17 MURRAY (1953), p. vii.
18 *Hansard* vol. 286, para. 707.
19 *Ibid* para. 713. N.B. Parliament was meeting in Church House because of blitz damage to the House of Commons.
20 *The Times*, 16 January 1941, quoted in GOSDEN (1976), p. 271.
21 CRUICKSHANK (1963), p. 141.
22 The Roman Catholic authorities remained unable to accept the agreement that was finally decided with the Anglican and Free Churches.
23 See CRUICKSHANK (1963) and GOSDEN (1976) for discussions of this.
24 BOARD OF EDUCATION (1943) para. 36.
25 See HULL (1975) for a discussion of the pre-war handbooks.
26 CHURCH OF ENGLAND BOARD OF EDUCATION (1970), p. 16.
27 INSTITUTE OF CHRISTIAN EDUCATION (1954), pp. 54–69.

28 University of Sheffield Institute of Education (1961), p. 47.
29 Martin (1981), pp. 15–16.
30 Vidler (1971), p. 269.
31 The Second Vatican Council initiated a parallel movement within the Catholic Church.
32 Robinson (1963).
33 Vidler (1971), p. 274.
34 This is discussed in Ferris (1964), pp. 268–77.
35 Schools Council (1968), pp. 56–62.
36 Loukes (1961, 1965).
37 Acland (1963).
38 See Goldman (1964) and the curricular implications, in Goldman (1965a).
39 Published in *Learning for Living* vol. 5(1), p. 16, 1965.
40 Lowndes (1969), p. 259.
41 Department of Education and Science (1968), pp. 92–3. The comparable figure for another 'shortage subject', mathematics, was seventy per cent.
42 The renaming of the major professional journal has reflected the changing character of agreed syllabuses: *Religion in Education*, 1934–1960; *Learning for Living*, 1961–1977; *British Journal of Religious Education* after 1977.
43 Published in *Learning for Living* vol. 5(3), pp. 18–19, 1966.
44 Church of England Board of Education (1970). See especially Chapter 4.
45 See Hull (1975), pp. 102–4 for a discussion of this point.
46 Schools Council (1971).
47 It was a university department of Religious Studies, not Theology, and the school syllabuses reflected the approach to the subject pioneered in that department. The Schools Council Working Paper was only the first product of a much larger curriculum project that was based at Lancaster.
48 Martin and Pluch (1977); p. 26. King (1973) reports similar responses to school assemblies.
49 Martin, D. (1978). See especially pp. 12–19.
50 Birmingham (1950), p. 8.
51 Birmingham (1975), p. 4.
52 The ILEA (1968) conference was the first to include representatives from non-Christian religions, by an extension of the term 'other denominations' in Schedule V of the 1944 Act.
53 The DES limited its involvement to the question of whether so brief a document constituted a legal syllabus. It was the LEA's lawyers who advised the removal of the communism theme.
54 Tulloch (1977); see also Order of Christian Unity (1973).
55 Free Church Federal Council (1976).
56 British Council of Churches (1976).
57 For this reason the teaching of communism was frequently described as 'indoctrination' by those who objected most strongly to the Birmingham syllabus.
58 An indication of this is the fact that there are currently (1983) discussions taking place within ARE as to whether the organization should seek to amalgamate with CEM.

59 HOLM (1975), p. 1.
60 BERGER (1967), p. 9.
61 MARTIN, D. (1967), p. 55.
62 GOLDMAN (1965b).
63 For a discussion of this, see WILSON (1976), especially pp. 16–26.
64 Using these terms in the sense outlined by BERGER (1967).
65 Ironically, some opposition to the recent 'phenomenological' definition of RE comes from groups of immigrant parents who find it so archetypically Western as to be more threatening than the traditional confessionalist position. (I am indebted to W.J.H. EARL for this point.)
66 HULL (1975), p. 114.


## References/Bibliography

ACLAND R. (1963) *We Teach Them Wrong*, London, Gollancz.

AVON (1976) *Religious Education: Avon Agreed Syllabus*, Avon Education Committee.

BALL, S.J. (1982) 'Competition and conflict in the teaching of English: a socio-historical analysis', *Journal of Curriculum Studies*, 14, 1, pp. 1–28.

BERGER, P.L. (1967) 'The secularization of theology' in *Journal for the Scientific Study of Religion*, 6, 1, pp. 3–16.

BIRMINGHAM, (1950) *Agreed Syllabus of Religious Instruction*, City of Birmingham Education Committee.

BIRMINGHAM (1975) *Agreed Syllabus of Religious Instruction*, City of Birmingham Education Committee.

BOARD OF EDUCATION (1943) *Educational Reconstruction*, Cmd 6458.

BRITISH COUNCIL OF CHURCHES (1976) *The Child in the Church*, London.

CARLISLE, CUMBERLAND AND WESTMORLAND (1951) *Agreed Syllabus of Religious Instruction*, Carlisle, Cumberland and Westmorland Education Authorities.

CHURCH OF ENGLAND BOARD OF EDUCATION (1970) *The Fourth R*, London, National Society: SPCK. (Durham Report).

COOPER, B. (1983) 'On explaining change in school subjects', *British Journal of Sociology of Education*, 4, 3, pp. 207–222.

CRUICKSHANK, M. (1963) *Church and State in English Education*, London, Macmillan.

DEPARTMENT OF EDUCATION AND SCIENCE (1968), *Statistics of Education, Special Series No. 1*, London, HMSO.

FERRIS, P. (1964) *The Church of England*, Harmondsworth, Penguin.

FREE CHURCH FEDERAL COUNCIL (1976) *Religious Education in County Schools*, London.

GOLDMAN, R.J. (1964) *Religious Thinking from Childhood to Adolescence*, London, Routledge and Kegan Paul.

GOLDMAN, R.J. (1965a) *Readiness for Religion*, London, Routledge and Kegan Paul.

GOLDMAN, R.J. (1965b) 'Do we want our children taught about God?' *New Society*, 27 May, pp. 8–10.

GOODSON, I.F. (1981) 'Becoming an academic subject: patterns of explanation and evolution', *British Journal of Sociology of Education*, 2, 2, pp. 163–180.

GOODSON, I.F. (1982) *School Subjects and Curriculum Change: Case Studies Social History of Curriculum*, London, Croom Helm.

GOSDEN, P.H.J.H. (1976) *Education in the Second World War*, London, Methuen.

HOLM, J. (1975) *Teaching Religion in Schools*, London, Oxford University Press.

HULL, J.M. (1975) 'Agreed syllabuses, past, present and future' in SMART, N. and HORDER, D. (Eds.) *New Movements in Religious Education*, London, Temple Smith, pp. 97–119.

INNER LONDON EDUCATION AUTHORITY (1968) *Learning for Life*, ILEA.

INSTITUTE OF CHRISTIAN EDUCATION (1954) *Religious Education in Schools*, London, National Society: SPCK.

KING, R. (1973) 'School rituals' in *New Society*, 12 July, pp. 71–72.

LOUKES, H. (1961) *Teenage Religion*, London, SCM Press.

LOUKES, H. (1965) *New Ground in Christian Education*, London, SCM Press.

LOWNDES, G.A.N. (1969) *The Silent Social Revolution*, London, Oxford University Press.

MARTIN, B. (1981) *A Sociology of Contemporary Cultural Change*, Oxford, Blackwell.

MARTIN, B., and PLUCK, B. (1977) *Young People's Beliefs*, London, General Synod Board of Education.

MARTIN, D. (1967) *A Sociology of English Religion*, London, Heinemann.

MARTIN, D. (1978) *The Dilemmas of Contemporary Religion*, Oxford, Blackwell.

MURRAY, A.V. (1953) *Education into Religion*, London, Nisbett.

MUSGROVE, F. (1968) 'The contribution of sociology to the study of curriculum' in KERR, J.F. (Ed.) *Changing the Curriculum*, London, University of London, pp. 96–109.

MUSGROVE, F. (1979) 'Curriculum, culture and ideology' in TAYLOR, P.H. (Ed.) *New Directions in Curriculum Studies*, Lewes, Falmer Press, pp. 57–69.

NORTHAMPTONSHIRE (1980) *Religious Education in Northamptonshire*, Northamptonshire Education Committee.

ORDER OF CHRISTIAN UNITY (1973) *Ways Whereby Christian Education in State Schools Should be Saved*, London.

PRIESTLEY, J.G. (1981) 'A world of harmonious confusion' in LEALMAN, B. (Ed.) *Implementating the Agreed Syllabus*, London, CEM.

ROBINSON, J., BISHOP OF WOOLWICH (1963) *Honest to God*, London, SCM Press.

SCHOOLS COUNCIL (1968) *Enquiry 1: Young School Leavers*, London, HMSO.

SCHOOLS COUNCIL (1971) *Religious Education in Secondary Schools*, London, Evans/Methuen.

SURREY (1945) *Syllabus of Religious Instruction*, Surrey County Council.

TULLOCH, F. (Ed.) (1977) *Curriculum Christianity; Crisis in the Classroom*, London, Unity Press.

UNIVERSITY OF SHEFFIELD INSTITUTE OF EDUCATION (1961) *Religious Educa-*

*tion in Secondary Schools*, London, Nelson.

VIDLER, A. (1971) *The Church in an Age of Revolution*, Harmondsworth, Penguin.

WEST RIDING (1966) *Suggestions for Religious Education*, County Council of the West Riding of Yorkshire.

WILSON, B. (1976) *Contemporary Transformations of Religion*, London, Oxford University Press.

WILTSHIRE (1967) *Religious Education in Wiltshire*, Wiltshire County Council.

# Modern Languages and the Curriculum in English Secondary Schools

*Harry Radford*

From Wales to Quebec, from Brussels to Soweto, foreign languages in the modern world have been perpetual sources of strife. Likewise, in the politics of the school curriculum no less than in the world arena, languages have been a perennial source of friction and controversy. Since modern foreign languages first established a real foothold in the secondary schools of nineteenth century Britain, the history of language teaching has been a chronicle of dissension — of extravagant claims, conflicting theories, diverse objectives and defeated hopes. The struggle for recognition, for enhanced prestige and resources, not only brought the partisans of modern languages into competition with rival disciplines — classics, the sciences, English — but also caused tensions within the subject between traditionalists and progressives, or more recently pressure from the teachers of so called 'minority' languages to overthrow the despotism of French. Eventually, such rivalries and sub-factions crystalized in the formation of a number of professional groups, each defending particular sectional interests.

Modern languages, then, have been at the heart of the curriculum conflict, especially as a discipline commonly associated with failure. In fact, the debate surrounding them encompasses almost every major contentious issue in the wider discussion about the curriculum as a whole — the function of compulsory education; the impact of public examinations; the problem of educating the unintelligent; elitism versus egalitarianism; the rhetoric of the educationist and the reality of the classroom; subject-centred as against child-centred learning; tradition and the implementation of change; the influence of external factors (social, political, commercial and technological) upon the content of study programmes. In short, as a central battleground of the forces contesting the territory of the secondary school curriculum, modern languages are a singularly rewarding field for any student interested in the vicissitudes of the struggle and the evolution of the modern curriculum.

## Early Trends — The Origins of the Utilitarian and Academic Traditions in Language Teaching

In 1974, the former headmaster of a leading comprehensive school called attention to the diversity of aims which in recent history have bedevilled teachers of what the French felicitously call 'living languages': 'In no subject are the tensions between a traditional academic emphasis (a language leading to a literary study) more curiously at odds with notions of international understanding or communication (all pupils to be able to order an ice-cream in French)'.[1] Such tensions, however, were virtually unknown for centuries following the implantation of first Latin, then French, in this country as a result of foreign invasion. Latin, as the 'common tongue of Christendom',[2] and later French as the language of the Norman invaders, were learned of course by the ruling classes as indispensable vocational tools for the business of everyday life. Thus they were studied not as foreign, but as almost indigenous languages freely encountered in the environment outside the classroom — a process of language acquisition which Hawkins[3] has labelled Immersion Learning (IL), to distinguish it from the highly artificial conditions of Foreign Language (FL) learning as we usually know it today (children of Welsh-speaking communities learning English provide an obvious contemporary analogy).

The early history of language teaching in Britain has already been carefully documented in studies by Watson,[4] Lambley,[5] and the valuable but largely unknown survey in French by Clapton & Stewart,[6] which owes much to Lambley's work. But a brief outline of the salient features of a period that coincides with England's growth to nationhood seems essential for an adequate understanding of more recent developments.

After the Norman Conquest, French became the medium of communication among the upper classes, whilst the vernacular was only spoken by the peasantry. Latin also, of course, remained very much in active use certainly until the seventeenth century; in medieval times it was the language in which the business of Church and state was transacted, all knowledge transmitted, all scholarly activity conducted. During the fourteenth century, growing contempt for 'Anglo-French' (dismissed as a corrupt dialect by Frenchmen themselves), together with the rise of national consciousness in England, caused French to be viewed increasingly as a foreign tongue, though it continued to pervade the judicial system.[7] In fact, a mastery of Parisian French was to remain until the modern era an indispensable passport to high society or a career in the diplomatic service for young men of rank.

As the prestige of French culture increased throughout Europe, so demand for knowledge of the French language redoubled, sustained by recurrent wars and royal marriages. It is said to have been a language particularly favoured in Court circles during the Tudor period, with Italian and Spanish also in evidence.[8] Henry VIII is alleged to have had a fluent command of French, and to have found the language of Ronsard a natural medium for his courtship of Anne Boleyn.[9]

The striking feature of this long period of contact with the French language, however, is that it was generally learned from native-speakers outside the formal school system and its acquisition was essentially utilitarian. For this purpose wealthy families employed French-speaking tutors, recruited from the large numbers of refugees, mainly Huguenots or Walloons, who were driven from the continent by religious persecution, especially in the sixteenth and seventeenth centuries.[10] Thus, many students from the rigidly traditional grammar schools — for example, Sir Philip Sydney who was educated at Shrewsbury — acquired a knowledge of French as an extra accomplishment in this way from a private foreign tutor.[11] Similarly, William Shakespeare is reputed to have owed his familiarity with the language to a Huguenot, Christopher Montjoy, whose home he frequented for several years.[12]

In the latter half of the sixteenth century, private academies for language teaching (often associated with a religious community) sprang up in London and in a number of provincial cities, whilst a constant stream of textbooks and dictionaries for English students of French appeared,[13] mostly from the pens of enterprising French settlers like the famous Claude de Sainliens (Holyband), as demand for instruction in colloquial French spread to the merchants and professional classes in Elizabethan society.[14] A century later, during the period of exceptional 'Gallomania' which followed the restoration of the Stuart monarchy when the power and prestige of France under Louis XIV had reached their zenith, the vogue for the French language in England had become even stronger. Boyd remarks that for the English aristocracy 'a perfect knowledge of French as the cosmopolitan language was of course essential, and acquaintance with Italian was scarcely less important'.[15] Lambley has also concluded that 'to be unacquainted with French was accounted a great deficiency in a gentleman'.[16]

Tuition in French had normally occurred outside the old schools and colleges; it had been conducted by native speakers, often on an individual basis, and directed towards active use of the language, though essential grammar was certainly not ignored. By contrast, inside the schools — as their name of course implies — grammar, especially Latin (but also Greek after the Renaissance and in some schools Hebrew too, formed the nucleus of the curriculum. William of Wykeham in his statutes for Winchester College (1382) is said to have expressed the prevailing view of education: 'Experience ... plainly teaches that grammar is the foundation, gate, and source of all the other liberal arts'.[17] This attitude, which was to endure until the twentieth century and ultimately influence the study of modern languages profoundly, is particularly significant when we recall that in Wykeham's day mastery of spoken Latin was a necessity for any ambitious young man. Watson claims that the need for colloquial competence in the language during the Middle Ages extended from scholars and clerics to architects, philosophers, lawyers, physicians and even merchants.[18] This demand for communicative skills in Latin among scholars and professional men naturally affected the schools; scrutiny of the statutes of eighteen foundations reveals that all stipulated the exclusive use of Latin within the school precinct.[19] As late as the sixteenth century, the apostle of the new Humanism, Erasmus, showed that the language of Cicero remained the 'lingua franca' of Europe: 'Speaking only Latin and his native Dutch, he was equally at home among the scholars of Holland, France, England, Germany and Italy'.[20]

Inevitably, when after the seventeenth century spoken Latin fell into disuse, the schools and universities in whose curricula the 'dead' languages remained solidly entrenched, grew increasingly remote from everyday life and remained dark retreats of medieval scholasticism, impervious to social change. It was against this fossilized system of education that Milton and later John Locke reacted.[21] In his book *Some Thoughts Concerning Education* (1693), Locke firmly rejected the analytic approach to language study, based on laborious learning of rules and exceptions: 'I would fain have anyone name to me that tongue that anyone can learn, or speak as he should do, by the Rules of Grammar'.[22] For Locke the content of education should be strictly relevant to the needs of everyday life; consequently he proposed that his pupil should be taught both Latin and French by the direct method.

However, the defenders of the traditional grammar-translation approach had two powerful arguments to deploy, the academic and the religious. Kelly reminds us that one of the supreme values traditionally ascribed to language learning, especially to the study of Latin and Greek, was mental discipline — a reason often invoked as 'an emergency device when the other aims of language teaching are becoming confused'.[23] But as well as this intellectual argument, the other major factor in the ascendancy of the 'dead languages' was their association with the Bible; Latin, Greek and Hebrew were the 'holy' languages[24] to seventeenth century educators. Charles Hoole, the translator of Comenius and himself a grammar school teacher, offered the following advice to young schoolmasters: 'Every morning read six or ten verses . . . out of the Latine Testament into English, that thus they (the scholars) may be become acquainted with the matter and words of that most holy book'.[25] Kelly in turn argues that for the status of the ancient languages, 'their value as tools of established religion was most important'.[26]

These ideas of the 'transfer of training', the moral and humane value of the classical languages, especially for those destined for high office in government,[27] were to dominate the curriculum of most British secondary schools from the Renaissance until the early years of the twentieth century. As the authors of *Educating the Intelligent* (1962) remarked, 'there can be few more curious episodes in the long history of education than the way in which the *grammaticus* of ancient Rome . . . cast his shadow into the future'.[28] The long shadow of the Latin grammarians was to darken particularly the teaching of modern languages when eventually these subjects found grudging acceptance in the grammar or public schools in the nineteenth century. Until that period, tuition in French (and much less commonly, Italian or Spanish)[29] continued to flourish outside the endowed schools and ancient universities, though colonies of expatriate Frenchmen settled in both Oxford and Cambridge,[30] as well as in other cities, profiting from the steady demand for French lessons. The Revocation of the Edict of Nantes in 1685, and a century later the Revolution of 1789, brought further cohorts of refugees from France to perpetuate the now established practice of teaching French through private tutors or language schools to the widening circle of clients, from aristocrats and professional men to soldiers and merchants, now eager to acquire such knowledge.[31] By 1830, the French author of one of the numerous manuals of instruction published for English students estimates that as many as thirty-five thousand of his fellow-countrymen were making their living by teaching French in Britain.[32] Stressing the importance of conversational French, especially for every 'young lady of rank', Porquet expressed amazement at the 'immense sums . . . at five to ten shillings per lesson' often wasted upon incompetent foreign tutors.[33]

Meanwhile, during the eighteenth century, the growth of the so-called Dissenting Academies[34] had provided an alternative source of instruction in modern languages and other subjects which remained excluded from the ancient universities and schools. According to Irene Parker, whereas in the older institutions the purpose was to insulate education from everyday life, the Academies considered it imperative that education should include 'as many utilitarian subjects as possible ... English early received attention, as also did French, and in some cases German, Italian and Spanish'.[35] By contrast, the torpor and sterile formalism of the official classical curriculum was enshrined in the very statutes of the grammar schools, as Lord Eldon's judgment in 1805 underlined, when efforts to divert funds for the teaching of French and German at Leeds Grammar School were declared illegal.

## The Emergence of French as a School Subject in the Nineteenth Century

The legendary Dr Thomas Arnold, Headmaster of Rugby from 1828–42, is said to have been the first headmaster of a major school to break the monopoly of classics by allowing modern languages, like interlopers, to enter the hallowed garden of the traditional curriculum.[36] In spite of Arnold's initiative, the cult of Latin and Greek in the schools was not seriously challenged until the end of the nineteenth century. Thus, in his evidence to the Clarendon Commission — whose report on the nine leading public schools, in 1864, actually reaffirmed the supreme value of classical studies — the one teacher of French at Eton College could still describe himself as a mere 'objet de luxe'.[37] Another witness, this time at Harrow School, where French and German had been incorporated in the curriculum in 1855, revealed that 'idleness' was more common in modern language lessons than in any other subject.[38]

In fact, a salient feature of the curriculum in the nineteenth century as new subjects were tentatively introduced was the exceptionally low status accorded to modern languages. Not only was the time allocation — at best a mere two hours weekly — totally inadequate, but there was also a crippling dearth of properly qualified teachers of French and German. Furthermore low pay, the absence of promotion prospects, the notorious indiscipline in language classes often entrusted to incompetent foreigners, and above all the neglect of modern languages in the universities of Oxford and Cambridge, where the lack of entrance scholarships or College Fellowships in these subjects inevitably caused French or German to be viewed contemptuously in the schools as frivolous, undemanding pastimes for inferior intellects — all these factors served to ensure that until the twentieth century, the position of modern languages in the secondary school curriculum remained precarious. On paper, the addition of these subjects, in accordance with the recommendations of the Clarendon Report (1864) and also the Taunton Report (1868) on the 782 endowed grammar schools in England and Wales, was certainly reassuring for parents anxious that their sons and daughters should receive a more 'relevant' education. Headteachers, too, were glad to impress potential clients by including in their staff-list of solid university men the occasional foreign name with the prefix 'Mons.'[39] In practice, however, modern languages were to remain until the last decade of the Victorian age the Cinderella of the school curriculum — neglected, despised, and grossly maltreated.

At first, the task of teaching French (by far the most popular modern language in Britain for centuries past) was commonly allocated to classicists or semi-retired churchmen, since 'foreign gentlemen' like the individual encountered by Mr Podsnap,[40] were generally viewed with distrust and disdain. Consequently, from the moment of its appearance on the traditional school curriculum, French was taught as a 'dead' language. For men like Arnold of Rugby and Butler of Harrow, this approach was a deliberate and reasoned policy. Dr Arnold believed all pupils should be given 'a thorough grounding in grammar' and the ability to read 'an ordinary French author with facility'. Defending his policy in a letter to the chairman of Governors, he continued: 'I assume . . . that boys at a public school never will learn to speak or pronounce French well under any circumstances'.[41] Likewise, the Headmaster of Harrow, Dr Butler, in his evidence to the Royal Commission in June, 1862, dismissed any attempt to promote oral proficiency as unrealistic, arguing that the objective should be to teach the rudiments of grammar and some ability to read the modern language as a basis for further study.[42]

Whether through planning, inertia or improvization, the practice of modelling instruction in French on the ritual method applied to the 'dead' languages proved distressingly futile. In many schools, French lessons became an additional chore for form masters; there was no coordination of the teaching syllabus, each master adopting whatever manuals or texts he pleased. Marks were often discounted in assessing form 'orders', so that French was inevitably devalued for the pupils. Lessons were generally relegated to early morning or late afternoon sessions, the weekly time allocated was only one sixth of that assigned to Latin, yet French was also treated 'as a corpse to be dissected' — a subject almost any university man could 'teach' by checking the words beforehand.[43] Predictably, horror stories abounded. Mr Paton, for example, recalled that French consisted of one lesson per week 'encroached on at one end by prayers and at the other by the anticipation

of breakfast', whilst a typical advertisement of the day read: 'Wanted —
a master to teach French, German, chemistry and book-keeping'.[44]
Another victim of such 'teaching' cited the example of the master who
always inflicted upon his pupils the same three Molière texts, the titles
of which he mispronounced as 'Tar-tough' (*Tartuffe*); 'Lez Farm
Save-aunt' (*Les Femmes Savantes*); and 'Ler Miss Anthrowp' (*Le
Misanthrope*); the only boy with a natural French accent was ridiculed
and obliged to imitate 'the manly British accent of his master'.[45] Texts of
course were laboriously 'construed' in class, Dumas and Daudet being
subjected to the same treatment accorded to Xenophon or Caesar.
Time was lavished on the subtleties of syntax and accidence, on 'peculiar
plurals and strange feminines ... unknown to the majority of
Frenchmen'.[46]

Such bungling amateurism could only be described as a farce[47] and
the subsequent inability of leading statesmen and Cabinet Ministers to
show a minimal working knowledge of the key language of European
diplomacy proved a major indictment of the traditional curriculum: 'Mr
Balfour speaks no French. Lord Grey speaks a French disgraceful on the
lips of a Foreign Secretary. Mr Asquith's French is excessively bad ...
Mr McKenna speaks excellent, fluent, conversational (though not
colloquial) French. But then, Mr McKenna never went to one of our
great public schools'.[48] Despite the initiatives of the more progressive
Headmasters such as Butler and Kennedy at Shrewsbury, or Arnold and
his successor Tait (later Archbishop of Canterbury) at Rugby, reforms
in the classical curriculum had been slow to spread in the more ancient
foundations. However, it should be noted that the movement towards a
more modern programme of studies had gathered strength from the
foundation of proprietory colleges and other new public schools in the
first sixty years of the nineteenth century — schools such as Mill Hill
(1807), where by 1821 boys were taught French by a Frenchman,[49]
Cheltenham (1841), Marlborough (1843), Rossall (1844), Wellington
(1853) and Clifton (1862). These schools together with private
academies linked to religious denominations, were more responsive to
popular demand for the inclusion of new subjects such as mathematics,
natural science, English, history, French and German. It was in a
number of the newer schools that the first Modern Sides were
established.[50]

For girls, the traditional instruction in religion, reading, writing,
keeping accounts and needlecraft had been extended in the eighteenth
century to include more modern fashionable accomplishments such as
French, Italian, music and drawing. But even at the beginning of the
Victorian era, the education of women was still haphazard and super-

ficial, limited to inferior private schools or ill-qualified governesses.[51] Serious learning was generally considered inappropriate for young women, and even in the more expensive schools the main objective of the instruction in languages, music, and dancing was merely social display.[5.] This frivolous approach to girls' education was vehemently denounced by one of the most influential critics of contemporary educational practice, Herbert Spencer. In July 1859, Spencer's essay entitled 'What knowledge is of most worth' was published in the *Westminster Review* and a few months later in book form; with all the vigour of the iconoclast, Spencer demolished the arguments upholding the conventional curriculum with its cult of the ancient languages, but also explored the question of the relative value of various disciplines in respect of the time necessary to master them. Knowledge was too often valued, not for its intrinsic benefit to the pupil but for 'its extrinsic effects on others'.[53] Thus, girls were required to study modern languages because 'a knowledge of those tongues is thought lady-like',[54] so that they might parade their accomplishments by singing an Italian or German song. Similarly, Spencer argued that the mainstay of the classical curriculum was prestige or merely conformity, ornament rather than utility: 'As the Orinoco Indian puts on paint before leaving his hut, not with a view to any direct benefit, but because he would be ashamed to be seen without it; so a boy's drilling in Latin and Greek is insisted on, not because of their intrinsic value, but that he may not be disgraced by being found ignorant of them ...'.[55]

## The 'Great Reform' in Modern Language Teaching and the Struggle for Recognition

Whilst this awesome tradition of high culture and intellectual power conferred prestige upon the classical curriculum, it caused the newer languages to be viewed condescendingly as trivial pursuits, cheap pabulum for second-rate minds. Indeed, the history of their role in English schools during the fifty years which separated the publication of the Taunton Report in 1868 from that of the Leathes Committee at the end of the Great War, is a record of an upward thrust for status constantly hampered by the stigma of utilitarianism. Paradoxically, this struggle for supporters of modern languages for a greater share of curriculum time, and for proper recognition of their discipline in the two most prestigious universities, coincided with a radical reform in teaching methods which, by according new prominence to the spoken language, appeared to make rejection inevitable.

The origins of the Great Reform movement in modern language

teaching have been carefully researched elsewhere.[56] It is evident from the comments about aims and methods in the reports of the Public Schools Commission (Clarendon), 1864, and the Schools Inquiry Commission (Taunton), 1868, that the 'grammar-translation' method was almost universally favoured; perceiving the main objective as discipline for the mind, Gilbert notes that the commissioners 'were suspicious of oral methods and attempts to impart mere fluency in conversation'.[57] Moreover, the proliferation of the new influential examinations — the London Matriculation, the Oxford and Cambridge Locals, the Indian Civil Service and Army entrance examinations, the College of Preceptors — whilst helping to promote the study of modern languages, also served to reinforce the traditional obsession with grammar and philology. During the 1870s and 1880s, the partisans of French and German recognized that their crusade would only succeed if university dons and sceptical headmasters could be persuaded that the disciplinary or academic value of modern languages was comparable with that of classics.[58] Modern languages, hitherto learned for practical reasons and excluded from the grove of Academe, had no such tradition behind them; but as Kelly has emphasized, 'to be accepted in the schools as having the same educational, moral and intellectual values as Latin, they had to be taught with the same methods …'.[59]

It was this belief that caused the enemies of utilitarianism to vilify 'courier' French. Thus, in an outspoken article published in the monthly *Journal of Education* in July 1887, Dr R.W. Hiley proclaimed the alleged value of mental discipline imposed through 'hard and dry studies'; grammar, he urged, should be 'rigidly learnt', for it was 'the pith and marrow of a language, and not the mere jabbering taught by a "bonne"'.[60] This last contemptuous jibe was a clear retort to the mighty Jowett, Master of Balliol, who had intervened in the language teaching controversy a few months earlier unexpectedly on the side of the 'moderns'. In a historic address to the congress of French-speaking teachers resident in England on 13 January, 1887, Dr Jowett as a great Hellenic scholar had expressed surprisingly enlightened views about the need for improvements in the teaching of modern languages, including the desirability of beginning 'with conversation, not with book exercises'. Though he claimed that French was already an optional subject in some elementary schools, he saw little hope of real progress until the universities gave the subject due recognition. No university student should be awarded a degree without demonstrating 'reasonable knowledge' of a modern foreign language: 'ignorance of French, like ignorance of Latin, should be regarded as involving a sort of discredit'.[61]

Jowett's utopian view was countered within a month by a more gloomy and cynical assessment of the educational scene in England. R.H. Quick noted how an overloaded curriculum in Germany had prompted efforts to solve the problem through systematic reform, but saw no prospect of educators in Britain — now faced with the same pressures — heeding developments abroad: 'We English inhabit the polar regions of the educational world, and . . . seem, like the Eskimos, to manage our own affairs without much reference to what is going on in Europe'.[62] There was every likelihood, he continued, that we should proceed 'in our happy-go-lucky fashion, trying small alterations to show that we are moving with the times and then congratulating ourselves on having kept things substantially as they are'.[63] Science masters and teachers of modern languages would be appointed, but 'given twice as many pupils as they can teach'.

Whatever the obstacles, however, the Reform movement in language teaching rapidly gathered strength as the nineteenth century neared its end. German linguists like Viëtor and Francke,[64] advocating the primacy of the spoken word and the use of 'immersion' techniques in the classroom reminiscent of the methods which had long characterized language instruction outside the grammar schools, found energetic disciples in England such as W.S. MacGowan, of Cheltenham College, W.H. Widgery of University College School and the phonetician Henry Sweet. The new science of Phonetics, which was to facilitate and accelerate the change in the classroom to the development of oral proficiency, had been promoted since the mid-seventies by scholars like Sayce and Sweet; it was further strengthened in 1886 when the International Phonetic Association was founded by the great French linguist, Paul Passy. A few years earlier, in 1882, another milestone in the advance of modern language teaching in England had been reached by the establishment of an official body representing the numerous French-speaking teachers employed in British schools, the Société Nationale des Professeurs de Français en Angleterre.[65] As well as organizing national competitions with book prizes and medals for the best students of French, the new society exercised considerable influence through its annual congress, such as the meeting at Oxford addressed by Jowett in 1887. Typical of their activities was a paper by G. Petilleau at this same historic sixth congress, attacking the bondage of so many French teachers — the 'maîtres esclaves' — to an obsolete academic tradition which produced examples of grotesque incompetence in translation. Petilleau also inveighed against the plague of French grammars aimed at the lucrative school market, and ridiculed the equally popular annotated editions of French texts, citing one example which had four pages of philological notes on the single word 'violon'!

The only time to use English in the classroom, he urged, was to send a pupil into detention for not talking French.[66]

This new utilitarian emphasis on practical skills rather than knowledge of grammatical rules, on speech instead of writing, was manifestly unlikely to find acceptance in the existing educational climate. Goodson has recently reminded us how practical and 'useful' subjects have been traditionally ascribed an inferior status in the curriculum hierarchy by comparison with academic disciplines concerned with abstract, examinable knowledge.[67] The consequent tendency of subject groups to seek to acquire a more intellectual image, a certain academic *gravitas*, thereby enhancing their prestige and power to command resources, has become a familiar feature of curriculum evolution.[68] In spite of the utilitarian pressures generated by the Industrial Revolution, the curriculum in Victorian England — like society itself — remained firmly stratified; to promote a subject on the grounds of its utility alone would have been to offer a hostage to fortune. An illustration of this was the prolonged and acrimonious debate in connection with the establishment of the crucial academic base for modern languages at the two ancient universities. At Cambridge, the Medieval and Modern Languages Tripos, set up in 1886, was contemptuously dubbed the 'Courier Tripos' by its opponents, yet involved no oral test. Oxford, despite the advantage of the Taylor Institution opened in 1845, delayed the inauguration of the Honour School of Modern Languages until 1903.[69] In both universities, the study of medieval texts and philology loomed large, to safeguard academic respectability.

Although Hawkins has concluded that 'there was real progress between 1868 and 1912',[70] with language classrooms becoming 'more interesting and intellectually stimulating places', he also concedes that in most schools the momentum of change slackened after 1914. Actually, several factors had combined to inhibit widespread radical innovations in classroom practice — the requirements of external examinations, from University Boards to Woolwich, Sandhurst and the Civil Service; the continuing lack of competent teachers, acknowledged by the Board of Education in its Memorandum of 1912;[71] and particularly a shrewd awareness among the leading exponents of the Reform (or Direct Method, as it was loosely described) that the only hope of denting the supremacy of classics was to maximize the potential of modern language study as an intellectual discipline worthy of comparison with Latin and Greek. Distrust of French and German as 'easy', 'useful' and consequently 'soft' options had to be dispelled: 'Does anyone really doubt', asked one Oxford classics don in 1916, 'that Latin prose exercises the sinews of the mind as well as gymnastics exercise those of the body, or deny that to attempt to get the same result out of a modern language is like supposing that the muscles will be satisfactorily developed by changing from one chair into another?'.[72]

Confronted by attitudes of this kind, men like Widgery, MacGowan, Von Glehn, Rippmann, Storr and Eve, as leading spokesmen for the modern language lobby, did not allow their commitment to the principle of giving pupils a practical command of French to divert them from the goal of achieving academic respectability and a semblance of parity with classics. For the reformers, as F.B. Kirkman pointed out, the spoken word was only a means to a more noble end, the key to 'the literary treasure-house of a foreign nation'.[73] Cultivation of a rudimentary oral competence to satisfy the whims of materialist parents would simply enable a pupil 'to prove himself a fool in whatever country he may choose to conduct his business'.[74] On August 7, 1883, Henry Weston Eve, Headmaster of University College School, reiterated his view that the chief objective of language teachers should be to discipline the mind, concentrating upon accuracy rather than fluency, 'on those parts of the grammar which, like the German order or the French subjunctives, involve close and delicate reasoning ... I am convinced that it is only by such scholarly treatment that French and German can furnish the disciplinary element in education which Classics have so long supplied'.[75] Similarly, in 1890, from the platform of the historic Cheltenham Conference, W.S. MacGowan of Cheltenham College, after proclaiming his belief that 'grammar was made for man, not man for grammar', strongly denied that the new 'inductive' approach, setting authentic examples before precepts, implied any wish to belittle the importance of systematic teaching of grammar: 'This is a real education to a pupil, and in these days when the tendency is to assign the dominant place to purely utilitarian subjects, we cannot afford to let (the pupil) neglect it. It gives him a power of abstract thinking, and may be obtained just as easily from a modern as from an ancient language'.[76] More than ten years later, in January 1901, addressing a conference at Liverpool, MacGowan again felt it necessary to reaffirm that the acknowledged utilitarian value of French and German should not cause their educative value to be underrated; in view of the inferior status of modern languages, it was vital to concentrate on 'the task of proving their literary value as instruments of humanistic culture'.[77]

In fact, the columns of the journals during this period were littered with similar views. For example, in 1903 P. Atherton still ventured to argue that the main aim of language teaching was to exercise the mind: 'no subject, however useful in itself, can find a place, or at least a prominent place, in the curriculum if it fails to satisfy this requirement'.[78] Writing in 1905, Cloudesley Brereton in his turn exhorted those concerned to advance the cause of French and German to demonstrate that these subjects could provide a thoroughly liberal education 'not hopelessly inferior to that given by the best classical curricula'[79]; in short, modern languages must no longer be treated dismissively as simply a utilitarian workshop for mediocre minds. Continuing the same strategy, a special sub-committee appointed by the Modern Language Association to draw up 'an Ideal Curriculum in Modern Languages', introduced their report with an unequivocal statement of their principles: 'The committee desire, in the first place, to express their conviction that the object of teaching modern languages, as of all teaching, is primarily educational and not merely practical'.[80] Even for students specializing in commercial French, the committee recommended that some time should be allocated to 'the reading and discussion of works of pure literature'.[81] Soon afterwards, in yet another analysis of the place of language study in the secondary curriculum, A.C. Benson deplored the fact that too often the student of Latin had been compelled to loiter endlessly 'in the ante-room of grammar', but maintained that a genuinely 'liberal' education must combine practical with cultural aims.[82] Likewise, Dr Karl Breul, who had long been an influential Cambridge protagonist for the cause of German and French, in 1911 defined the 'Aims and Claims of Modern Languages' in a statement evidently inspired by the same humane ideals which were to be the mainstay of language teaching until the second half of the twentieth century. Breul acknowledged that teachers of French and German could not ignore 'certain practical and utilitarian considerations', but in emotive terms he enjoined his fellow linguists not to forfeit literary taste and sound scholarship: '. . . the overwhelming majority of us teachers of modern languages will never consent to sacrifice literary training to mere mechanical drill in the practical use of the language. Surely we want to remain different from the old "maîtres de langues"!'[83]

It was precisely this desire to remain different and aloof from the mundane activities of everyday life which was reflected not only in the education dispensed at the major universities, but also in the influence transmitted from those seats of higher learning to the curriculum of secondary schools — via teachers themselves as well as through external examinations. Long before the establishment of the School Certificate and Higher School Certificate in 1917, which effectively was to perpetuate the dominance of the old triumvirate — grammar, translation, literature — until after 1950, protests were voiced about the negative influence of examination requirements upon classroom practice. For instance, in 1906 a study of the problems confronting language teachers by F. Dorr was very critical of the adverse effects in schools caused by the multitude of divergent examinations 'as plentiful as strawberries in June';[84] while shortly afterwards in 1907, an inquiry into the impact of the new methods of language teaching in secondary schools revealed that in a majority, innovation was confined to the elementary classes, due largely to 'the requirements of examining bodies'.[85] Indeed, from 1902 onwards the Board of Education's inspectors found widespread evidence of cramming, over-pressure, conflicting demands and restrictive effects on methods and curricula attributable to these tests.[86] One of the few common features of the examinations in modern languages was the absence of a compulsory oral test. When the Oxford and Cambridge Schools Board introduced a voluntary French Oral Test in 1901, only 122 candidates (10 per cent — two-thirds girls) attempted it, and 62 per cent of this total passed.[87]

A further potent force in establishing and shaping the study of modern foreign languages in British secondary schools during the years before the Great War was of course the Modern Language Association, which held its inaugural meeting on 22nd December, 1892, in London. The Society brought together university dons such as Dr Breul and Professor Spiers, and schoolmasters such as Somerville (Eton), Moriarty (Harrow), Siepmann (Clifton), and MacGowan (Cheltenham). Welcoming the formation of this new body, the *Journal of Education* predicted that it would soon 'exert a powerful influence on school curricula, methods of study and examinations'.[88] The first President of the MLA was Professor Max Müller, who held the Chair of Comparative Philology at Oxford. By a succession of shrewd selections for the office, from headmasters of the great public schools like Mr Eve, Dr Haig-Brown, Mr Laffon and Dr Welldon as well as eminent scholars like Müller or Dr Warren (Oxford), Professor Skeat and Dr Breul (Cambridge), the Association ensured that its activities carried maximum weight. Among its declared aims were raising the standard of modern language instruction in the schools and also providing a forum — through its conferences and, from 1897, its journal – for discussion of language, literature, philology, phonetics and teaching method. But its cardinal objective was: 'To obtain for modern languages the status in the educational curricula of the country to which their intrinsic value, as instruments of mental discipline and culture, entitles them — apart from their acknowledged commercial and utilitarian importance.'[89]

As we have seen, it was this adroit balance between serious academic pretensions and an enlightened, practical approach which characterized the Association's work in those vital early years of its existence and accounted for its success. Membership rose steadily from a figure of about 350 in 1900, to almost 900 subscribers by 1910. On 7 January, 1910, at the MLA Annual Dinner in St John's College Cambridge, Sir Robert Morant assured guests that the Board of Education welcomed proposals for reforms from such specialist bodies and would do all in its power to implement them.[90] However, this assurance must have sounded faintly ironic to those members like Breul, Fiedler, Milner-Barry, Storr and Rippmann who in November 1908 had signed an open letter to the Board, urging positive steps to arrest the 'lamentable decline in the study of German'[91] in Britain. The Board's response, rejecting this appeal on the grounds that Latin was more important for university applicants (it was compulsory for all Arts Degree courses),[92] had been strongly attacked in the MLA journal in June 1909.[93] Repeated efforts to persuade the Oxford and Cambridge colleges to offer more scholarships in modern languages had also met with limited success; in the year 1910–11, awards in classics still numbered ten times the figure for modern languages.[94] Nevertheless, the new Association — which by 1911 had branches in six major provincial centres — succeeded in obtaining improvements in public examinations (particularly the addition of optional oral tests);[95] promoted exchange visits to Europe, and encouraged LEAs to offer scholarships tenable at centres abroad; persistently attacked the policy of appointing foreign teachers and particularly foreign professors; and initiated a number of major inquiries into problems of special importance such as the Decline of German, the Conditions of Modern Language Instruction in Secondary Schools, and the Qualifications and Training of Modern Language Teachers (the latter chaired by the Vice-Chancellor of Cambridge University, E.S. Roberts).[96] Moreover, through its conferences and authoritative articles, the Association achieved maximum publicity for its cause, certainly keeping modern languages in the forefront of public attention.[97] Perhaps a sign of its success was the founding of the Classical Association in 1903, to prevent classical studies from being 'absolutely excluded' from the education of the young.[98]

Although the drive for parity of esteem with classics as an intellectual discipline, whilst teaching French and German as useful living languages, were the MLA's primary objectives, additional arguments to justify an increasing share of the curriculum for those subjects also emerged. Of the three agents of curriculum change identified by Ivor Goodson — the academic, the utilitarian and the pedagogic[99] — the last was to become most prominent after 1960, but had already surfaced briefly in the heyday of the Reform between 1892 and 1914. The theories of the eccentric French reformer, François Gouin, which became the canons of the Natural Method, apparently converted many disciples in this country, following the translation into English of Gouin's book: *L'Art d' enseigner et d'étudier les langues* (1880) by Betis and Swan in 1892.[100] Walter Rippmann considered that one of the virtues of the 'New Method' was that it harmonized with the principles of the child-centred, active education favoured by Pestalozzi and Froebel.[101]

Although apostles of all three educational creeds — the academic, the utilitarian and the pedagogic — could henceforth find in modern languages justification for their beliefs, there exists one other group of educators whose adherents find in language teaching an almost unique platform for their ideals. For this group, the place of foreign languages on the curriculum is legitimized by their potential contribution to cementing international friendship and understanding. Like the Esperantists, they see in language learning a key to a happier, more peaceful world. Thus, to the values commonly ascribed to all major subjects in varying degrees — to the intellectual, the useful, the pedagogic — must be added another exclusive benefit claimed to be inherent in foreign language study, the humanitarian.

This view of modern languages was eloquently expressed by Sir Richard Jebb, MP., in a memorable address to the Modern Language Association on June 26, 1901, in Oxford. After urging linguists not to be diverted by narrow utilitarian goals from the highest cultural aims, Sir Richard likened French and German to a 'modern humanism' with a formidable international mission: 'It is, I think, no exaggeration to say that, over and above the educational reasons for promoting modern languages, there is this further reason that such a study will greatly tend to promote international goodwill, and thereby, to safeguard the peace of the world'.[102] These words echoed the sentiments of that tireless spokesman for the languages lobby, MacGowan of Cheltenham, who some months earlier in a speech at University College, Liverpool, to the annual conference of the MLA, had portrayed the modern language teacher as 'a consul of cosmopolitan culture, an unofficial diplomatist whose business is to promote the universal brotherhood of man'.[103] Among many similar utterances, this humanitarian argument was frequently used by those pressing for action to halt the decline in the study of German. If this language was more widely taught in English schools, it was argued, misunderstanding and prejudice might well be reduced.[104] Lord Fitzmaurice in his presidential address to the MLA on January 12, 1909, in Oxford, elected to devote his talk to the question of languages and their bearing on international relations. Fitzmaurice maintained that to combat national prejudice 'the only remedy is a knowledge of languages so that different races and nations may understand each other and not perish in fratricidal contests . . .'.[105] He attributed the 'entente cordiale' to 'the widespread knowledge of the French language and literature in this country', and described the efforts to promote German in our schools as a mission 'to carry the light of peace and goodwill into the obscure regions of mistrust and doubt'.[106] As war loomed, this crusading zeal produced other examples of such rhetoric. Languages were compared to international highways leading to Peace, Truth, Justice;[107] whilst in a tribute to the late King Edward VII, the journal *Modern Language Teaching* declared: '. . . we, too, are peacemakers, and in our efforts to bring closer the great foreign nations whose languages we teach, we may justly see some kinship to the life-work of the wise monarch whose loss we mourn'.[108] Two years later, with Anglo-German relations even more strained, another MLA President, Mr Paton, expressed his conviction that attitudes to Germany would be much more cordial if English pupils could only read German instead of *The Daily Mail*. He saw the teacher of modern languages as 'the indispensable instrument of Progress'; if the 'grim terror of a European war' was to be averted, said Paton, 'next to the work of the Christian Churches, I place the work of the modern language teachers.'[109]

Such flights of fancy might be seen as typical of the delusions of grandeur sometimes cherished by language teachers, prone to exaggerate their own importance to society as if goaded by some unconscious desire to enhance their self-image. Even the cataclysm of 1914–18 did not destroy this belief in the power of foreign languages to cement the League of Nations.[110]

### The Leathes Report and the Inter-War years

In 1918, the committee appointed by the Prime-Minister (August, 1916) to examine the position of Modern Languages in the educational system of Great Britain, published its report, *Modern Studies*. Though dismissing the notion that ignorance of German attitudes and aspirations had been a cause of war, the committee (chaired by Stanley Leathes) agreed that ignorance of our foe and of our allies had hampered Britain's preparation for, and prosecution of, the conflict.[111] Noting the intense pressures on the school curriculum during the previous twenty years, the committee recognized that the position of modern languages was still unsatisfactory: 'In the scramble for inadequate resources, inadequate staff, and inadequate school-time, Modern Studies have improved their position during the last ten or fifteen years, though there is still much ground to make up'.[112] In their definition of the aims of language teaching in secondary schools, the committee set great store by the disciplinary, educative aim: the need for scholarship.[113] Practical aims, they argued, could only have any validity if the student left school with sufficient mastery of one language to be able to progress unaided.[114] This somewhat cautious, conservative view of classroom objectives combined with the new examination machinery set up by the Board of Education in 1917 (in an attempt to remedy the proliferation of disparate tests) was enough to ensure that language teaching in the inter-war period regressed to a predominantly traditional pattern, based on the written rather than the spoken word. Prose translation into the foreign language became the keystone of the new School Certificate examination, whereas the oral test was a mere irksome formality carrying only a negligible percentage of marks.[115] These priorities, of course, were duly reflected in the classroom. The Board of Education's inspectors criticized the 'harmful influence' of external examinations in the 'modern' schools,[116] and found that headteachers justified the inclusion of language study on cultural rather than utilitarian grounds.[117] The Hadow Report in 1926 had urged the inclusion of a modern language in the curricula of the 'modern' schools, on the grounds that the subject 'has ... at once a disciplinary, a literary and a practical value'.[118] But the committee also noted the continuing serious shortage of teachers capable of using practical oral methods.[119]

The onset of the Great Depression and economic stagnation were soon followed by the publication of a report by the committee on *Education for Salesmanship* (1930) — a forerunner of the recent British Overseas Trade Board Report[120] — renewing the periodic appeal for more linguists to help boost Britain's foreign trade.[121] However, despite official reports, questions in Parliament and a chorus of press criticism, the schools muddled on as before, generally adopting the 'compromise' method with some concession to phonetics and elementary conversation only in the early years. In January 1933, the President of the Board of Education, Lord Eustace Percy, denounced 'that almost impossible synthesis between discipline and utility which the English instinct so clamorously demands',[122] unequivocally identified reading ability and a taste for literature as the most worthy aims of foreign language study, and called for 'a coherent educational policy' for modern language teaching.[123] This 'lack of an organized plan' was also criticized by Dr Frank Hedgcock, who blamed the Modern Language Association for failing to give firm leadership in this respect,[124] though still condemned the School Certificate Examination as 'the greatest obstacle'.[125] The Spens Report (1938) had also complained that secondary education was prejudiced by the undue influence of the university curriculum',[126] and recognized that the School Certificate Examination[127] was inimical to the welfare of many children.

### The Fate of Languages other than French

The force of inertia within the school curriculum and the way in which that curriculum is harnessed to university requirements is particularly apparent in the case of German (and other 'minority' languages). During the Victorian era, the supremacy of Greek for Oxford and Cambridge applicants decimated German groups, whilst the Board of Education's insistence on Latin as the second foreign language (since Latin was compulsory for all Arts degree courses) caused an alarming decline in the numbers of pupils studying German after 1904, which a vigorous MLA campaign failed to check. The aftermath of war left German even more unpopular. To improve the situation, the Board's inspectors proposed in 1929 that the curricula of neighbouring secondary schools be differentiated so that provision for learning German should be available in at least one school in a given area.[128] The usual practice of making the second foreign language an alternative to Latin in third-year 'options' inevitably discouraged many bright pupils from choosing German or Spanish, in view of the importance of Latin to potential university students. Statistics for the year 1939 show that candidates in German for the School Certificate represented only 11.8 per cent of the total entries in modern languages (compared with 83.3 per cent in French).[129] Other European languages, such as Spanish or Russian, were very seldom taught in schools, though MLA sub-committees for both Russian and Spanish had been active since 1917 and 1931 respectively.

Ironically, the hegemony of French over other modern languages was partly due to that same cultural prestige which had earlier ensured the ascendancy of Latin and Greek. The Norwood Report in 1943 made a number of constructive suggestions designed to achieve greater diversification in the languages studied in English secondary schools.[130] Yet by 1956, a Ministry of Education pamphlet reported little sign of progress towards a wider choice of languages, whilst noting the effect of 'recent wars' in retarding the expansion of German, Spanish and Italian. The Annan Committee in 1962 made a further strong bid to break the existing pattern, and whilst the minority languages as a whole steadily improved their position relative to French up to 1980,[131] numbers of pupils remained extremely small and lately have been seriously jeopardized by falling school enrolments. A research study by the Schools Council in 1981 noted an 'astonishingly regular' decline in A-level entries in all modern languages as a percentage of total subject entries between 1965 and 1978, German slipping to only 1.4 per cent, Spanish to 0.46 per cent, Italian to 0.14 per cent, and Russian to the brink of extinction at 0.09 per cent.[132] The same study concluded that curriculum change was often impeded by trivial matters of internal school organization — unsympathetic timetabling or a misconceived system of options[133] — as much as by lack of planning. Yet the absence of regional and national blueprints has continued to provoke criticism. A staff inspector of Modern Languages in 1976 compared the chaos of the secondary curriculum to 'an open market place, where wares of all sorts, some valuable, some worthless, can be put up for sale'.[134] Paradoxically, the latest DES consultative paper revives the idea outlined half a century ago for setting the provision of second modern languages on a rational basis,[135] at a time when their very survival in many comprehensives is threatened by financial cuts and falling rolls.

## The Audio-visual Revolution and the Role of the Universities

By the middle of the twentieth century, in the post-war grammar schools modern languages had achieved a position of high status and academic prestige, despite lingering suspicions in some university circles.[136] The tenacity of the literary and intellectual tradition in school language courses is manifest in the statement of principles published in a government pamphlet in 1956: 'Whatever the claims of modern languages to an important place in the curriculum, it must be said at the outset that they cannot be justified unless the course contains intellectual discipline'.[137]

At that time, of course, only about 30 per cent of the school population had access to instruction in a foreign language, and of these a mere 7 per cent normally completed a full seven year course in a language.[138] But during the sixties, three seismic shock-waves undermined the structure of the language teaching monolith — new technology, non-selective schools and the relaxation by universities of their foreign language entrance requirements.

Hastened by the embarrassing shortage of military personnel with an adequate command of modern languages during and after the war, the advent of tape recorders, language laboratories and audio-visual materials coincided with growing social and economic pressures for more investment in language teaching. It was an epoch memorable for its brash slogans — 'language is a set of habits', 'language is speech not writing', 'teach the language, not *about* the language'; for its hallowed sequence of skills — 'listen, speak, read, write'; and above all for its boundless confidence in the new techniques. Scholars speculated that 'the four-language pupil ... might become the norm among grammar school leavers', even claiming that once 'practical language teaching' was established from the primary school upwards, the notion of apprentice mechanics reading the workshop manual of a Mercedes in German or of junior clerks understanding correspondence in Italian or Russian, could be envisaged.[139] In 1962, a major new professional group, the Audio-Visual Language Association, complete with six regional branches, was inaugurated. The initial membership numbered roughly three hundred linguists from schools and further education; the first issue of their journal proudly boasted that no other discipline except physics offered teachers 'a greater abundance of wires, knobs, machines and technicalities upon which to meditate'.[140] Such meditation, however, gradually lost its appeal as the equipment proved unreliable and the new methods ineffectual. On September 1, 1977, the name of the society was tactfully changed to the British Association for Language Teaching (BALT), in recognition of the wider scope of its activities; its respected journal, more school-based than the MLA counterpart which has a stronger literary and academic flavour, likewise assumed a different title in 1980.[141]

Meanwhile, a cluster of other professional groups had emerged, each — with its own publications — an active cell and an agent of change: the Associations of Teachers of Spanish (1947), German (1958), Russian (1959), Italian (1966); the Centre for Information on Language Teaching (1966); the National Association of Language Advisers (1969).

Whilst the new audio-visual aids had brought renewed pressure for a more utilitarian approach to language teaching, this lobby was further strengthened by the massive expansion and democratization of French teaching in the mid-sixties. Grammar, the symbol of the academic tradition, was dethroned just as the selective schools to which it had lent its name began to disappear. Henceforth, teachers of French had to contend for the first time with children of low intelligence. To render the subject more palatable and accessible to this unreceptive clientele, a practical approach shifting the emphasis away from the written word and cognitive skills seemed indispensable.[142] The familiar association of low-status, skill-based learning and poor intellectual endowment was simply re-asserting itself; French, it appeared, was reverting to its pre-Victorian humble status as a useful accomplishment like handicraft, book-keeping, fencing or callisthenics. The Newsom Report suggested that the growth in travel to Europe provided 'a strong motive for acquiring at best a "tourist" knowledge of another language',[143] also reviving the pedagogical argument for language study as a means of increasing confidence, self-respect and language awareness in non-academic pupils. This democratic, or egalitarian, view of foreign language study as an instrument of education appropriate for all, irrespective of aptitude or ability, was endorsed by a Council of Europe Resolution proclaiming that '. . . knowledge of a modern language should no longer be regarded as a luxury reserved for an élite . . .'.[144] A similar view was also upheld by the Schools Council[145] in England. British pupils, however, appeared less convinced of the advantages and 'enjoyment' said to be conferred by the study of French, remaining stubbornly impervious to the attractions of audio-visual materials. Boys especially, in the fourth, fifth and sixth forms of comprehensive schools, abandoned the subject in huge numbers.[146]

A further blow undermining the strong academic base which modern languages had established in the secondary school curriculum was the abolition by the universities, in the fiercely competitive post-Robbins era, of the compulsory foreign language entrance require-ment — a decision which removed the major incentive for historians, economists or engineers to continue their language studies.[147] Priorities had evidently changed from the days when all students reading for an honours degree in either natural or applied science were expected to follow a course in a modern language as a subsidiary component[148] — a significant factor in the expansion of French teaching in schools. Indeed, throughout the history of modern language teaching in Britain the universities had naturally exerted a crucial influence upon the destiny of the subject in schools. Until about 1880, English univer-sities had accorded scant recognition to modern languages. The existence of Regius Professorships in History and Modern Languages at Oxford and Cambridge since 1724, the bequest to the University of Oxford by Sir Robert Taylor of the Taylorian Institute (opened in 1845), had failed to stir the prevailing apathy. Even after the establishment of a Medieval and Modern Languages Tripos at Cambridge in 1886, and the Honour School of Modern Languages at Oxford in 1903, philology and the study of ancient texts became the nucleus of the course, to provide the necessary academic ballast.[149] Professor Mansell Jones in a recollection of his own undergraduate experiences before 1910, has described the deleterious influence of the classical tradition upon university departments of French: 'The living tongue was not taught at all, except through weekly exercises in written composition on the Latin prose model'.[150] Too many French departments, he complained, were 'in the charge of elderly German philologists, whose oral power was negligible'.[151] In 1918, the Leathes Report had also been strongly critical of the staffing in university departments of modern languages, complaining that ten of the fifteen professors of French, and nine of eleven professors of German were foreigners — a situation attributed to the poor stipends and career prospects which reflected the low esteem still accorded to modern languages in academic circles.[152] The growth of the new 'redbrick' universities had helped in boosting the number of French honours graduates (England and Wales) from a mere sixty in 1904 to over 300 by 1923;[153] but the strong conservative influence of university language faculties upon future schoolteachers, as well as the predominance of grammar, translation and literary history in the Higher School Certificate examinations, combined with university entrance requirements to give dons an exceptional measure of control over language teaching in the schools — at least, until the 1960s. Gradually, notable advances (greater emphasis upon oral proficiency; a more enlightened approach to literary studies) could be observed in existing courses, and a welcome diversity of provision for linguists was eventually introduced by new foundations like the universities of Sussex, Kent, Essex and York, and the polytechnics, which pioneered courses radically different from the old 'language and literature' pattern. Other factors tending to loosen the stranglehold of traditional university courses were the rapid increase in non-graduate teachers of French after 1963, the new CSE syllabuses available after 1964, and the pressures within universities themselves for removal of the compulsory foreign language entry qualification in an era of severe competition for the most able students. Yet the danger perceived by Dr. Stern of 'a regrettable split between an *academic* study of languages in the universities and the *practical* training of linguists in other institutions'[154] still looms; indeed, it currently threatens to disrupt the study of languages at school level.

## The Crisis in Modern Language Teaching

Talk of the 'crisis' in modern language teaching became increasingly common in the mid-seventies, particularly after the disappointing outcome of the ten-year research project on Primary French[155] and the controversial HMI survey, *Modern Languages in Comprehensive*

*Schools*. Various commentators described language teaching in English schools as 'a disgrace',[156] deplored 'the grim state of most language teaching in comprehensives',[157] or viewed it as 'the great disaster area of modern state education'.[158] The upheaval of the Sixties had left teachers trapped between new oral-based utilitarian objectives and old-style public examinations evaluating performance mainly in terms of written accuracy. All too often, the result was that pupils neither learned to speak French nor to pass examinations in it. The forbidding reputation of modern languages as difficult examination subjects gained fresh notoriety;[159] even bright children increasingly turned away from them.[160]

Naturally, some scholars began to question the claims of modern languages to a central place in the comprehensive school curriculum. Their middle class, elitist image is an affront to the egalitarian ideals of many contemporary educators, a perfect example of 'the triple alliance between academic subjects, academic examinations and able pupils (which) ensures that comprehensive schools provide similar patterns of curriculum differentiation to previous school systems'.[161] Thus, Rée proposed that languages should be taught not in schools but in specialist academies,[162] whilst Munn[163] and Barrow[164] disputed the case for including a foreign language as a compulsory element in an irreducible common curriculum. More recently, David Hargreaves has stated categorically that modern languages are

> a good example of the grammar school curriculum now being imposed on all in the comprehensive school ... I see no point in making a foreign language part of the core curriculum.... I am not persuaded that all pupils should spend so much time in learning the rudiments of a language they will soon forget.[165]

Partly from egalitarian and political motives, partly through idealism, and partly for reasons of self-interest (if languages for the less able cannot be justified, then jobs will be threatened), the modern languages lobby has persisted in its determination to advocate that 'foreign languages should be included in the curriculum of every pupil'.[166] Summarizing the views of the professional associations and eminent individual contributors to the debate, James groups the unique advantages claimed for language study into four main categories: educational, social, political and economic. Most of the well-rehearsed arguments are re-stated: development of linguistic and cognitive skills, promoting international understanding and tolerance of other cultures, meeting the needs of British industry and the Civil Service, providing slow learners with opportunities to consolidate basic concepts (number, time, colour, direction) and thereby experience 'the socially liberating potential of language study'.[167] It is conceded that those benefits will not be gained by all pupils, but there is again evidence of 'optimism that the problems can be solved'.[168]

This latest wave of euphoria springs from the 'graded-test' movement, developed regionally during the last ten years in an effort to break the stranglehold of traditional examinations. The central purpose of the new schemes (now numbering over sixty throughout Great Britain) is to dismantle the existing five-year examination course, replacing it with a series of interim goals (or levels) based upon clearly defined language tasks, with a strong emphasis on the oral functions of language and the learner's presumed needs as a visitor abroad. The watchword of this crusade for graded objectives in modern languages (GOML) is 'communicative competence'. This bold utilitarian approach, designed to accommodate a much wider ability range, is reflected in the published national criteria for the proposed 16+ examination.[169] The recent DES consultative paper also subscribes to this new orthodoxy: 'Schools should concentrate more on the skills of communication, particularly in the spoken form'.[170]

The obvious practical constraints which render such an objective unrealistic in normal school conditions have been dealt with elsewhere.[171] The history of the Direct Method could repeat itself; large classes, limited time, fewer foreign assistants, the absence of reliable procedures for oral assessment, not to mention consumer resistance or the imminent availability of electronic 'phrasebooks', could again torpedo this renewed attempt to make schoolboys speak French. More vulnerable still, however, in the context of an overloaded curriculum is the dubious premise that children's educational 'needs' are best served by a foreign language course imprisoned in clichés about the communicative function of languages. Although in many traditional courses the neglect of practical skills is undeniable, to rest the case for language study almost exclusively upon oral skills seems equally misconceived, particularly in the case of less able pupils. Long before this notion was challenged by contemporary scholars such as Hornsey (1973), White (1973), Barrow (1976), Hawkins (1981), Hargreaves (1982) and Byram (1982), a meeting of linguists at Oxford addressed by Sir Richard Jebb on 26th June, 1901, had been alerted to the danger of facile phrasebook learning: 'It is of importance ... to make the utilitarians see that even for their own objects, modern languages if they are to be useful must be learned thoroughly'.[172] Similarly, in 1925 the headmaster of Rugby School, Dr Vaughan, after welcoming the new emphasis on spoken French in the nation's classrooms, urged teachers to beware of trivializing a subject 'which would be useful not only in a passage across the Channel, but also in the passage through life'.[173] More recently, the persistent association of 'communicative strategies' with pupils of low attainment has, regrettably, tended further to devalue courses with mainly utilitarian objectives. However, sensibly applied, the communicative techniques should help to banish tedium from many language lessons and promote effective learning.

To conclude, the history of modern language teaching in Britain can be divided into four distinct phases. The first long period, extending roughly from the Norman Conquest to the Napoleonic Wars, was the era of the private tutor when languages (principally French) were learned by the rich and ambitious from native speakers for practical purposes, or in the case of girls as a fashionable accomplishment. The second phase, occupying most of the nineteenth century, was marked by the struggle for recognition in the leading schools and the universities, where modern languages were commonly despised as the poor man's Latin; efforts to emanicipate French and German from this serfdom to the classics were long hampered by the suspicion that anything useful like a 'living' language must be necessarily unworthy of serious academic respect. By 1918, after a brief flirtation with the 'Direct Method', modern languages were securely established in Britain's schools and universities. There followed a third phase of expansion and rising status, but the price of university rank was to leave the traditional cult of grammar, literature and the written word dominant in schools until the dynamic innovations of the sixties. Finally, the modern era has been characterized by renewed tension as linguists have sought to defend their base on the over-crowded curriculum of comprehensive schools. Recent initiatives — new 'functional' syllabuses and behavioural objectives — have envenomed the debate between ancients and moderns, between the aristocratic view of foreign languages as avenues to culture and the democratic approach to them as instruments of communication. For the sake of our pupils, a more balanced view of the aims and value of modern language study seems desirable; neither 'croissants' nor Camus should be excluded.

## Notes

1 H. JUDGE: *School Is Not Yet Dead* (1974), pp. 12–13.
2 E. JAMES: *An Essay on the Content of Education*, p. 13.
3 E. HAWKINS: *Modern Languages in the Curriculum* (1981), pp. 98–9.
4 F. WATSON: *The Beginnings of the Teaching of Modern Subjects in*

*England* (1909; reprinted 1971); also *The English Grammar Schools to 1660* (1908).

5 K. LAMBLEY: *The Teaching and Cultivation of the French Language in England during Tudor and Stuart times* (1920).

6 G. CLAPTON & W. STEWART: *Les études françaises dans l'enseignement en Grande-Bretagne* (1929).

7 *Ibid.*, pp. 43–5.

8 LAMBLEY: *Op Cit.*, pp. 64–7.

9 *Ibid.*, p. 71.

10 *Ibid.*, pp. 114–5.

11 CLAPTON & STEWART: *Op. Cit.*, p. 53.

12 LAMBLEY: *Op. Cit.*, pp. 125–7.

13 *Ibid.*, p. 131 *passim*.

14 CLAPTON & STEWART: *Op. Cit.*, p. 52.

15 W. BOYD: *The History of Western Education* (7th edition, 1964), p. 263.

16 LAMBLEY: *Op. Cit.*, p. 260.

17 Quoted in JAMES: *Op. Cit.*, p. 14.

18 F. WATSON: *The English Grammar Schools to 1660* (1908; reprinted 1968), pp. 306–7.

19 *Ibid.*, pp. 316–18.

20 BOYD: *Op. Cit.*, p. 174.

21 JAMES: *Op. Cit.*, pp. 17–20.

22 J. LOCKE: *Some Thoughts Concerning Education* (1693; edited R. QUICK, 1889), p. 145.

23 L. KELLY: *25 Centuries of Language Teaching*, (1969), p. 380.

24 F. WATSON: *The English Grammar Schools to 1660* (1968), p. 536 & p. 539.

25 C. HOOLE: *A New Discovery of the old Art of Teaching Schoole*, (1660; reprinted and edited E. CAMPAGNAC, 1913), p. 310.

26 L. KELLY: *Op. Cit.*, p. 369.

27 *Ibid.*, p. 374.

28 M. HUTCHINSON & C. YOUNG: *Educating the Intelligent*, (1962), p. 62.

29 F. WATSON: *The Beginning of the Teaching of Modern Subjects in England*, (1909), p. 446, p. 470.

30 CLAPTON & STEWART: *Op. Cit.*, p. 56.

31 K. LAMBLEY: *Op. Cit.*, p. 400.

32 L. FENWICK DE PORQUET: *The Fenwickian System of Learning and Teaching the French Language* (1830), p. 10.

33 *Ibid.*, p. 9.

34 CLAPTON & STEWART: *Op. Cit.*, p. 70.

35 I. PARKER: *Dissenting Academies in England*, (1914), pp. 133–34.

36 CLAPTON & STEWART: *Op. Cit.*, p. 74.

37 *MLQ*, I, 2. (June, 1898), p. 142.

38 *Ibid.*, p. 326.

39 *JE.*, March, 1892, p. 144.

40 C. DICKENS: *Our Mutual Friend*.

41 F. STORR in *Public Schools from Within* (1906), p. 38.

42 *MLQ*, I, 2, (June, 1898), p. 326.

43 *MLT*, II, 1, (Feb. 1906), p. 23; also *MLQ*, IV, 1, (May, 1901), pp. 17–19.

44 *JE*, (July, 1901), p. 437.
45 D. SAVORY in *MLT* (Feb. 1906), p. 24.
46 *Ibid.*, p. 24.
47 *q.v.* F. STORR in: *Public Schools from Within*, (1906), p. 38.
48 Quoted in P. GORDON & D. LAWTON: *Curriculum Change in the 19th and 20th Centuries*, (1978), p. 172.
49 Board of Education: *Differentiation of the Curriculum in Secondary Schools*, (1923), p. 9.
50 *Ibid.*, pp. 11–12.
51 *Ibid.*, p. 22.
52 *Ibid.*, p. 23.
53 H. SPENCER: *Essays in Education*, (ed. C.W. ELLIOTT, 1911), p. 4.
54 *Ibid.*, p. 3.
55 *Ibid.*, p. 2.
56 *q.v.* articles by M. GILBERT in *The Durham Research Review*, September, 1953; Sept. 1954; Sept. 1955. Also, E. HAWKINS: *Modern Languages in the Curriculum*, 1981, pp. 117–153.
57 *DRR*, Sept. 1953, p. 2.
58 GILBERT: *Op. Cit.*, p. 4.
59 KELLY: *25 Centuries of Language Teaching*, (1969), p. 375.
60 R.W. HILEY: 'The study of Modern Languages in England', *J.E.*, 1887, pp. 307–10.
61 *JE*, (Feb. 1887), p. 114.
62 *JE*, (Feb. 1887), p. 85.
63 *Ibid.*
64 HAWKINS: *Op. Cit.*, pp. 117–124.
   GILBERT: *DRR*, (Sept. 1954), pp. 9–18.
65 *q.v.* HAWKINS: *Op. Cit*, p. 121.
66 *JE*, (Feb. 1887), p. 113.
67 I. GOODSON: *School Subjects and Curriculum Change*, (1983), pp. 26–27.
68 *Ibid.*, p. 3; p. 34.
69 *q.v.* SIR C. FIRTH: *Modern Languages at Oxford*, 1724–1929, (1929).
70 HAWKINS: *Op. Cit.*, p. 137.
71 *Memorandum on the Teaching of Modern Languages*, Circular 797, (1912), p. 4.
72 R.W. LIVINGSTONE: *A Defence of Classical Education*, (1916), p. 233.
73 *MLT*, II, 7, (Nov. 1906), pp. 204–5.
74 S. WILKINSON: *The Nation's Need*, (1903), p. 192.
75 'On the curriculum of a modern school', *Conference in Education*, (1884), pp. 283–4.
76 *JE*, (June, 1890), p. 337.
77 *MLQ*, III, 3, (Jan. 1901), p. 169.
78 *Ibid.*, IV, 3 (Dec. 1903), p. 169.
79 *MLT*, I, 1, (March, 1905), p. 27.
80 *MLT*, I, 8, (Dec. 1905), p. 241.
81 *Ibid.*, p. 244.
82 *Ibid.*, III, 1, (Feb. 1907), p. 14.
83 *Ibid.*, VII, 1, (Feb. 1911), p. 18.
84 *MLT*, II, 7, (Nov. 1906), p. 210.

Matters for Discussion, 3, London, HMSO.

—— (1978) *Curriculum 11–16: Modern Languages*, London, HMSO.

HOOLE, C. (1913) *A New Discovery of the old Art of Teaching Schoole* (originally pub. 1660) republished Ed E. CAMPAGNAC, Liverpool, The University Press.

HOPKINS, A. (1978) *The School Debate*, Harmondsworth, Penguin.

HORNSEY, A. (1973) 'A foreign language for all: the questions to be answered', *Modern Languages in Scotland*, May, pp. 32–41.

HUTCHINSON, M. and YOUNG, C. (1962) *Educating the Intelligent*, Harmondsworth, Penguin.

JAMES, C., 'Foreign languages in the school curriculum' in G. PERREN (Ed.) *Foreign Languages in Education*, NCLE Papers and Reports 1, CILT.

JAMES, E. (1949) *An Essay on the Content of Education*, London, Harrap.

JUDGE, H., (1974) *School is not yet Dead*, London, Longman.

KELLY, L. (1969) *25 Centuries of Language Teaching*, Rowley, Massachusetts Newbury House.

LAMBLEY, K. (1920) *The Teaching and Cultivation of the French Language in England during Tudor and Stuart Times*, Manchester, Manchester University Press.

LEATHES COMMITTEE, (1918) *Modern Studies*, London, HMSO.

LIVINGSTONE, R. (1916) *A Defence of a Classical Education*, London, Macmillan.

LOCKE, J., (1889) *Some Thoughts Concerning Education*, (originally published 1693) republished Ed. R. QUICK, London, Cambridge University Press.

MANSELL JONES, P., (1913) *The Assault on French Literature and other Essays*, Manchester, University Press.

MINISTRY OF EDUCATION (1956) *Modern Languages*, Pamphlet No. 29 London, HMSO.

—— (1963) *Half Our Future* (Newsom Report) London, HMSO.

MOORE, H. (1925) *Modernism in Language Teaching*, Cambridge, Cambridge University Press.

MUNN, J. et al (1977) *The Structure of the Curriculum in the 3rd and 4th Year of the Scottish Secondary School* (Munn Report), London, HMSO.

PARKER, I. (1915) *Dissenting Academies in England*, Cambridge, Cambridge University Press.

POWELL, R. and LITTLEWOOD, P. (1982) 'Foreign languages — the avoidable options', *British Journal of Language Teaching*, Winter.

RADFORD, H. (1981) 'Language Barriers', *The Times Educational Supplement*, 8 May.

REÉ, H. (1972) 'A license to learn languages', *The Times Educational Supplement*, 8 December.

RIDDY, D.C. (1967) in Council for Cultural Cooperation, *Modern Languages in Great Britain and Ireland*, AIDELA.

SCHOOLS COUNCIL, (1969) *Development of Modern Language Teaching in Secondary Schools*, Working Paper No. 19, London, HMSO.

SCHOOLS COUNCIL MODERN LANGUAGES COMMITTEE (1981) *Languages other than French in the Secondary School*, London, Schools Council.

SPENCER, H. (1911) *Essays on Education*, (originally published 1860) republished with an introduction by C.W. ELLIOTT, London, Everyman's Library.

STERN, H.H. (1967) in Council for Cultural Cooperation, *Modern Languages in Great Britain and Ireland*, AIDELA.

STEVENS, A. (1980) *Clever Children in Comprehensive Schools*, Harmondsworth, Penguin.

STORR, F. *et al* (1906) *Public Schools from Within*, London.

WATSON, F. (1968) *The English Grammar Schools to 1660* (originally published 1908) republished Cambridge, Cambridge University Press.

—— (1971) *The Beginnings of the Teaching of Modern Subjects in England* (originally published 1909), republished London, Pitman.

WHITE, J. (1973) *Towards a Compulsory Curriculum*, London, Routledge and Kegan Paul.

WIGRAM, M. (1977) 'A national plan for modern languages', *Modern Languages*, LVIII, 1, March.

WILKINSON, S. (1903) *The Nation's Need*, London, Westminster.

# The Social Efficiency Movement and Curriculum Change* 1939–1976

*Barry M. Franklin*

If one wishes to identify an uniquely American contribution to curriculum thought and practice, one is, I think, drawn almost immediately to that period of educational reform during the first half of this century known as the social efficiency movement. It was under the rubric of social efficiency that so many of the ideas we typically identify as representing an American contribution to curriculum work, namely curriculum differentiation, curriculum integration, and scientific curriculum making, as well as the belief that the school programme must prepare youth for immediate life situations, first made their appearance. No comparable effort at educational change has been so in touch with such American characteristics as a belief in the methods of science, a trust in business expertise, and a faith in the progressive nature of technology than has this attempt to create a more utilitarian school programme.

If there is a conventional wisdom within the contemporary field of curriculum studies, one of its central tenets would no doubt be that efficiency ideas have been a dominant force in shaping not only curriculum studies as an academic discipline within the university but the American school curriculum itself. This belief in the commanding influence of social efficiency ideas seems to be almost taken for granted among those contemporary American educators who write and speak on the subject of curriculum theory.

---

* The research required for this chapter could not have been completed without the assistance of the staff of the Information Service Center of the Minneapolis Public Schools. I am particularly indebted to Dr August Rivera, Director of the Information Service Center, for his help in using the general files of the Minneapolis Public Schools, the source of most of the data for this research.

The American curriculum field, so this conventional wisdom goes, was established by a group of individuals with a special fondness for the practices of early twentieth century American business and industry. It was in fact the principal industrial innovation of the day, the idea of scientific management, to which these first curriculum workers turned in their efforts to establish a methodology of curriculum construction and to define the role of the school curriculum in American life. Under the rubric of social efficiency, they and their intellectual heirs would go on during the first half of this century to build a school curriculum to prepare youth for their occupational and citizenship roles in an urban, industrial society.

As a result of their efforts, a school curriculum directed toward the goal of mental training at the beginning of this century would by the end of the second world war be transformed into a more directly functional school programme, designed first to sort and then to channel youth to their assigned place in the nation's industrial workforce and its social class system. Except for a brief hiatus in the 1960s, when curriculum workers temporarily abandoned their adherence to efficiency ideas during a period of discipline-centred curriculum reform, the social efficiency movement has continued to exert a dominant influence on curriculum thought and practice. The almost singular devotion of curriculum workers to efficiency ideas, this line of research concludes, has made American schools society's principal agency for adjusting youth to the demands of life in a corporate, industrial society.[1]

Despite the wide appeal this conventional wisdom seems to enjoy, a close examination of various instances of this interpretation reveals a glaring weakness. Almost uniformly, those who advance this view rely for their evidence, first on the writings of efficiency-minded proponents, such as Bobbitt, Charters, and Tyler, who have defined the supposed purpose of this curriculum reform movement, and secondly, on the reports of those national committees, such as the Commission on the Reorganization of Secondary Education and the Commission on Life Adjustment Education, which have throughout this century recommended the reorganization of the curriculum along efficiency lines. They have rarely, if ever, presented any evidence about what was occurring within the schools in the way of curriculum development or change. Their evidence does seem to support the claim that efficiency ideas have exerted a dominant influence on the work of those theorists who established and built the curriculum field. It is less certain, however, that their evidence tells us anything about what has occurred in the schools.

During the last three years, a number of scholars have undertaken investigations of the implementation of efficiency-oriented curriculum changes in a number of American school systems during the first half of this century. These studies taken together suggest that efficiency-minded curriculum reform was not the monolithic movement many contemporary educators seem to believe. It was a movement that seems to have had diverse influences on American schools. In some instances the introduction of efficiency-minded curriculum changes did transform the school programme, although not always in the precise direction suggested by our field's conventional wisdom. In other instances, however, the introduction of these same reforms had, at best, a marginal effect on the existing curriculum.[2] These studies seem to indicate, then, that the direction which the curriculum was taking in American schools during the first half of this century may have been different from what a reading of Bobbitt or the *Cardinal Principles of Secondary Education* would suggest.

If, as I believe, these recent investigations of the implementation of efficiency-minded curriculum change are accurate, we need to pay more attention than we have in the past to the relationship between curriculum theory and curriculum practice. We need, first, to examine what has occurred when school people committed to the ideas of social efficiency have attempted to introduce these ideas into the actual school curriculum. Second, we need to examine what connection, if any, has existed between those proposals for curriculum change that have been advanced by educators as representing a theory of social efficiency and actual school practices that have been introduced in the name of efficiency. Third and finally, we need to examine the claim that under the influence of efficiency ideas, American schools have become prime instruments for socializing youth to the demands of a corporate, industrial economy. In this chapter, I will explore these issues by examining one historical case, in Minneapolis, Minnesota, of an effort to introduce one efficiency-minded curriculum reform within an actual school system.

In the Fall of 1939, the Minneapolis Public Schools introduced an integrated, functionally oriented twelfth grade social studies course known as Modern Problems. Following the recommendation of the 1916 Social Studies Committee of the Commission on the Reorganization of Secondary Education (CRSE), the Minneapolis school administration had instituted this curricular addition as part of an effort to reorient their social studies programme along efficiency lines.[3] Organized around a number of specific social issues or problems thought to be of concern and interest to high school youth about to enter adult society, such as health, education, crime, and recreation, to name a few, the course, the administration believed, would place the twin goals of preparation for citizenship and work at the heart of the social studies programme.

The history of Minneapolis' Modern Problems course offers a good case study for two reasons. First, Minneapolis school administrators, specifically those involved with curriculum planning and development, have been committed, at least throughout the first half of this century, to the goals of social efficiency. In his 1931 annual report to the Minneapolis Board of Education, Superintendent Carroll Reed signaled the important role that social efficiency ideas had come to play and would continue to play in the city's schools for another three or four decades. Using terminology more common to the corporate boardroom than to the schoolroom, Reed announced in the report, which he aptly titled 'The Product of the Minneapolis Public Schools', that the success of the schools depended on '. . . the ability of the young people who are the product of the public schools to adjust themselves to the life of the community with a minimum of lost time and with few costly mistakes'. 'That school system is most successful,' he went on to say, 'which turns out the largest percentage of young men and women able to take their places in the community as efficient and self-regulating citizens.'[4] A school system so singularly committed to the ideas of social efficiency offers a good place to examine the actual influence of this movement on the school programme.

Second, Modern Problems was, as we shall see, a central concern of Minneapolis curriculum workers for almost forty years. The reform which Modern Problems exemplified — the integrated, functionally oriented social studies course — has been in all probability the most successful and enduring legacy of the social efficiency movement. Examining the history of a course over so long a period of time that has been so inextricably linked with the social efficiency movement offers a good way to evaluate the influence which this movement has had on the school curriculum.

The focus of this chapter, then, will be on the history of the Modern Problems course in Minneapolis. I will first look at the efforts of Minneapolis educators, beginning in the mid-1920s, to reorganize the social studies curriculum along efficiency lines. I will then examine the introduction of the Modern Problems course in the late 1930s and trace its development through the 1960s. Finally, I will look at the demise of the course during the early 1970s.

I will argue, first, that an examination of the history of this course in Minneapolis does indicate that the social efficiency movement played a significant role in shaping the curriculum in at least one major American school system during this century. The impetus for curriculum change in Minneapolis from the mid-1920s through at least the 1950s was the commitment of its key curriculum workers to the goal of remaking the curriculum along efficiency lines. Their commitment, however, did not lead to the simple translation of the theories of Bobbitt, Charters, and others into curriculum practice. There was, in other words, no one-to-one correspondence between the ideas advanced by efficiency-oriented curriculum theorists and the practices of school people in Minneapolis. Curriculum change is, I think, a far more complex and ultimately ambiguous process for that kind of similarity to exist.

Second, I will argue that central to this instance of efficiency-oriented curriculum reform was the existence of certain local factors that served to mediate what change occurred. These factors, which included such things as legal requirements, teachers' attitudes and talents, the nature of the existing curriculum, and the organization of the school year — to name but a few ═ acted to limit the ability of the Minneapolis school adminstration to implement this efficiency oriented change in anything but a marginal way. In the end, it was these mediating factors far more than the ideas of any efficiency minded curriculum theorist that determined the fate of Modern Problems in Minneapolis.

The proposals of efficiency-oriented curriculum theorists and the recommendations of efficiency-oriented curriculum committees have, I think, only provided a rough indication of the direction that a segment of the American educational establishment during this century has hoped the school curriculum would take. Our study of the Modern Problems course in Minneapolis will show that the curriculum in at least one American city has been, for better or worse, only an inexact beacon of those hopes.

### Origins of Modern Problems in Minneapolis

In 1925, the Minneapolis Public Schools undertook a revision of their high school curriculum. As part of that revision, they adopted a social studies curriculum similar to the one recommended in 1916 by the Social Studies Committee of the Commission on the Reorganization of Secondary Education.[5] For the senior year, the Committee had recommended, as we have already noted, a course organized around the social problems of secondary age youth. They suggested either the introduction of courses in political science, economics, or sociology that dealt with these problems or the development of a single, integrated social science course with the same focus on social problems, which they called Problems of Democracy.[6] Minneapolis' programme was similiar to the Committee's first recommendation and included a one semester required course in American government and semester electives in economics, sociology, and commercial law.[7]

A year earlier, Superintendent of Schools W.F. Webster had appointed Prudence Cutright, who had been Assistant Superintendent of the La Crosse, Wisconsin Public Schools, as Director of Minneapolis' Bureau of Research and Curriculum Construction. In 1934, she would be promoted to Assistant Superintendent for Instruction and would from that position serve for almost another two decades as Minneapolis' principal architect of efficiency-oriented curriculum reform. Her earliest work in Minneapolis was clearly indicative of her devotion to the ideals of efficiency. Her Master's thesis, which she completed in 1927 at the University of Minnesota under the supervision of Leo Brueckner, an expert of the day in mental measurements, was a study of the relative efficiency of different types of dictation exercises in improving students' use of correct punctuation.[8] In one of the first curriculum revisions Cutright undertook at the Research Bureau, she developed the objectives for an elementary citizenship programme by having teachers identify the 'faulty behaviour' of students in the light of correct adult citizenship practices. And in another early project, she used Bobbitt's ten classes of human activities to develop composition topics to identify the common spelling errors of elementary children.[9]

Cutright approached the task of curriculum construction from what she called the 'scientific point of view'. The approach, similar to that advocated by Bobbitt and Charters, saw the first task of the curriculum worker as that of establishing the aims or objectives of education.[10] There were, she noted, again mirroring the views of those who advanced the principles of scientific curriculum making, two basic ways of identifying these objectives. A curriculum committee could undertake a 'community survey' of how individuals used a particular subject 'in their everyday activites'. The survey would reveal the most appropriate objectives for the study of that subject. Or a committee could by 'consensus' select certain objectives from a larger available pool of objectives identified by an examination of certain 'authoritative writings'.[11]

Cutright not only shared the methodology of scientific curriculum making, she shared its efficiency goals. She opposed, for example, the pattern of curriculum selection and organization she found upon her arrival in Minneapolis, a pattern she later labelled as the 'old subject matter preparatory curriculum'.[12] In the 1937 annual report of the Division of Instruction, she attacked this school of thought because of what she believed was the inefficiency of its allegiance to the goal of mental training:

> Experiments have shown that while a child may be very accurate in solving mathematics problems, this accuracy did not carry over to practical affairs and to other matters to any great extent. Therefore, a teacher who still teaches as if the thing she was trying to do was to train the mind as we train muscles of the body is to a large extent wasting a child's time and effort.[13]

What was required in Minneapolis, she argued, was a curriculum that prepared students 'to meet life-like problems and situations rather than merely covering and memorizing textbooks'.[14]

The twelfth grade social studies programme that Minneapolis introduced in 1925, had only partially met Cutright's goal for a curriculum to prepare students for the demands of adult society. The sociology course that was added emphasized the study of the discipline of sociology and not the examination of social problems. As Superintendent Webster noted in his 1929 annual report, 'Minneapolis now offers a course in sociology that would do credit to a junior college. The text used is in fact a college text.'[15] Similarly, the course in American government involved a study of the organization and operation of the federal and state governments, which the CRSE's Social Studies Committee had warned in its 1913 preliminary report stood in direct opposition to the goals of social efficiency.[16]

The source of the problem seemed to be that some Minneapolis educators viewed the social studies as a number of distinct disciplines. In an October 1939 memorandum to the city's high school principals outright questioned the practice of appointing separate department chairmen in each high school for geography, history and government. She was concerned that this practice might indicate that teachers held the erroneous view that the social studies were 'three separate and distinct subjects' when in fact there should be 'a minimum of sharp breaks in the curriculum'.[17] Treating the social studies as a number of separate subjects was incompatible, she felt, with the goal of establishing a more functionally oriented curriculum:

> Since the purpose of education is to develop the ability to meet problems and situations with increasing effectiveness, it is obvious that the curriculum must give more prominent place to *actual* experiences in dealing with situations and problems.

There was no problems that fall neatly into one subject-matter division. Real problems override subject-matter boundary lines....[18]

To deal with this problem, Earl Peckham, the Supervisor of Secondary Education in Cutright's Division of Instruction, recommended to a citywide social studies committee in 1937 the development of a senior level contemporary problems course.[19] Peckham forwarded two proposals for such a course to the committee. One was composed of three suggested units: 'taxation and the common man,' 'world wars and who pays for them,' and 'making a living'. The second proposal, developed by Milton Schadegg, a social studies teacher at the city's Central High School, was a complete course of seventeen units, including such topics as 'sobriety,' 'social inadequacy,' and 'social misfits'.[20] What Peckham was in effect proposing was a course similar to the Problems of Democracy course recommended by the CRSE's Social Studies Committee twenty-one years earlier.

Two years later, a new integrated twelfth grade social studies course, known as Modern Problems, was introduced. During the next five years, Modern Problems was offered as an alternative to the existing senior level social studies programme. Students were allowed to take Modern Problems I in lieu of taking the required semester course in American government. Modern Problems II was an elective which students could take instead of taking a course in sociology, economics, or commercial law.[21]

Despite Cutright's hopes for this new course, it did not, as implemented, appear all that different from the existing twelfth grade social studies offerings. The course description for Modern Problems I was virtually the same as the description of the course in American government. The course was, unlike the government course, to include a unit on 'occupational adjustment'. This unit, however, it seems, was never added. In 1944, five years after Modern Problems was first introduced, the senior high school social studies committee recommended that a unit on vocational guidance needed to be added to Modern Problems. The description of Modern Problems II included the study of such issues as 'population, labour, housing, family life, and consumer needs'. Similar issues, however, were already a part of the sociology, economics, and commercial law courses.[22]

Some Minneapolis teachers evidently saw little difference between Modern Problems and the existing course in American government. The West High School history faculty, for example, viewed Modern Problems as just another course in government. Modern Problems, they pointed out at their October 1940 department meeting, was '. . . a full year subject using American Government as the core subject and about a semester for Modern Problems. The subject could be named Civics, Modern Problems, or American Government.' The name of the course had more to do with meeting 'the credit requirements of the state department' than with its content.[23]

Why might it be that these teachers at West High School saw so little change as a result of this addition to the curriculum? To understand this, we need to look further at the events surrounding the introduction of Modern Problems. In April of 1940, Barbara Wright, head of the Counseling Division, informed Assistant Superintendent Cutright that the University of Minnesota might not accept Modern Problems for its social science entrance requirement, which allowed for courses in history, American government, commercial geography, economics and sociology. Wright went on to suggest that perhaps the State Department of Education could assist Minneapolis in obtaining the University's approval of Modern Problems for this requirement.[24]

That same month, Superintendent Carroll Reed wrote to State Commissioner of Education John Rockwell to inform him that Modern Problems met state high school graduation requirements for a course in the social sciences that included the study of American government. This requirement is met, he noted, 'by intensive study in a one semester course required of all seniors'. He requested Rockwell's assistance in obtaining University approval of the course.[25] Rockwell in turn wrote to Royal Shumway, Assistant Dean of the University's College of Letters, Sciences and Arts to notify him that Modern Problems appeared to meet state requirements for a senior year 'Introduction to Social Science' course. Minneapolis, he stated, did not have to offer a specific course in either economics or sociology to meet this requirement because these disciplines '. . . may be involved in the various problems considered in this course'.[26] A week later, Shumway wrote back to Rockwell to tell him that the University would abide by his interpretation and accept Modern Problems as meeting the social science entrance requirement.[27]

The following month, A.B. Caldwell, Deputy State Commissioner of Education, wrote to Cutright to ask if the difficulty involving Modern Problems had been resolved. Cutright replied that the matter was 'cleared up'. 'It will,' she added, 'simplify bookkeeping on credit in high school enormously.'[28] For the next four years, Minneapolis continued to offer both semester courses in American government, sociology, economics, and commercial law as well as the new, two semester Modern Problems course. In 1944, the separate social science courses were dropped from the curriculum and a one year Modern Problems course, involving one semester devoted to the study of American government and one semester for the consideration of contemporary problems, became the required senior year social studies course.[29]

Why, however, was the study of American government confined to one semester, thereby limiting the possibility of curriculum integration? The State Department of Education and the University were only interested in insuring that government was taught, not how instruction was organized or how the subject was taught. All Minneapolis students, as it turned out, were not able to take both semesters of Modern Problems. Students taking vocational courses only had enough room in their programmes to take one semester of social studies during their senior year. If they were to meet the state graduation requirement in government, it was necessary that the subject be taught in one semester. There was, then, not enough time in this one semester course to complete the required work in government and to treat contemporary problems.[30]

The interplay of three factors, then, seemed to have limited the ability of Minneapolis educators to use Modern Problems to fully transform the curriculum along efficiency lines. First, Modern Problems to be a viable course needed to be accepted by the University in fulfilment of its social science entrance requirement. Second, the course, again to be viable, had to be accepted by the State Department of Education as satisfying its high school graduation requirement for the study of American government. Third, the study of government to be accessible to all high school students needed to be offered in a one semester course. Taken together, these three factors, university admission requirements, state high school graduation requirements, and the demands of the existing school programme, necessitated the development of a Modern Problems course in which one semester was devoted to the study of government and the other to the integration of sociology and economics around the social problems of high school youth. It was this anomaly between the goal of Minneapolis curriculum workers and what they achieved with the implementation of Modern Problems that apparently caught the attention of the West High School history faculty and accounted for their scepticism concerning the supposed change brought by the introduction of Modern Problems. In the end, then, it was the mediating role played by certain factors in Minneapolis more than any theory of a Bobbitt or any recommendation of a national committee that determined the outcome of this effort at efficiency-oriented curriculum reform.

## Discontent with Modern Problems

By all odds, Modern Problems should have been a popular and successful curriculum reform. It was a change that matched the efficiency viewpoint of the school administration. Teachers, too, seemed favourably inclined towards the notion of an integrated course. In 1937, a number of Minneapolis teachers met to organize a social studies club, which would in the 1950s become the Minneapolis chapter of the National Council for the Social Studies. One of the two principal objectives of the teachers in proposing the club was to secure the integration of the social studies curriculum '... in order that our teaching may help the youth of the city to develop as worthy members of the society in which they find themselves.'[31]

In addition to its seeming popularity, Modern Problems represented a change that should have fitted the concerns of the moment during the early 1940s to use the curriculum as an instrument in support of the nation's war effort. In 1943, the senior high school social studies policies committee recommended that social studies teachers devote time to the discussion of such current problems as manpower, rationing, and civil defense.[32] These were the very kinds of issues which a course such as Modern Problems was designed to address. And similarly as the war drew to a close, Modern Problems seemed to be the perfect vehicle for meeting Minneapolis' post war goal of re-adjusting those who had served in the military and war related work to the demands of civilian life.[33] In this vein the citywide committee on global living and citizenship training recommended that such topics as employment trends, labour legislation, and social security be included in the Modern Problems course.[34]

Yet, there were efforts made to alter the Modern Problems requirement. At their December 1946 meeting, the city's senior high school principals recommended that Modern Problems be made an elective course. They noted that while the state required only two years of social studies, Minneapolis offered a three year programme, an elective in world history in the tenth grade and required courses in American history and Modern Problems in the eleventh and twelfth grades. Students who took all three years of social studies had little opportunity, the principals argued, for other elective courses. No action, however, was taken on the recommendation.[35] Two years later, the Social Studies Steering Committee considered abandoning the course altogether. What prevented them from making this recommendation was the belief of the chairman Ed Haynes, a social studies teacher at Roosevelt High School, that the course was required by the State Department of Education.[36]

The reason for this dissatisfaction with Modern Problems is not entirely clear. One difficulty that may have led some Minneapolis educators to want to abandon it or at least make it an elective was the issue of identifying appropriate content. It seems that Modern Problems became the required twelfth grade social studies requirement before any definite decision was made about how to use contemporary problems to integrate the social science disciplines that made up the course. In the year that Modern Problems became the sole senior level social studies course, Laurel Burkle, a curriculum assistant under Cutright, had suggested that the schools might need to have some experience with Modern Problems before they 'evolve a successful approach to the course and discover how the social and economic problems may be integrated.'[37] It seems, then, that the school administration had introduced Modern Problems before some Minneapolis educators had determined what to do with this innovation.

Despite some apparent doubts about the suitability of Modern Problems, the course continued unchanged as the twelfth grade social studies requirement for the remainder of the decade. During the 1950s, in the wake of a nationwide assault on the social efficiency movement, Modern Problems would undergo changes. As we shall see, however, these changes had more to do with local factors unique to Minneapolis than they had to do with any ideological shifts in the larger society away from efficiency ideals.

## Modern Problems and the Efficiency Controversy in Minneapolis

If the conventional wisdom I described at the beginning of this chapter were to hold true, we would expect that during the 1950s Minneapolis educators would have come under increasing attack for their devotion to the ideals of social efficiency. This was, after all, the decade that began with the criticisms of Albert Lynd and Arthur Bestor that the academic quality of American schools had deteriorated under the influence of life adjustment education, that later saw a national debate over the viability of American education spurred on by the fear of a technological Armageddon in the wake of Sputnik, and ended at Woods Hole with the emergence of a new discipline-oriented curriculum reform movement.[38]

There was what we might think of as the beginning of a controversy over the efficiency movement in Minneapolis during the early 1950s. In 1952, thirty-three members of the University of Minnesota faculty signed a resolution then circulating nationwide for presentation to the upcoming meeting of the American Historical Association denouncing the '"anti-intellectual" trend of American public schools'. The resolution went on to call for the establishment of a committee of university scholars and scientists to examine existing programmes of teacher education and proposals for changing the content and organization of the secondary school curriculum.

A.C. Krey, chairman of the University's History Department and former head of the American Historical Association's Commission on the Social Studies during the 1920s and 1930s, did not sign the resolution, but he did comment to *The Minneapolis Tribune* on his assessment of the situation in the Minneapolis Public Schools. He noted that 'some Minneapolis schools — Washburn, West, and North High in particular — do a fairly satisfactory job of preparing students for college'. Their work was, he went on to say, 'not good enough'. 'The schools have to keep the youngsters happy,' which had led them to reduce their academic standards. 'Education and schools,' he concluded, 'are no longer synonymous.'[39]

Angered by Krey's comment, Harry Cooper, Assistant Superintendent for Secondary Education, who after Cutright's retirement in 1950 had become Minneapolis' chief champion of efficiency-minded curriculum reform, wrote to Krey asking for evidence to support his charge about the inadequate preparatory programme of some of the city's high schools.[40] A few days later, Krey responded to indicate that while he had not intended to single out particular schools for criticism, he stood by his statement.[41] The following month, Cooper again wrote to Krey to tell him that Minneapolis had sent students to a number of universities and that they were 'making remarkable records'. He also noted in his letter to Krey that at present there were six graduates of Minneapolis high schools attending Yale University, and all of them were on the dean's list.[42]

Despite this criticism, Minneapolis school administrators were not swayed from their commitment to the social efficiency movement. In 1953, Minneapolis issued a statement of its educational objectives in its curriculum guide. Of the nine objectives, seven matched those stated in the efficiency-oriented *Cardinal Principles of Secondary Education*.[43] There was, however, one setback to the efficiency movement in 1950 involving an integrated, problems-oriented course known as Common Learnings. Five years earlier, the administration had introduced Common Learnings, a programme to integrate English and social studies around the problems of youth, as a requirement in the city's junior and senior high schools in lieu of traditional courses in English and social studies. In 1950, the Board of Education in response to parental pressure required that Common Learnings be made optional and that separate courses in English and social studies be available to students who desired them. The administration was, however, able to maintain Common Learnings within the curriculum for another twenty years as an integrated, problems-oriented, albeit optional, course.[44]

For the most part, the administration tended to dismiss criticism of the schools as the propaganda of anti-public school forces. In a 1957 memorandum, Kopple Friedman, the Supervisor of Secondary Social Studies, commenting on a criticism of public education in *The Wall Street Journal*, noted that the Defense Department was responsible for 'our lagging behind Russia in producing satellites'. The schools, he argued, were a convenient 'scapegoat' for this criticism, 'the result of perennial hostilities which are coming to the surface again with a new excuse'.[45] A year later in a memorandum to Superintendent Rufus Putnam, Friedman stated that there was little evidence to support the charge that the life adjustment movement was dominating the public schools.[46]

Why, we need to ask, in the midst of an assault on efficiency ideals, was there so little controversy over this movement in Minneapolis? One factor that may have accounted for this lack of discord, at least with respect to the social studies, was the public support voiced for the existing social studies curriculum in the 1957 report of the Citizens Committee on Public Education, an independent lay committee of citizens concerned about public education in Minneapolis. There was, the committee noted, no undue weight given to issues of 'personal and social adjustment' in Modern Problems and other social studies courses. The subject was only addressed indirectly, they pointed out, while the student was studying the 'content of geography, history, and civics'. The Committee's Board of Directors in fact warned against any overreaction to the charge that the quality of education in Minneapolis was declining. It was necessary, they argued, to '... keep a balance between the pressure of Sputnik and the need for proper emphasis on cultural values and preparing for citizenship'.[47] It is, of course, difficult to judge the impact of this report. It would seem, no doubt, to have, at the least, strengthened the resolve of Minneapolis administrators to maintain their commitment to efficiency ideals. It may even have created the kind of public climate that would have forestalled widespread community criticism of Minneapolis' social studies programme.

## Modern Problems during the 1950s

Although the shift away from efficiency ideals in the nation as a whole did not seem to have much influence on Minneapolis curriculum workers, they did nonetheless introduce changes in Modern Problems during the 1950s that struck at the core of its uniqueness, its integrated content and its organization around contemporary problems. In 1955, the Social Studies Scope and Sequence Committee recommended that certain high schools be allowed to offer in addition to Modern Problems any or all of six, year long, so-called equivalent courses, Problems of Government, Current World Problems, Economics in Everyday Life, Social Problems and Community Study, Psychology of Daily Living, and Occupational Relations. In each of the equivalents, thirty weeks would be devoted to the same core content, which was similar to but less extensive than the content of Modern Problems. The remaining eight weeks of the year would be devoted to additional study of the particular subject emphasized by each equivalent. Economics in Daily Life, for example, would cover the same basic material as did Modern Problems and the other equivalent courses. There would, however, be additional opportunity for the study of economics not available in the other alternative courses.[48] The administration accepted this recommendation and introduced equivalent courses a year later.[49]

The effect of introducing equivalent courses was to return, at least with respect to the government, economics and psychology equivalents, the social science disciplines to a more central role in the curriculum. This modification in Modern Problems had little to do with any criticisms of the efficiency rationale of the course. Rather, the social studies committee recommended the addition to deal with a problem posed by the apparent overload of content in the Modern Problems course. It was not possible given the scope of content in Modern Problems, the committee felt, to examine course material in any depth and still cover all that was required. The equivalents would address this difficulty by providing a common core of content for all students which approximated what was taught in Modern Problems without precluding an in-depth study of at least one topic.

From 1955 to 1958, Minneapolis underwent a major examination of its secondary curriculum known as the Study of the High School Day. In its 1959 report, the study committee noted that a critical problem of the existing school programme was the presence of almost identical content in a number of different subject areas. Family living, they pointed out, was covered in the social studies, home economics, physical education and science. To resolve this problem, the study committee recommended that one single home economics course, Home and Family Living, be devoted to instruction in this area.[50] To accommodate this recommendation, a number of topics that had been a part of Modern Problems were transferred to this home economics course. They included, 'preparation for marriage', 'requirements for successful marriage', 'responsibility for wise selection of a mate', and 'requirements for successful parenthood'. The study committee further suggested that instead of examining the problems of family life, Modern Problems should address the sociology and economics of the family. As a result, there was a shift in the emphasis of Modern Problems away from the study of contemporary problems and toward the study of the disciplines of sociology and economics.[51]

Our examination of Modern Problems during the 1950s, just as our examination of the origins of the course in the previous decade, poses problems for our conventional view of the influence of the social efficiency movement on the curriculum. There was not, as we might have expected, much in the way of public opposition to efficiency reform in Minneapolis. The opposition that existed, however, did not seem to dissuade Minneapolis curriculum workers from their commitment to efficiency reform. We argued that perhaps the favourable report on the social studies issued by the Citizens Committee on Public Education may have acted to undercut whatever local opposition there was to an efficiency-oriented social studies programme, as well as to strengthen the devotion of Minneapolis curriculum workers to their programme of efficiency reform.

The changes in Modern Problems that did occur — the introduction of the equivalent courses and the de-emphasis on contemporary problems — were the result of efforts of Minneapolis educators to deal with such local concerns as the overload of content in the Modern Problems course and the duplication of content across the curriculum. In the end, then, what happened to Modern Problems during the 1950s had less to do with any shift that may have occurred in educational thinking than it did with the mediating influence of several local factors affecting the day-to-day operation of Minneapolis high schools.

The changes that occurred in Modern Problems during this decade although slight were not unimportant. They did set the stage for other changes during the next fifteen years that would lead ultimately to the elimination of this course from the curriculum. These changes, too, as we shall see had less to do with the prevailing current of educational thought than they did with local factors involved in the ongoing functioning of schooling in Minneapolis.

### The Demise of Modern Problems

In addition to altering the content of Modern Problems, the Study of the High School Day recommended a complete review of the course. Several high schools had reported that they were having continual difficulties in deciding what aspects of the course to emphasize and in allocating time adequately among all the topics covered in the course. Throughout 1960, the social studies departments of the city's high schools examined a number of possible solutions to this problem. The three that gained the widest support included increasing the length of the course to one and a half years, replacing Modern Problems and the equivalents with semester courses in the various social science disciplines, and doing nothing. The citywide Secondary Social Studies Committee then asked all high school principals and social studies teachers to vote on which of these three proposals they preferred. The committee also examined a number of social studies curricula in other school systems around the country to determine how they had organized their senior year programme. They noted that only one school system had a year course in social problems while the remainder offered semester courses in either social problems or in various social science disciplines.[52]

In June 1961, the committee reported its recommendations for changes in Modern Problems, which the administration, in turn, accepted. Each high school, beginning in September of 1962, would be able to offer both a year course in Modern Problems and semester electives in any or all of six social science disciplines — government, economics, geography, psychology, sociology, and world affairs. Students would be able to take either the year Modern Problems course or a one semester course in government and, if their programmes allowed, an additional semester chosen from one of the five remaining electives.[53] In instituting these new semester electives in place of the year long equivalent courses, the administration seemed to have moved one step further away from the idea of course work in social problems and toward work in the social science disciplines. Under this new programme, students would now take a course in economics instead of Economics in Everyday Life or a course in psychology instead of Psychology of Daily Living.

We can see this change in emphasis when we look at the new semester elective in economics. The Study of the High School Day had recommended the establishment of an economics course to prepare students to be more effective consumers.[54] The economics course that was actually implemented in 1962, however, placed more emphasis on 'economic theory and less on everyday economics'.[55]

When we try to account for this change, we find, as we did in our discussion of Modern Problems previously, that the prevailing educational thinking of the moment had little influence. It was during the 1960s that the criticisms of efficiency ideas found expression in an attempt, known as the structures of the disciplines movement, to reassert the centrality of the academic disciplines in the organization of the curriculum. In the social studies, this movement resulted in a number of discipline-centered curriculum projects in history and the social sciences, known collectively as 'the new social studies'.

By the middle of the decade, Minneapolis educators were certainly aware of the shift in educational thinking exemplified by the new social studies. During the 1965–66 academic year, the city's social studies teachers concerned about upgrading their programme reviewed many of these new, discipline-centered curriculum projects. One of them, a project in economics education, was introduced into some high schools. The entire issue of the March 1968 *Social Studies Bulletin*, one of the house organs for Minneapolis social studies teachers, was devoted to reprinting excerpts from the writings of such well known advocates of the new social studies as Edwin Fenton, Hilda Taba, and Bruce Joyce.[56] The introduction of twelfth grade social science electives occurred, however, at least three years before this interest and involvement in the new social studies was much in evidence. It is doubtful, then, that the principal changes that were made in Modern Problems during the 1960s, which occurred at the beginning of the decade, had much to do with any impact that the new social studies had on Minneapolis educators.

More important in bringing about the creation of semester social science electives was a growing dissatisfaction of the school administration with either the willingness or ability of high school social studies teachers to teach Modern Problems adequately as an integrated course. Kopple Friedman, for example, noted that he now had doubts about the suitability of the integrated, problems-oriented course he had once supported. 'I continually observe the inability of some teachers to handle curriculums that represent any departure from textbooks. I often question the handling of general courses, such as the typical twelfth grade problems course, even by teachers who have social studies majors'.[57]

At the April 1963 meeting of the city's senior high school principals, the principals from Roosevelt and Henry High Schools indicated that it had been difficult to get Modern Problems teachers to cover all the material required in the course. Many of them, they noted, had simply used the course to teach either American or world history. The introduction of the social science electives, these two principals thought, had been helpful in avoiding this problem because it offered teachers the opportunity to teach in their areas of specialization.[58] Two months earlier, at the Secondary Social Studies Committee meeting, the Principal of North High School indicated a similar problem. He had resolved it by allowing the Modern Problems teachers to teach only one of the two semesters of the course, thereby affording them some opportunity to develop an area of specialization within the course. He suggested that this practice had been an excellent first step toward the wider use of semester electives at his school.[59]

The introduction of semester electives allowed an alternative senior year programme for those high schools that were dissatified with Modern Problems for one reason or another. In 1966, six of the city's high schools offered only Modern Problems. Of the remainder, three offered a choice between Modern Problems and semester electives, and two high schools dropped Modern Problems in favour of the electives.[60] During the next six years, more high schools began to introduce semester electives. In 1972, two schools that had only offered Modern Problems, South and Southwest High Schools, introduced the electives. One school, Edison High School, abandoned Modern Problems in favour of electives.[61] Over the next four years, other high schools, in turn, abandoned Modern Problems until by the middle of the decade the course ceased to exist within the Minneapolis school curriculum.

There were several good reasons why Minneapolis school administrators would have favoured the elimination of Modern Problems during the 1970s. There was at least some community criticism of the academic value of the course. In April 1970, T.B. Corlett, Director of Minneapolis' Water Works, complained to Superintendent of Schools John Davis that the Modern Problems requirement was interfering with his son's preparation to enter the engineering programme at the University of Minnesota. The course, he claimed, was a waste of time since it would not be accepted for admission by the University's Institute of Technology. It was a similar situation, Corlett noted, to the one he had encountered during the 1930s when faced with this same requirement as a student at the city's Washburn High School. 'Why', he asked, had Minneapolis for forty years placed a 'stumbling block' in the way of students preparing to be scientists 'by requiring a course be taken only for the satisfaction of the Minneapolis school system?'[62]

Modern Problems also seemed to be out of step with the current thinking of social studies educators. In a 1976 report to the administration on developments in the social studies, John Bastolich, the Social

Studies Consultant, noted that 'at the secondary level there is a trend toward dividing social studies into topics, mini courses, options, etc, rather than describing the social studies in larger blocks of content such as world history, US history, modern problems, etc'.[63]

Finally, Minneapolis during this decade was under court order to desegregate its schools. As part of its court approved desegregation plan, the administration agreed to develop a multi-ethnic social studies curriculum involving courses in minority group history and culture.[64] What was needed, it seemed, were not all inclusive courses such as Modern Problems but narrow, more specialized courses that would address existing concerns as well as this new interest in race and ethnicity.

Although these considerations, reflecting larger societal concerns, no doubt influenced the fate of Modern Problems, the precipitating event in the elimination of the course was something local in nature, a change in the school calendar. In 1976, Minneapolis high schools abandoned their longstanding practice of dividing the academic year into two ninety day semesters in favour of shorter, sixty day periods or trimesters.[65] To institute this change it was necessary to reorganize existing semester courses into shorter, trimester courses. Rather than restructuring Modern Problems to fit this pattern, the high schools still offering the course simply dropped it from the curriculum and added new trimester social science electives and several new multi-ethnic courses, including Street Law and Youth in the Pursuit of Justice.[66] Ultimately, then, the elimination of Modern Problems had less to do with what was occurring in the realm of educational theory than what was happening locally in Minneapolis in response to an administrative adjustment in the organization of the high school calendar.

## Conclusions

Our examination of the Modern Problems course in Minneapolis from 1939 to 1976 does indicate that in at least one American school system, the social efficiency movement did exert the dominant influence suggested by our field's conventional wisdom. Yet our study also indicates that we should use the term 'dominant' advisedly. Minneapolis school administrators seemed throughout this period to be committed to efficiency ideals, a commitment they maintained in spite of outside criticism and shifts in prevailing educational thought.

When we look, however, at the content and organization of

Modern Problems, we note some important departures from efficiency principals. At its inception, the interplay of three factors — university admission requirements, state high school graduation requirements, and the demands of the existing school programme — prevented the course from attaining the kind of content integration that was the hallmark of efficiency-minded curriculum change. Thereafter, other factors, the overloaded content of the course, the duplication of content across the curriculum, and the difficulty which teachers experienced in teaching the course, resulted in changes in Modern Problems that undermined its integrated content and its problems orientation.

It was, we argued, the existence of these and other local mediating factors involving the day to day operation of the schools that account for the disparities between Minneapolis' Modern Problems course and efficiency ideals. These factors, we suggested, seemed to limit the ability and willingness of Minneapolis educators fundamentally to transform the senior social studies curriculum along efficiency lines.

One of the important effects of these mediating factors, we noted, has been to disrupt what our conventional wisdom has told us is a simple correspondence between efficiency ideas and school practices. If what we have found about the relationship between curriculum theory and practice in Minneapolis is true for other school systems, we will need to revise our understanding of that relationship. To determine this connection, we will have to undertake additional historical studies of the efforts of school people to implement curriculum ideas into practice in actual school systems.

Central to our field's conventional wisdom about the social efficiency movement has been the view that the school curriculum and the school itself under the influence of efficiency ideas have become direct agents of the American state in realizing its long term political and economic goals. Contemporary curriculum theorists are divided in their interpretation of this linkage. Some take a positive view and argue that the development of a functionally oriented school curriculum has represented a vehicle for social mobility and equal opportunity in urban industrial America for a school population that has throughout this century become increasingly diverse in ability, social class, and ethnic background. Others, however, have been less sanguine about the impact of efficiency ideas on the curriculum. They maintain that the sorting and channeling of students that has occurred in the schools under the influence of social efficiency ideas has served to reproduce and perpetuate existing inequalities in American society. The long term effect of these practices, they argue, has been to propel certain segments of the nation's school population — the poor, immigrants, and racial minorities — into courses of study that have prepared them for subordinate economic and political positions in American society.[67]

The principal characteristic of either of these interpretations is that they link the efforts of curriculum workers in the schools to larger economic and political movements outside the schools. Curriculum workers appear, then, as either liberals or conservatives committed to either equalizing the life chances or socially controlling the poor and ethnic minorities. They appear, in other words, as the agents or counterparts of individuals involved in the various economic and political struggles that characterize twentieth century American life.

In this chapter, we have not really addressed the larger political and economic effects of efficiency-minded curriculum reform. Our examination of the history of the Modern Problems course does, however, tell us something about the linkage between the efforts of curriculum workers in the schools and those of others in the political and economic realm. In considering the role that Minneapolis curriculum workers played in the implementation of the Modern Problems course, it seems that for the most part they were preoccupied with adjusting the curriculum to a number of technical problems associated with managing a complex organization. Minneapolis curriculum workers seemed to pay little, if any, attention to the impact that their Modern Problems course had on the political and economic life of the larger society. What did concern them was the impact that Modern Problems had on such matters as their relationship with the State Board of Education and the University of Minnesota, on other subject areas within the curriculum, and on teacher performance. Rarely, except when they sought to defend the schools from outside criticism, did Minneapolis curriculum·workers address what we might think of as larger political and economic questions.

I do not mean to suggest that Minneapolis educators carried on their work untouched by outside influences. This was obviously not the case. After all, the impetus behind their attempts to remake the Minneapolis social studies curriculum was the same commitment that guided a host of other American reformers, both inside and outside the schools, who were seeking during the first half of this century to transform all of American society along efficiency lines. Nor do I mean to suggest that Minneapolis curriculum workers were politically neutral. The very fact that in designing the Modern Problems course, they seemed to take for granted the prevailing political and economic arrangements of American society would insure that their efforts at change would have political effects.

Rather, my point is that in introducing the Modern Problems

course, in later altering the course, and finally in abandoning it altogether, these curriculum workers were operating at their own behest as professionals whose job it was to change the school programme.[68] Our study provides virtually no support for the claim advanced by many contemporary curriculum theorists that these efficiency-oriented curriculum workers were the agents of one segment of society or another involved — at their direction — either explicitly or implicitly, in the pursuit of larger political goals. The efforts of Minneapolis curriculum workers may have ultimately served to change our political and economic institutions, or to preserve them, or more likely to do a little of both. Our study of the Modern Problems course, however, suggests that this concern was hardly on the minds of Minneapolis curriculum workers as in 1939 they set about reorganizing the social studies programme along efficiency lines.

### Glossary

*Assistant Superintendent*  A member of the administrative staff of a school system responsible for a particular aspect of the system's operation (for example curriculum, instruction, elementary education).

*Commission on Life Adjustment Education*  A Commission organized by the United States Office of Education that met from 1947 to 1954 and defined the principal efficiency-oriented curriculum reform of the post-World War II period, the life adjustment education movement.

*Commission on the Reorganization of Secondary Education*  A Committee of the National Education Association that met from 1913 to 1918 which sought to restructure the American secondary school curriculum along efficiency lines. Its most famous statement was the 1918 *Cardinal Principles of Secondary Education*.

*Consultant*  An administrative position within the Minneapolis Public Schools responsible for curriculum work within a particular subject area (for example social studies consultant).

*Curriculum Assistant*  An administrative position within the Minneapolis Public Schools during the 1940s involving curriculum planning and research.

*Curriculum differentiation*  The development of different curricular programmes within the secondary school (for example college preparatory, vocational) for students of different interests and abilities.

*Curriculum integration*   The organization of the curriculum around social issues or social problems instead of around traditional academic disciplines.

*Department chairman*   A teacher who in addition to his or her regular instructional duties administers the affairs of a particular subject area and its faculty within a school (for example chairman of the history department).

*Discipline-centered curriculum reform*   A curriculum reform movement during the 1960s committed to reasserting the primacy of the academic disciplines in the organization of the school programme.

*Elective*   An optional course that students can select according to their needs and interests.

*High school principal*   The administrative position that directs the affairs of a secondary school which typically encompasses grades nine to twelve.

*Junior College*   An institution of higher education that provides for two years of post-secondary instruction in the liberal arts and training in various technically oriented occupations.

*Scientific curriculum-making*   The effort of efficiency-oriented curriculum workers such as Franklin Bobbitt and W.W. Charters during the 1920s to use the so-called scientific management procedures of industry, particularly the practice of activity analysis, to design the school curriculum.

*Secondary education*   The period of schooling betwen grade seven (approximately age 12) and grade twelve (approximately age 18). The period of schooling encompassing junior and senior high school.

*Semester*   One half of a school year (usually 18 weeks).

*Senior year*   The last year of high school (grade 12).

*Social efficiency movement*   The period of educational reform in the

United States from the years around World War I through the 1950s during which educators sought to redirect the school programme from its traditional goals of mental training and college preparation toward the goals of social and vocational adjustment.

*State Commissioner of Education*  The chief executive officer of a school system within a state (for example State Commissioner of Education for Minnesota). In some states the commissioner is elected by popular vote while in others he or she is appointed by the state governor.

*Supervisor*  An administrative position, usually under an assistant superintendent, responsible for one segment of the school system (for example secondary education, elementary education, social studies).

*Superintendent of Schools*  The chief executive officer of an urban, rural or surburban school district. The superintendent is typically appointed by the Board of Education.

*Woods Hole*  A conference site in Massachusetts where in 1960 a number of scholars first articulated the ideas underlying the discipline-centered curriculum reform movement of the 1960s. One of the participants, the psychologist Jerome Bruner, summarized the conclusions of the conference in a small volume titled *The Process of Education*.

### Notes

1 See for example, APPLE (1979), chap. 6; APPLE and FRANKLIN (1979), pp. 178–201, FRANKLIN (1976), pp. 298–309, KLIEBARD (1971), pp. 74–93, KRUG (1972), pp. 4, 346–351, SEGUEL (1966), chap. 4, and SELDON (1977).
2 See FRANKLIN (1982), O'CONNOR (1980), RINGEL (1981), URBAN (1981).
3 Commission on the Reorganization of Secondary Education (1916), pp. 52–56.
4 REED (1931), p. 7.
5 Commission on the Reorganization of Secondary Education, *op. cit.* p. 12, *Senior High School Course of Study* (1925–1931), pp. 4–5.
6 Commission on the Reorganization of Secondary Education, *op. cit.*, p. 52.
7 *Senior High School Course of Study, op. cit.*, p. 5.
8 CUTRIGHT (1927).
9 CUTRIGHT (1928), pp. 158–159, 163.
10 CUTRIGHT (1934), p. 120, (1940), p. 2.
11 General Files, *Curriculum Bulletin No. 277* (February 29, 1936), p. 2.
12 CUTRIGHT (1941), p. 5.

13 General Files, *Report of the Division of Instruction* (1937), p. 20.
14 General Files, *Curriculum Bulletin No. 642* (1940), p. 2.
15 WEBSTER (1929), p. 43.
16 *The Scope of the Senior High School* (1935), pp. 13–14, Commission on the Reorganization of Secondary Education (1913), p. 17.
17 General Files, Cutright to High School Principals (October 26, 1939).
18 CUTRIGHT (1938), p. 2.
19 General Files, *Curriculum Bulletin No. 400* (November 8, 1937).
20 General Files, *Curriculum Bulletin No. 424* (December 8, 1937).
21 General Files, *Curriculum Bulletin No. 701* (October, 1939).
22 General Files *Curriculum Bulletin No. 198* (March 29, 1944), *Senior High School Course of Study* (1938–1939), p. 11, (1941–1942), pp. 11–12, (1943–1944), pp. 12–12.
23 General Files, *Minutes, Department of History, West High School* (October 19, 1940).
24 General Files, Wright to Cutright (April 4, 1940).
25 General Files, Reed to Rockwell (April 29, 1940).
26 General Files, Rockwell to Shumway (May 6, 1940).
27 General Files, Shumway to Rockwell (May 14, 1940).
28 General Files, Caldwell to Cutright (June 5, 1940), General Files, Cutright to Caldwell (June 11, 1940).
29 General Files, *Curriculum Bulletin No. S-201* (April 13, 1944).
30 General Files, *Report to the Teachers of Social Studies in Grades 7–12* (February–June, 1944), p. 6.
31 General Files, *Minutes of the Meeting of Social Studies Teachers* (May 13, 1937).
32 General Files, *Report of the Senior High School Social Studies Policies Committee* (February, 1943).
33 *Minneapolis School Bulletin* (March 23, 1944), pp. 1–4, (April 13, 1944), p. 3.
34 General Files, *Curriculum Bulletin No. S-178* (February 15, 1944).
35 General Files, *Minutes of the Senior High School Principals Meeting* (December 10, 1946).
36 General Files, *Minutes of the Social Studies Steering Committee Meeting* (October 21, 1948).
37 General Files, *Report to the Teachers of the Social Studies in Grades 7–12*, op. cit., p. 7.
38 See CREMIN (1961), pp. 338–347 and McCLURE (1971).
39 *Minneapolis Morning Tribune* (December 30, 1952), p. 13.
40 General Files, Cooper to Krey (January 6, 1953).
41 General Files, Krey to Cooper (January 8, 1953).
42 General Files, Cooper to Krey (February 3, 1953).
43 Compare, General Files, *Achieving the Objectives of Education: A Guide for Curriculum Development* (September, 1953), p. 7 with Commission on the Reorganization of Secondary Education (1918), pp. 11–16.
44 FRANKLIN (1982), pp. 22–28.
45 General Files, Memorandum from Kopple Friedman to Arthur Lewis (November 17, 1957).
46 General Files, Memorandum from Robert Bennett, Kopple Friedman, and

Harvey Jackson to Rufus Putnam (April, 24, 1958).

47  Citizens Committee on Public Education (April, 1958), pp. 10, 13.

48  General Files, *Report to Principals of Senior High Schools on Social Studies Curriculum Study* (March 2, 1955), pp. 2–3.

49  General Files, *Illustrative Material from the Social Studies Curriculum Study* (August, 1956), p. 13.

50  General Files, *Study of the High School Day* (February, 1959), p. 12. Minneapolis Board of Education Minutes (February 24, 1959), p. 106.

51  *Social Studies Newsletter* No. 6 (March 25, 1960), p. 2.

52  General Files, *New Social Studies Curriculums* (September 20, 1960).

53  *Social Studies Newsletter No. 8* (June 1, 1961), p. 4.

54  *Minneapolis Board of Education Minutes, op. cit.*, p. 106.

55  General Files, Memorandum from Adner I. Haggerston to High School Principals (February 1, 1962).

56  General Files, *Lines of Communication for Curriculum Development in Minneapolis Public Schools* (September, 1966), *Social Studies Bulletin No. 2* (March 8, 1968).

57  General Files, Memorandum from Kopple Friedman to the National Council for the Social Studies Committee on the Social Studies and National Interest (December 7, 1962).

58  General Files, *Minutes of the Senior High School Principals Meeting*, (April 17, 1963), p. 2.

59  General Files, *Minutes of the Social Studies Committee (February* 11, 1963).

60  *Social Studies Newsletter No. 2* (September 26, 1966), p. 2.

61  South High School (1972–1973), pp. 49–50, Southwest High School (1972–1973), p. 23, Edison High School (1972–1973), pp. 19–20.

62  General Files, Corlett to Davis (April 1, 1970).

63  General Files, Memorandum from John Bastolich to William Phillips. (January 2, 1976).

64  Minneapolis Accountability Project (1974), p. 35.

65  *Directory of Minneapolis Public Schools* (1976–1977), p. 3.

66  *A Description of Social Studies Grades 7–12* (1980). It is difficult to determine the exact date of the eliminaton of Modern Problems because Minneapolis did not pubish any curriculum guides for the social studies from 1957 to 1980. John Bastolich, Minneapolis' Social Studies Consultant, supports the view that the introduction of the trimester calendar led those high schools still offering the course to drop it.

67  KLIEBARD and FRANKLIN (1983), pp. 141–143.

68  For a discussion of the view that human service professionals tend to act in their own interests as individuals whose job it is to bring about change see MOYNIHAN (1965). For a discussion of this view as it relates to curriculum workers see BOYD (1978, pp. 589–594).

## References/Bibliography

APPLE, M. (1979) *Ideology and Curriculum*, London, Routledge and Kegan Paul.

APPLE, M. and FRANKLIN, B. (1979) 'Curriculum history and social control', in GRANT, C. (Ed.) *Community Participation in Education*, Boston, Allyn and Bacon, pp. 178–201.

BOYD, W. (1978) 'The changing politics of curriculum policy making for American schools', in *Review of Educational Research*, 48, 4, pp. 577–628.

CITIZENS COMMITTEE ON PUBLIC EDUCATION (1958) *Social Studies Makes Citizens: a Report on the Social Studies Program of the Minneapolis Public Schools*, Minneapolis, Citizens Committee on Public Education.

COMMISSION ON THE REORGANIZATION OF SECONDARY EDUCATION (1913) *Preliminary Statements by Chairmen of Committees of the National Education Association on the Reorganization of Secondary Education*, Bulletin 41, Washington, DC, Government Printing Office.

COMMISSION ON THE REORGANIZATION OF SECONDARY EDUCATION (1918) *Cardinal Principles of Secondary Education*, Bulletin 35, Washington, DC, Government Printing Office.

COMMISSION ON THE REORGANIZATION OF SECONDARY EDUCATION (1916) *The Social Studies in Secondary Education*, Bulletin 28, Washington, DC, Government Printing Office.

CREMIN, L. (1961) *The Transformation of the School: Progressivism in American Education, 1876–1957*, New York, Vintage.

CUTRIGHT, P. (1940) *Biographical Sketch of Curriculum Study and Construction in the Minneapolis Public Schools*, Minneapolis, Information Service Center, Minneapolis Public Schools.

CUTRIGHT, P. (1941) *The Curriculum and the World Today*, Minneapolis, Information Service Center, Minneapolis Public Schools.

CUTRIGHT, P. (1934) 'How to use the scientific method in curriculum studies', in RANKIN, P. (Ed.) *Seventh Yearbook of the Department of Supervisors and Directors of Instruction of the National Education Association*, New York, Teachers College, pp. 114–31.

CUTRIGHT, P. (1938) *Some Guiding Principles for Teaching and for Curriculum Development*, Minneapolis, Information Service Center, Minneapolis Public Schools.

CUTRIGHT, P. (1928) 'The use of research in supervision and curriculum construction', in HOSIC J. (Ed.) *First Yearbook of the National Conference on Educational Method*, New York, Teachers College, pp. 157–175.

CUTRIGHT, P. (1927) 'What Effect has the Systematic Use of the Dictation Exercise on the Ability of Children to Use Selected Marks of Punctuation', Unpublished Masters thesis, University of Minnesota.

*A Description of Social Studies for Grades 7–12*, Minneapolis, Information Service Center, Minneapolis, Public Schools.

*Directory of Minneapolis Public Schools* (1976–1977), Minneapolis, Information Service Center, Minneapolis Public Schools.

EDISON HIGH SCHOOL (1972–1973) *Curriculum Guide*, Minneapolis, Information Service Center, Minneapolis Public Schools.

FRANKLIN, B. (1976) 'Curriculum thought and social meaning: Edward L. Thorndike and the curriculum field', *Educational Theory*, 26, 3, pp. 298–309.

FRANKLIN, B. (1982) 'The social efficiency movement reconsidered: curriculum change in Minneapolis, 1917–1950', in *Curriculum Inquiry*, 12, 1, pp. 9–33.

GENERAL FILES (1920–1980), Minneapolis, Information Service Center, Minneapolis Public Schools.

KLIEBARD, H. (1971) 'Bureaucracy and curriculum theory', in HAUBRICH, V. (Ed.) *Freedom, Bureaucracy, and Schooling*, Washington, DC, Association for Supervision and Curriculum Development, pp. 74–93.

KLIEBARD, H. and FRANKLIN, B. (1983) 'The course of the course of study: History of curriculum', in BEST J. (Ed.) *Historical Inquiry in Education: A Research Agenda*, Washington, DC, American Educational Research Association, chap. 7.

KRUG, E. (1972) *The Shaping of the American High School, 1920–1941*, Volume 2, Madison, University of Wisconsin Press.

McCLURE, R. (1971) 'The reforms of the fifties and sixties: A historical look at the near past', in McCLURE R. (Ed) *The Curriculum: Retrospect and Prospect*, Seventieth Yearbook of the National Society for the Study of Education, Part 1, Chicago, University of Chicago Press, pp. 47–75.

MINNEAPOLIS (1935) *The Scope of the Senior High School*, Minneapolis Public Schools.

MINNEAPOLIS ACCOUNTABILITY PROJECT (1974) *Curriculum Development in the Minneapolis Schools*, Minneapolis, Minneapolis Accountability Project.

*Minneapolis Board of Education Minutes* (1959), Minneapolis, Board of Education.

*Minneapolis Morning Tribune* (December 30, 1952), p. 13.

*Minneapolis School Bulletin* (1944), Minneapolis, Information Service Center, Minneapolis Public Schools.

MOYNIHAN, D. (1965) 'The professionalization of reform', *The Public Interest*, 1, pp. 6–16.

O'CONNOR, C. (1980) 'Setting a standard for suburbia: innovation in the Scarsdale schools, 1920–1930', *History of Education Quarterly*, 20, 3, pp. 295–311.

REED, C. (1931) *The Product of the Minneapolis Public Schools*, Report of the Superintendent of Schools to the Board of Education, Minneapolis, Board of Education.

RINGEL, P. (1981) 'Cooperative industrial education: The Fitchburg plan', unpublished paper prepared for the meeting of the American Educational Research Association, Los Angeles, California.

SEGUEL, M. (1966) *The Curriculum Field: Its Formative Years*, New York, Teachers College Press.

SELDON, S. (1977) 'Conservative ideology and curriculum', in *Educational Theory*, 27, 3, pp. 205–222.

*Senior High School Course of Study* (1925–1944), Minneapolis, Information Service Center, Minneapolis Public Schools.

*Social Studies Bulletin* (March, 8, 1968), Minneapolis, Information Service Center, Minneapolis Public Schools.

*Social Studies Newsletter* (1960–1970), Minneapolis, Information Service Center, Minneapolis Public Schools.

SOUTH HIGH SCHOOL (1972-1973), *Tiger Fare: A Description of Classes and*

*Programs Offered at South High School*, Minneapolis, Information Service Center, Minneapolis Public Schools.

SOUTHWEST HIGH SCHOOL (1972–1973) *Educational Programs*, Minneapolis, Information Service Center, Minneapolis Public Schools.

URBAN, W. (1981) 'Educational reform in a new south city: Atlanta, 1890–1925', in GOODENOW, R. and WHITE A. (Eds.) *Education and the Rise of the New South*, Boston, G.K. Hall, chap. 6.

WEBSTER, W. (1929) *Minneapolis Public Schools Annual Report, 1928–1929*, Minneapolis, Information Service Center, Minneapolis Public Schools.

# Social Studies and Political Education in England since 1945[1]

## Geoff Whitty

Overt social and political education has never commanded the wide-spread support in England that education for citizenship appears to command in the USA. Although there have been successive attempts to legitimate greater curriculum provision in this field, they have often fallen foul of a considerable resistance amongst English educators to the idea that education should 'serve the needs of society' in any direct or obvious manner. Practical and vocational education has always enjoyed low status within the English educational system when compared with an education grounded in liberal humanist conceptions of culture and this has tended also to militate against anything which might smack of citizenship training. As a relatively stable society, England has generally favoured implicit means of socialization into the *status quo* and has thus been much less overtly obsessed with the need to inculcate pupils with its dominant ideology than societies experiencing rapid social change or trying to legitimate a new political regime. Unlike the USA, England was not faced in the early years of this century with welding together a disparate immigrant population and, unlike the Soviet Union, it was not faced with the initiation of pupils into a new political ideology. This has contributed to a situation in which high status knowledge in English education has been firmly associated with the academic disciplines and hence with knowledge that tends to be literate, abstract, differentiated and unrelated to everyday life.[2] During the course of this century (at least until very recently), overt state control of the school curriculum has been progressively reduced and control has, certainly since the second world war, been exercised largely through teachers' professional ideologies and a particular conception of professionalism.[3] Taken together, these features of the English educational system have helped to give it an appearance of relative autonomy from its economic and political conditions of existence.

This is not, of course, to claim that education in England is without economic and political significance. Various writers have suggested not only that such autonomy is often more limited than it appears, but also that apparently autonomous educational systems play a vital role in social and cultural reproduction.[4] Nor, indeed, has social and political education been absent from English schools. What I am pointing to here is a difference in the form in which, and perhaps in the degree to which, it has been a major feature of our schools when compared with those in many other countries. The dominant tradition of social and political education has remained that which was derived from the English public schools in which the children of the ruling class have traditionally been educated. Here implicit socialization via the experience of the school's regime combined with the study of ancient Greece and Rome to provide what social and political education was deemed necessary. As mass secondary education developed during this century, this high status curriculum (somewhat updated) was aped by the grammar schools. Though academic history and geography courses grew in importance as classical studies declined, any suggestion that they were or should be vehicles for overt political education (as opposed to components of a 'liberal education') was always hotly contested. It is interesting to note, in view of my earlier remarks about social and political education being most in evidence where there was a perceived problem of social control, that what overt and explicit education for citizenship *has* always existed in English schools has been directed largely towards the children of the working class. Thus, for instance, a rather passive concept of education for citizenship, in the form of civics and similar courses, was a significant feature of the curriculum of the secondary modern schools but, even before these combined with the grammar schools to form comprehensives in the 1960s and 1970s, the grammar school tradition had tended to become the dominant one.

While overt education for citizenship has continued to exist in the lower streams of the comprehensive schools, it has generally been considered a low status activity amongst teachers when compared with academic history and geography teaching, and teachers of these latter subjects have consistently distanced themselves from those concerned with social studies, social education and citizenship. A Royal Geographical Society memorandum of 1950[5] deplored the growth of social studies in secondary modern schools and urged geographers to resist any further incursions by the social studies lobby, especially in the grammar schools. It claimed that social studies, even with a geographical bias, would not be as effective in producing 'intelligent and enlightened citizens' as a curriculum which included a conventional geography syllabus. It suggested that the effect of social studies on learning was similar to the effect of squeezing a lemon — 'the juice is removed, and only the useless rind and fibres remain'. Its defence of the educational value of geography teaching was echoed by Burston's defence of traditional history teaching in an Historical Association pamphlet of 1954,[6] though in somewhat more measured terms. Similar defences of the curricular *status quo* have continued ever since and these entrenched traditions have made change in this area of the curriculum difficult even in circumstances where it has been supported by powerful interests outside the educational system.

I now want to discuss three specific attempts to change the nature of social and political education within the secondary school curriculum. These attempts — by the social studies movement of the 1940s and early 1950s, the new social studies movement of the late 1960s and early 1970s and the political education movement of the late 1970s and early 1980s — have all sought in their different ways to make explicit teaching about and/or for life in contemporary society a more central feature of the school curriculum. In looking at attempts to challenge the prevailing state of affairs, we can see something of the complexity of the influences that have sustained the mainstream curriculum model and contributed to its reproductive effects. Proponents of the three reform movements under consideration differed in the particular visions of society that they espoused but they shared a view that curriculum reform in the area of social and political education could contribute to a reduction in the mismatch between their vision of the 'good society' and unacceptable aspects of society as it was or as it looked like becoming.

Yet all three have so far failed to make the impact on the school curriculum that they desired, let alone achieved the broader social ends to which they felt their respective approaches would contribute. In tackling the problem of change in different ways, the experiences of all three movements help us to recognize important elements in the dynamics of curricular continuity and change. However, it is only in bringing the three cases together that we begin to understand how it is the articulation between political and professional processes that generates reproductive or potentially transformative effects. We can then also recognize the need for any effective strategy of change to be operative at both these levels (and probably more) if it is to change the existing pattern of provision and contribute to the sorts of broader ends that some proponents of all these reform movements intended.

## The Social Studies Movement

The fate of the social studies movement of the 1940s and 1950s has been chronicled many times.[7] This rather amorphous movement was heralded with extravagant claims which have, in fact, made precious little impact upon the English educational scene. Whilst it was certainly not a really radical movement and one of its major obsessions was to develop education to fit the changing demands of British capitalism and democracy after the war, it did propose significant changes in our system of schooling. It opposed the prevailing elitism of the English educational system and proposed alternatives which would open the way for a more 'healthy' society. The argument was that social studies should form a backcloth to more specialist studies and allow 'every child to feel himself [sic] to be closely associated with the past and present struggles and achievements of mankind, and to have a personal contribution to make towards future progress'.[8] James Hemming explicitly argued that pupils following courses 'broadened by social studies carried on with plenty of project work' were 'adventurous in outlook, approachable and articulate, eager to give their minds to new problems'. Those who followed a curriculum composed entirely of academic subject-based courses had, on the other hand, 'a marked tendency to be parochial in outlook, reserved, conditioned *against* change'. Hemming's ideas had a lot in common with the ideas of American progressivism, and there was a further parallel in the concern of two other influential writers of this time, Dray and Jordan, to ensure 'orderly change' in a society facing the dual threat of totalitarianism or anarchy.[9] It may, of course, be argued that had the social studies movement succeeded in transforming the educational system to produce the creative, flexible and tolerant citizens which Hemming envisaged, it woud have bolstered British capitalism more successfully than has in fact happened. It remains the case, however, that, despite making some initial headway in secondary modern schools, this movement fell foul of the traditionalism of the British school system even before its impact on the outside world could really begin to be assessed.

The strength of 'subjects' as the central organizing category for the English school curriculum, combined with the jealous defence of the occupation of existing slots by more traditional subjects, made the foothold of social studies increasingly tenuous as the secondary modern schools came under strong pressure to compete with the grammar schools on the latter's terms. The introduction of grammar streams into many secondary moderns, together with the eventual acceptance of the idea that they could enter pupils for academic examinations, made the struggle of a new and relatively unconventional subject to survive in the climate of English secondary education an unequal one. There was a romantic, even epic, quality to the efforts by Hemming and his associates to transform the nature of the curriculum and one which, of course, they have not yet entirely abandoned.[10] In the 1950s, however, the reforming promise of the social studies movement was certainly not fulfilled. Only the more explicitly conservative features of the tradition remained as a target for its successor, the 'new' social studies movement of the 1960s. The divisiveness by which social studies often found itself restricted to the bottom streams of secondary modern schools ultimately served only to maintain the elitism of English schools and society. The incorporation of social education into the 'pastoral' rather than the 'academic' provision of many schools, especially for so-called Newsom pupils, also served to reinforce its low status in relation to increasingly dominant grammar school traditions. Even the limited legacy that did survive was hardly the active one which Hemming envisaged, but rather a passive one in which activity and involvement did not seem to go beyond the ability to fill in an income tax form, remember the name of the local mayor or decorate some old lady's kitchen without pausing to consider why she was permitted to exist in such squalor anyway. Small wonder that their critics dismissed such courses in 'life-adjustment' as 'social slops' and sought for alternatives which encouraged pupils to look critically at society rather than passively accepting their lot in a society seemingly beyond their control. The social studies movement, although it had consciously challenged the prevailing social relations of the school, had ultimately made no significant impact either there or in society at large.

It may now prove useful to consider its fate in terms of the three curricular traditions which Goodson[11] calls academic, utilitarian and pedagogic. If we do so, we can see that, in refusing to conform to the requirements of the first of these and combining elements of the other two, the social studies movement was doomed to marginalization in a situation where the academic tradition was reasserting its dominance even in schools supposedly intended to foster the alternatives.[12] This was the case despite the fact that proponents such as Hemming[13] and Dray and Jordan[14] often tried to present their arguments in terms of the benefits that the new approaches would bring to society as a whole. At this time, however, political priorities for the education system were far more directed towards an expansion of the pool of educated labour than towards the precise nature of the political socialization of the workforce. The social studies movement was thus not in a position to benefit from either the professional or the political priorities of its time.

## The New Social Studies

It may be that the future will provide a more fertile climate than the 1950s for Hemming's attempt to challenge the hegemony of the academic subject at the heart of professional curricular thinking, but it is clear that the first social studies movement of the postwar period of reconstruction died partly as a result of the reassertion of its hegemony at that time. On the other hand, the emergent movement of the 1960s, that of the new social studies, chose to make a virtue out of what it saw as necessity. Far from challenging the central values of the English education system, this movement sought to establish itself by celebrating at least some of those values and adapting itself to them. The problem for the new social studies movement was not so much the form of the curriculum as its content, even if it did envisage some degree of weakening between what Bernstein[15] was later to term the classification between different contents and between school and the outside world. Even then, classification between school knowledge of the outside world and street knowledge of that world was kept strong, as is evident in the data of Keddie[16] and Gleeson and Whitty.[17]

Initially the new social studies movement in England combined an overt attack on the uncritical nature of existing social studies courses in secondary modern schools, and on the lack of rigour in Hemming's alternatives, with a rather more implicit critique of the lack of relevance in the conventional academic curriculum of the grammar schools. Thus Lawton and Dufour, in the standard reference book for the new social studies in England, mounted a dual case in support of the inclusion of social science in the school curriculum:

1  The practical need for young people to develop an awareness and understanding of their own society, illustrated by the statements made in such reports as Crowther and Newsom that young people need to be 'less confused by' or to be able to 'find their way about' in a complex, industrial (and welfare) society.

2  The fact that our world is increasingly a social-scientific world, *ie* that social science as a form of knowledge is increasingly important to a balanced understanding of the universe ....[18]

The first of these seems, in some ways, little different from the rhetoric of some of the more conservative forms of citizenship education designed to fit pupils into society as it is, while the second can be read as an appeal to the advocates of a liberal education based on initiation into 'public forms of knowledge'[19] not to ignore the social sciences as a form of knowledge which ought to be represented in the school curriculum. But it seems clear that many of the advocates of the new social studies saw their subject as offering a much more critical perspective on society than their public rhetoric of legitimation revealed. Rather than being committed to the fine tuning of society in terms of its traditional values and ideals, even some of the more cautious members of new social studies movement argued on occasions that a social science-based social studies should encourage 'a critical approach to the values of society'.[20] Others implied that the exposure of pupils to the knowledge generated by the social sciences would remedy 'half-truths' and make pupils 'critically aware' of the extent to which their own commonsense ideas were distorted by bias and prejudice. The alternative firm foundation of 'true knowledge of the social structure and the social processes',[21] generated by the social sciences, would seemingly provide a basis for critical thinking about social reality. Social justice within education would be achieved by making the 'best' knowledge available to all and some clearly harboured the hope that social justice in society might ultimately be served by the use of such knowledge as a basis for changing the world. At the very least, the teaching of the supposedly universalistic knowledge generated by the social sciences was expected to free pupils from the parochial and implicitly conservative outlook which many earlier social studies courses had merely served to reinforce.

However, while the rhetoric of the movement stressed both rigour and relevance, and while some of its advocates saw it as having considerable radical potential, it was so obsessed with the need to avoid the fate of Hemming's earlier initiative that, in practice, rigour was stressed at the expense of relevance. Unlike Hemming, the advocates of the new social studies recognized quite clearly the particular role of academic subjects in English education. Most conventional subjects, and certainly those with high status, had a strong sense of continuity with subject communities in higher education. Newcomers were recruited to the profession via a narrow process of professional socialization that, for grammar school teachers, was almost exclusively subject-based. Clearly, the stress on the subject and initiation into its mysteries relates closely to prevailing patterns of segmentation within the teaching profession in England,[22] and the new social studies movement tried to use this feature of the situation to its advantage. Recognizing that the fate of earlier social studies movements had been tied up to a lack of commitment by its teachers to a subject, and the tendency of schools to allocate to it teachers with other subject identities or none, the new social studies movement was determined to give social studies as strong a subject identity in conventional terms as possible. Most of those associated with the movement were social scientists, as was the case with the American New Social Studies Movement, but in the English case the lobby was essentially one of sociologists seeking to establish sociology in the curriculum for the first time. English historians and geographers do not regard themselves as social scientists, while at that time economists and political scientists seemed content with the rather limited place they occupied within sixth form academic studies. What the sociologists sought to do was both establish their own discipline at examination level and reform low status social studies courses by injecting into them the academic rigour of sociological perspectives. This was clearly recognized as providing the best route to status and resources for the subject and its teachers and hence as providing the best chance of placing what the proponents saw as a valuable educational experience on the curriculum of all pupils. In view of the ways in which other subjects had received recognition in the past,[23] this was arguably an appropriate occupational strategy.

The thrust of the movement was, then, to establish sociology and a sociology-based social studies as a subject like any other in the school curriculum. While some of those involved would now say that this was a conscious attempt to use the space offered by the academic emphasis in English education for radical purposes, such a perspective was often lost in the quest to achieve equal status with other academic subjects. This meant that the earliest social science courses in English schools were often based on the transmission of the sort of implicitly functionalist sociology which was already beginning to be rejected by radical students in higher education as a form of conservative ideology though it still constituted the basis of respectable academic sociology. More significantly, the social relations of social science teaching in schools were generally based on a traditional transmission model of learning, even if the methods employed often involved worksheets rather than chalk-and-talk. Above all, the emphasis on emulating other academic subjects led to the relative neglect of the dimension of relevance and thus detracted from the meaningfulness of the subject to pupils. As Denis Gleeson and I have argued at length elsewhere,[24] this served to defuse most of the radical potential that the movement may initially have held. Even when the earlier content was replaced with supposedly more 'critical' concepts and perspectives, it was often taught with scant regard for its meaningfulness and relevance to pupils and, in particular, to working class pupils. The undue emphasis on teaching the concepts and structures of the social sciences as a basis for increasing critical awareness produced a social studies which was sometimes even less meaningful to pupils than the earlier conservative and parochial approach. Concepts only become tools of critical analysis and the basis of action in the real world if they are first of all recognized as meaningfully related to the world as it is experienced by pupils. This is not to argue, as some people have implied, that a radical approach to social studies would consist of an uncritical celebration of working class culture, but rather that social studies has to be meaningful before it can become critical in any strong sense of the term. In the absence of this, social science tends to be perceived by pupils as having little more than certification value and, as such, articulates with their 'cultural capital' in a similar way to other academic subjects and thus performs a similar role in the process of social reproduction. In this sense, as in others, the new social studies followed what Goodson[25] sees as a common 'evolutionary profile' for aspiring school subjects.

It is, however, one of the ironies of the situation that the attempt to establish social science as another high status academic subject not only militated against its being meaningful to students, and hence a possible basis for social action for change, it also seems to have failed even in that quest to establish the subject firmly in the curriculum. In the changing political context, there has been growing demand that subjects should be 'useful' and the curriculum has once again come under scrutiny from extra-professional quarters. To some extent this has been successfully resisted by defenders of the liberal humanistic conception of education,[26] but what is noticeable is that sociology and social science-based social studies figure hardly at all either in external demands for useful subjects or in the defence advanced by liberal humanists that certain subjects have an inalienable right to a place in the curriculum irrespective of their immediate utility. While part of the explanation may lie in sociology's (largely unwarranted) reputation for being a critical and subversive subject, it seems possible that it is as much a result of its reputation as largely irrelevant to the real world. Even those approaches which have attempted to meet earlier criticisms of the new social studies on this score seem to have done so too late to command favour. For the present, sociology remains as a somewhat marginal examination option subject in schools, much more vulnerable to the effects of falling rolls than either history or geography, and as a significant examination subject in further education, where it is nevertheless potentially susceptible to the renewed emphasis on vocationalism in that sector. Elsewhere in the curriculum the influence of the new social studies movement has been limited and regionally varied. Though there are now many social studies and humanities courses with some social scientific content, they have by no means replaced other approaches or succeeded in overcoming the subject's relative marginality and lack of status.

In Goodson's terms, then, we might say that, although initially the new social studies movement paid some lip service to the alternative utilitarian and pedagogic traditions in English education, its central thrust involved the acceptance of the values of the dominant academic tradition. It therefore had to pay the price of renouncing 'practical connections and relevance to the personal and to the industrial and commercial world'.[27] Yet, at the same time, it did not unequivocally receive the full fruits of joining that tradition in terms of resources, status, and so on. Indeed, its only partial success in terms of Goodson's 'evolutionary profile' left it vulnerable at a time when falling school rolls were putting pressure on the curriculum as a whole and when all but the most secure academic subjects were being subjected to renewed political demands that they should conform more to the utilitarian model.

## Political Education

The third movement which I wish to discuss here is the political education movement which rose to prominence in the late 1970s after a decade of quiet gestation. Its intention is to ensure that a particular form of political education relevant to the real world in which pupils live becomes part of every pupil's curricular experience. This involves developing pupils' 'political literacy', which it defines as involving 'the knowledge, skills and attitudes needed to make a person informed about politics, able to participate in public life and groups of all kinds and to recognize and tolerate diversities of political and social values'.[28] This entails a dual strategy of pressing for political education courses in schools while also fostering the political literacy approach in existing subjects. It also seeks to get away from the over-academic approach to politics represented in most existing GCE syllabuses in the subject. The political education approach to social and political education might then seem well placed to provide meaningful starting points upon which a genuinely critical pedagogy could be built and thus to avoid the pitfalls of the strategy of the new social studies. Indeed, there is a strand of thinking within the movement which argues that this is the case, seeing a parallel between attempts to develop the political 'literacy' of English school pupils and Paulo Freire's work in developing critical conscious-ness via adult literacy programmes in the third world.[29] However, in general terms, the movement seems more concerned to preserve rather than improve upon the form of society in which we live. It is this that has helped to place its ideas on the national political agenda and put it more clearly in line with 'national priorities' than either of the other movements we have been considering.

Despite the disparate nature of the educationists involved in the political education movement, many of the public statements emanating from it show that it is far from clear that its leading members are committed to providing the context for a genuinely meaningful and critical education. The lobby's major publication, *Political Education and Political Literacy*, illustrates the problems. When it was published in 1978 it certainly cleared up some of the ambiguities about the movement's stance, but it also exposed many points of contradiction and glossed over other potential ones. While some of the work suggested in it might encourage the development of 'critical awareness', other examples might well produce the sort of quietism or 'domestication' which were the outcome of traditional low status citizenship courses. Yet other examples seem to treat political education as another packaged commodity for pupils to consume, even though 'politics is *par excellence* a field to be mastered by learning by doing, by discovery through active experience'.[30] The experiential element of the featured courses consists largely of visits, speakers, debates and simulations. Very little work is reported that is based upon active involvement in the politics of the community and the ideas of the more radical wing of the political literacy movement are certainly not in evidence in the report. However, if this leaves room for doubt about the central thrust of political education, the clearest indication of the movement's preferred strategy of legitimation can be seen in the way its spokesmen have described its work to the public and politicians. Here there is a clear tendency to shift the focus of the movement sharply towards a concept of political education as the production of uncritical, conforming citizens.

Thus, for example, in publicizing *Political Education and Political Literacy* in a radio interview,[31] Crick was asked whether more political education in schools would lead to demands for pupil power. He responded that, on the contrary, the pupil power movement had been the result of a *lack* of political education and he then went on to make the point that, while the political education movement felt that schools should give consideration to extreme points of view, they should do so only after 'having gone through the ordinary, acceptable beliefs and institutions of society'. Even this is perhaps some advance on the academic version of Crick's ethnocentrism where he seems to suggest that politics ceases when compromise and conciliation ceases — or, to quote Berridge's succinct statement of Crick's position: 'He offers us the politics of liberal-democracies as politics period'.[32] But to argue that we should offer pupils evidence of alternatives in ways which try to predetermine their attitude towards them suggests a form of education only marginally more open than offering them no such evidence at all. Another example comes in an appendix to *Political Education and Political Literacy*. There it is suggested that the decline in public confidence in British political institutions is 'less to be associated with failings within the institutions themselves than with a failure to present . . . the broad principles and practice of parliamentary politics to the public . . . in a systematic and purposeful way'. The writer, the chairman of the Politics Association, goes on to tell us that his association seeks to end the long neglect of political education as the best long-term means of ensuring that 'the whole works' does not fall apart. It does not wish to exclude the '*consideration* of alternative ways of doing things', but it is in no doubt that schools and colleges should '*support* the principles and practice of parliamentary politics' (my emphases). In these circumstances the commitment to recognize its shortcomings and the existence of alternatives seems little more than a formality. And, although this position is scarcely surprising since the Programme for Political Education is sponsored by the Hansard Society for Parliamentary Government, and this particular paper was addressed to an audience of MPs, it is hardly encouraging to those who believe political education should involve a genuinely open consideration of alternatives.

The initial stimulus for the acceptance of political education onto the national political agenda lay in official anxieties about the confrontations between political groupings of the extreme right and left on the streets of London in the summer of 1977. In announcing grants for political education work by the National Association of Youth Clubs and the British Youth Council, members of the then Labour government explicitly drew attention to the drift towards extremism amongst the young and the need to win them back to the middle ground of British politics. More fundamentally, some observers have argued that the political education movement is part of an attempt to re-establish hegemony in a new phase of corporate capitalism. Explicit political education is seen as necessitated by the collapse of the social democratic ideology in the face of contradictions in the system exposed by the re-emergence of mass unemployment.[33] Certainly the linking, in the Labour Government's Green Paper on Education,[34] of studies of the democratic political system and studies of industry (whose role in the way 'the nation earns and maintains its standard of living' we are told elsewhere in the paper children should learn to 'properly esteem') was an early indication of the intimate connection in official thinking between political education and the defence of present economic arrangements. As in a whole range of official pronouncements on economic and social policy, there was an almost Hegelian assumption that our current forms of political and social organization were the ultimate end-point of human achievement and the role of education was therefore conceived in terms of defending them and extolling their virtues. Thus a senior Conservative Party spokesman on education, Norman St John Stevas, MP,[35] demanded that teachers of political education should give an undertaking to uphold the crown and constitution, a demand clearly in conflict with recent traditions of autonomy within British education. There is then a fair amount of *prima facie* evidence that the success of the political education movement in mobilizing support from politicians was associated with their belief that it could assist in preserving the *status quo* and in bolstering respect for it in a period of economic crisis.

It therefore seems that many of those involved with the political education movement tended to seek sponsorship from those who advocate a utilitarian rather than an academic approach to curriculum planning. Certainly many of its proponents sought to distance themselves from the kinds of academic syllabuses that have traditionally constituted politics as an examination subject. In the context of the Great Debate and its aftermath, and the apparent political priorities of the period, it would thus seem that the political education movement was more clearly in tune with the ideological climate of the times than was either of our other two cases. Yet, even in a situation where the traditional autonomy of the educational system has been under attack from powerful political forces, professional resistance to the introduction of political education has been remarkably strong and, at least to date, successful. Though the movement's own surveys indicate a not insubstantial amount of politics teaching in schools, much of this consists of long-standing examination courses or minor adjustments to the pastoral curriculum rather than an acceptance of a need either for a compulsory period of political education on the timetable or for the fostering of political literacy in the curriculum as a whole. It would therefore be wrong to infer, as might have been possible from our earlier two cases, that the capacity of professional and institutional processes to resist reform is entirely contingent on the tacit agreement of hegemonic political forces in the wider society to let educationists manage their own affairs. Traditional professional values and practices remained remarkably strong and resistant to change even when educationist proponents of change were receiving overt support from powerful political interests outside the education system. Despite the undoubted value of a utilitarian rhetoric of legitimation in mobilizing the support of such external interests, such a stance still experienced considerable difficulty in countering the continuing dominance of academic values within the system. In the case of political education, resistance to change was no doubt aided by a greater ambivalence by the Conservative government towards the movement than had been shown by its Labour predecessor,[36] but even before then the portents for political education were far from good. How far and how long resistance to sustained external political pressure could be maintained in the long run remains, of course, a matter for curricular futurology rather than curricular history.

## Discussion

I want now to make some brief comments about the relevance of studying reform movements of this kind for our understanding of the dynamics of curricular continuity and change and of the relationship between the curriculum and society. My initial comments will concern the extent to which data of the kind reported here can be related to sociological theories about the curriculum and the linkages between schooling and capitalism. I shall then consider the significance of these observations for those who wish to embark upon curriculum reform in the area of social and political education and especially for those who regard it as a radical enterprise.

In looking just at the social studies movement and the new social studies movement, it would have been possible to infer that their impact was limited partly because (despite the claims of their proponents) their proposed reforms were out of line with the perceived political priorities of hegemonic forces within the wider society. Indeed, even regardless of the perceptions of those involved, it would be possible to argue in these cases that, although the *mechanism* of exclusion consisted of professional processes within the educational system, its *function* could best be interpreted in terms of the reproductive needs of society. Thus, the failure of these reforms, and in particular their more radical elements, could easily be understood in terms of some of the general theories adopted by sociologists to characterize the relationship between schooling and the reproductive needs of capitalism.[37] It might be argued that, at the time of these reform movements, the traditional model of a grammar school curriculum was serving to reproduce the social relations of capitalism in much the same way Bourdieu and Passeron[38] suggest has been the case with the high-status curriculum in France. In such contexts, there was little that reform groups could do to enlist the support of hegemonic interests outside the educational system to counter the internal hegemony of established professional interests within it. The reformers therefore had to face a choice between marginalization, the route taken by the earlier movement, and the acceptance of a standard 'evolutionary profile' for their subject, the preferred but not entirely successful solution chosen by the new social studies group.

However, even were such an interpretation entirely sustainable in these first two cases (which, I would argue, it is not), the case for the political education movement is much less clear-cut in these terms. In this case, despite the existence of a small radical wing to the movement, its political thrust was very much in line with the expressed priorities of powerful political forces seeking to influence the educational system in the 'national interest'. This was a time when the autonomy of the education system was frequently identified in official pronouncements as a problem for British capitalism and, when in curricular terms, a 'utilitarian' approach was being officially sponsored as an alternative to the traditional academic emphasis. Yet, to date, prevailing curricular arrangements have generally been maintained in the area of social and political education. Despite the strength of political support for change, the minor adjustments that the political education movement might have stimulated in the subject option system or the pastoral curriculum have certainly not significantly altered the curricular balance of power in such a way as to transform the ideological messages being transmitted or received. Therefore it might be argued that in this context the relative autonomy of professional processes from the direct imperatives of capital or liberal democracy obstructed, rather than facilitated, the efficient reproduction of the sorts of social relations that would be maximally functional to capital in the present conjuncture. Any changes in the standard 'evolutionary profile' for curricular subjects that might have been expected in the changing economic, political and ideological climate had certainly not become evident. In appealing to external forces to a greater degree than to professional interests, the political education movement thus underestimated the power of traditional professional values even at a time when they were under attack.

To this extent, detailed studies of curricular history can perhaps help to make us sceptical of the cruder forms of sociological theory that regard the education system in general, and the curriculum or professional processes in particular, as expressing in some direct manner the reproductive needs of capitalism. However, the data produced by such studies can, in no sense, be considered inconsistent with the majority of contemporary sociological theories, Marxist or otherwise, which specify a general rather than a specific or constant relationship between schooling and capitalism. Those theories which see the relationship between capitalist production, the state and schooling in terms of contradictions and relative autonomies would clearly have little difficulty in accounting for the data presented here.[39] Nevertheless, detailed studies in curricular history can help us to interrogate and refine those theories and this, in turn, can generate a form of theory better able to inform future studies of curricular continuity and change.

To what extent, though, can such work be of value to curricular reformers themselves? Certainly our three case studies make it clear that social and political educators in the past have often based their strategies on an inadequate analysis of the context in which they have chosen to intervene. Thus, as we have seen, the social studies movement of the late 1940s displayed virtually no sociological understanding of the nature of the English school system and the professional values and processes associated with it. The new social studies movement of the 1960s, on the other hand, was extremely conscious of the status hierarchies of English schooling, but displayed only a limited insight into the ways in which they contributed to social and cultural reproduction. While recognizing the social significance of the existing divisive forms of curricular provision, it shared the widespread assumption that social justice would best be served by making available high-status academic knowledge to all pupils. It certainly lacked the sort of insight subsequently offered by Bourdieu and Passeron[40] about the way in which an academic curriculum can itself be profoundly inegalitarian in its effects. It further failed to recognize the extent to which the espousal of conventional modes of professional practice could lead to cooption into an essentially conservative system and thus to the frustration of much of the radical promise initially held by the movement. Equally, it did little to cultivate a political constituency outside the educational system that might have helped to sponsor its efforts. The political education movement of the late 1970s, however, was clearly aware of the importance of mobilizing powerful political forces behind its conception of curriculum reform, though its more radical elements were somewhat naive about the extent to which their rhetoric could be used to generate hegemonic rather than oppositional discourse. At the same time, all wings of the movement seem to have underestimated the strength of traditional academic values and their associated professional processes.

In a sense, then, perhaps the central lesson to be drawn from all this is that curriculum reform movements should beware of studying and reacting to the fate of their immediate predecessors alone. The new social studies movement chose a strategy based on its reading of the causes of failure of the earlier movement, while the political education movement was often consciously concerned to distance itself from the strategies associated with the new social studies. What the account given here certainly argues against is the drawing of strategic conclusions from such limited experience. Rather it argues for the development of historical and comparative studies of curriculum reform movements which, in a cumulative way, can contribute to the development of the kind of theory that can help us understand the complexities of curriculum change and its relationship to social change in a particular conjuncture. What the specific studies reported here demonstrate is that such understanding must embrace both professional and political processes in and around the curriculum if it is to be of value in informing the strategies of future reform movements.

For radical social and political educators, such understanding would seem to be particularly important, since it is the aspirations of this group that seem most consistently to have been thwarted in the developments discussed here. Not only do they need to define their own purposes more clearly, they must also make the fullest possible use of the available empirical and theoretical tools to understand the complex and contradictory nature of the professional and political contexts into which those purposes are inserted. If, as I have argued elsewhere,[41] one of the purposes of a radical approach to social studies teaching itself is to assist students in an active exploration of *why* the social world resists and frustrates their wishes and how social action might focus upon such constraints, then it seems only fitting that curriculum reformers in this field should themselves be engaged in a similar enterprise!

## Notes

1 This paper is adapted from WHITTY, G. 'Society, social justice and social/political education', *Teaching Political Science*, 8 (3), 1981. A more extensive treatment of the arguments developed here will be found in WHITTY, G. *Sociology and School Knowledge*, Methuen, (forthcoming).
2 YOUNG, M. (Ed.) (1971).
3 GRACE, G. (1978).
4 BOURDIEU, P. and PASSERON, J–C (1977).
5 ROYAL GEOGRAPHICAL SOCIETY (1950), pp. 181–85.
6 BURSTON, W.H. (1954).
7 eg. CANNON, C. (1964); LAWTON, D. and DUFOUR, B. (1973).

8 HEMMING, J. (1949), p. 25.
9 DRAY, J. and JORDAN, D. (1950), pp. 13–19.
10 HEMMING, J. (1980).
11 GOODSON, I. (1983), p. 27.
12 BANKS, O. (1955).
13 HEMMING, J. (1949).
14 DRAY, J. and JORDAN, D. (1950).
15 BERNSTEIN, B. (1971).
16 KEDDIE, N. (1971).
17 GLEESON, D. and WHITTY, G. (1976).
18 LAWSON, D. and DUFOUR, B. (1973), p. 26.
19 HIRST, P. and PETERS, R. (1970).
20 LAWTON, D. (1968), pp. 1–2.
21 DUFOUR, B. (1970), p. 96.
22 WARWICK, D. (1974).
23 GOODSON, I. (1983).
24 GLEESON, D. and WHITTY, G. (1976).
25 GOODSON, I. (1983).
26 WHITTY, G. (1978), p. 140.
27 GOODSON, I. (1983), p. 202.
28 CRICK, B. and PORTER, A. (1978), p. 1.
29 PORTER, A. (1979).
30 WRIGHT, N. (1978), p. 22.
31 *The World This Weekend*, BBC Radio, 4, 16 July 1978.
32 BERRIDGE, G. (1978), p. 233.
33 JONES, P. (1978).
34 DES (1977), p. 41.
35 Quoted in 'Tories take stand on morality', an article in *The Times Educational Supplement*, 27 January 1978, p. 9.
36 For some discussion of the ambivalence of the Thatcher government about whether to support an academic or a utilitarian approach to the curriculum see WHITTY, G. (1983), p. 175–87.
37 ALTHUSSER, L. (1971), BOWLES, S. and GINTIS, H. (1976).
38 BOURDIEU, P. and PASSERON, J–C (1977).
39 See YOUNG, M. and WHITTY, G. (1977); and APPLE, M. (1982).
40 BOURDIEU, P. and PASSERON, J–C (1977).
41 GLEESON, D. and WHITTY, G. (1976), p. 102.

## References/Bibliography

ALTHUSSER, L. (1971) 'Ideology and ideological state apparatuses' in *Lenin and Philosophy and other essays*, London, New Left Books.
APPLE, M. (1982) *Education and Power*, London, Routledge and Kegan Paul.
BANKS, O. (1955) *Parity and Prestige in English Secondary Education*, London, Routledge and Kegan Paul.
BERNSTEIN, B. (1971) 'On the classification and framing of educational

knowledge' in YOUNG, M. (Ed.) *Knowledge and Control*, London, Collier Macmillan.

BERRIDGE, G. (1978) 'Crick and the curriculum', *Teaching Politics*, 7, 3.

BOURDIEU, P. and PASSERON, J–C (1977) *Reproduction in Education, Society and Culture*, London, Sage.

BOWLES, S. and GINTIS, H. (1976) *Schooling in Capitalist America*, London, Routledge and Kegan Paul.

BURSTON, W.H. (1954) *Social Studies and the History Teacher*, London, Historical Association.

CANNON, C. (1964) 'Social studies in secondary schools', *Educational Review*, 17.

CRICK, B. and PORTER, A. (1978) *Political Education and Political Literacy*, London, Longmans.

DEPARTMENT OF EDUCATION and SCIENCE (1977) *Education in Schools: a consultative document*, London, HMSO.

DRAY, J. and JORDAN, D. (1950) *A Handbook of Social Studies*, London, Methuen.

DUFOUR, B. (1970) 'Society in the school', *Education and Social Science*, 1.

GLEESON, D. and WHITTY, G. (1976) *Developments in Social Studies Teaching*, London, Open Books.

GOODSON, I. (1983) *School Subjects and Curriculum Change*, London, Croom Helm.

GRACE, G. (1978) *Teachers, Ideology and Control*, London, Routledge and Kegan Paul.

HEMMING, J. (1949) *The Teaching of Social Studies in Secondary Schools*, London, Longman.

HEMMING, J. (1980) *The Betrayal of Youth*, London, Marion Boyars.

HIRST, P. and PETERS, R. (1970) *The Logic of Education*, London, Routledge and Kegan Paul.

JONES, P. (1978) 'The politics of political literacy', unpublished MA dissertation University of London Institute of Education.

KEDDIE, N. (1971) 'Classroom knowledge' in YOUNG, M. (Ed.) *Knowledge and Control*, London, Collier Macmillan.

LAWTON, D. (1968), reported in ATSS Newsletter No. 9.

LAWTON, D. and DUFOUR, B. (1973) *The New Social Studies*, London, Heinemann.

PORTER, A. (1979) 'The programme for political education: a guide for beginners', *The Social Science Teacher*, 8, 3.

ROYAL GEOGRAPHICAL SOCIETY (1950) 'Geography and "social studies" in schools', Memorandum from the Education Committee to Council, June.

WARWICK, D. (1974) 'Ideologies, integration and conflicts of meaning' in FLUDE, M. and AHIER, J. (Eds.) *Educability, Schools and Ideology*, London, Croom Helm.

WHITTY, G. (1978) 'School examinations and the politics of school knowledge' in BARTON, L. and MEIGHAN, R. (Eds.) *Sociological Interpretations of Schooling and Classrooms*, Driffield, Nafferton Books.

WHITTY, G. (1983) 'State policy and school examinations, 1976–82' in AHIER, J. and FLUDE, M. (Eds.) *Contemporary Education Policy*, London, Croom Helm.

Geoff Whitty

WRIGHT, N. (1978) 'One man's mainstream ...', *The Times Educational Supplement*, 27 January.
YOUNG, M. (Ed.) (1971) *Knowledge and Control*, London, Collier Macmillan.
YOUNG, M. and WHITTY, G. (Eds.) (1977) *Society, State and Schooling*, Lewes, The Falmer Press.

# Curriculum Change and the Evolution of Educational Constituencies: The English Sixth Form in the Nineteenth Century

*William A. Reid*

## Introduction

The question I raise in this chapter is: how can the study of curriculum history help us understand (for practical as well as theoretical purposes) the nature of curriculum change? I answer the question in a way which is both general and particular: general in that it suggests a broad framework for understanding curriculum change, and particular in that the framework as presented is explored through consideration of a concrete case — the evolution of the curriculum of the English sixth form through the nineteenth century.

Two matters of explanation need to be settled first. These are: what meanings of 'curriculum', 'curriculum change' and 'curriculum history' am I working with; and, what do I see as the deficiencies of the available account of curriculum change and why do I suppose that curriculum history provides a suitable means for strengthening them?

I do not, in this instance, understand curriculum simply in terms of the subjects of which it is comprized or of the contents of those subjects. Of more fundamental importance are questions of the aims associated with the teaching of particular subjects or content and of the overall form and structure of the curriculum. In terms of texts read and constructions mastered the curriculum of the nineteenth century sixth form appeared to enjoy a long period of stability. But the aims of teaching shifted, with the appearance of a new middle class clientele, from the 'finishing' of the aristocrat to the induction of salaried administrators into careers. And the structure and ambience of the students' curriculum experience underwent a radical change with the introduction of standard grammars, the growth of public examining and the move from schoolroom to classroom. Stability of subject content tends to mask important shifts in the curricular meanings and significances which the transaction of that content has for teachers, students and wider publics. Curriculum history is more than the tracking of new elements or techniques and keeping a record of the loss of old ones: it is the recovery and explanation of how the curriculum comes to have new meaning, or the production of accounts of why, in some circumstances, meanings can remain stable for long periods. Such accounts may or may not centre on changes in curriculum content as listed in lesson plans, syllabuses and prospectuses.

The theories commonly invoked to explain curriculum change differ according to the emphasis they place on the role of external or internal forces. They also differ in the extent to which they represent change as resulting from purposive action or from the effects of forces over which there can be little or no control. Externally driven change can be described within a frame of reference which stresses functionalist or determinist interpretations of social forces, or, alternatively, it can be seen as resulting from the mobilization of political and administrative resources targetted on policy goals. Equally, internally driven change can be represented as stemming from the actions of individuals who are actuated by societally determined self-interest, or as emanating from espousal on the part of key organizational figures of programmes of educational reform. The most commonly encountered accounts of curriculum change are, on the one hand, those that emphasize external, determinist influences and, on the other, those that give pride of place to the directive actions of policy-makers internal to the educational system. Thus, to borrow their own language, revisionist historians of education in the United States explain change in the high school curriculum in terms of superstructural responses to dialectical evolution in the politico-economic infrastructure of American capitalism,[1] while historians of science education on both sides of the Atlantic have offered accounts of the 'reform' movements of the 1960s which stress change as the result of conscious, goal-directed activity on the part of educators for whom external events provided merely a rhetorical focus for action.[2]

Clearly, both perspectives have something to be said for them. Links between economic and political trends and the forms and structures of curriculum are too well documented for there to be much dispute about their importance. On the other hand, it is equally evident that some kinds of change and some aspects of change are traceable to initiatives on the part of educators. The question is not whether one kind of account is right and the other wrong, but how these partial accounts which grow from differing presuppositions can be brought together within a common framework of understanding. One such attempt has been made by Westbury[3] who conceptualizes the potential for curriculum change in terms of internal 'invention' and external 'climates'. Educators are productive of social and technical inventions (classrooms, for example) which have a potential for institutionalizing curriculum change. They also take over inventions supplied by the outside world (books, microcomputers). But the question of whether the potential of an invention is realized depends on the cultural climate external to the schools. Thus, in his study with McKinney of the Gary schools, Westbury points to the fact that the inventive resources for reforming the science curriculum were available there long before change in the external climate in the 1960s released the needed financial and ideological support for the introduction of a new curriculum. This formalization provides a useful basic ground for bringing together internal and external forces in a common perspective.

A tighter articulation of the internal and external is offered by Goodson[4] who sees educators as spontaneous actors, though constrained by aspects of the structure of schooling resulting from prior actions and policies which transcend the boundary of the school. On this view, educators pursue goals which they believe will lead to improvements in the quality of schooling (to use his example, the institution of an environmental studies curriculum in senior secondary classes in England) but in order to attain their goals are forced to adopt priorities which may be in conflict with their original intentions (for instance, to stress the abstract knowledge content of the environmental studies curriculum when their educational purpose was to offer something more immediate and practical). This goal displacement results from features of the structure of the educational system brought about by past translations of ideologies into concrete form. In the case quoted, support for 'decontextualized' learning led to the promotion of structures supportive of it — channelling of resources through specialist academic subject departments within schools, the linking of teacher careers to departmental status, and the creation of an external examination system conferring legitimacy on certain kinds of subjects and contents. These are the realities which have to be confronted by educators who propose new subjects and new contents. Thus, Goodson represents the internal and the external as interpenetrating components in the change process. Educators have to 'play the game' according to externally mandated rules which become internalized for schools and teachers because they are reflected in the shaping of the environment within which change has to be effected: on the other hand, schools and teachers are able to promote innovation and to work to change the ways in which environments encourage or restrain certain types of action.

Both Westbury and Goodson arrive at their formulations of the change problem through applying an historical perspective. McKinney and Westbury studied how the curriculum of the Gary schools evolved over a period of 30 years, while Goodson researched the evolution of curricula in geography, biology, and environmental studies in English schools over a similar time span. Westbury, working with data from a decentralized education system, emphasizes the fortuitous aspects of conjunctions between local curricular aspirations and the unlocking of federal and state resources which can make them productive of institutionalized change. Goodson, viewing action within a context which is more closely integrated at the national level through centralized resource allocation and a common system of public examining, highlights the interlocking of individual career with pervasive traditions which shape the terrain the innovator must traverse. There is certainly evidence here of the potential of historical work for assisting in the construction of change theories which can accommodate the internal and the external, directive action and structural constraint, in formulations of some subtlety and sophistication. But what more might history offer?

First of all, we might anticipate that history which concerned itself with the particulars of places, people and institutions, but over even longer timespans, might enable us to build up a view of curriculum change which sees the education system itself as variable in character. School systems, schools and classrooms are socio-cultural inventions (to borrow Westbury's terminology) which assume different meaning and significance according to the state of the community or society within which they operate. We would not expect that a fully elaborated change theory would propose that the same change mechanisms are salient at all times and in all places. This obervation has practical as well as theoretical importance. Periods of socio-political stability alternate with periods of rapid evolution. If one reason for pondering on change theory is a wish to understand and manage curriculum today, we should take account of the possibility that education systems in Western societies may be on the brink of a major adjustment in role and status. Weiler[5] has documented the recent precipitate decline in confidence in education as a public institution; governments in the United Kingdom and North America are pursuing policies which tend to de-emphasize the standing of public education as a uniform nationwide system importantly connected with consensually held values and priorities. If our attempts to guide curriculum change are posited on theories which assume the stability and permanence of national education systems as conventionally understood we may be led to endorse irrelevant or misguided policies and proposals.

Secondly, we could expect that historical studies of the curriculum might enable us to move away from representations of external forces which show them on the one hand as monolithic or on the other as capricious. Education systems are complicated and comprise a range of activities which respond to the wants and ambitions of a variety of social groups. It is unlikely that curriculum change in a rural secondary school, closely integrated with community interests, is to be explained in the same way as change in a suburban school with a cosmopolitan orientation and a heavy investment in college preparatory programmes. This too may be a point with current significance. Modern society is tending to become more diversified in its groupings and interests; there is more emphasis on specialism of career and idiosyncracy of life style; curriculum change is drawn towards the particular need or demand rather than general or universal priorities (press on the part of authorities for uniform 'basic skills' learning can be seen as a rearguard attempt to control what may still be controllable rather than the signal of a new curricular uniformity[6]).

Change theories need, ideally, to be capable of being applied to a wide range of educational contexts, according to whether local or national interests are at issue, or whether the curriculum is under the control of private or public jurisdictions. What kind of conceptions might guide the historical studies which could be drawn on to build or elaborate such theories? No doubt a wide variety of these could be identified according to the orientation of the writer. In this paper, I want to draw attention to one conception which seems to provide a necessary link between curricular activity, enterprises of curriculum innovation and socio-cultural climates affecting the values and meanings attached to teaching and learning.

### The Idea of a Constituency

The conception I wish to pursue is that of 'educational constituencies'. The idea of the constituency that supports, or demands change in particular curricular arrangements was raised for me in the course of an investigation into the evolution of the curriculum of the English sixth form in the nineteenth century.[7] The object of the study was a curricular category which persisted, in a recognizably continuous tradition, throughout the period in question, but which experienced fundamental change both in terms of content and of its significance for the students who followed it. At no point, however, was there any precise articulation between this evolution and initiatives on the part of central or local governments. In spite of this, the sixth form was, by the latter part of the century, clearly to be understood as a national institution. How, then, was its curricular evolution to be explained?

The fact that the sixth form curriculum in the nineteenth century was a private and not a public affair (in spite of occasional attempts, as in the case of the Clarendon Commission, to bring public pressure to bear on its form and content) pointed to the need to import the notion of 'constituency' as a means of explaining the nature of the changes it underwent. In the absence of visible legal frameworks which legitimate certain kinds of curricular arrangement, or which define whose view of appropriate arrangements shall prevail, the question of what gains support and why is clearly a question about the publics or constituencies which actually pay for education and about their motives for doing it. This idea of the constituency which provides the link between what schools do and competing visions of what they might do is obscured for those whose studies of curriculum change start with the assumption of a state education system and the concomitant assumption of the existence of a public which understands the idea of nationally significant categories of educational experience. Writers who are imbued with the modern notion of the universality of educational forms find it hard to construe national systems as an innovation which drove out a previous conception of education as private or domestic and shaped to individual circumstances. But the study of history teaches us that the linking of curricula to nationally understood statuses and careers was a nineteenth century invention which went along with the honing of devices to secure uniformity of practice (grant regulations, textbooks, examining) and the rise of conceptions of teacher professionalism. Prior to that, as Rothblatt reminds us, 'A liberal education could be offered in boarding or grammar schools, or in Dissenting academies and private educational establishments, or it could be acquired by the wealthy on a grand tour of the continent. Locke thought a tutor would provide it, and while his influence lasted tutorial instruction was one major source of liberal instruction'.[8] This historical shift from private to public conceptions of education has to be understood in terms of the willingness of individuals or small groups to prefer shared educational experience, provided through common forms and structures, to personal experience gained through idiosyncratic styles of learning. In other words, it is a matter of the emergence of educational constituencies consisting of people who believe that they have interests in common which can be served by certain kinds of more or less uniform curricula. The justifications for this choice are embodied in rhetorical language which connects the preferred forms of educational experience with praiseworthy statuses, careers or life styles. To preserve and further their perceived common interest constituency members are prepared to follow the imperatives of the rhetoric and make available the resources of economic and ideological support needed to ensure the preservation of symbolically important curricula. This process can take place with or without the support of local or national jurisdictions. The invocation of these may mark a step in the consolidation of constituencies which gain the support of legal powers, though at the cost of freedom of manoeuvre.

The idea of 'constituency' can provide a link that is at once stabilizing and flexible between the inventions and initiatives of educators and the restraint or impulse of outside forces. It helps us to see how change, even quite rapid change, may be possible in circumstances where the structures of schooling seem to embody only obstacles to evolution, for the rhetorics of universalism may conceal the existence of variegated and unstable constituencies, offering points for experimentation, innovation and the institutionalization of new curricula. On the other hand, a stable and ideologically unified constituency may be able to block the efforts of reformers even when these are armed with legal powers and backed by the pronouncements of national reports. Key questions to be asked if constituencies are to be the object of historical study are: how do they come into being, how do they evolve, and how do they decline? How do they symbolize their perceived common interest, and what connections do they make between these symbols and the categories of educational experience? What marks of constituency membership are conferred by the experience of education? The connections to be studied between constituencies and curricula are connections which are rhetorically or symbolically made; they are about meaning and significance more than they are about knowledge and achievement. Thus the key curricular question becomes that of the experience of the student. Unfortunately, this is one which, though squarely in the province of historical investigation, is not readily amenable to research. Unless, like Costello, we are able to 'pick over the contents of the . . . student's wastepaper basket'[9] the mind of the learner is hard to penetrate and has to be approached through second hand testimony. Paradoxically, Costello's study was of the seventeenth century student. With the spread of books and the ready availability of paper the contents of the basket were less and less likely to be prized. For the nineteenth century they are rare. For the twentieth practically non-existent.

## The Sixth Form Constituency

The sixth form had its origin in a small number of independent boarding schools. By the eighteenth century these had become, sometimes despite the wishes of their founders, schools for the sons of aristocratic families where they might stay to the age of 18 or 19. They were not, however, at that stage, an essential part of the experience of being confirmed into aristocratic status. Upper class boys, as well as girls, were, as we have seen, often tutored at home. Social customs such as making 'the grand tour' were also sources of education. And in so far as education depended on a knowledge of texts it was not thought essential that this should be acquired through the mediation of a teacher. The schools themselves followed no common patterns of eduation, though they agreed on taking the study of Latin and Greek as the main component of the curriculum. Each evolved its own unique forms of organization with idiosyncratic vocabularies to describe them. The boys inhabiting one end of the schoolroom at Westminster were known as 'the shell' from its apsidal 'conch-like shape'[10] — a name which subsequently spread to other schools. Winchester, at the time of the investigations of the Clarendon Commissioners in the 1860s, still preserved ancient 'peculiarities in classical teaching' by the names of 'pulpiteers', the 'vulgus', and 'standing up week'.[11] The place of education was, everywhere, the large schoolroom in which all students were accommodated. Instruction proceeded, generally, through the giving of 'lessons to learn' which then had to be orally reproduced, but the content of instruction in terms of classical texts and grammars was a matter of local arrangement. 'Each schoolmaster or teacher or tutor felt it incumbent upon himself to make his own selection of texts ... This being the case, schoolmasters did not, on the whole, worry about continuity in studies from one place of education to another, either from the home to the school, from one school to another, or from school to university'.[12] Where students were divided into 'forms' (a term referring originally to the benches on which they sat) this was done in a rough and ready manner for the convenience of teaching and not with the idea of establishing a hierarchy of ability or a sequence of learning. The first 'form' to establish a definite identity was the 'sixth'. The idea of having six 'forms', with sub-divisions where numbers demanded it, had spread from Winchester which was a school of sufficient antiquity and reputation to be copied by other, equally venerable, establishments. The sixth was the 'highest form' in that it contained the best (not necessarily the oldest) scholars and was therefore fit to be taught by the headmaster who, in terms of status and learning, was in a different category from the assistant masters.

The sixth form at the end of the eighteenth century was a 'private' institution which assumed a different character and significance in different places and which was only marginally linked with the future status of its occupants. Membership in it was not essential either for entry to the universities of Oxford and Cambridge or for membership in a social class (an idea that was, in any case, only just beginning to take shape). The nature of society was, however, changing. Industrialization, coupled with the demands for national co-ordination of resources made by the Napoleonic Wars, was beginning to shift the focus of interest and action for the upper echelons of society from the local to the national stage. Following the French Revolution, concern with confirming the unity of the elite which provided leadership in government and administration was heightened. There were, as Rothblatt points out, the beginnings of a shift of attention from civility and sociability to the Victorian virtues of duty and responsibility.[13] As the aristocracy became more aware of itself as a consensual interest group and as the goals of action became more and more those associated with public arenas, it acquired a greater willingness to support organizations such as schools which could claim to assist in the production of consensus and of the virtues demanded of those with civic responsibility.

It was about this time that the word 'public' began to be used in association with the long established boarding schools to denote a general educational category, though 'it was only in the period after 1840 that the phrase "public school" came normally to mean a boarding school and the place to which well-to-do parents almost automatically sent their sons'.[14] But around the turn of the century the public school constituency was a small one and a broad and uniform category was not what was wanted. Indeed, the preservation of the uniqueness of old established schools was more to the point. Small, discriminating constituencies want to be offered hand-crafted goods, not mass-produced articles. Their members are well informed and well acquainted with one another. They can appreciate the finer points of choosing between variations on a quality product. Thus, although the categories of 'public school sixth form' and 'public school sixth former' were current, the question of curriculum change was one that could be answered only in terms of what individual schools and headmasters were doing to adapt to the evolution of society. Though the staple of the curriculum — Greek and Roman texts — remained, modifications began to be made in a variety of ways to the experience of being a sixth former. At

Shrewsbury, Butler worked hard to raise academic standards in his sixth form — to such good effect that some of his students won university prizes which were then available for open competition. At Winchester the notion was developed of the sixth as a source of example and authority for lower forms.

By 1830 a further evolution in the constituency was apparent. The increasing demands which were being placed on resources of government and administration outran the capability and willingness of the aristocracy to supply them. The new cadres of public servants had to come from another class which began to prepare itself for service in the public arena for, as Bagehot noted, 'the deference of the people to the spectacle of power can, in a modern state, only be secured by the inconspicuous collaboration of the middle class'.[15] But consensus of interest between middle class and aristocracy was to be the goal and the schools were to be an important means of achieving this. The Clarendon Commissioners, in 1864, were repeating what was by then a piece of conventional wisdom when they said in their Report: '. . . all the boys should, in their general education, pursue the same studies in kind, though not in degree, on the grounds . . . that . . . education . . . should generate as much sympathy as possible between the leaders of different departments, and also between the leaders and their followers'.[16] The precept was put into practice not only in the Clarendon schools, but more importantly in the new schools founded in the 1840s and 50s on the pattern of these to extend public school and sixth form education to an enlarged constituency.

The 'middle class' was an invention of the early nineteenth century and soon rhetorical connections began to be made between it and categories of schooling; promoters of educational reform spoke of 'middle class schools' and even 'middle class examinations'. But the newly self-conscious class did not see it as in its interest to foster categories of education that were significantly different in meaning from those patronized by the aristocracy. Nor, on the other side of the picture, was there any reason why the upper class should depart from the consensual ideology which enabled it easily to absorb new elements. The extension of the sixth form constituency came about through the transplanting of the category to new schools where, in spite of curricular differences such as the addition of 'modern subjects' (history, foreign languages), categorical meaning was preserved. Thus, a first step was taken towards transforming the 'private' institution of the sixth form into a category with some of the characteristics of a national institution. That is, one which can be seen as linked to a constituency which is defined not by race, creed, class or locality, but by commitment to a rhetoric connecting particular forms of educational experience with nationally significant roles and statuses. Salient features of the rhetoric which joined middle class and aristocracy in a shared consciousness of affinity with nationally defined responsibility and privilege were an emphasis on christianity which did not exclude any particular sect; on loyalty and devotion to duty; on the value of solidarity and consensus. The old and the new public schools, through curriculum change, were able to reflect just such a rhetoric.

The needed change had to bring about an identity of interest between organization (the school or schools) and institution (the educational category as understood by the constituency). Such adjustments come about through movement, initiative, and accommodation on both sides. In the case under discussion, the middle class was seeking an identity that was, as yet, not clear. Nor was it yet obvious what part education should play in the shaping of that identity or whether that education should be supplied by existing schools, by new schools, by private initiative or government intervention (Matthew Arnold argued strongly for the latter). Identity crystallized as educators proffered models of practice, and practice evolved according to the response of the publics it was aimed at. Schools and constituency collaborated in the development of the informing rhetoric — in this instance centred on concepts of 'manliness', 'gentlemanly conduct', and 'intellectual excellence'. The process was aided by important mediators who produced the books, stories and sermons which served as texts for the shaping and preservation of the categorical rhetoric. Much of this writing, in the 1850s, clustered around Arnold's Rugby which embodied some of the most significant inventions, and notably the projection to a more morally significant status of the sixth form as a source of authority in the school. Ahead of his time, Arnold was also a promotor of the classroom against the schoolroom, something noted by historians but not by propagandists, and, retrospectively, was credited by Thomas Hughes and others with the invention of organized games as part of the school curriculum — something for which he was not responsible. Such is the fate of those who are raised to be important legitimators of practice. The rhetoric, once established, became the means of shaping and stabilizing what schools did. Inventions contributed to a curricular orthodoxy and could be changed only to the extent that the orthodoxy was not interfered with. On the other hand, deviant, inefficient, or ignorant practice could exist provided that it could be represented as in tune with the rhetoric. This was especially true for schools with powerful reputations. At a time when much was made of 'intellectual excellence' it could be said that 'hardly any amount of ignorance prevents a boy's coming to Eton'.[17]

Thus, change in the curriculum of the sixth form over the period of roughly 1830–1860 is to be thought of as, on the one hand, the trying out of inventions and, on the other, the development of a national middle class constituency allied to and in some ways identified with the already existing aristocratic sixth form constituency. It also has to be thought of in terms of the construction of rhetorics connecting curriculum to constituency and providing a means whereby each can assume a coherent identity. The significant inventions were: the association of membership in the sixth form with the exercise of moral authority, the development of a 'mimetic' tradition of sixth form teaching, and the fusing of religious and classical elements of the curriculum into an undogmatic Christian humanism. The exercise of moral authority, as fostered by Arnold in the Rugby sixth, began the process of marking off the curricular experience of sixth formers from that of other students, thus enabling the act of becoming a sixth former to assume the quality of a status passage. Now it could be a means not simply of confirming students in the social standing of their families but of marking a movement to a new status. This possibility was reinforced by the particular emphasis given to the role of the headmaster in sixth form teaching. The mimetic theory of education holds that what the teacher most significantly provides is not knowledge or skilled instruction but example. To become educated is to imitate and internalize the manners, tastes, enthusiasms, and preferences of the teacher. In the public schools, access to the role model of the head, who was on a different plane from other teachers, was restricted to members of the sixth form. The pivotal importance of the head also contributed to the transformation of the sixth from a school based institution to one which transcended these bounds to become a national one. Uniformity of theory and practice grew up through personal contact among a small number of men who, in any case, shared the common educational background of Oxford or Cambridge (to quote a small, but significant example of this, Kennedy of Shrewsbury produced his Latin Primer when, in the 1830s, 'the public school headmasters decided on the desirability of a common textbook'[18]). Finally, the merging of classical and religious themes in the curriculum to make the former 'the complement of Christianity in its application to the culture of the human being'[19] enabled non-Anglicans to share in the experience of being a sixth former, while, at the same time, the moral aspects of that experience continued to be buttressed by religious principle.

Research has shown that schools such as Rugby appealed to a new middle class clientele and did not merely extend the provision for those already catered for by public schools with longer established reputations such as Eton and Winchester. They provided what the newly evolving constituency needed: a means of conceiving of itself as a nationally significant group sharing symbols and interests with the ruling elite and fitted to embark on careers in the public service. They fostered a rhetoric centering on the reviving notion of chivalry[20] which could provide both educational aims plausibly connected to curriculum content and standards of honour and loyalty by which the new constituency could recognize itself. The idea of a chivalric order offered a basis for the creation of a new group which was cohesive, yet made up of people from different social origins. On the one hand, this was a model for the status passage experience of becoming a sixth former; on the other, it was a rationale for the life and careers of constituency members.

## The Sixth Form as a National Educational Category

Recognition on the part of government that sixth form education had assumed national significance was accorded incidentally as a consequence of its perception that the education offered by the major public schools had become a national issue. This was marked by the setting up, in 1861, of the Clarendon Commission to 'inquire into the Revenues and Management of Certain Colleges and Schools'. There was apparently much to criticize, in the view of some, in the way the schools were organized and in the teaching they provided and a good deal of the evidence the Commissioners heard was to their detriment. Charles Neate, Fellow of Oriel College, testified that the classical languages, the heart of the curriculum, 'are now so ill taught, or at least so little known by the great majority of those who are supposed to have learnt them, that half the time now bestowed upon their acquisition would be a great deal too much to give for the result obtained'.[21] But the Commission did not on that account conclude that the schools were unsuccessful. While admitting some shortcomings, they instead drew attention to the fact that they:

> have been the chief nurseries of our statesmen; in them, and in schools modelled after them, men of all the various classes that make up English society, destined for every profession and career, have been brought up on the footing of social equality, and have contracted the most enduring friendships, and some of

the ruling habits of their lives; and they [sc. the schools] have had perhaps the largest share in moulding the character of an English Gentleman.[22]

The language used here by the Commissioners shows a fine appreciation of the fact that what matters to a supportive constituency is not the learning of a curriculum but the experience of it (learning might, in some circumstances be at issue, but not inevitably). The description given of the virtues of the schools records the change which had taken place in the curriculum over the previous half century — in spite of the persistence of Greek and Latin texts as its staple content. The significance of learning is now public, not private, national, not local. The curriculum has become a symbol of common experience looking forward to public service careers, emphasizing group solidarity and lending significance to belief and action through the rhetoric surrounding the concept of the gentleman.[23] The fact that the Clarendon Commission was set up at all is evidence of the connection that had been made between the character and ability of the governing classes and the nature of the education they had received — a connection which would not have been at all obvious fifty years earlier.

The Clarendon Report provides a marker of the successful fusion of upper and upper middle class elements through schooling. But already events were moving on. As the demand for induction into 'gentlemanly' roles through education expanded and the constituency grew, the problem of the connection between the legitimating rhetoric and the forms of the curriculum took on new dimensions. Firstly, the need arose for tangible proofs of the quality of teaching. The comment that boys left Rugby with 'stagnant and ill-formed minds' could be shrugged off because Rugby was Rugby.[24] But as the Rugby sixth form, which had been copied in the newer public schools, spread even further afield after 1860 to the reviving endowed grammar schools, the boundary between curriculum experience which was categorically acceptable and that which was not had to be clearly marked or the whole notion of the extended constituency would collapse. The inventions which could supply this need were those tending towards uniformity and predictability of curriculum. But secondly there was a concomitant need for curriculum variation. The teaching of the classics demanded either the conjunction of highly qualified teachers and highly committed students or, as at Eton, a centuries old reputation which allowed poor performance to pass unremarked. For the newer schools, especially the grammar schools, this posed a problem. On the other hand, there was a positive demand from those who would take up lower status careers for more 'utilitarian' studies: English, history, modern languages, as well as mathematics which was already taught in the universities and some public schools.

The invention which did most to promote uniformity of curriculum while tolerating or even encouraging some variety of content was the public examination. Beginning in the 1850s, entry to the army and the home and overseas civil service moved towards selection by examination for which the schools prepared sixth form pupils. At the same time, demand on the part of schools for evidence that their teaching programmes were categorically acceptable resulted in the offering of public examinations by the College of Preceptors and the Local Examinations Syndicates of the universities of Oxford and Cambridge. These examinations were seen just as much as tests of schools as of students. For example, when the Secretary of the College of Preceptors was interviewed by the Taunton Commissioners and asked whether the effect of examinations had been to improve 'middle class education', he replied that:

> A school examined for the first time by us ... is generally speaking very unsuccessful in the examinations. ... but they persevere ... and you see a gradual improvement, until at last some of these schools distinguish themselves even above others.[25]

All this took place without any intervention on the part of central authorities, providing a good illustration of the fact that the institutionalization of national categories is not to be confused with the centralization of educational policy-making. The growth of examining on a national level paved the way for success in sixth form studies to be tied to uniform tests of achievement, clarified in the mind of a broader constituency the conception of sixth form work, and enabled the places where that conception was implemented to be identified (so that, to this day, arguments about where real sixth form work is done are conducted by pamphleteers who base their conclusions on the statistical manipulation of examination results).

Even more important for the sixth forms of the late nineteenth century were the entrance examinations set by the universities of Oxford and Cambridge. These tightened and formalized the link which had long existed between sixth form and university and fostered a pattern of curriculum that has persisted ever since.

As Annan explains:

... the Oxford and Cambridge scholarships were far more influential than the reformers ever dreamed. They transformed the pattern of national secondary education. If anyone asks why it is that children specialize at such an early age at school ... and why so many arts graduates are innumerate, the answer is simple. The Oxford and Cambridge scholarships were the blue riband of sixth form education.[26]

The specialization which was thus permitted and encouraged enabled commonality to be combined with variety. While students following other studies could share in the experience of the sixth, the true scholars and leaders could continue to pursue the classics.

Examining was not the only invention which enabled sixth form experience to assume a more standardized character. This trend was also greatly assisted by the move away from the system of having everyone taught in the big schoolroom and towards the consistent use of separate classrooms. Those of us who have always thought of classrooms as the conventional arena for the transaction of a curriculum might wonder why, once the idea and possibility of classrooms existed, their virtues were not immediately perceived. The reason lies in exactly the area which we are exploring. The supportive rhetoric of the schoolroom meshed with the career anticipation of the constituency — as long as this was broadly aristocratic. This is quite clear from the Clarendon Report which came down against any rapid extension of the classroom system precisely because of the understanding it held of the constituency of the nine schools:

> ... it may admit of doubt whether ... schools are not moving faster than the world, for which they are a preparation, has followed or will be able to follow them. It is necessary at the Bar, and in other careers in life, and in the Houses of Parliament, that much mental work should be done of all kinds, amidst many outward causes of distraction.[27]

The schoolroom lived because it was an invention which had meaning beyond the immediate tasks of the accomplishment of teaching. But its days were numbered. Classrooms came with their own wider meanings centering around collectivist sentiments of sympathy and emulation which were to be unlocked by the new teacher professionalism which class teaching made possible.[28] These meanings made more appeal to the new majority bound for lesser administrative posts than those of the schoolroom which were suited to a minority of leaders. Not surprisingly, the more aristocratic schools clung longest to the old traditions. But by 1885 even at Winchester the 'once thronged room was derelict'. And when in the 1890s the Headmaster summoned his sixth form to meet him there he 'was shocked to find that it was not longer known where to sit or what to do in School'.[29]

The uniformity brought by classrooms and examining counteracted the other imperative of the enlargement of the constituency — that the content of learning become more diversified. To begin with, the introduction of new subjects created difficulties. Butler of Harrow reported that:

> At a large school, where tradition and emulation act so power-fully, boys are not likely to work vigorously at any subject in which the majority of their companions are not keenly in-terested. . . . If exempted from . . . regular work, or from any part of it, they are likely to become listless and idle.[30]

The experience of being a sixth former depended on doing what was seen as 'regular work', a point made even more forcibly by Westcott of Harrow:

> A boy may rise most rapidly into the upper sixth form without being at any time distinguished for scholarship, by the help of modern languages and mathematics . . . it happens continually that a boy reaches the upper sixth who is a very bad scholar.[31]

Or, cast in a logical form, only scholars should be sixth formers, one can only become a scholar by studying classics, therefore only classicists can be sixth formers. That the contest between those who took this view (and supported the old constituency) and those who urged the introduc-tion of new subjects (and therefore supported the new) was resolved in favour of the latter was due to the opportunities offered by examina-tions and by class teaching for holding together diverse interests in a common framework. These were the inventions which permitted the realization of the aim for middle class education expressed by a head of one of the new public schools, Bradley of Marlborough:

> [It] should be at once *general*, *ie*, like the education of other classes, and *special*; and *special* in two senses, first, as putting forward certain subjects more prominently than they are brought forward in ordinary education; secondly, as trying to form tastes which will in some degree counteract the hardening and deadening influences of engrossing occupations, which are not in themselves of an elevating or refining nature.[32]

The evolving curriculum framework allowed the definition of sixth form status to be not scholarship, as conventionally defined, but specialization, whether in classics, modern studies or, later, the sciences. In this way experience could be shared but at the same time varied and the broader constituency could embrace a range of interests and aspirations.

These new contents and frameworks for the curriculum brought with them a new justificatory rhetoric. For the most part, the vocabulary was the same as that which had supported Arnold's new model sixth, but the significance of the words had been modified. 'Manliness' which had been linked to the assumption of Christian moral responsibilities was gradually transmuted into the manliness of the games field — 'honour, loyalty, skill at games, and a certain stoical acceptance of pain'.[33] The militant Christianity of Empire replaced the earlier concern with personal rectitude and avoidance of sin. Control over others associated with captaincy and prefectship was more emphasized than responsibility exercised on a personal level. If the curriculum in its overall form was more uniform and predictable, so were personal conduct and relationships, down to niceties of dress, posture and demeanour. And when the time came for the national institution of the sixth form to be incorporated into a centrally controlled system of education after the passing of the Education Act of 1902, it was this powerful rhetoric meshed with the curricular forms to which it gave meaning which ensured that many issues of policy which might have seemed open to debate were not in fact so open. Should upper secondary education be on the pattern of the curriculum of the higher grade school or of the independent public school? Should the curriculum provide choices between specialisms or a general range of studies for all on the model of the Baccalaureate or the Abitur? Should secondary education rest on the foundation of the elementary school or should it represent a different but parallel educational experience? All of these seemed to be contentious issues. They were not. The constituency understood what sixth form education was and acted in accordance with that understanding, with important consequences for the whole future development of secondary education.

## Conclusion

This brief study of the evolution of the sixth form curriculum in the nineteenth century suggests the importance of the notion of constituency in explaining change. Left to itself the educational community had transformed an idiosyncratic, aristocratic form of curriculum into a national institution capable of holding together a diverse population of mainly middle class students and initiating them into a kind of freemasonry where they could share common values with the governing class and move into the cadres of public servants and administrators needed to run a complex industrial society and an overseas Empire. Both the content and the significance of the curriculum had changed. How is this change to be accounted for? Directive initiatives on the part of public authorities are part of the story but cannot stand on their own as explanations. If we look at the national level, while it is true that government concern with secondary and sixth form education grew over the period under review, control was minimal and exercised indirectly through the restructuring of private funding by the Charity Commissioners, the channelling of small amounts of public funding through the Science and Art Department, and the publication of reports of Royal Commissions. Government action was sometimes of considerable significance, as for example, in the introduction of science teaching into sixth forms, but it does not assume major importance in an account of curriculum change. At the local or private level, the inventions of headmasters, textbook writers, and examining boards are factors which play a critical role in any account of curriculum innovation. But, without the backing of central authorities, what was it that enabled them to be significant? The case of the classroom is instructive. It was not a superior technical device which drove out the inferior. As the Clarendon Commissioners noted: 'All the teaching of all the classes at Winchester School has for centuries been conducted in one room' and 'there has been a considerable amount of efficient teaching'.[34] The contest was between technical systems which grew from and supported different accounts of desirable educational experience. We have to enquire into the reasons why one form of experience was favoured at Rugby and another at Winchester.

If, on the other hand, we look to explanations which stress the primacy of social and economic forces, perhaps pointing to the development of class conflicts as the effects of industrialization moved the basis of power from 'land and consols' to the management of risk capital, we again face the problem of making connections between such forces and the reformist inventions of public school headmasters. Butler, Arnold, Thring, Kennedy and Farrar set out to devise and promote forms of teaching and learning connected to the realization of well articulated social and cultural aims. Were the Rugby prefects, the Winchester classrooms, or the Uppingham playing fields called into being by determinist forces rather than by conscious agents? If we dismiss internal, directive explanations altogether, curriculum change has to be represented as 'meaningless' whereas the most significant thing that emerges from the study of nineteenth century educators is the extent to which they concerned themselves with meaning and the connection of meaning with forms of schooling and with personal and professional careers.[35]

Obviously, the importance of the constituency as bearer of meanings which mediate between reformist invention and the broader forces of social and economic evolution is thrust to the fore when the instance under discussion relates to a form of education which can be seen as 'private'. But what about the case where public authorities have assumed control of education and the system is 'national' not just in the sense that the sixth form in the nineteenth century became a national institution, but in the sense that policy and administration are provided through central government agencies?

The contention of this paper is that, while the intervention of central authorities certainly acts to modify the ways in which constituencies relate to curricular forms, it is not necessarily the case that such intervention detracts from the importance of constituencies as critical integrating agencies in the explanation of change. This is particularly the case when, as in England, government does not assume central direction over the form and content of the curriculum or rely on the use of mandates and directives. The idea of constituency could, for example, extend and enrich the understandings of modern examples of curriculum change provided by Goodson.[36] The meanings carried by and responded to by educational constituencies can provide an important key to his discussion of the encounter between reformist aspirations and the organizational structures which hinder or subvert them. Secondary schooling has been shaped in ways that favour certain kinds of hierarchical arrangements and promote certain kinds of career patterns because the policies which brought this about — allocation of funding, definitions of qualification — have been the expressions of meanings attached by constituencies to the educational categories they support. For example, support for subject specialism was not simply something which weighed in the scale when decisions about resource allocation were being made: it formed part of a coherent rhetoric connecting forms of education with constituency beliefs about how men should relate to society and build careers within it. Goodson's story is different from the story of the sixth form in the nineteenth century because his protagonists can use central authorities as a resource when constituency interests are challenged: a resurrected notion of 'regular subjects' which alone confer sixth form status could be promoted with the active support of

Schools Council subjects committees with jurisdiction over the sanctioning of A-level syllabuses.

The picture is also complicated in that, once education is legally promoted and controlled, constituencies can act through local and national political systems as well as in direct concert with schools. For example, an account of how and why the curriculum changes associated with the introduction of comprehensive schools in the 1960s and 70s came about would have to work with a rather elaborate conception of the nature of the constituencies of secondary education and the scope for action open to them. It seems likely, however, that studies focused on the notion of constituency would shed more light on the complex development of the comprehensive secondary curriculum than studies of administrative action or of the inventions of educators pursued in isolation.

The richness of historical enquiry will no doubt lead us to other ideas which can provide a connective tissue between partial and sometimes conflicting accounts of how the curriculum changes, but the notion of constituency seems to be an example of the kind of conception which helps us to understand the process of curriculum change under a great variety of conditions and to evaluate, for any given occasion, the relative importance of other, and perhaps more obvious, sources of explanation.[37]

## Notes

1 See, for example, KATZ (1971) or BOWLES and GINTIS (1976).
2 WARING (1979). See also the accounts of the introduction of new science courses in HEATH (1964).
3 McKINNEY and WESTBURY (1975). WESTBURY (1982).
4 GOODSON (1983).
5 WEILER (1983).
6 *Ibid.*, p. 140.
7 REID and FILBY (1982), chapters 1–5.
8 ROTHBLATT (1976).
9 COSTELLO (1958).
10 OED.
11 Report (1864).
12 ROTHBLATT, *op. cit.*, pp. 45–6.
13 *Op. cit.*
14 SEABORNE (1971), pp. 79 and 246.
15 BOWLES (1954), p. 259.
16 Report, *op. cit.*, Vol. 2, p. 68.
17 *Ibid.*, Vol. 2, p. 127 (Evidence of William Johnson (Cory)).
18 OLDHAM (1952).

19 Report, *op. cit.*, Vol. 2, p. 43 (Letter from W.E. Gladstone).
20 GIROUARD (1981).
21 Report, *op. cit.*, Vol. 2, p. 49.
22 *Ibid.*, Vol. 1, p. 56.
23 Though Eton held on to the older tradition, resisting, in the person of its head, Dr Balsdon, Lord Clarendon's suggestion that it should 'render obligatory a thing (French) which they thought ought to be part of an English gentleman's education' (*Ibid.*, Vol. 1, p. 85).
24 *Ibid.*, Vol. 2, p. 314.
25 Report (1868), Vol. 4, pp. 5–6.
26 ANNAN (1981), p. 862.
27 Report (1864), Vol.1, p. 287.
28 HAMILTON (1980).
29 FIRTH (1949), p. 155. Socio-technical inventions once abandoned are lost forever, despite the heavy meanings they may once have carried.
30 Report (1864), Vol. 1, p. 218.
31 *Ibid.*, Vol. 1, p. 217.
32 Report (1868), Vol. 4, p. 419.
33 WORSLEY (1940), p. 98.
34 Report (1864), Vol. 1, p. 287.
35 WESTBURY's notion of 'invention' gains power as an explanatory concept if we extend the scope of the word beyond the cataloguing of technical attributes (seating in a classroom, allocation of space) to include the *meanings* an invention might be able to bear for those who encounter it (sympathy, emulation, hierarchy). Inventions are adopted into systems not by virtue of their technical efficiency, but because of their consonance with meanings which constituencies project onto the forms of schooling.
36 *Op. cit.*
37 The ideas contained in this paper draw heavily on the work of JOHN MEYER, and especially his paper in BIDWELL and WINDHAM (1980). See also REID (1982).

## References/Bibliography

ANNAN, NOEL (1981) 'A spontaneous liberality', *The Times Literary Supplement*, 31 July.
BIDWELL, C.E. and WINDHAM, D.M. (Eds.) (1980) *The Analysis of Educational Productivity*, Vol. 2, *Issues in Macroanalysis*, Cambridge, Mass., Ballinger.
BOWLES, J. (1954) *Politics and Opinion in the Nineteenth Century*, London, Cape.
BOWLES, S. and GINTIS, H. (1976) *Schooling in Capitalist America: Education and the Contradictions of Economic Life*, New York, Basic Books.
COSTELLO, W.T. (1958) *The Scholastic Curriculum at Early Seventeenth-Century Cambridge*, Cambridge, Mass., Harvard University Press.
FIRTH, J. d'E. (1949) *Winchester College*, London, Winchester Publications.
GIROUARD, M. (1981) *The Return to Camelot: Chivalry and the English Gentleman*, New Haven, Yale University Press.

GOODSON, I. (1983) *School Subjects and Curriculum Change*, London, Croom Helm.

HAMILTON, D. (1980) 'Adam Smith and the moral economy of the classroom system', *Journal of Curriculum Studies*, Vol. 12.

HEATH, R.W. (Ed.) (1964) *New Curricula*, New York, Harper and Row.

KATZ, M.B. (1971) *Class, Bureaucracy and Schools: the Illusion of Educational Change in America*, New York, Praeger.

McKINNEY, W.L. and WESTBURY, I. (1975) 'Stability and change: the public schools of Gary, Indiana, 1940–1970', in REID, W.A. and WALKER, D.F. (Eds.).

MEYER, J.W. (1980) 'Levels of the educational system and schooling effects', in BINDWELL, C.E. and WINDHAM, D.M. (Eds.).

OLDHAM, J.B. (1952) *A History of Shrewsbury School, 1552–1952*, Oxford, Blackwells.

REID, W.A. (1982) 'Curricular topics as institutional categories', paper presented to the conference on the History and Sociology of School Subjects, St Hilda's College, Oxford.

REID, W.A. and FILBY J.L. (1982) *The Sixth: an Essay in Education and Democracy*, Lewes, Falmer Press.

REID, W.A. and WALKER, D.F. (Eds.) (1975) *Case Studies in Curriculum Change: Great Britain and the United States*, London, Routledge and Kegan Paul.

Report of H.M. Commissioners appointed to inquire into the Revenues and Management of Certain Colleges and Schools, etc. (CLARENDON) (1864).

Report of the Schools Inquiry Commission (TAUNTON) (1868).

ROTHBLATT, S. (1976) *Tradition and Change in English Liberal Education*, London, Faber and Faber.

SEABORNE, M. (1971) *The English School: its Architecture and Organization, 1370–1870*, London, Routledge and Kegan Paul.

WARING, M. (1979) *Social Pressures and Curriculum Innovation*, London, Methuen.

WEILER, H. (1983) 'Education, public confidence, and the legitimacy of the modern state: is there a "crisis" somewhere?' *Journal of Curriculum Studies*, Vol. 15.

WESTBURY, I. (1982) '"Invention" of curricula: some notes directed at opening a theme for discussion', paper presented to the conference on the History and Sociology of School Subjects, St Hilda's College, Oxford.

WORSLEY, T.C. (1940) *Barbarians and Philistines: Democracy and the Public Schools*, London, Robert Hale.

# Pioneers of an 'Alternative Road'? The Association of Heads of Secondary Technical Schools, 1951–64

*Gary McCulloch*

According to A.S. Humpheryes, the President of the Association of Heads of Secondary Technical Schools (AHSTS) in 1960–61 and Headmaster of Slough Technical School, 'Secondary technical schools have been pioneers in the "practical" approach in education — an approach providing an intellectual challenge to able pupils and leading to the conception of "The Alternative Road"'.[1] This view has become a received wisdom in recent years. *The Times Educational Supplement* has referred nostalgically to the 'spirit' of the technical school, though without clarifying the exact nature of this spirit.[2] Moreover, it has been suggested that the new Technical and Vocational Education Initiative (TVEI) is squarely in the tradition of the 'practical' approach in education, as pioneered by the secondary technical schools. However, closer examination of the 'Alternative Road' in its historical context suggests several problems of relevance to such assumptions and initiatives.

In March 1956 the Minister of Education, Sir David Eccles, asked the Central Advisory Council for Education to consider the education of boys and girls between the ages of 15 and 18: under the chairmanship of Sir Geoffrey Crowther, deputy chairman of the Economist Newspaper Ltd, the Council's report was published in December 1959. Several recommendations in the report attracted widespread interest, particularly the raising of the school-leaving age from 15 to 16, and the provision of compulsory part-time education for all young persons of 16 and 17 who were not engaged in full-time education. But perhaps the most important section of the report, certainly in the opinion of Crowther himself,[3] was Chapter 35, entitled 'The Alternative Road'. The dominant approach to education, it alleged, was 'the academic tradition which inspires and is embodied in our grammar schools and universities'.[4] However, it suggested, not all pupils were attracted or motivated by such an approach. There were, in fact, 'two kinds of minds', which should be treated in different ways.[5] The first kind of mind was the academic type, 'which is readily attuned to abstract thinking and can comprehend the meaning of a generalisation'.[6] These were best catered for by grammar school education. However, '. . . there are other minds which cannot grasp the general except by way of the particular, which cannot understand what is meant by the rule until they have observed the examples.'[7] Such minds, which 'move more easily from the practice to the theory', or which 'reason better in non-verbal ways', were 'not necessarily inferior', and more provision should be made for them.[8] Indeed, 'If the country is to benefit fully from the intelligence of all its able boys and girls, it will be necessary to rehabilitate the word "practical" in educational circles — it is often used in a pejorative sense — and to define it more clearly.'[9] It was therefore vital to make this alternative tradition of 'artistic or creative education', which was being stimulated by the innovations and demands of a technological age, 'as much a respectable part of the general educational system as the largely analytical tradition of the schools'.[10] This alternative approach, the report stressed, was marked not by 'narrow vocational interest' but rather by a 'broad scientific curiosity'.[11] For such pupils there should be an alternative, 'practical' route of education, and for this role the Crowther Report commended the secondary technical schools which were then in existence.

The secondary technical schools comprised one element in the tripartite system of secondary education (grammar, technical and modern) which had emerged from the second world war. The Spens Report of 1938 had recommended that a number of junior technical schools should be elevated to secondary status alongside the grammar schools,[12] and the Norwood Report of 1943 elaborated upon the 'types of minds' for which each kind of school was intended.[13] After the war, secondary technical schools were set up, aiming at a less academic approach than that associated with the grammar schools but hoping for an equal quality of intake and 'selecting the sphere of industry or commerce as their particular link with the adult world'.[14] However, these schools, created amid great optimism, struggled and ultimately failed to maintain an independent stance. By the time the Crowther committee was drafting its report, there were still four grammar schools to every technical school, and six grammar school pupils to every technical school pupil. In 1958, there were 279 secondary technical schools in England and Wales, with a total of 95,239 pupils — amounting to only 3.7 per cent of the total number of secondary school pupils. Of secondary school pupils aged 15, out of a total of 171,000, there were 12,000 boys and 7000 girls at secondary technical schools. Moreover, over 40 per cent of local education authorities did not provide any secondary technical schools, usually preferring to rely instead upon the technical departments of modern schools, or on the comprehensives which by the late 1950s were making important political advances.[15]

From the beginning, the secondary technical schools laboured under several crippling handicaps. First and foremost, they suffered from a widespread social prejudice against technical education itself. As the *TES* pointed out, 'Like everything else in technical education they were heirs to that long tradition of prejudice and suspicion by which the English have always supposed that technical studies mean dirty hands and the artisan.'[16] The image of the trade schools and junior technical schools from which most of them had sprung did not help their claim for equal status with grammar schools. Moreover, as Olive Banks noted with great clarity:

> Parents are not likely to accord equal favour to all three types of secondary education while the grammar schools — enjoying in any case the reflected glory of their former esteem — still provide the chief avenue, within the state system of education, to occupations of the highest social and economic standing.[17]

In many cases the technical schools were hampered by being situated within the premises of particular technical colleges and thus becoming 'a junior version of the technical college, both in atmosphere and in actual work', with a 'very limited corporate life' of their own.[18] Also, they tended to be expensive to establish and maintain as independent institutions, involving as they did expenditure on specialist staff, buildings and equipment. As Sir Graham Savage, the Education Officer of the London County Council, observed wryly: 'If you really want a cheap education, there is nothing better than a course in the classics.'[19]

In practice, too, it was found difficult to devise a reliable system of selection and assessment for technical schools. In order to be able to compete with the grammar schools, technical schools needed to be able to select pupils at the 11+ stage, yet A.A. Part, principal private secretary at the Ministry of Education, could note as early as April 1946 that:

> The psychological experts, with few exceptions, seem to think that it is not practicable to select children adequately for secondary technical schools at an age earlier than 13. This view is

supported, I believe, by some at least of H.M. Inspectors and by various other people.[20]

By the 1950s, such scepticism had become widespread. As the *TES* concluded, 'Entry is the key, and selection is made difficult since tests, while they will sift with rough efficiency between the academic and the non-academic, fail to discriminate between those with a practical bent and those without.'[21] At the same time, many technical school headmasters were suspicious of examinations, particularly those organized on a national basis, because of their reliance on written skills, their association with university interests and their lack of contact with local needs and industries. Yet there was also much hostility among the technical schools to the idea of a 'Ninth Examining Body' which would cater specially for technical pupils.[22] This was probably in part because it was felt that such an examining body would be of lower standing than were those which already existed. However, the special committee on technical education set up by the National Union of Teachers also noticed that 'There was a mistaken idea that it would be compulsory for Secondary Technical teachers to take examinations set by this body.'[23] After the eventual establishment of the new examining body entitled The Associated Examining Board, there was continuing discontent within the secondary technical schools regarding their role, often because it seemed to be 'aiming at too wide a clientele' rather than 'meeting the needs of the secondary technical schools'.[24]

These problems combined to undermine support for the secondary technical schools. For many local authorities, such as Cheshire, the cheapest and most convenient option was to encourage bilateral and multilateral secondary schools;[25] while some Chief Education Officers, such as Dr Gurr in Middlesex and W.G. Stone of Brighton,[26] became actively hostile to the actual principle of independent technical schools. Dr William Alexander, the influential secretary of the Association of Education Committees, was initially sympathetic to the tripartite system, but by the mid-1950s problems of selection and expense led him to suggest that technical courses should be provided within general secondary education for the majority of pupils, rather than in separate institutions.[27] Meanwhile, although the Federation of British Industries education committee was involved in encouraging greater appreciation of applied science and engineering in schools in the 1950s, it was usually content to direct its attention and resources towards the public and grammar schools, as was the 'Industrial Fund' of the same period.[28] Professional scientific institutions,[29] and even university engineering departments and professional engineering institutions, also tended to ignore the secondary technical schools.[30] Nor could the technical schools look to the Labour Party for support. Despite the encouragement given to such schools by Ellen Wilkinson, Labour's first post-war Minister of Education,[31] the Labour Party and the Trades Union Congress were generally hostile to this type of education at the secondary level, fearing as they did that it would be exploited by employers and might help to perpetuate traditional social and work patterns. Thus the TUC told the Crowther committee in no uncertain terms:

> ... it is educationally and socially undesirable that young people should be unduly segregated on the basis of their possession or otherwise of certain specific abilities, especially if such segregation is related also to different fields of future employment and consequently to different degrees of social status.[32]

The various educational, professional, industrial and political interest-groups of the time each had their own reasons for neglecting or opposing the secondary technical schools, but together they ensured that the schools were in general starved of attention and resources.

Thus, the secondary technical schools found it most difficult to compete with well established grammar schools, and were hampered by problems with regard to finance, accommodation, selection and assessment throughout their existence. But besides all these difficulties, the technical schools also suffered from a basic lack of clarity over what their own role should be, and the nature of their distinctive approach to education. There existed many differences between the technical schools which could not be attributed to a healthy variety of opinion, and which added to the general confusion and suspicion about their status. There were still many schools directed towards particular trades or industries rather than industry and commerce in general, and these schools usually accepted pupils for entry at 13+ rather than 11+, and lacked sixth forms. Technical teachers and heads came from many different backgrounds, and their previous experiences often influenced their approach to secondary technical education.[33] Meanwhile, technical education for girls raised special problems with regard to rationale and aims. M. Collison, the headmistress of Stroud Technical School for Girls in Gloucestershire, declared firmly that 'From the beginning ... all girls must have the broadest training, and the approach to all subjects must be both theoretical and practical.'[34] However, for example, while Miss Walkden's school in Manchester involved girls in 'technological' work suitable for the professions, the Doncaster Technical School for Girls under Miss M. Woollett was less ambitious and preferred simply to develop such subjects as domestic science, biology and housecraft.[35]

In general, too, the technical schools were badly affected by a problem which had also bedevilled the engineering profession since the nineteenth century. Beginning from a position of low status within the scientific community, the engineering profession had developed its own internal rivalries and snobberies. Moreover, it was torn between conforming to the intellectual and academic ideals of scientists, and stressing the more practical and industrial aspects of engineering as an activity.[36] This conflict of strategy and self-image was also apparent in the technical schools, and even sympathetic observers could be confused by the differences which it generated. One account of secondary technical education, seeking to demonstrate a coherent approach, noted that the head of a certain technical school had 'paused outside a school workshop, saying: "Not plumbing ≏ non-ferrous metal work. We teach them why — not how." '[37] Not surprisingly this was rapidly followed by an indignant letter from T.C. McNeill, Head of Portsmouth Building School, complaining:

> . . . are we trying in some oblique fashion to make the secondary technical school respectable? . . . We suffer too much today, and particularly in the secondary technical schools, from individuals who, unaware of the significance of their work, spend much of their time apologizing for the fact that their school is not a grammar school and trying to put an academic veneer on what is in itself a thoroughly cultural effort giving an experience of values which no 'academic' education can equal.[38]

Increased publicity and public sympathy would not be enough when the schools themselves had such incoherent and contradictory aims. And so the AHSTS came into being not only to defend the existence of secondary technical schools and resolve their problems of selection and assessment, but also to try to find a coherent and meaningful rationale. A conference for technical school heads took place in Birmingham in June 1947, and its participants concurred with the views expressed in the recent Ministry of Education pamphlet, *The New Secondary Education*, which defended the tripartite system.[39] Moves towards the formation of an association of technical school heads were then encouraged when it transpired that none of the examining bodies apart from the University of London was prepared to accept 'technical subjects' in the new General Certificate of Education examinations for matriculation purposes. A meeting took place at Towneley Technical High School in Burnley in February 1950 to decide how to influence the Northern Universities Joint Matriculation Board, and it was agreed to form a northern Association.[40] A Southern Region was inaugurated later the same year, and a National Association was formed in February 1951. The first annual conference of the new Association was held in Blackpool in May 1951, although this event attracted very little publicity.[41] Membership grew steadily — from 22 heads in February 1951, to 93 by the start of 1955,[42] to a peak of 121 at the end of 1957.[43] From this point membership fell as the schools came under pressure from many LEAs and were replaced in several areas by bilateral, multilateral and comprehensive schools.

The leaders of the Association felt that they and their schools were being persistently misunderstood and misrepresented, and that this largely accounted for the failure of the schools to establish themselves. Such was the strength of this feeling that the Association tended to react in a very prickly manner even to constructive and sympathetic criticism of the secondary technical schools. In May 1953 the Association's secretary, J. Safkin, 'drew attention to the ignorance of both authorities [*ie* the LEAs] and the public generally to secondary technical education'.[44] In 1956 its Council was offended by the publication of a new book by Dr Olive Banks, *Parity And Prestige In English Education*, and sent a letter to its publishers expressing 'complete disagreement'.[45] In 1960, displeasure was expressed even over a generally sympathetic and thoroughly researched study on the subject of the secondary technical school, written by a local education officer, Reese Edwards.[46] When the National Union of Teachers offered to publish a booklet describing some of the experiments taking place in secondary technical schools, it was noted that 'there was a good deal of suspicion about the NUT interfering in this — suspicion that the booklet would not accurately represent technical schools.'[47] The AHSTS's general sense of grievance was perhaps well justified. But this feeling of isolation and embattlement led the Association to be suspicious, reserved and often uncooperative in its dealings with other educational bodies, rarely to its own advantage.

The Association tended to explain what it saw as the dominant prejudice and apathy concerning technical schools by way of a distinctive social critique, buttressed by a particular view of history. It was argued that English society and education had been and continued to be dominated by attitudes which undervalued 'practical' approaches to contemporary problems. Moreover, it was alleged, this situation had effectively reduced the competitiveness of British industry, and thus contributed to the decline in her world role and the relatively slow growth of the national economy. The principal target of the AHSTS's historical interpretation was Sir Robert Morant, the moving force behind the Education Act of 1902, who had promoted the classical and liberal values of the public and grammar schools at the expense of technical education. According to A.J. Jenkinson, the Principal of Bolton Technical College and editor of *Vocational Aspect*, the main reason for the failure of secondary technical schools to make a strong impact was the fact that educational policy was dominated by ' a group with a common educational and cultural background': 'It is, almost without exception, a grammar (and public) school group. Its members have been produced by Morant and the 1904 Regulations rather than by Donnelly, Huxley and the Science and Art Department'.[48] Dr H. Frazer, head of the Gateway School in Leicester and a member of the Crowther committee, argued that the Education Act of 1902 had embodied the views of the 'traditionalists in education', and claimed that this fact had already damaged national competitiveness and prosperity:

> For fifty years the grammar schools have resisted the introduc-
> tion of technical subjects into the curriculum . . . This attitude is
> a luxury which the country cannot any longer afford . . . At this
> moment Great Britain and America are competing for a two-
> thousand-million-pound order for atomic power stations in
> Western Europe. Had technical education been introduced into
> this country fifty years ago, there would be no doubt of our
> obtaining the order.[49]

This view of society and history, involving some hostility to traditional English culture as well as a sense of the technical schools' potential importance for national power and prosperity, united the members of the AHSTS rather more visibly than did any particular conception of technical education.

Resentment at the dominance and high status of grammar school education therefore helped to give the AHSTS its motivation and such cohesion as it possessed; but the problem of the relationship which technical schools should have with grammar schools served to create further divisions within the Association. The official view of the Ministry of Education was that grammar and technical schools should coexist as equal partners, with the grammar schools pursuing their traditional pure, academic approach and the secondary technical schools evolving an 'applied' approach of equal stature. The White Paper *Technical Education*, published in February 1956,[50] the Crowther Report of 1959 and successive Ministers of Education all advocated the maintenance of this fragile balance.[51] The *TES* faithfully reflected this hope for cooperation, arguing that the technical school should 'look forward, not to a nominal parity, but to real equality with the grammar schools', thus creating 'an avenue to the university departments of science and technology in company with the grammar schools'. But it stressed that 'grammar and technical schools need to be partners, not rivals.'[52] In fact, however, there was always an undercurrent of hostility against the grammar schools within the AHSTS. Dr Frazer was particularly aggressive in his attitude, and announced that '*We* have found the answer' — secondary technical education being not only a particular kind of education but the only relevant education for a technological age.[53]

But equally there were increasing numbers within the AHSTS who were willing to concede that the secondary technical schools were beset with too many problems, and that if necessary the Association should abandon the defence of the schools themselves in order to advocate the practice and extension of technical education in all schools. As the journal *Technology* observed, the policy of 'independence' was the 'radical' option, while the strategy of 'absorption' was the 'reformist' one: '. . . we may put all our energy into making real the ideal technical schools of 1944, or we may make do and mend by integrating technical studies in the grammar and public schools.'[54] There was always strong resistance to a policy of integration, and a statement of policy agreed by the Association in 1953 was firm in declaring that

> If secondary technical education is organized as a stream in a comprehensive or multilateral school, there is a danger that the technical bias may be diluted, the sense of purpose less clearly marked and the essential vitality lost. The Association considers, therefore, that wherever possible, secondary technical education should be provided in secondary technical schools.[55]

However, the strategy of absorption gained ground by the end of the 1950s. One of the earliest advocates of the change in tactics was Edward Semper, head of the Doncaster Technical High School for Boys and, from the late 1950s onwards, probably the dominant figure in the Association.[56] In 1964, influenced by Semper and the steady advance of the comprehensives, the AHSTS changed its name to the 'Association for Technical Education in Schools'.[57] Paradoxically, however, in the few years before its demise the Association under Semper's guidance came closer to a coherent notion of its role, and of the type of education which it represented, than it ever had before.

Edward Semper, born in Bradford in 1913, was educated first at a grammar school and then at Bradford Technical College. After being involved in technical training for cadets during the second world war, he quickly became aware of the basic problems which the new secondary technical schools would encounter.[58] In an MEd thesis entitled 'The Curriculum of the Technical High School', which he completed at the University of Leeds in 1946, Semper pointed to the confusion of purpose among the new schools. In this thesis, he urged that they should avoid a narrowly vocational approach, but should also avoid merging with grammar school education, by appreciating the 'educative value of technics'. The pupil at a technical school should differ from a grammar school pupil by being interested in knowledge not for its own sake, but in its application to practical problems. He argued in favour of 'a new and more practical approach to learning' which would balance the claims of science and technology, strengthen the impulses which stimulate discovery, and 'restore a sense of vocation to the technician'. He did not shirk the industrial connotations of this view, stressing that technical schools should have close links with local industries and that 'industry must form the corner-stone of the curriculum'. In general, he observed,

> Whereas the usual method of teaching the sciences is that of beginning with their systematic theoretical development, occasionally making a belated effort at practical application of the theory, the method used in the technical high school should be that of developing a coherent body of scientific knowledge from some of the observed applications.[59]

What was still not clear was exactly how this should be attempted.

Semper became headmaster of the Doncaster Technical High School for Boys in 1952, and spent the next few years trying to work out the practical implications of his approach. His staff was inexperienced and accommodation was restricted, but by 1959 his school had sixty sixth-formers and a new building in which craft work was practised as an 'instrument of general education'.[60] He was ready to publicize his approach in clear terms:

> The Doncaster Technical High School differs from a grammar school mainly in that it has a broad vocational aim and is unashamedly science-based. The applications of science are used to bring intelligent interest to the crafts and to create an awareness of our cultural heritage as well as to vitalise the teaching of pure science. The ethos of the school is conditioned by technology which, far from restricting the process of educa-

tion, provides a most engaging means of stimulating interest and sustaining effort.

In the junior school, the curriculum was as broad as possible, but according to Semper 'In the senior school applied science becomes the central theme of the curriculum and the distinctive character of the school emerges.' There were three separate groups, according to ability. The first group studied mechanics, applied physics and chemistry; the second took applied physics and mechanics; the third took engineering science. All boys studied English, history, geography, geometrical and engineering drawing, and either woodwork or metalwork. Sixth-formers studied three subjects to GCE A-level, as well as taking a course in general studies and undertaking a personal project. Physics, mechanics and chemistry were closely related to cars, engines, turbo-generators, etc.: 'The process of learning becomes exciting when scientific principles are deduced from or linked with the performance, construction, and design of machines.'[61]

Above all else, Semper stressed the educational value of this approach, rather than its vocational ends: 'It is important to appreciate the effectiveness of engineering as a basis of general education.' Work-shops in schools stimulated 'inventive thinking' and the 'unity of hand and mind'.[62] At the same time, its relevance to society was that it could help 'a nation of shopkeepers and colonial administrators to become a nation of technologists'.[63] Semper's emphasis upon the educational value of technology and engineering in schools was widely echoed among other technical school heads. According to J. Safkin, headmaster of the Nelson Secondary Technical School as well as being the first secretary of the National Association, 'the secondary technical school is justifiable, not because it produces engineers or plasterers, but because its realistic content and practical application are very well suited to stimulate, encourage, and guide the development of adolescents.'[64] This was also an important element in the notion of the 'Alternative Road' which the Crowther Report advanced in 1959, and Semper immediately seized the opportunity presented by the publication of the Crowther Report to press for further publicity and recognition for this approach. At a meeting of the northern region of the AHSTS on 4 February 1960, he demanded a further inquiry into the 'practical approach'.[65] At a weekend conference held at Huddersfield Training College for Technic-al Teachers later that month, Semper stressed the importance of Chapter 35 of the Report.[66] In July of that year, he called for the Ministry of Education to set up a further committee to inquire into the idea of the 'Alternative Road':

> The plain truth is that we have scarcely begun to develop a
> practical approach to education in our schools, that is, a practical
> education making progressively exacting intellectual demands.
> Research and planning are essential if we are to make any real
> progress in this aspect of education.

Thus, Semper acknowledged that the secondary technical schools had so
far failed to create a coherent 'practical' alternative to traditional
grammar school education. Moreover, he warned, the 'Alternative Road
will remain a pipe dream unless the Minister takes prompt action to
stimulate enquiry and foster research into the many problems associated
with it.'[67] But Semper was a determined man, imbued with a strong
sense of personal mission. As he later recalled, 'I felt sure that with the
onset of comprehensive education my work would die with me ...
unless measures were taken to promote developments of a similar kind
in all schools.' He set out to use the admittedly 'inadequate machinery'
of the AHSTS to this end.[68]

The annual conference of the AHSTS in 1961 was held at Doncaster
Technical College, and the 'Alternative Road' was its central theme. At
this conference, the technical school heads called unanimously for the
Minister of Education to appoint another committee on the 'Alternative
Road'.[69] Discussions on this theme were immediately started with
industrial organizations and the Principals of the Colleges of Advanced
Technology.[70] On the basis of these discussions Semper decided to
organize a curriculum research project on the 'Alternative Road' idea,
although, as he agreed, 'It was most important that the Research Project
should not become a PhD Research of the standard type, which would
just gather dust on Education Department shelves.'[71] So in July 1962
Semper led a small delegation to visit Professor Boris Ford of the
Institute of Education at the University of Sheffield, and a Development
Committee was set up.[72] At the same time, Semper was seconded by his
LEA to a lectureship in technical education at Sheffield from November
1962 to February 1963, and was the secretary of the Development
Committee which met for the first time under Ford's chairmanship on
18 January 1963. A long discussion took place at this meeting on the
meaning of the 'Alternative Road' notion and the need for further
research. W.S. Brace, head of the Thomas Linacre School in Wigan,
secretary of the AHSTS and a close ally of Semper, attempted to define
the idea of the 'Alternative Road' in a way which might attract
widespread support, or at least avoid predictable forms of criticism:

> It must be quite clear, he said, that this study is not an attack
> upon grammar schools. It is an attempt to devise an alternative

to grammar school work which, it is thought, would be much more acceptable to certain people. It is not an attempt to channel people into engineering or what have you at an early age, it is not a question of adding subjects to the curriculum, and it is certainly not a question of instituting a craft approach. What is envisaged is the provision of a learning situation in which theory grows out of practice and in which what is done has an end in itself viz. the development of intellectual grasp and understanding.[73]

The members of the committee exchanged ideas for possible research which might be relevant to this problem, generally agreeing that it was important to encourage 'creativity' and 'inventive thinking' at the secondary school level. It was also agreed that the 'practical' approach, if it could be defined, should involve intellectual demands. Ford suggested that the 'Alternative Road' should offer an alternative 'to both the merely theoretical and the rather narrowly technical'.[74] The practical approach which was here envisaged, perhaps rather vaguely, stressed educational aims more than vocational ends.

For some members of the committee, including George Bosworth of the English Electric Company who had been an influential member of the Crowther committee, further research was not needed, particularly if it was to involve analysis of such 'airy-fairy' ideas as creativity.[75] But the committee went on to devise a programme of research into the 'teaching of science by investigations and problem-solving activities based upon the application of science'.[76] A wide-ranging set of problems was tabled, and it was agreed to test them on 'a wide variety of schools located in dissimilar geographical areas'.[77] But such an experiment would require extensive funding, and despite approaches to several private foundations and to the new Department of Education and Science, this was not forthcoming. However, in October 1964 a Labour government came to power with a prime minister, Harold Wilson, committed to encourage all aspects of the 'white heat' of the technological revolution;[78] and Semper was emboldened to write to him to seek finance for a wider investigation of technical education in schools from the new Schools Council. At an interview with Semper in January 1965, the joint secretaries of the Schools Council announced that they would either give a small grant to Semper for an independent inquiry, or take over the whole project under their own auspices.[79] The prospect of a national inquiry, probably followed by a major development project, with all the resources at the command of the Schools Council, was hard to resist, and Semper handed over the project —

which ultimately evolved into 'Project Technology', headed by Geoffrey Harrison at Loughborough.[80]

Semper's efforts certainly constituted an 'Alternative Road' to that pursued by grammar school science teachers, who at the same time were seeking to reform their own syllabuses by stressing the pure, abstract, academic and cultural elements of science.[81] Dr Henry Boulind, a lecturer at the Department of Education at Cambridge University and chairman of the Science Masters' Association's Science and Education Committee, argued that all 'responsible' members of society 'should be trained to observe and think scientifically, and to know something of the way in which scientists work'.[82] But his definition of 'responsible' members of society was a highly limited one. He was clear and insistent in his demand for radical change: 'school physics and chemistry have for a long time now stopped short at the year 1900 — or even 1800; it is time that the schools entered the twentieth century.'[83] As an example of a modernized school science course, he suggested a new syllabus in atomic physics. But this would only be 'aimed at the top 25 per cent of the brightest and most able pupils', and its presentation must be based upon 'sound scientific principles', to provide 'the logical development of important physical concepts'.[84] In general, the 'main object' of science education in Boulind's view was 'to make pupils *think*, to lead them to formulate problems clearly, and to attempt to solve them in a common-sense, scientific manner'.[85] Moreover, he was strongly opposed to the introduction of engineering for 'intelligent' pupils:

> Engineers and others concerned with the problem are apt to say: why don't we teach engineering in schools? I strongly suspect that, if pinned down and made to say what they would like taught, it would turn out that they still wanted a sound background in mathematics, physics and chemistry. I do not think that more woodwork and metalwork, more copper ashtrays and more iron toasting forks, is what is wanted in grammar schools.[86]

There was a chasm between Boulind's views and those put forward by Semper and the AHSTS. Whereas Semper's activities led directly to the development of the Schools Council Project in Technology, and also encouraged the Joint Matriculation Board to set up an A-level in Engineering Science from 1969,[87] the reform proposals of the Science Masters' Association and the Association of Women Science Teachers were taken up and extended by the Nuffield Foundation Science Teaching Project, launched in 1962.[88] These contrasting ventures were remarked upon by Semper himself: 'note was taken of the Nuffield

Research Project in pure science to which, it was felt, a programme based upon the applications of science would be complementary'.[89] The columnist 'Astryx' in the *TES* (Leonard Jackson, the editor of the journal *Technology*) felt that Semper's group would be able to create 'a technical competitor to Nuffield'.[90] Even so, despite Semper's energy and determination, it is by no means clear that his research proposals amounted to a coherent and generally applicable conception of secondary technical education.

As Ivor Goodson has observed, much curriculum debate 'can be interpreted in terms of conflict between subjects over status, resources and territory'.[91] Technical and craft subjects have always carried low status within secondary education, and this is still the case today. The secondary technical schools, and their Association, were torn between imitating the academic traditions of the grammar schools, and rejecting them in favour of a more 'relevant' approach. The idea of the 'Alternative Road' presented a *via media*, a solution to this dilemma, by combining intellectual and academic pretensions with an insistence upon the value of engineering, applied science and craftwork within the school environment. In the light of Harold Silver's recent discussion of the various attempts to 'liberalize' technical education in order to render it more widely acceptable,[92] it is noteworthy that, in those few cases where applied science was taught in grammar and public schools, it was almost always motivated by the idea of the 'Alternative Road'.[93] But it was an idea which permitted varying interpretations, and this meant that it could be invoked to support differing and even conflicting approaches to the introduction of applied science and technology in schools.

The conception of the 'Alternative Road' had attracted Semper and the AHSTS because it provided a distinctive rationale for secondary technical education which combined academic and practical aims. But it ultimately failed to raise the status, increase the resources or broaden the territory of such education. Semper, perhaps in despair, once went so far as to suggest that 'perhaps the word "technical" was now misleading, what was wanted was an adjective suggesting "purposeful", "creative", "inventive" or "imaginative".'[94] Certainly, the changing name of the Association reflected a continuing search for wider appeal. It was altered in 1964 to the 'Association for Technical Education in Schools', and was later changed again to become the 'Association for Technological Education in Schools'. Moreover, although its support for the idea of the 'Alternative Road' gave the AHSTS some claim to a coherent notion of a 'practical' approach to education, the 'Alternative Road' itself embraced many differences of opinion and emphasis. Even at the first meeting of Semper's development committee in January

1963, there was disagreement over priorities and ends. But such differences became even more evident when the Schools Council Project in Technology attempted to act upon its own interpretation of the 'Alternative Road'.

From a very early stage, the Schools Council project appeared to be strongly associated with craft teaching. Its alleged 'craft approach' alienated science teachers, even those who favoured greater recognition for applied science. But it was also criticized by many advocates of the 'Alternative Road'. Semper, for example, stressed the importance of 'creativity' and 'inventive thinking' more than traditional craftr education, and was disappointed with the general outlook as well as the impact of the Schools Council project.[95] Yet the project was itself largely inspired by the concept of the 'Alternative Road'. A Schools Council curriculum bulletin published at this time explained the historical background and the problems of technical education in terms which were almost identical to the analysis offered by the Crowther Report,[96] but in practice the attitudes of the leaders of the Schools Council project differed significantly from those of other sympathizers of the 'Alternative Road' concept. The project ultimately failed to resolve the dichotomy between 'craft' and 'science', or to raise the status of technical education. It also highlighted the persistent ambiguities and tensions which sheltered behind the slogan of the 'Alternative Road'. The idea provided not one ' "practical" approach to education', but legitimation for various 'practical' approaches to education. Its supporters had in common a coherent social and historical explanation for the problems of secondary technical education, and a desire to combine 'academic' and 'practical' goals within secondary education; but they were as divided as ever when it came to positive proposals for action.

The legend of the 'Alternative Road', created by the Crowther Report and seized upon by the AHSTS, accounts for much of the high reputation enjoyed by the secondary technical schools among current academics and legislators. In recent years, the studied detachment which was once noted by E.H. Carr[97] has tended to give way to attempts to explain the relative national decline which has been experienced by Britain since the late nineteenth century. The history of scientific and technical education has come to be seen as a symbol and partial explanation of an 'English disease' which has inhibited social development and promoted national decline. Such analyses, usually drawing upon such social and historical interpretations as have been offered by groups like the AHSTS, have suggested a general formula by which Britain might have avoided long term decline and the discontents of the 1980s: the 'practical' approach in education. Corrélli Barnett, for example, has attributed Britain's low industrial productivity to the social attitudes reflected in and reproduced by education: 'the general ethos and thrust of British education are, if anything, hostile to industry and careers in industry'.[98] He argues that only an increase in 'practical' education, which he describes as 'education for capability', can arrest the relative decline which he perceives; indeed, 'education for capability alone can keep Britain an advanced technological society and save her from becoming a Portugal, perhaps even an Egypt, of tomorrow.'[99] It is in reality most difficult to predict either the general economic and social requirements of the future, or the specific industrial consequences of changes in education and training.[100] Also, the 'practical' approach itself permits many different interpretations, now as in the past. However, once Barnett's assumptions are taken for granted, it is possible to argue that Britain's relative decline might have been avoided by means of an 'Alternative Road' involving the 'practical approach'.

A recent book by Martin J. Wiener provides an impressive and elaborate version of this kind of argument. Wiener discerns 'a cultural *cordon sanitaire* encircling the forces of economic development — technology, industry, commerce',[101] and contrasts these forces with the ethos of the leading public schools. Thus, 'when science teaching finally arrived in the public schools, it came late, marked by a social stigma and a bias against those aspects that bordered on engineering.'[102] According to Wiener, moreover, the officials of the Board of Education, particularly Morant, encouraged the public school ethos in establishing the new system of secondary education from 1902, and thus prevented the emergence of an alternative, more practical tradition in education which might have helped Britain to avoid its relative economic decline. Wiener's social and historical explanation for the problems of 'practical' education does in fact bear a close resemblance to the arguments put forward by such groups as the AHSTS. But he gives little in the way of analysis of the tensions, ambiguities and differences between the various proponents of a more practical approach to education, and this leaves a misleading impression of coherence.

This tendency is particularly noticeable in some recent work of Gordon Roderick and Michael Stephens. The 'British disease', they argue, is 'synonymous with relative economic failure and an inability to match our industrial productivity to that of our competitors'.[103] They trace this failure from the Victorian period, and ask *Where Did We Go Wrong?* In answering this question, they stress the continuity of the 'Great Debate' on the 'British malaise', and point out that the social criticisms made by such figures as Baron Playfair and T.H. Huxley in the nineteenth century have strong affinities with those advanced by

Lords Snow and Bowden, among others, in the 1950s and 1960s. But they leave the strong impression that there were no significant differences between the various advocates of a more 'practical' approach. Huxley, Snow and the like are depicted as lofty statesmen protesting to no avail against the reactionary attitudes of Sir Robert Morant and his kind. In general, the picture of national decline drawn by Roderick and Stephens is one of a continuing conflict between progressives and the forces of reaction.

Fifty years ago, Herbert Butterfield saw the Whig interpretation of history as 'the tendency in many historians to write on the side of Protestants and Whigs, to praise revolutions provided they have been successful, to emphasize certain principles of progress in the past and produce a story which is the ratification if not the glorification of the present'.[104] Butterfield was writing at a time when it was still possible to see the 'British constitution' as the culmination of progress. But some recent attempts to explain 'national decline' seem predicated upon an assumption which is no less Whiggish than that described by Butterfield. The Whigs are still the heroes in such history, but where they were once triumphant in their battles against reaction, now they are portrayed as tragic losers. In explaining the persistent problems of 'practical' education, the temptation encouraged by such an attitude is to exaggerate the coherence of thought of the many educational and social critics of the last century. This historiographical tendency has recently been described as 'lumping' as opposed to 'splitting': 'Instead of noting differences, lumpers note likenesses; instead of separateness, connection'.[105] It may well be that there is currently a need to resist the temptation to 'lump' in this field of historiography.

A deepening perception of 'national decline' has also influenced political attitudes to scientific and technical education in Britain. Since the early 1960s, active state involvement in education, science and technology has steadily grown. Planning on these issues was initially intended to maximize economic growth. But increasingly in the late 1960s and 1970s, the purposes of government intervention in education, science and technology were associated with the need to minimize the effects of economic recession. The development in direct government involvement has accelerated since the launching of the 'Great Debate' in the autumn of 1976. In a widely publicized speech at Ruskin College, Oxford, the prime minister, James Callaghan, stressed the need to change social and educational attitudes, especially to relate education more usefully to society and industry.[106] Since then this theme has become highly familiar, increasing in urgency and stridency as the economic and industrial difficulties of the nation have increased.

Education in general, and the low social status of technical education in particular, have been widely taken as a major cause and symbol of 'national decline'. One sign of such concerns was the Finniston Report on the engineering profession, published in January 1980: 'Unless urgent actions are taken, continued relative and possibly absolute industrial decline is inevitable with unpredictable but certainly undesirable social consequences.'[107] Another was the launching of the TVEI in November 1982. Norman Tebbit, Secretary of State for Employment, described the new 'technical educational initiative' as the 'rebirth of technical education' which was vital if British was to compete with its chief industrial rivals.[108]

Tebbit's depiction of this new scheme as a 'rebirth' of technical education which could help to arrest 'national decline' implied the existence of an 'Alternative Road' by which Britain might have avoided many of its worst problems. It reflected not only the view that the TVEI would be a significant factor in ending relative economic decline, but also the assumption that it was in the same broad tradition as past initiatives in technical education. Other spokesmen made it clear that the TVEI was particularly influenced by lessons drawn from the experiences of the postwar secondary technical schools. David Young, the chairman of the Manpower Services Commission (MSC), declared that in setting up the planned ten projects in England and Wales by September 1983, 'Our objective is to create a vocational technical high school which can be replicated'.[109] Young's own experience of technical schools had been in France and elsewhere, but a clear parallel between these schools and the earlier existence of secondary technical schools in England itself was widely drawn:

> Technical schools, providing vocational secondary education [sic], have almost disappeared from the United Kingdom under secondary reorganization. But they continue to thrive in France as part of mainstream provision. Mr David Young, the MSC's chairman, says that his determination to bring some vocational options back into Britain's schools is strongly influenced by the success of some of the French technical schools.[110]

Dr Rhodes Boyson, junior minister with responsibility for schools at the Department of Education and Science, recalled that 'the old technical schools had been seen as second rate to the grammars and this affected their selection'. He hoped that the TVEI would provide a solution to this problem by 'setting up "mini-schools" within existing non selective schools'.[111] The Education Secretary, Sir Keith Joseph, also made a direct comparison between the approach adopted by the secondary technical schools and that of the TVEI: 'There were technical schools, a small number, under the 1944 Act. They never spread as was originally intended, and I think that we want to encourage the reintroduction of the technical stream within the present schools.'[112] The basic theme of such accounts was that the secondary technical schools, despite their ultimate failure, had been pioneers of an 'Alternative Road', the practical approach in education, and that their example should now be followed.

Yet although the spokesmen of the TVEI stressed the general continuity of the tradition in 'practical' education, with particular reference to the example of the secondary technical schools, the differences between the approach of the TVEI and that of the AHSTS are as significant as their similarities. First, the secondary technical schools were intended to be selective in nature, competing with the grammar schools on equal terms. They rarely achieved this aim in practice, but the Minister of Education could still assure a delegation of the AHSTS as late as 1959 that 'we equate the secondary technical school with the grammar school as being selective, which we certainly hope to defend from wholesale comprehensive schools'.[113] The initiators of the TVEI did not pursue such an aim. Tebbit hoped that the initiative would 'attract a broad spectrum of ability', but added that 'for those who do not fancy the rich academic diet we are providing them with a rather more nourishing technical diet'.[114] Young sought to involve a 'wide range' of academic ability in the schools, but aimed particularly for the '15 to 85 percentiles of the ability range'.[115] Sir Keith Joseph placed more emphasis upon the needs of the 'bottom 40 per cent' in schools in this context.[116] But the 'selective' rationale which was an integral part of the outlook of the AHSTS was nowhere apparent in the launching of the TVEI.

Also, the rationale of the secondary technical schools as expressed by the AHSTS was educational much more than vocational. The Crowther Report emphasized 'broad scientific curiosity' rather than 'narrow vocational interest'. Semper and the AHSTS in general sought a balance between 'academic' and 'practical' goals, and perceived the 'Alternative Road' as providing such a balance. By contrast, the TVEI was conceived primarily as a vocational device. It was controlled by the MSC, which was accountable to the Department of Employment. David Young stressed the improved employment prospects which the TVEI could offer: 'By the time they leave our youngsters will be highly employable.'[117] Moreover, the initiators of the TVEI had less respect for liberal and academic values than had been shown by the AHSTS. Bill

Bonnen of the CBI's Special Programmes Unit, a supporter of the new initiative, argued:

> Within the harsh context of restricted resources and the absolute need to achieve a cost-effective economy, I see no place for education merely for its own sake. Educational 'purists' who parade the liberal education banner in our schools are naively misguided. In the market-place of world competition such vague thinking is a luxury we cannot afford.[118]

Another characteristic of the TVEI in its initial stages was its somewhat dismissive attitude towards established educational interests. The launching of the scheme was announced without any prior consultation with such interests, but Young was unapologetic: 'Supposing we had decided to launch a debate about technical education or the lack of it. We might have had a royal commission and it might have taken five years or even ten to get off the ground. Now we have a pilot project due to start by September next year.'[119] The initiative was associated with the 'resolute approach' of a Conservative government which had emerged triumphantly from the Falklands war. The Conservatives' dominance was likely in due course to subside, if only partially. Thus the TVEI, which had little educational support — because it had sought none — also rested upon a narrow political base. Again, this situation contrasts sharply with the circumstances which surrounded the creation of the secondary technical schools. These schools were established in the 1940s with the support of educational interests and as part of a wide educational and political consensus. Support for the schools soon waned, and the consensus slowly crumbled. But the important point here is that the AHSTS was acutely aware of the need to retain such support, and tried to maintain the political consensus of the 1940s, whereas the TVEI paid little attention to such problems.

It may be that the TVEI will inherit 'that long tradition of prejudice and suspicion' which afflicted the secondary technical schools. But the AHSTS and the leaders of the TVEI had very different ideas of the 'practical' approach in education. Few secondary technical schools actually lived up to the ideal of the Crowther Report, and even the leaders of the AHSTS failed to formulate a wholly coherent notion of the 'Alternative Road'. Even so, their general aims contrast sharply with those of the later initiative which claimed to be inspired by their example. In fairness, it should be added that the LEA schemes which were eventually adopted by the TVEI bore little resemblance to Young's original objectives.[120] Also, many opponents of the scheme seemed under the same misapprehension as its originators in arguing that the TVEI would revive 'tripartism'.[121] But it seems clear that the TVEI was influenced strongly by an idealized view of the secondary technical schools, and a misplaced faith in the coherence of an 'Alternative Road' which could arrest Britain's relative economic decline. Edward Semper has argued that the AHSTS, and then the Association for Technical Education in Schools, 'exerted an influence altogether out of proportion to the size of their memberships'.[122] Their influence was indeed strong, and their contribution distinguished. However, the idea that they were pioneers of an 'Alternative Road' has encouraged a distorted view of history and maintained the belief that there exists a single practical approach in education. It has also helped to legitimize a very different enterprise, the TVEI. Indeed, the original rationale of the TVEI shows how 'raids' on the past, involving highly selective interpretations of history, may be employed for the purposes of current policy aims.

## Notes

1 A.S. Humpheryes, letter to *TES*, 6 January 1961.
2 *TES*, 18 June 1982, 'Comment': 'Making and doing'.
3 *Technology*, January 1960, leading article, 'Looking Forward'.
4 Ministry of Education, *15 To 18: A Report Of The Central Advisory Council For Education (England)*, vol. I (1959), 391.
5 *Ibid.*, 394.
6 *Ibid.*, 394.
7 *Ibid.*, 394.
8 *Ibid.*, 468.
9 *Ibid.*, 391.
10 *Ibid.*, 392.
11 *Ibid.*, 393.
12 Board of Education, *Report Of The Consultative Committee On Secondary Education, With Special Reference To Grammar Schools And Technical High Schools* (1938).
13 Board of Education, *Curriculum And Examinations In Secondary Schools: Report Of The Committee Of The Secondary Schools Examinations Council* (1943).
14 Ministry of Education, *The New Secondary Education* (pamphlet no. 9, 1947), 23.
15 Relevant statistics are in the Crowther Report, 16–27. Also R. Edwards, *The Secondary Technical School* (1960), Appendix I. Further details may be found in G.F. Taylor, 'Developments in Secondary Technical Education, 1944–1960' (Sheffield MA thesis, 1965). For the rise of the comprehensives, see K. Fenwick, *The Comprehensive School 1944–1970: The Politics Of Secondary School Reorganization* (1976).

16 *TES*, 26 February 1960, leading article, 'Threatened School'.
17 O. BANKS, *Parity And Prestige In English Secondary Education: A Study In Educational Sociology* (1955), 7.
18 A.A. PART, minute, 'The Secondary Technical School', 2 April 1946 (Ministry of Education papers, Ed./136/789; Public Record Office). EDWARDS (1960) felt that the 'biggest handicap to the proper development of secondary technical education' was 'the serious shortage of suitable school accommodation' (*The Secondary Technical School*, 35).
19 *TES*, 9 February 1951, report, 'Absorption or Independence?'
20 A.A. PART, minute, 'The Secondary Technical School', 2 April 1946 (Ministry of Education papers, Ed/136/789).
21 *TES*, 2 April 1954, leading article, 'Bias and bent'.
22 Association of Heads of Northern Secondary Technical Schools (AHNSTS), meeting, 4 May 1950, minute 3, and 1 June 1951, minute 7. Also NUT special committee on technical education, 9–10 June 1950 (file T5, c/o NUT).
23 NUT, special committee on technical education, 8–9 June 1951, minute 2.
24 FBI education committee 15 September 1953, minute 4; AHSTS Council 16 October 1954, minute 8(a); and Meeting of Principals of Colleges of Advanced Technology with representatives of the AHSTS, 9 April 1962 (AHSTS paper). I am most grateful to Mr E. SEMPER, OBE, for making these papers and his personal archive and recollections available to me.
25 *Technology*, January 1958, report, 'The Grammar of Technology'.
26 *Technology*, December 1957, report, 'Southall Rumpus: Technical School?' DR GURR was quoted as remarking that 'The technical school is an anachronism.' Also *TES*, 9 February 1951, report, 'Absorption or Independence?'
27 W. ALEXANDER, 'The Organization of Secondary Education', in *Education*, 5 March, 1954, 391–5. Also AHSTS, report of meeting with DR ALEXANDER, 1 May 1958 (AHSTS papers).
28 e.g. FBI education committee, 25 January 1955, minute 1; and 9 October 1956, minute 85. (FBI papers, Modern Records Centre, Warwick University). Also Industrial Fund, *The Industrial Fund For The Advancement Of Scientific Education In Schools: Final Report* (1963).
29 See e.g. C.A. RUSSELL, with N. COLEY and G.K. ROBERTS, *Chemists By Profession: The Origins And Rise Of The Royal Institute Of Chemistry* (1977), esp. 267–76.
30 FBI education committee, 1 June 1954, minute 3. Also SIR JOSEPH POPE, interview with the author, 24 September 1982.
31 A.A. PART, minute to R.A.R. TRICKER, 24 June 1946 (Ministry of Education papers, Ed./147/195).
32 TUC, 'The Education of Boys and Girls between 15 and 18'; memorandum to Crowther committee, 1957 (Raybould papers, University of Leeds).
33 EDWARDS, *The Secondary Technical School*, 165. J.C. KINGSLAND, 'Cray Valley Technical High School for Boys (Kent)', in *British Secondary Education: Overview And Appraisal*, ed. by R.E. GROSS (1965), 335–68 is a useful account of the author's personal experience of teaching in first a grammar school, then a junior technical school, and then a secondary

technical school.

34 M. COLLINS, 'Technical Education for Girls: More Than Sentimental', in *TES*, 13 July 1962.

35 M. WOOLLETT,, 'The Technical High School for Girls', in *Technical Education*, 1/8 (October 1959), 4–6.

36 See e.g. W.J. READER, *Professional Men: The Rise Of The Professional Classes In Nineteenth-Century England* (1966), and J.E. GERSTL, S.P. HUTTON, *Engineers: The Anatomy of A Profession. A Study Of Mechanical Engineers In Britain* (1966). London, Tavistock.

37 *TES*, 11 June 1954, report, 'Secondary Technical School: 1 — Visiting the Craft Rooms'.

38 T.C. MCNEILL, letter to *TES*, 2 July 1954.

39 *TES*, 28 June 1947, report, 'Technical School Headmasters'.

40 J. SAFKIN, 'The Association of Heads of Secondary Technical Schools', in *Vocational Aspect*, 6, May 1951, 170–72.

41 *TES*, 11 May 1951, report, 'Technical Schools: First Conference of Heads'.

42 AHSTS Officers' meeting, 12 February 1955, minute 6(iii).

43 AHSTS Council, 1 February 1958, minute 5.

44 AHSTS Council, 16 May 1953, minute 8(ii).

45 AHSTS Council, 3 July 1956, minute 3.

46 AHSTS Council, 12 November 1960.

47 NUT Advisory Committee for Secondary Technical Schools, meeting, 29 September 1961.

48 A.J. JENKINSON, 'Reservoirs of Talent — The Secondary Technical School', in *Research*, 10/11 (November 1957), 418.

49 H. FRAZER, 'Note on the Secondary Technical School'; memo to Crowther committee, 8 May 1957 (Raybould papers).

50 Ministry of Education, *Technical Education* (Cmd. 9703), 1956.

51 e.g. LORD HAILSHAM, address to AHSTS Annual Conference, 8 March 1957; and AHSTS, 'Deputation to Minister of Education' (Sir DAVID ECCLES), 16 March 1959.

52 *TES*, 11 May 1951, 'Comment in Brief'.

53 *TES*, 16 March 1956, report, 'Industry's Prep Schools'. Also report of AHSTS Annual Conference, 9–10 March 1956. This view was elaborated upon by A.J. PETERS, 'The Changing Idea of Technical Education', in *Br. Jnl of Educational Studies*, 11/2 (1963), 142–66. An earlier version of this paper had been prepared for the NFER in 1957, and was known to the Crowther committee, but was not published.

54 *Technology*, January 1958, 'Commentary'.

55 AHSTS Annual Conference, 20–21 March 1953.

56 AHNSTS, meeting, 10 May 1958, and AHSTS Council, 22 June 1963.

57 AHSTS Council, 5 October 1963. The official change took place at a study-conference at Sheffield, April 1964.

58 E. SEMPER, interview with the author, 24 May 1982.

59 E. SEMPER, 'The Curriculum of the Technical High School: With Special Reference to Bradford' (MEd. thesis, University of Leeds, 1946).

60 *Technical Education*, 1/4 (May 1959), 'Doncaster Technical High School — A Pictorial Survey', 23–5.

61 E. SEMPER, 'The Technical High School Approach', in *Technical Educa-*

*tion*, 1/6 (July 1959), 10–12.

62 E. SEMPER, 'Handicraft and applied science' (n.d.; c. 1962, in Semper papers).

63 E. SEMPER, 'The place of engineering in the sixth-form curriculum', in *Technical Education*, 8/6 (June 1966), 258–61.

64 J. SAFKIN, 'The Secondary Technical School', in *Jnl of Education*, April 1954, 165–7.

65 AHSTS, Northern Region, meeting, 4 February 1960.

66 *TES*, 11 March 1960, report, 'Crowther a Hit at Huddersfield: Technical Teachers'.

67 E. SEMPER, 'The Need for a Report on the Alternative Road', in *Technical Education*, 2/7 (July 1960), 19–20.

68 E. SEMPER to SIR H. HARTLEY, 6 May 1969 (Hartley papers, Churchill College, Cambridge, Box 328. I am grateful to SIR CHRISTOPHER HARTLEY for allowing me access to these papers.)

69 Report of AHSTS Annual Conference, 8–10 June 1961.

70 AHSTS Council special meeting, 8 July 1961; meeting, 27 January 1962; and meeting, 26 May 1962.

71 AHSTS Council, 26 May 1962.

72 FORD had been the editor of the *Journal of Education*, which was highly sympathetic to the cause of secondary technical education. He took over at Sheffield from H.C. DENT, who also had close links with the secondary technical schools.

73 'Report of the First Meeting of the Development Committee', 18 January 1963 (Semper papers). Also W.S. BRACE, letter to the author, 5 July 1982.

74 *Ibid.*

75 2nd Meeting of Development Committee, 7 June 1963 (Semper papers); and G. BOSWORTH, letter to the author, 10 June 1982.

76 E. SEMPER, *Technology And The Sixth-Form Boy — The Teaching Aspect* (1964), 21.

77 E. SEMPER, memorandum, 'Curriculum research project in applied science and technology' (n.d.; 1963, Semper papers).

78 *Labour Party Conference Report* (1963), 133–40, printed by the Labour Party.

79 E. SEMPER, circular to members of the Development Committee, 4 February 1965 (Semper papers). Also D.I.R. PORTER, Schools Council internal memo, 'Engineering Science in Secondary Schools' (1965).

80 See B. MACDONALD and R. WALKER, *Changing The Curriculum* (1976), esp. 103–22, and R. WALKER, 'Project Technology', in *Curriculum Research And Development In Action*, ed. by L. STENHOUSE (1980), 115–38, for further details on the creation of the Schools Council Project in Technology.

81 See e.g. Science Masters' Association, policy statement, *Science And Education* (1957).

82 H. BOULIND, letter to *New Scientist*, 20 June 1957.

83 H. BOULIND, 'Atomic Energy and Education', in *School Science Review*, March 1959, 332.

84 *Ibid.*, 331–2.

85 H. BOULIND, 'Accommodation and equipment', in *Science In Schools*, ed.

by W.H. PERKINS (1958), 63. Art 9.

86  H. BOULIND, address to Parliamentary and Scientific Committee, 15 December 1964.

87  DR C.G. WILLIAMS, 'NUJMB Engineering Science syllabus: discussion with Professor Edels at Liverpool University, March 25th, 1968' (Hartley papers, Box 302).

88  Nuffield Foundation Science Teaching Project, *Progress Report* (1963). London, printed and circulated by Nuffield Foundation.

89  E. SEMPER, memorandum, 'Curriculum research project in applied science and technology' (Semper papers, n.d.; 1963).

90  'ASTRYX', 'The Alternative Road', in *TES*, 17 April 1964.

91  I. GOODSON, *School Subjects And Curriculum Change* (1982), 3.

92  H. SILVER, 'The liberal and the vocational', in his *Education As History: Interpreting Nineteenth- And Twentieth-Century Education* (1983), 153–72.

93  G.T. PAGE, *Engineering Among The Schools* (report for the Institution of Mechanical Engineers, 1965).

94  AHSTS Northern Region meeting, 24 May 1963, minute 5(a).

95  SEMPER told SIR HAROLD HARTLEY in May 1969 that 'Project Technology has foundered and failed to evolve beyond the feasibility study stage.' (Semper to Hartley, 6 May 1969, in Hartley papers, Box 328).

96  Schools Council Curriculum Bulletin no. 2, *A School Approach To Technology* (1967).

97  E.H. CARR, *What Is History?* (1961), 37.

98  C. BARNETT, 'Technology, Education and Industrial and Economic Strength', in *Jnl of the Royal Society of Arts*, 5271 (February 1979), 120.

99  *Ibid.*, 127.

100  See e.g. S.B. PRAIS, *Vocation Qualifications Of The Labour Force In Britain And Germany* (1981), London, National Institute of Economic and Social Research and K.G. GANNICOTT and M. BLAUG, 'Manpower forecasting since Robbins: a science lobby in action', in *Higher Education Review*, 2/1 (autumn 1969), 56–74.

101  M.J. WIENER, *English Culture And The Decline Of The Industrial Spirit, 1850–1980* (1981), ix.

102  *Ibid.*, 19.

103  G. RODERICK, M. STEPHENS (eds.), *The British Malaise: Industrial Performance, Education And Training In Britain Today* (1982), 3. Also G. RODERICK, M. STEPHENS (Eds.), *Where Did We Go Wrong? Industrial Performance, Education And The Economy In Victorian Britain* (1981).

104  H. BUTTERFIELD, *The Whig Interpretation Of History* (1931; Pelican edn 1973), 9.

105  J.H. HEXTER, *On Historians* (1979), 242.

106  *TES*, 22 October 1976, report, 'What the PM said'.

107  *Engineering Our Future: Report Of The Committee Of Inquiry Into The Engineering Profession* (Cmnd. 7794, January 1980), 4.

108  *Times*, 13 November 1982, report, 'Tebbit starts technical education scheme'.

109  *Education*, 19 November 1982, news in review, 'Mailed fist and velvet glove from Mr David Young'.

110 *TES*, 19 November 1982, report, 'ORT: The French Connexion'.
111 M. JACKSON, report, 'Technical comeback for schools', in *TES*, 19 November 1982.
112 *TES*, 25 February 1983, platform, 'Good enough for your child?'
113 AHSTS, 'Deputation to Minister of Education', 16 March 1959.
114 *Times*, 13 November 1982, report, 'Tebbit starts technical education scheme.'
115 *Education*, 19 November 1982, news in review, 'Mailed fist and velvet glove from Mr David Young'. Also House of Commons Education, Science and Arts Committee, minutes of evidence, 20 December 1982, 16.
116 *TES*, 25 February 1983, platform, 'Good enough for your child?'
117 *Education*, 19 November 1982, news in review, 'Mailed fist and velvet glove from Mr David Young'.
118 B. BONNEN, letter to *TES*, 11 March 1983.
119 *Times*, 22 November 1982, report, 'David Young's £7m secret'.
120 *Education*, 11 March 1983, news in review, 'Mixed bag of schemes for the Young initiative'.
121 See for example — M. HOLT, 'The great education robbery', in *TES*, 3 December 1982.
122 E. SEMPER, 'Teaching for Technology', in *School Technology*, March 1981.

## References/Bibliography

ALEXANDER, W. (1954) 'The organization of secondary education', *Education*, 5 March, pp. 391–5.
ASSOCIATION OF HEADS OF NORTHERN SECONDARY TECHNICAL SCHOOLS (1950) meeting, 4 May, minute 3, AHSTS Papers (E. Semper holdings).
——— (1951) meeting, 1 June, minute 7, AHSTS Papers.
ASSOCIATION OF HEADS OF SECONDARY TECHNICAL SCHOOLS (1953). AHSTS Council, 16 May, minute 8(ii), AHSTS Papers.
——— (1955) Officers' meeting, 12 February, minute 6(iii), AHSTS Papers.
——— (1956) Council, 3 July, minute 3, AHSTS Papers.
——— (1958) Council, 1 February, minute 5, AHSTS Papers.
——— (1959) Deputation to Minister of Education (Sir David Eccles), 16 March, AHSTS Papers.
——— (1963) Northern Region meeting, 24 May 1963, minute 5a, AHSTS Papers.
BANKS, O. (1955) *Parity And Prestige In English Secondary Education: A Study In Educational Sociology*, London, Routledge and Kegan Paul.
BARNETT, C. (1979) 'Technology, education and industrial and economic strength', *Journal of the Royal Society of Arts*. 5271, pp. 117–30.
BOARD OF EDUCATION (1938) *Report Of The Consultative Committee On Secondary Education, With Special Reference To Grammar Schools And Technical High Schools*, London, HMSO (SPENS REPORT).
BOARD OF EDUCATION (1943) *Curriculum And Examinations In Secondary Schools: Report Of The Committee Of The Secondary Schools Examinations Council*, London, HMSO (NORWOOD REPORT).
BOULIND, H. (1958) 'Accommodation and equipment', in PERKINS, W.H.

(Ed.), *Science in Schools*, London, Butterworth Scientific Publications.
—— (1959) 'Atomic energy and education', *School Science Review*, March.
BUTTERFIELD, H. (1973) *The Whig Interpretation of History*, Harmondsworth, Penguin Books.
CARR, E.H. (1973) *What is History?*, Harmondsworth, Penguin Books.
EDWARDS, R. (1960) *The Secondary Technical School*, London, University of London Press.
FEDERATION OF BRITISH INDUSTRIES EDUCATION COMMITTEE (1954) 1 June, minute 3, FBI Papers, Modern Records Centre, University of Warwick.
—— (1955) 25 January, minute 1, FBI Papers.
—— (1956) 9 October, minute 85, FBI Papers.
FENWICK, K. (1976) *The Comprehensive School 1944–1970: The Politics Of Secondary School Reorganization*, London, Methuen.
FINNISTON, SIR M. (1980) *Engineering Our Future: Report Of The Committee Of Enquiry Into The Engineering Profession*, Cmnd 7794, London, HMSO.
FRAZER, H. (1957) 'Note on the Secondary Technical School', memorandum to Crowther Committee, 8 May, Raybould Papers.
GANNICOTT, K.G. and M. BLAUG (1969) 'Manpower forecasting since Robbins: a science lobby in action', *Higher Education Review*, 2, 1, autumn, pp. 56–74.
GERSTL, J.E. and HUTTON, S.P. (1966) *Engineers: The Anatomy of a Profession. A Study of Mechanical Engineers in Britain*, London, Tavistock.
GOODSON, I. (1982) *School Subjects And Curriculum Change*. Kent, Croom Helm.
HEXTER, J.H. (1979) *On Historians*, Cambridge, Mass., Harvard University Press.
INDUSTRIAL FUND (1963) *The Industrial Fund for the Advancement of Scientific Education in Schools: Final Report*.
JENKINSON, A.J. (1957) 'Reservoirs of talent — the secondary technical school', *Research*, 10, 11, pp. 417–21.
KINGSLAND, J.C. (1965) 'Cray Valley Technical High School for Boys (Kent)', in GROSS, R.E. (Ed.) *British Secondary Education: Overview And Appraisal*, London, Oxford University Press, pp. 335–68.
LABOUR PARTY (1963) *Conference Report* printed by the Labour Party.
MACDONALD, B. and WALKER, R. (Eds.) (1976) *Changing The Curriculum*, London, Open Books.
MINISTRY OF EDUCATION (1946) 'The secondary technical school', minute by A.A. PART, 2 April, Ed/136/789, Ministry of Education Papers, Public Record Office.
—— (1946a) Minute by A.A. PART to R.A.R. TRICKER, 24 June, Ed./147/195, Ministry of Education Papers.
MINISTRY OF EDUCATION (1947) *The New Secondary Education*, pamphlet no. 9, London, HMSO.
MINISTRY OF EDUCATION (1956) *Technical Education*, Cmd 9703, London, HMSO.
MINISTRY OF EDUCATION (1959) *15 To 18: A Report Of The Central Advisory Council For Education (England)*, London, HMSO (CROWTHER REPORT).

National Union of Teachers (1950) Special Committee on Technical Education, 9–10 June, File T5, NUT.

—— (1951) Special Committee on Technical Education, 8–9 June, minute 2, File T5, NUT, London.

—— (1961) Advisory Committee for Secondary Technical Schools, 29 September, NUT.

Nuffield Foundation Science Teaching Project (1963) *Progress Report*, London, printed and circulated by the Nuffield Foundation.

Page, G.T. (1965) *Engineering Among The Schools*, London, Institution of Mechanical Engineers.

Peters, A.J. (1963) 'The changing idea of technical education', *British Journal of Educational Studies*, 11, 2, pp. 142–66.

Porter, D.I.R. (1965) 'Engineering science in secondary schools', internal memorandum, Schools Council. AEC Papers File A.31(c).

Prais, S.B. (1981) *Vocation Qualifications of the Labour Force in Britain and Germany*, London National Institute of Economic and Social Research.

Roderick, G. and Stephens, M. (Eds.) (1981) *Where Did We Go Wrong? Industrial Performance, Education And The Economy In Victorian Britain*, Lewes, Falmer Press.

Roderick, G. and Stephens, M. (Eds.) (1982) *The British Malaise: Industrial Performance, Education And Training In Britain Today*, Lewes, Falmer Press.

Safkin, J. (1951) 'The Association of Heads of Secondary Technical Schools', *Vocational Aspect*, 6, pp. 170–72.

Safkin, J. (1954) 'The secondary technical school', *Journal Of Education*, 86, 1017, pp. 165–7.

Schools Council (1967) *A School Approach To Technology*, curriculum bulletin no. 2, London, HMSO.

Science Masters' Association (1957) *Science and Education: policy statement*, London. S.M.A.

Semper, E. (1946) 'The Curriculum of the Technical High School: With Special Reference to Bradford', Leeds, MEd thesis.

Semper, E. (1959) 'The technical high school approach', *Technical Education*, 1, 6, pp. 10–12.

Semper, E. (1960) 'The need for a report on the Alternative Road', *Technical Education*, 2, 7, pp. 19–20.

Semper, E. (n.d., c.1962) 'Handicraft and applied science', Semper Papers, *mimeo*.

—— (1965) Circular to members of the Development Committee, Semper Papers.

Semper, E. (1964) *Technology And The Sixth-Form Boy — The Teaching Aspect*, lecture to science teachers' course, University College, London, Shell.

Semper, E. (1966) 'The place of engineering in the sixth-form curriculum', *Technical Education*, 8, 6, pp. 258–61.

Semper, E. (1981) 'Teaching for technology', *School Technology*, March, pp. 6–7, 25.

Silver, H. (1983) 'The liberal and the vocational', in *Education As History:*

*Interpreting Nineteenth- And Twentieth-Century Education*, London, Methuen, pp. 153–72.

TAYLOR, G.F. (1965) 'Developments in Secondary Technical Education, 1944–60', Sheffield, MA thesis.

TRADES UNION CONGRESS (1957) 'The education of boys and girls between 15 and 18', memorandum to Crowther Committee, Raybould Papers, University of Leeds.

WALKER, R. (1980) 'Project Technology', in STENHOUSE, L. (Ed.) *Curriculum Research And Development In Action*, London, Heinemann, pp. 115–38.

WIENER, M.J. (1981) *English Culture And The Decline Of The Industrial Spirit, 1850–1980*, Cambridge, Cambridge University Press.

WILLIAMS, C.G. (1968) 'NUJMB engineering science syllabus: discussion with Professor Edels at Liverpool University, 25 March', Hartley Papers, Box 302.

WOOLLET, T.M. (1959) 'The technical high school for girls', *Technical Education*, 1, 8, October, pp. 4–6.

# Subjects for Study

*Ivor Goodson*

This chapter scrutinizes the part which social histories can play in the study of the curriculum. The introduction to this collection began by claiming that at this present time it was important to bring together in one volume historical work (some 'primary', other 'secondary') on the school curriculum conducted by historians, sociologists and curriculum specialists. It was noted that such an exercise was a necessary precursor to developing curriculum history as a fully-fledged intellectual synthesis. Such a synthesis cannot be built by sociologists and curriculum specialists 'doing bits' of history; nor by historians pursuing a course which does not engage with the complexity of the curriculum. It is worth returning to the dangers of partial engagement before going on to argue how historical work allows hypotheses to be examined and reformulated. By this view, a 'sequence to theory' emerges from historical work which not only extends the range of our studies, but, by posing questions about current theories, can aid in generating new theories and agendas.

Partly because *Knowledge and Control* was an influential starting point for my own historical studies I want to examine briefly the use that has been made of history by some of the sociologists who contributed to this volume. I am aware that this is to generalize dangerously from the particular; I am also aware of the excellent past and recent sociological work that has employed historical perspectives, for instance, that of Margaret Archer. Nonetheless, I think the example will establish some general points especially as Young and Bernstein have, since *Knowledge and Control*, come to argue for historical work. Young has said that 'one crucial way of reformulating and transcending the limits within which we work, is to see . . . how such limits are not given or fixed, but produced through the conflicting actions and interests of man in history'.[1] Likewise Bernstein has argued that 'if we are to take shifts in the content of education seriously, then we require histories of these contents, and their relationships to institutions and symbolic arrangements external to the school.'[2] In practice however much of the work of these sociologists to date can be characterized in two ways: either history is not used, or alternatively history is misused, or to use Silver's elegant word 'raided'.[3] Much of the work actually ignores historical background, no evolutionary historical process is provided. Studies develop, so to speak, horizontally working out from theories of social structure and the social order. When historical evidence is presented it is provided as a snapshot from the past to prove a contemporary point.

The use of Layton's work by Young (1977) is a good example of how history is used in this manner. Layton was describing a particular movement led by Richard Dawes towards 'The Science of Common Things' and its fate in a particular period during the nineteenth century. Layton was clear that there were striking similarities between many of the issues which engaged science educators in the mid-nineteenth century and those which occupy their latter-day counterparts, but in the first paragraph of his conclusion he warned:

> Within the last century and a quarter the social environment of science education has been radically transformed. At the time when Davies and Moseley fought their cause science was a national enterprise of limited scale, operating at the level which Derek Price has termed 'little science'. State and science had not begun to interact in any significant way and the limits of the principles of voluntaryism and *laissez-faire* applied to the growth of scientific activity were only just becoming clear. Today, in contrast 'big science' is not only heavily dependent on state patronage, but has become inextricably interwoven into the economic, political and ethical problems of the age. Concomitantly, there has arisen a national system of secular education in which the importance of scientific studies is recognised at all levels.[4]

Young, however, uses Layton's work to question Professor Jevons' *contemporary* view that in science 'we are up against something in the cognitive structure of science itself'. A historical snapshot is used to question a view about science today; moreover the implication is that our conceptions of school science can be understood from evidence of this particular period of conflict. Young is aware that 'it is not possible to draw any direct parallels with science education today' but nonetheless implies if not parallels, direct continuities: 'what is emphasized is the historical emergence and political character of the most basic assumptions of what is *now* taken to be school science'.[5] In fact, without direct parallels and with no evidence produced of continuities, it is difficult to move to *any* understanding of the basic assumptions of contemporary school science from the specific historical evidence presented from Layton's work.

Clearly the danger of 'raiding' history is that such moves can span centuries of change at all levels of content and context. A more systematic *evolutionary* understanding of how the curriculum is negotiated is therefore needed. One is concerned to ensure that histories make evolutionary connections partly to secure against 'raiding' but more constructively to facilitate the use of such histories in developing theoretical frameworks. A continuity thesis cannot be assumed (as in the Young example) but has to be established over time. It is surely at the centre of the sociological as well as historical enterprise to examine curriculum transformation and reproduction at work over time: such complex undertakings simply cannot be elucidated by 'snapshots' of unique events which may be entirely aberrant and without general significance. The *recurrence* of events however can help in discerning explanatory frameworks in which structure and interaction interrelate. One is reminded of the humility of Lowe's comment in his seminal article on the divided curriculum:

> While it is well known that the major educational enquiries of the mid-nineteenth century culminated in an analysis of the educational needs of society by the Taunton Commissioners which in some ways prefigured (this) twentieth century tripartism, it is not widely realised that the evolution of ideas on a structured and hierarchical system of secondary education was both gradual and continuous from that time.[6]

Historical studies therefore should seek to establish the 'gradual and continuous' nature of curriculum change and do so in ways which examine negotiation and action. By this view to seek to provide from the macro level, theories of curriculum without related empirical studies of how the curriculum has been negotiated at micro level over time is a dangerous sequence through which to proceed. This article will argue that pursuing an understanding of the complexity of curriculum action and negotiation over time is a meaningful sequence through which to test, and formulate, theory.

### Subjects for Study

Having made a polemical plea for the potential of curriculum history in furthering our understanding of schooling I want to provide some instances of historical work which begins to explore that potential. By citing some of the work which is brought together in *School Subjects and Curriculum Change* I hope first to characterize the kinds of insights and hypotheses which are generated through undertaking curriculum histories, and secondly to illustrate the capacity of such histories to aid the examination of sociological theories.

My original interest in undertaking curriculum history grew out of my teaching experience. Certainly after Countesthorpe (recently described as an 'unemulated educational maverick') I was susceptible to the arguments presented by R.A. Nisbet in *Social Change and History*. Nisbet argues that we are often deluded into thinking fundamental social change is taking place because we do not take account of a vital distinction

> between readjustment or individual deviance within a social structure (whose effects, although possibly cumulative are never sufficient to alter the structure or the basic postulates of a society or institution) and the more fundamental though enigmatic, change of structure, type, pattern of paradigm.[7]

To pursue Nisbet's crucial distinction into the field of curriculum demands, I think, that we undertake historical work. This is true whether we seek to understand how change is contained as 'readjustment or individual deviance' as at Countesthorpe or to analyze more fundamental changes of structure over time.

In the curriculum histories undertaken, I focused on subject groups and sub-groups in action. The particular historical context was the emergence of the environment as an influential idea and area of concern and of environmental education as a viable curriculum possibility. The location of the environmental climate of opinion within a broader structural *milieu* has been dealt with in a number of studies but here my particular concern was to understand how subject groups and sub-groups responded to the change in 'climate' (one subject advocate spoke of the 'changing climate' and argued that his subject group would have to 'adapt or perish'); beyond this was the need to investigate the manner in which the subject group and sub-groups scrutinized the new climate for opportunities of promoting their interests; and why it was that one sub-group decided to promote a new subject at A-level in

Environmental Studies; and, finally, why other sub-groups and subject groups responded so strongly against this initiative as to threaten its viability.

Eventually a strategy for this historical investigation was designed and divided into three sections which aimed to focus on the conflict over Environmental Studies in the 1960s and 1970s. Beyond this paramount concern, where possible, the sections were designed so as to test hypotheses and to examine theories which related to the content studied. The first and second sections focused on the origins and evolution of the three subjects involved in the emergence of Environmental Studies: geography, biology and rural studies. Here the concern was to understand the process of becoming a school subject and patterns of internal change. The third section dealt with 'external relations' between subjects and with the conflict over Environmental Studies, in particular the moves to promote an A-level syllabus for the subject. Hence the sections evolve chronologically: the subjects are scrutinized under construction and as they pursue status and resources; the groups, traditions and alliances within subjects are analyzed; these subjects and groups are then analyzed in the culminating conflict over Environmental Studies. For the purposes of this paper I do not however want to provide a summary account of *School Subjects and Curriculum Change* but rather to concentrate on the way in which in constructing that account hypotheses were tested and reformulated and theories examined.

## Testing Hypotheses

In the three sections of the book noted above three main hypotheses are examined within the context of the history of three subjects involved in the conflict over Environmental Studies:

1  That subjects are not monolithic entities but shifting amalgamations of sub-groups and traditions. These groups within the subject influence and change boundaries and priorities;
2  That in the process of establishing a school subject (and associated university discipline) base subject groups tend to move from promoting pedagogic and utilitarian traditions towards the academic tradition;
3  That in the conflict over environmental studies much of the curriculum debate can be interpreted in terms of conflict between subjects over status, resources and territory.

Obviously the pattern of the first hypothesis would appear most strongly in subjects representing 'fields' rather than 'forms' of knowledge. The history of geography, for instance, shows that in the early stages the subject was made up of a variety of idiosyncratic local versions devised or taught by specialists from other disciplines. During the period in curriculum history that is the concern of this book, the battle over environmental education in the late sixties and early seventies, the sub-groups within geography can be seen 'pursuing different objectives in different manners'.[8] So much so that in 1970 Professor Fisher wrote that 'The light-hearted prophecy I made in 1959 that we might soon expect to see the full 57 varieties of geography has been almost literally fulfilled, and my personal collection of different categories of geography that have seriously been put forward in professional literature now stands at well over half that number.'[9] At about the same time, the President of the Geographical Association was warning that 'new' geography created a problem because 'it leads towards subject fragmentation', so that ultimately 'the question must arise as to how much longer the subject can effectively be held together'.[10] The potential danger of new versions of geography was touched on by Walford who argued that 'unity within the subject' was 'a basic requirement for its continued existence'.[11]

The tendency to fragmentation in geography through the proliferation of sub-groups and sub-versions is a recurrent feature of the subject's history, and was echoed by the Norwood Report's fear about the 'expansiveness of geography'. At this earlier stage, 1943, they saw geography as 'The study of man and his environment from selected points of view' — a definition at that time leading to fears that through its expansiveness geography was becoming 'a "world citizenship" subject, with the citizens detached from their physical environment'.[12] As a result 'by then, geography had become grievously out of balance; the geographical synthesis had been abandoned'. The problem was fairly rapidly addressed and a decade later Garnett claimed that most departments were headed by specialists so that 'The initial marked differences and contrasts in subject personality had been blurred or obliterated'.[13]

The means by which the fragmentary sub-groups were monitored, controlled and periodically unified will be dealt with later. However, in the period of the battle over 'environmental education', two, or more accurately three, major sub-groups within the subject were actively concerned: the regional geographers, the field geographers and, the fastest-growing sub-group, the 'new' geographers. The first two groups, representing strong traditions within the subject had large support among school geography teachers. The latter group was largely derived from new developments in the subject within the universities. The first two sub-groups were considerably more sympathetic to environmental initiatives than the new geographers. This was because the environmental lobby offered aid and sustenance to the field and regional geographers. Hence, we find eminent regional geographers like Professor Bryan promoting conferences in environmental studies because this expressed more clearly than new geography 'his own life's work and ambitions as a geographer'.[14] P.R. Thomas explained the affection for environmental approaches entirely in terms of the struggle for survival of the regional sub-group[15] and a college lecturer in geography judged that the new crisis among geography sub-groups 'caused traditional (i.e. regional and field) geographers to flee into environmental studies for a time.'[16] This flirtation proved a short-run phenomenon because of the overwhelming desire for fully-fledged academic status among all geographers; because new geography carried within it the seeds of this final acceptance; and because the activities of the Geographical Association and the university schools of geography together helped manage the change towards a new 'geographical synthesis' where once again the sub-groups were 'delicately held together'.

The pattern discerned among geography sub-groups in the period of environmental education's emergence is partly echoed when considering biology. Again the subject began with a variety of idiosyncratic versions and groupings devized and taught by specialists from other disciplines, in botany and zoology. By the 1960s biology had also developed a major sub-group whose concern with ecology and field biology bordered on the new environmental approaches. For a time this sub-group gained considerable momentum from initiatives like the Keele Conference which saw this version of biology as promoting environmental awareness.

Alongside field biology a sub-group promoting biology as a 'hard science' based in laboratories gained increasing adherents. The rise of molecular biology, symbolized by the Nobel prizewinning work of Crick and Watson in the late 1950s gave renewed impetus to the work of this group. In the new universities opening up in the 1960s and in many schools following the Nuffield project, this group managed to dominate the versions of biology that were accepted. Hence the 'hard science' version was embodied in the new laboratories that were then being built and in the departments that were set up. So dominant did the 'hard science' group become in biology, that for a time the ecology and field biology sub-group developed defensive connections with environmental studies. As with geography a number of professors associated with the sub-group appeared at events or in publications sponsored by the National Association for Environmental Education. However, although only a sub-group on the defensive within biology, the field biologists were actively pursuing opportunities elsewhere and secured a dominant position (along with the field geographers) in the Field Studies movement which grew rapidly as the 'environmental lobby' gained momentum. The field biology sub-group was thereby able to develop important new 'territory' inside the growth area of field studies which partially compensated for losing the battle for mainstream biology to the hard science sub-group. By securing this leading role in field studies any permanent alliance with the rural studies groups promoting environmental studies was rendered both unnecessary and undesirable.

In both geography and biology the sub-groups allied to distinctive versions of the subject often gathered very different degrees of support according to whether school or university groups were being considered. Sometimes this reflected a time-lag effect as the new versions of the subject only slowly worked their way into the schools with new graduates taking up teaching posts in them. This was, for instance, the case in the battle between the original geography and new geography groups; a long time after new geography was well-established in universities, regional geography retained the allegiance of the vast majority of school teachers.

In rural studies the varying support according to whether one concentrates attention on school or university groups, was never an issue as the subject was not taught in universities and beyond certain individuals there was no academic reference group. The sub-groups within rural studies therefore concentrated on particular versions of the subject within schools. In the period when environmental studies was launched, the two main groups were those who wanted quickly to attach rural studies to a new examination subject with some connections in the tertiary sector and those who wanted to retain traditional rural studies as a subject of outstanding appeal to the more 'practical' pupil. The battle which ensued over the name of the subject association and the new subject was essentially a battle between these two sub-groups and ended in resounding victory for the first group led by Sean Carson, when the name of the subject and its association was changed from rural studies to environmental studies.

The second hypothesis examined within the book relates to three major 'traditions' discerned in school subjects: the academic, the utilitarian and the pedagogic. As this has been dealt with in considerable detail in *Becoming a School Subject* I will provide only the briefest of commentaries. It was thought that an evolutionary profile of the school subjects under study would show a progressive movement away from stressing utilitarian and pedagogic versions of the subjects towards increasing promotion of more academic versions. We have already seen when discussing the nature of school subjects that sub-groups representing new geography, 'hard science' biology and examinable environmental studies, had come to be leading promoters of their subjects by the early 1970s. The process and rationale behind this outcome require fairly detailed understanding as they represent the culmination of a contest between a range of well-supported alternative definitions within each of the subjects.

The model of subject establishment towards a culminating 'academic' discipline was found to be closely applicable to both geography and biology. Once successfully promoted as an academic discipline the selection of the subject content is clearly considerably influenced 'by the judgment and practices of the specialist scholars in the field'. Subjects defined in this way require a base of 'specialist scholars' working in universities to continue the definition and legitimation of disciplinary content.

The strategy for achieving this final stage received early recognition in geography. MacKinder's 1903 four-point plan provides an explicit statement of a subject aspiring to academic acceptance:

> Firstly, we should encourage university schools of geography, where geographers can be made ...

> Secondly, we must persuade at any rate some secondary schools to place the geographical teaching of the whole school in the hands of one geographically trained master ...

> Thirdly, we must thrash out by discussion and experiment what is the best progressive method for common acceptation and upon that method we must base our scheme of examination.

> Lastly, the examination papers must be set by practical geography teachers.[17]

The key to the strategy was the first point, the establishment of 'university schools of geographers where geographers can be made'. To complete the control of the subject's identity, geography teaching and examination construction was to be placed in the hands only of teachers 'made in the universities'. The mediation between university and school was in geography partially placed in the hands of the Geographical Association. The Association, founded in 1893, played a central role in the promotion of geography, since in its early days the subject was confined to idiosyncratic schools-based versions and had obtained a tentative place in only a few universities. The close linkage between the growth in schools and the establishment of the subject elicited regular comment in the pages of *Geography*. The President of the Geographical Association paid homage to the 'fruits of inspired teaching' which have led to the 'intense and remarkable upsurge in the demand to read our subject in the universities.' The result has been 'the recognition of our project's status among university disciplines ... together with the costly provision made available for its study'.[18] The latter point shows the direct link between academic status and resources in our educational system: the triumph of the 'academic' tradition over the utilitarian and pedagogic traditions which played such a prominent part in geography's early days needs to be understood partly in these terms.

The establishment of 'discipline' status inside the universities which had been so systematically pursued since MacKinder's 1903 proclamation provided a range of material improvements in the subject's place within schools. In 1954 Honeybone could claim that 'at long last, geography is forcing its complete acceptance as a major discipline in universities and that geographers are welcomed in to commerce, industry and the professions, because they are well educated men and women'.[19] From now on geography could claim its place in educating the most able children, and thereby become established as a well-funded department inside schools staffed with trained specialists on graded posts. By 1967 Marchant noted that geography was 'at last attaining to intellectual respectability in the academic streams of our secondary schools'.[20] But he noted that the battle was not quite over and gave two instances where the subject was still undesirably taught as a 'less able' option. With the launching of new geography the subject finally attained total acceptance as an academic discipline in universities and as a fully-fledged A-level subject in all schools, with the resources and 'costly provisions' which such status attracts.

In biology the evolution of the subject is distinguishable from geography because from the beginning there was an associated and well-established university base in the form of botany and zoology. For this reason and also because from the outset the subject benefited from the side-effects of the influential science lobby the task of subject promotion never totally resembled geography's 'beginning from scratch'. Biology's task was more to present a case for inclusion within the, by then well-established (and consequently well-resourced), science area of the curriculum. This task was often pursued within the overall arena of the Science Masters Association, who from the 1930s onwards played an active role in promoting biology. In 1936 an influential biology sub-committee was formed to promote biology syllabuses, and many articles in the Association's *School Science Review* argued the case for biology's recognition as an examination subject for the able student. The problem was best voiced by the Ministry of Education in 1960:

> The place which is occupied by advanced biological studies in schools ... is unfortunately that of vocational training rather than of an instrument of education.

The need to be seen as an 'instrument of education' meant that the promoters of the subject had to move away from the utilitarian towards more academic versions — only then could an A-level subject command sufficient pupil numbers to warrant 'departmental' status and resources in schools. Hence we find the common theme being advocated: biology must be treated 'as a comprehensive discipline in its own right'.[21]

In the final stages in the promotion of biology as an 'academic discipline' in the 1960s, the two main initiatives stressed the subject as a 'hard science' needing 'laboratories and equipment'. In the rapidly expanding universities it was this version of the subject which was widely introduced, thereby establishing the academic discipline base; likewise part of the Nuffield Biology Project for Schools centred on 'a crusade in terms of equipment and laboratory staff'. With the new generation of biology graduates trained in this hard science at universities, the establishment of the subject as a fully fledged academic O and A-level subject was finally assured.

Unlike biology and geography, rural studies remained for generations a low status enclave, stressing highly utilitarian or pedagogic values. This provides confirmation for Ben-David and Collins's contention that the move to a change in intellectual and occupational identity came at the time when the subject was faced with survival problems in a reorganizing educational system stressing academic examinations. The pervasive influence of this tradition can clearly be seen in the following quote:

> The lack of a clear definition of an area of study as a discipline has often been a difficulty for local authorities in deciding what facilities to provide ... It has been one of the reasons for the fact that no A-level course in rural studies exists at present.[22]

The Schools Council Working Party in 1968 confirmed this with the broad hint that there was the 'need for a scholarly discipline'.[23]

With no tertiary base and hence no specialist scholars involved, except random specialists from other disciplines, the Hertfordshire strategy was to develop an A-level syllabus from groups working in the secondary schools. This offered the promise of tailoring 'a course to the needs of the kids' and not to 'have to meet the requirements of other people's courses'. But the crucial reason in terms of the subject teachers' material self interest was often frankly admitted:

> I think we had got to prove that environmental studies was something that the most able of students could achieve and do something with . . . if you started off there all the expertize and finance that you put into it will benefit the rest — your teaching ratio goes up etc. and everyone else benefits.[24]

Likewise, another leading advocate admitted that they had seen that:

> the only way to make progress was to get in on the examination racket . . . the examination was essential, otherwise you couldn't be equal with any other subject. Another thing was that comprehensive education was coming in. Once that came in, no teacher who didn't teach in the fifth or sixth form was going to count for twopence. So you had to have an A-level for teachers to aim at.

The survival rationale was always a strong factor:

> I just thought if you're outside this you've had it in schools: it was already happening in some schools where a (rural studies) teacher was leaving, they didn't fill the place, because they gave it to someone in the examination set up. And beyond survival the reasons for an academic A-level were simply because if you didn't you wouldn't get any money, any status, any intelligent kids.[25]

The Hertfordshire A-level in environmental studies which was ultimately devized is a recognition of the factors defining the aspirations and efforts of these rural studies teachers. What has subsequently been denied is not that environmental studies represents a valid area of curriculum, but that it can thereby claim to be an academic discipline. Such claims it would appear are best validated through university scholarship and without a university base status passage to acceptance as an academic subject has been denied.

MacKinder's strategy of using the school subject base to help bring about the creation of university departments was correctly conceived. As Carson noted at the Offley conference, new contenders for academic status are often placed in an impossible situation since they are asked 'What evidence have you that universities would accept this sort of A-level?' On making enquiries to universities, the reply was 'show us the successful candidates and we will tell you'. A chicken and egg situation.[26]

The third hypothesis follows on as one moves from consideration of the patterns of internal evolution in school subjects to investigate the role that the pursuit of academic status plays in the relationship between subjects. In continuity with the second hypothesis we would expect established subjects to defend their own academic status at the same time as denying such status to any new subject contenders, particularly in the battle over new A-level examinations.

In the struggle to launch environmental studies as an A-level subject, the geographers reacted strongly, and the biologists much more mildly, following the lines of the hypothesis. MacKinder, the founding father of geography's road to academic establishment, would have understood this. In explaining the geologists' opposition to geography he saw their fear of the new subject making 'inroads in their classes' as the reason for their response and noted that 'even scientific folk are human, and such ideas must be taken into account'.[27] In continuity with this, the geographers strongly opposed social studies, an integrated package that pre-dated environmental studies by several decades. The geographers, it was claimed, 'saw the new proposals as a threat to the integrity and status of their own subject'.[28]

The growth of environmental studies was treated in similar manner by the geographers. The discussion of the Executive Committee of the Geographical Association show precious little concern with the intellectual or epistemological arguments for environmental studies. The discussion focused on 'the threat to geography involved in the growth of environmental studies'. Indeed, when the possibility of a dialogue with environmental studies teachers was suggested 'some members felt that to do so would be tantamount to admitting the validity of environmental studies'.[29] The most overt plea for defence rather than dialogue came in the Presidential Address to the Geographical Association in 1973. Mr A.D. Nicholls laid great emphasis on the 'practical realities' for 'practising teachers'. 'With constant pressure on teaching time, headmasters are ever searching for new space into which additional prestige subjects can be fitted, and the total loss of teaching time to environmental subjects may be considerable'. Beyond these practical fears about the material interests of geography teachers, environmental studies evoked a particularly emotional response among geographers because of its proximity to geography's continuing identity crisis. Nicholls provides an unusually frank admission of the need for territorial defence being placed above any intellectual imperatives:

Ten years ago almost to the day and from this platform, Professor Kirk said 'modern geography was created by scholars, trained in other disciplines, asking themselves geographical questions and moving inwards in a community of problems; it could die by a reversal of the process whereby trained geographers moved outwards in a fragmentation of interests seeking solutions to non-geographical problems'. Might not this be prophetic for us today? Could it not all too soon prove disastrous if the trained teachers of geography moved outwards as teachers of environmental studies seeking solutions to non-geographical problems?[30]

The fears which geographers expressed so strongly and emotionally about the emergence of environmental studies were not shared to the same degree by biologists. As we have seen only the field biology sub-group was threatened and they managed to expand into the growing territory of field studies. However in the negotiations at Schools Council the science sub-committee, which included a number of biologists, joined forces with the geographers in their opposition to the environmental studies A-level. In both sub-committees 'concern was expressed at the heavy overlap between this syllabus and syllabuses in both geography and biology'. The pursuance of this allegation involved a clever strategy. First the committees argued that the A-level must delete 'irrelevant topics' mainly content not related to geography or biology. Then the committees stated that 'if irrelevant topics were envisaged as removed, the effect would be to reveal how close the resulting syllabus would be to existing syllabuses'[31] in geography and to a lesser extent biology.

A judgment from Carson that the Schools Council sub-committees 'jealously guarded the preserves of their subject' was confirmed by the comments from the geography sub-committee when the decision on the A-level was finally announced. They were plainly fairly satisfied with their territorial defence and 'noted with approval that candidates could not take this examination together with geography'. A final point was added that there was 'as yet no indication that universities would be prepared to accept a pass in this subject as an entry qualification for degree courses'.[32] The restriction on environmental studies being offered with geography, together with an initial restriction to a five year 'experimental' period and to a limited number of schools placed enormous practical obstacles in the way of any widespread adoption of the subject. By ensuring these obstacles faced the new subject in the early years when the momentum for change was strong, the opponents of the new subject effectively extinguished its chances of establishment in the secondary school curriculum.

## Examining Theory: An Example

Since we began by instancing the non-use or misuse of history by sociologists who contributed to *Knowledge and Control* it would be instructive to examine their theories with respect to school subjects. This way we can examine an earlier contention that 'to seek to provide from the macro-level theories of curriculum without empirical investigation or understanding of how the curriculum has been negotiated at micro level over time is a poor sequence through which to proceed to theory'.[33]

The first point to recognize in Young *et al* is the assumption in a number of the papers that subjects are monolithic. This is hardly a promising starting point from which to develop the theme that the curriculum is subject to patterns of control by dominant interest groups. The papers in the book reflect Bernstein's contention that 'how a society selects, classifies, distributes, transmits and evaluates the educational knowledge it considers to be public, reflects both the distribution of power and the principles of social control'.[34] Young likewise suggests that 'consideration of the assumptions underlying the selection and organization of knowledge by those in positions of power may be a fruitful perspective for raising sociological questions about curricula'.[35] The emphasis leads to general statements of the following kind:

> Academic curricula in this country involve assumptions that some kinds and areas of knowledge are much more 'worthwhile' than others: that as soon as possible all knowledge should become specialized and with minimum explicit emphasis on the relations between the subjects specialized in and between specialist teachers involved. It may be useful, therefore, to view curricular changes as involving changing definitions of knowledge along one or more of the dimensions towards a less or more stratified, specialized and open organization of knowledge.

> Further, that as we assume some patterns of social relations associated with any curriculum, these changes will be resisted in so far as they are perceived to undermine the values, relative power and privileges of the dominant groups involved.[36]

The process whereby the unspecified 'dominant groups' exercise control over other presumably subordinate groups is not scrutinized although certain hints are offered. We learn that a school's autonomy in curriculum matters 'is in practice extremely limited by the control of the sixth form (and therefore lower form) curricula by the universities, both through their entrance requirements and their domination of all but one of the school examination boards'.[37] In a footnote Young assures that 'no direct control is implied here, but rather a process by which teachers legitimate their curricula through their shared assumptions about 'what we all know the universities want'.[38] This concentration on the teachers' socialization as the major agency of control is picked up elsewhere. We learn that:

> The contemporary British educational system is dominated by academic curricula with a rigid stratification of knowledge. It follows that if teachers and children are socialized within an institutionalized structure which legitimates such assumptions, then for teachers high status (and rewards) will be associated with areas of the curriculum that are (1) formally assessed (2) taught to the 'ablest' children (3) taught to homogeneous ability groups of children who show themselves most successful with such curricula.[39]

Young's explanation of patterns of curriculum control therefore hinges on his belief that universities 'control sixth form curricula' through 'their entrance requirements and their domination of all but one of the school examination boards'. Direct control is not apparently meant; rather indirect control through the shared assumptions into which teachers are socialized.

Curriculum histories present evidence of a more complex process at work. The role of dominant groups shows perhaps most clearly in the victory of the academic tradition in the early years of the twentieth century. This victory was embodied in the influential 1904 Regulations and most significantly, the 1917 School Certificate. *Once established* however these curricula patterns (and their associated financial and resource implications) were retained and defended in a much more complex way and by a wider range of agencies. It is therefore correct to assume that initially the rules for high status knowledge reflected the values of dominant interest groups at that time. But it is quite another issue to assume that this is *inevitably* still the case or that it is dominant interest groups themselves who *actively* defend high status curricula. It is perhaps useful to distinguish between domination and structure and mechanism and mediation.

By focusing on subjects in evolution and the conflict over A-level examinable knowledge the studies in the book clearly indicate the central role played by school subject groups and sub-groups. The most powerful of these agencies are those groups promoting the academic tradition — successfully in geography, and biology — but unsuccessfully in environmental studies. These groups *demanded* the creation of an academic discipline based in the universities. The 'academic tradition' subject groups act in this way because of the legacy of curricula, financial and resource structures inherited from the early twentieth century (when dominant interests *were* actively defended). Because of this legacy able pupils and academic examinations are linked and consequently resources, graded posts and career prospects are maximized for those who can claim academic status for their subject.

The evidence indicates not so much domination by dominant forces as solicitous surrender by subordinate groups. Far from teacher socialization in dominant institutions being the major factor creating the patterns discerned it was much more considerations of teachers' material self-interest in their working lives. Since the misconception is purveyed by sociologists who exhort us 'to understand the teacher's real world' they should really know better. High status knowledge gains its school subject adherents and aspirants less through the control of the curricula which socialize than through well-established connection with patterns of resource allocation and the associated work and career prospects these ensure. The study of curriculum histories argue that we must replace crude notions of domination with patterns of control in which subordinate groups can be seen actively at work. A tentative explanatory framework at this level is provided in the next section.

## School Subjects and Curriculum Change: An explanatory framework

*The structure of material interests: status, resources and careers*

The historical investigation of the curriculum conflict over 'environmental studies' suggests the pursuit of material interests as a major explanatory factor in understanding curriculum change. This is not to provide an overarching theory but to suggest that this aspect has been substantially neglected in previous accounts.

The similar aspirational patterns discerned in the subject histories provided directs our attention to the structuring of material interests — how resources and career chances are distributed and status attributed.

Essentially the structure emerged in the period 1904–1917. The 1904 Regulations defined the subjects suitable for the secondary, grammar schools. These were largely academic subjects and they were subsequently enshrined in the School Certificate examinations launched in 1917. From then on these examination subjects inherited the priority treatment on finance and resources directed at the grammar schools.[40]

The structure has effectively survived the ensuing changes in the educational system. Byrne, for instance, stated 'that more resources are given to able students and hence to academic subjects', (the two are still synonymous) 'since it has been assumed that they necessarily need more staff, more highly paid staff and more money for equipment and books'.[41]

The material interests of teachers — their pay, promotion and conditions — are broadly interlinked with the fate of their specialist subject communities. The 'academic' subject is placed at the top of the hierarchy of subjects because resource allocation takes place on the basis of assumptions that such subjects are best suited for the able students who, it is further assumed, should receive favourable treatment.

Hence in secondary schools the self-interest of subject teachers is closely connected with the status of the subject in terms of its examinable knowledge. Academic subjects provide the teacher with a career structure characterized by better promotion prospects and pay than less academic subjects. Seen from this viewpoint the conflict over the status of examinable knowledge is therefore essentially a battle over the material resources and career prospects available to each subject community.

### Subjects as 'coalitions'

The process model developed by Bucher and Strauss for the study of professions provides valuable guidelines for those studying school subjects. Within a profession, they argue, are varied identities, values and interests. Hence professions are to be seen as a 'loose amalgamation of segments pursuing different objectives in different manners and more or less delicately held together under a common name at particular periods in history'.[42] The most frequent conflicts arise over the gaining of institutional footholds, over recruitment and over external relations with clients and other institutions. At times when conflicts such as these become intense professional associations may be created or if already in existence become more strongly institutionalized.

The Bucher and Strauss model of professions suggest that perhaps the 'subject community' should not be viewed as a homogeneous group whose members share similar values and definition of role, common interests and identity. Rather the subject community should be seen as comprising a range of conflicting groups, segments or factions (referred to as subject sub-groups). The importance of these groups might vary considerably over time. As with professions, school subject associations (for example, the Geographical Association) often develop at particular points in time when there is an intensification of conflict over school curriculum and resources and over recruitment and training.

*Subject coalitions in evolution: internal curriculum change*

In the subjects studied (further work is of course needed) a pattern of evolution can be discerned in the process of becoming a subject. Initially a subject is a very loose amalgamation of sub-groups and even idiosyn-cratic versions, often focused on pedagogic and utilitarian concerns. A sub-group emerges arguing for the subject to become an academic discipline so as to be able to claim resources and status. At the point of conflict between earlier sub-groups and the proselytizing 'academic' sub-group, a subject association is often formed. The association increasingly acts to unify sub-groups into a *dominant coalition* promoting academic status. The dominant coalition calls for discipline status and the university departments to be set up to train its disciplinary specialists (see MacKinder's manifesto). Some subjects (for example, rural/environmental studies) are blocked at this point (university admissions policies play a role here).

For the successful subjects a final stage is the creation of a university discipline base. The subject is now defined increasingly by university scholars and it is to the structure of their material interests and resulting aspirational patterns that we must now look to explain curriculum change (for example, new geography, molecular biology) and to explain any resultant tensions for the school subject.

*Changing climates and external relations: defining a new subject*

The emergence of the environmental climate of opinion offered new opportunities for subject groups and sub-groups in the promotion of their interests. (I have not dealt with the structural origins of this new climate as other work has attempted this. For example, 'the climate of opinion which made environmental studies a credible label for curriculum innovation in the 60s and 70s is best understood in terms of the historical circumstances of post-war capitalism').[43]

In this respect Ben-David and Collins's hypotheses were substantially proven. They argued that for a new subject or discipline:

1   the ideas necessary for creation ... are usually available over a relatively prolonged period of time and in several places;
2   only a few of these potential beginnings lead to further growth;
3   such growth occurs where and when persons become interested in the new idea, not only as intellectual content but also as a potential means of establishing a new intellectual identity and particularly a new occupational role. They conclude 'the conditions under which such interest arises can be identified and used as a basis for eventually building a predictive theory'.[44]

Applying this to subject groups and sub-groups a number of factors would be relevant:

1   subject group/sub-group position in hierarchies of subjects (current power and status);

2   their current position regarding resource allocation in schools (current resources);

3   patterns of career and age position of practitioners (current career patterns).

Subjects with low status and resources and poor career patterns, like rural studies, therefore embrace the opportunity to establish a new intellectual identity and occupational role. Established high status subjects conversely ignored the opportunity but contested the new contenders' right to claim similar academic status (and thereby establish parity of status and resources and a share therein). Carson has provided the rationale for the rural studies sub-groups' move to promote an Environmental Studies A-level: 'because if you didn't you wouldn't get any money, any status, any intelligent kids'.

## Conclusion

In this chapter I have been concerned to show that curriculum histories can be a valuable complement, indeed at times an active agency, in the development of theoretical frameworks. The essential value of such histories (as of more general histories) is that they are immersed in the complexity of the social process. They develop from the desire to understand particular events not from a desire to prove particular theories. The curriculum historian will often travel with her/his ideological and theoretical baggage packed away. This implicitness, whilst avoiding the primacy of theoretical verification, should not however limit theoretical aspiration. The curriculum historian *should* be concerned to aid the generation of theories about actions and events in specific historical conditions. In this way the historian can play an important role in the theoretical enterprise and in the making of agendas for further studies.

Of course the specificity of curriculum histories often act against their capacity for generalization. The model of subject change developed here clearly has many limitations. What about pastoral systems, falling rolls, whole curriculum planning? Does this apply to subjects like classics, economics or, dare we mention it, sociology? What about subjects where industrial and external forces are more clearly involved? What are the factors behind 'the changing climates for action' that have been discerned? What about current changing climates where the autonomy of the educational system and the 'rules of the game' therein defined are challenged.

But beyond the problem of the specificity of curriculum histories lies the problem of the *nature* of curriculum histories. Clearly (following the first hypothesis!) history is no monolithic subject or method. In history there are schisms which resemble those in other subjects — notably the disagreement between the 'general law' school of historians and what we might call the 'uniqueness' school (for example, 'the special interest of the historian is not in classes of events but in the uniqueness of each event').

At one level the argument for curriculum histories merely reiterates the need to study how the curriculum has evolved, to understand historical background and origins so as to provide a context for contemporary inquiry. By this view historical studies can *extend* the range of our accounts. I would however want to go further than this and argue that histories are important because of their potential to *transform* our accounts: to pose fundamental questions and to point towards new agendas for study; for instance, reformulating notions of 'domination', changing the priority given to prior socialization in accounts of subject change or stressing the importance of professional subject groups in the evolution of the curriculum.

The specificity and nature of history leave us with a dual challenge in conducting future curriculum histories. Firstly, where possible, they must pursue the gradual and continuous nature of curriculum change (certainly in systems as decentralized as ours) so as to illuminate *contemporary situations*: this argues against too rigidly 'periodized' histories. Secondly, they must aspire not only to *extend* our range of data but to contribute to the examination and reformulation of hypotheses and theories, thereby offering the potential for *transforming* our accounts.

These aspirations have of course to be set against the limitations of the studies reported here. I hope, however, that some progress has been indicated as well. Curriculum histories point to the evolutionary nature of subjects as coalitions 'more or less delicately held together under a common name at particular periods'. The nature of these coalitions responds to both the structuring of material interests and the 'changing climates' for action. Because of the manner in which resources (and associated career prospects) are distributed, and status attributed, 'academic' subject groups normally develop as 'dominant coalitions'. The conflict over the status of examinable knowledge therefore becomes the crucial conflict arena where the subject coalitions (and their representative associations) contest the right to material resources and career prospects.

This chapter suggests that it is a dangerous enterprise to develop theories of curriculum whilst underusing or misusing historical studies. Particularly significant is the constant harking back to the early nineteenth century for analogies with which to support contemporary theory. Structural and interactional features are not continuous and to assume continuity is at best to oversimplify and at worst wilfully mislead.

A particular problem in those studies which generalize from the early nineteenth century to the contemporary situation has been identified in the work reported here. Namely that by raiding history in this way sociologists have been returning to a *pre-professional era* with respect to curriculum groups. The evidence presented here points to the power and importance of professional subject groups; they cannot be dismissed as powerless agencies in the face of structural change.

The use of socialization as a kind of black box theory of causation seems a common but inappropriate device; postulating causation without presenting evidence is poor theorizing, particularly when professionalization has been substantially ignored. The evidence presented here suggests that is not so much prior socialization as the structuring of material interest which provides the mediating mechanism between structural and interractional levels.

The dominance of 'academicism' can be shown over the last century or more. But historical studies pose questions about in whose interests this dominance prevails: professional groups, culturally dominant groups or industrial or financial capital. Academicism may be the past cultural consequence of previous domination rather than a guarantee of future domination. Through immersion in the complexity of social action the curriculum historian (like the ethnographer, of course) places her/himself among the participants in social action as they respond to and scrutinize the social structure. In such a position, by analogy, she/he is well placed to scrutinize macro-theory 'from the complexity below'. In particular curriculum histories may help in emancipating us from the grosser correspondence and dominance theories and give new meanings to concepts of relative autonomy where people can be recognizably viewed in action.

## Notes

1 M. YOUNG in M. YOUNG and G. WHITTY (Eds.) (1977) pp. 248–9.
2 B. BERNSTEIN (1974) p. 156.
3 H. SILVER (1977).
4 D. LAYTON (1973) p. 166.
5 M. YOUNG *op. cit.* p. 245.
6 R ROWE (1976) pp. 139–140.
7 R.A. NISBET (1969) in J.R. WEBSTER 'Curriculum change and crisis'. *British Journal of Educational Studies*, 3, October 1971, pp. 204–5.
8 R. BUCHER and A. STRAUSS (1976) p. 19.
9 C.A. FISHER (1970) pp. 373–4.
10 A. GARNETT (1969) pp. 388–9.
11 R. WALFORD (1973) p. 97.
12 *Norwood Report* (1943) pp. 101–2.
13 *Op. cit.* GARNETT p. 368.
14 R. MILLWARD (1969) p. 93.
15 P.R. THOMAS (1970) pp. 274–5.
16 Interview Scraptoft, 14 December 1976.
17 H.J. MacKINDER (1903).
18 *Op. cit.* GARNETT.
19 R.C. HONEYBONE (1954).
20 E.C. MARCHANT (1968).
21 Ministry of Education (1960).
22 S. CARSON Unpublished M.Ed. Thesis (Manchester 1967) p. 135.
23 *Schools Council Working Paper No. 24*, p. 19.
24 S. CARSON interview.
25 *Ibid.*
26 S. CARSON (1971) p. 6.
27 H.J. MacKINDER (1913).
28 C. CHANNON (1964).
29 Geographical Association Notes of meeting of Chairmen of section/ Standing Committee (28 September 1970)

30  A.D. Nicholls (1973) p. 201.
31  Letter Schools Council, Herts. File, 21 February 1973 SS/L/G/191.
32  *Ibid.*
33  I. Goodson *Towards a Social History of Subjects* (Mimeo)
34  B. Bernstein (1971).
35  M. Young *Ibid* p. 3.
36  *Ibid* p. 34.
37  *Ibid* p. 22.
38  *Ibid.*
39  *Ibid* p. 36.
40  See M. Smith (1980) p. 153–172.
41  E.M. Byrne (1974), p. 29.
42  *Op. cit.* Bucher and Strauss.
43  R. Gomm *Environment and Environmental Studies* (monograph).
44  J. Ben-David and R. Collins (1966) p. 452.


## References/Bibliography

Ben-David J. and Collins R. (1966) 'Social factors in the origins of a new science: the case of psychology' *American Sociological Review*, 31, 4, August.

Bernstein, B. (1974) 'Sociology and the sociology of education: a brief account' in Rex J. (Ed.) *Approaches to Sociology*, London, Routledge and Kegan Paul.

Bernstein, B. (1971) 'On the classification and framing of educational knowledge' in Young M. (Ed.) *Knowledge and Control*, London, Collier Macmillan.

Bucher R. and Strauss, A. (1976) 'Professions in process' in Hammersley M. and Woods P. (Eds.) *The Process of Schooling*, London, Routledge and Kegan Paul.

Byrne, E.M. (1974) *Planning and Educational Inequality* Slough, NFER.

Carson, S. (1967) unpublished M.Ed. Thesis 'The Use of Content and Effective Objectives in Rural Studies', Manchester.

Carson, S. (Ed.) (1971) *Environmental Studies, the Construction of an A-Level Syllabus* Slough, NFER.

Channon, C. (1964) 'Social studies in secondary school,' *Educational Review*, 17 January.

Fisher, C.A. (1970) 'Whither regional geography', *Geography*, 55, Part 4, November.

Garnett, A. (1969) 'Teaching geography: some reflections', *Geography*, 54, November.

Geographical Association Notes of meeting of Chairman of Section/ Standing Committee 28 September 1970.

Gomm, R. (1977) *Environment and Environmental Studies* Monograph.

Goodson, I. (1976) *Towards a Social History of Subjects* Mimeo.

Honeybone, R.C. (1954) 'Balance in geography and education,' *Geography*, 34, No. 186.

LAYTON, D. (1973) *Science for the People* London, George Allen and Unwin.

Letter, Schools Council, Herts. File, 21 February 1973, SS/L/G/191.

LOWE, R. (1976) 'The divided curriculum: Sadler, Morant and the English secondary school', *Journal of Curriculum Studies*, 8.

MACKINDER, H.J. (1903) *Report of the Discussion on Geographical Education*.

MACKINDER, H.J. (1913) 'The teaching of geography and history as a combined subject', *The Geographical Teacher*, 7.

MARCHANT, E.C. (1968) 'Some responsibilities of the teacher of geography', *Geography*, 3.

MILLWARD, R. (1969) 'Obituary: Patrick Walter Bryan', *Geography*, 54, Part 1, January.

MINISTRY OF EDUCATION, (1960) *Science in Secondary Schools*, Pamphlet No. 38 London, HMSO.

*Norwood Report* (1943) London, HMSO.

NICHOLLS, A.D. (1973) 'Environmental studies in schools,' *Geography*, 58, Part 3, July.

SMITH, M. (1980) 'The evaluation of curriculum priorities in "Secondary Schools 1903–4"'; *British Journal of Sociology of Education*, 1, 2 June.

*Schools Council Working Paper No. 24* (1969) London, Evans/Methuen Education.

SILVER, H. (1977) 'Nothing but the past, or nothing but the present?', *Times Higher Educational Supplement*, 1. July.

THOMAS, P.R. (1970) 'Education and new geography,' *Geography*, 55, Part 3.

WALFORD, R. (1973) 'Models, simulations and games' in WALFORD, R. (Ed.) *New Directions in Geography Teaching*, London, Longmans.

WEBSTER, J.R. (1971) 'Curriculum change and crisis', *British Journal of Educational Studies*, 3, October.

WILLIAMS, M. (1976) *Geography and the Integrated Curriculum*, London, Heinemann.

YOUNG, M. (1971) 'An Approach to the study of curricula as socially organized knowledge' in YOUNG, M. (Ed.) *Knowledge and Control* London, Collier Macmillan.

YOUNG, M. (1977) 'Curriculum change: limits and possibilities' in YOUNG, M. and WHITTY, G. (Eds.) *Society State and Schooling*, Lewes, Falmer Press.

An earlier version of this paper appeared in the *Journal of Curriculum Studies*, 15, 4, October–December, 1983.

# Contributors

**Stephen Ball** is Lecturer in Education and Director of Research in the Education Area of the University of Sussex. He is author of *Beachside Comprehensive* (Cambridge University Press, 1981) and it was through the fieldwork for that study that he first became interested in English teaching; he has written several other papers on changes in English, and is the British correspondent of the International Mother-Tongue Network.

**Adrian Bell** is Lecturer in Education at the University of East Anglia. Previously he worked for ten years in a college of education and before that in secondary schools in Birmingham. He is currently undertaking research into the social process by which new agreed syllabuses are disseminated within LEAs.

**Barry Cooper** is Lecturer in Education at the University of Sussex. After studying the natural sciences and education at Cambridge, he taught mathematics in a comprehensive school. He then studied sociology at Sussex University, where he carried out the work on which this article is based.

**Barry M. Franklin** is an Assistant Professor of Education and Chairperson of the Education Department at Augsburg College in Minneapolis, Minnesota where he teaches courses in curriculum, special education and urban education. His principal area of research and writing is the history of the curriculum. At present he is working on a book on the historical development of the idea of social control in American curriculum thought and conducting research on the development of the high school curriculum in St Paul, Minnesota in the early twentieth century. He earned his graduate degrees from the University of Chicago and the University of Wisconsin.

**Ivor Goodson** read history as an undergraduate and graduate student at University College and LSE. He trained as a teacher at the Institute of Education where he gained a distinction and went on to teach at Countesthorpe College and Stantonbury Campus. He completed his DPhil at Sussex University where he has been Director of the Schools Unit since 1979. He is author of *School Subjects and Curriculum Change* (Croom Helm, 1983) and *Essays in Curriculum History* (Falmer Press, forthcoming).

**Gary McCulloch** is Lecturer in Education at the University of Auckland, New Zealand. He read history at Christ's College, Cambridge, and completed his doctorate there on the British Left in the 1930s and 1940s. He was a Research Fellow at the School of Education, University of Leeds, from 1980 until 1983, and is the author (with Edgar Jenkins and David Layton) of *Technological Revolution? The Politics of School Science and Technology in England and Wales since the Second World War* (Falmer Press, 1984).

**June Purvis** is Lecturer in the Sociology of Education in the Faculty of Educational Studies at the Open University. She studied at the Universities of Leeds and Manchester, and then taught at Manchester and Portsmouth Polytechnics. She then went to the Open University, on a SSRC grant, to research the education of working class women in nineteenth century England. Her interests include a range of topics in the sociology of education and the history of education — women's education, school-teaching, the curriculum, adult education. She is currently working on a new Open University course, *Conflict and Change in Education: a Sociological Introduction*, to be presented in 1984.

**Harry Radford** took a First Class Honours Degree in French at the University of Liverpool, subsequently completing his MLitt at Emmanuel College, Cambridge. After national service in the Intelligence Corps where he qualified as an interpreter in Russian, he served for eight years as a schoolmaster and Head of the Modern Languages Department at Rossall School. Thereafter, he became Senior Lecturer in French at Culham College, before taking up his present appointment in 1973 as Tutor in Modern Languages at the University of Oxford Department of Educational Studies. He has recently served on a 16+ Working Party (French) and is currently a member of the Steering Committee for the new Oxford Certificate of Educational Achievement. He has contributed a number of articles on language teaching to *The Times Educational Supplement*.

**William Reid** is Senior Lecturer in Education in the Faculty of Education, University of Birmingham. He taught general subjects in a secondary modern school, and languages in a grammar school before moving to Birmingham in 1969 to direct a Schools Council Project on Sixth Form Curriculum. His research interests are in curriculum theory, curriculum history and upper secondary education. His books include *Thinking about the Curriculum* (Routledge and Kegan Paul, 1978) and *The Sixth: An Essay in Education and Democracy* (with J.L. Filby, Falmer Press, 1982).

**Christopher Stray** was born in Norwich in 1943. He read classics at Cambridge, then taught it for three years. After converting to sociology, he carried out research on classics teachers, on which his chapter is based.

**Mary Waring** was educated in Rhodesia (now Zimbabwe), South Africa and London. She describes herself as a 'disintegrated scientist'. Now retired, she was formerly a Lecturer at the Centre for Science Education, Chelsea College, University of London. She is author of *Social Pressures and Curriculum Innovation: A Study of the Nuffield Foundation Science Teaching Project* (Methuen, 1979).

**Geoff Whitty** graduated from Cambridge and London Universities and taught history and social studies in two secondary schools before moving to a lectureship in the School of Education at the University of Bath in 1973. He was visiting professor at the University of Wisconsin-Madison in 1979/80 and became coordinator of the higher degree programme in urban education at King's College, University of London, in January 1981. He has published widely on social studies teaching methods and the sociology and politics of education. He was co-author with Denis Gleason of *New Developments in Social Studies Teaching* (Open Books, 1976) and co-editor with M.F.D. Young of *Exploration in the Politics of School Knowledge* (Nafferton, 1976).

**Ivor Goodson** taught history in comprehensive schools (including both Countesthorpe College and Stantonbury) before taking up a post as Research Fellow at the University of Sussex where he is now Director of the Schools Unit in the School of European Studies. He is the author of *School Subjects and Curriculum Change*.

# Index